International Political Economy Series

General Editor: **Timothy M. Shaw**, Professor of Political Science and International Development Studies, and Director of the Centre for Foreign Policy Studies, Dalhousie University, Halifax, Nova Scotia

Titles include:

Francis Adams, Satya Dev Gupta and Kidane Mengisteab (*editors*)
GLOBALIZATION AND THE DILEMMAS OF THE STATE IN THE SOUTH

Randall D. Germain (*editor*)
GLOBALIZATION AND ITS CRITICS
Perspectives from Political Economy

Barry K. Gills (*editor*)
GLOBALIZATION AND THE POLITICS OF RESISTANCE

Dong-Sook Shin Gills
RURAL WOMEN AND TRIPLE EXPLOITATION IN KOREAN DEVELOPMENT

Don Marshall
CARIBBEAN POLITICAL ECONOMY AT THE CROSSROADS
NAFTA and Regional Developmentalism

Stephen D. McDowell
GLOBALIZATION, LIBERALIZATION AND POLICY CHANGE
A Political Economy of India's Communications Sector

Ronaldo Munck and Peter Waterman (*editors*)
LABOUR WORLDWIDE IN THE ERA OF GLOBALIZATION
Alternative Union Models in the New World Order

Ted Schrecker (*editor*)
SURVIVING GLOBALISM
The Social and Environmental Challenges

Caroline Thomas and Peter Wilkin (*editors*)
GLOBALIZATION AND THE SOUTH

Kenneth P. Thomas
CAPITAL BEYOND BORDERS
States and Firms in the Auto Industry, 1960–94

Geoffrey R. D. Underhill (*editor*)
THE NEW WORLD ORDER IN INTERNATIONAL FINANCE

Robert Wolfe
FARM WARS
The Political Economy of Agriculture and the International Trade Regime

International Political Economy Series
Series Standing Order ISBN 0–333–71708–2 hardcover
Series Standing Order ISBN 0–333–71110–6 paperback
(*outside North America only*)

You can receive future titles in this series as they are published by placing a standing order.
Please contact your bookseller or, in case of difficulty, write to us at the address below with
your name and address, the title of the series and one of the ISBNs quoted above.

Customer Services Department, Macmillan Distribution Ltd, Houndmills, Basingstoke,
Hampshire RG21 6XS, England

Globalization and the Politics of Resistance

Edited by

Barry K. Gills
Senior Lecturer in International Politics
University of Newcastle upon Tyne

Foreword by John Kenneth Galbraith

First published in Great Britain 2000 by
MACMILLAN PRESS LTD
Houndmills, Basingstoke, Hampshire RG21 6XS and London
Companies and representatives throughout the world

A catalogue record for this book is available from the British Library.

ISBN 0–333–79332–3

First published in the United States of America 2000 by

ST. MARTIN'S PRESS, INC.,
Scholarly and Reference Division,
175 Fifth Avenue, New York, N.Y. 10010

ISBN 0–312–23023–0

Library of Congress Cataloging-in-Publication Data
Globalization and the politics of resistance / edited by Barry K. Gills ; foreword,
John Kenneth Galbraith.
    p. cm. — (International political economy series)
Includes bibliographical references and index.
ISBN 0–312–23023–0 (cloth)
1. International economic integration. 2. Competition, International. 3.
Government, Resistance to. 4. Social movements. I. Gills, Barry K., 1956– II.
Series.
HF1418.5 .G58184   2000
337—dc21
                                                                99–051482

This book is printed on paper suitable for recycling and made from fully managed and sustained
forest sources.

10   9   8   7   6   5   4   3   2   1
09   08   07   06   05   04   03   02   01   00

Printed and bound in Great Britain by
Antony Rowe Ltd, Chippenham, Wiltshire

To all those who struggle for a better future

Contents

vii

Foreword: The Social Left and the Market System

John Kenneth Galbraith

I begin this preface with the diversity of designations accorded the socially concerned and active in similarly developed national communities in our time. In continental Europe and elsewhere there are democratic socialists and social democrats. In the United States we are liberals; in Britain, labour and social democrats. Elsewhere the reference generally is to the social left. The difference in designation is unimportant; in rewarding measure, all are united by the political purposes that we affirm, even more by the economic and political structures with which we live. To these I turn first.

Common to all economically advanced countries is the basic market system for the production of goods and services – the word 'capitalism', one notes, is now politically not quite correct. The market system produces goods and services in the favoured countries of the world in manifest abundance – an abundance so great that large sums of money and heavy literary and artistic effort must be spent to cultivate the wants it then supplies. We do not accept that this performance is without flaw; this I will sufficiently urge. In the more remote recesses of philosophical thought the present preoccupation with consumer satisfaction, original and contrived, may be regretted. There are also environmental problems and those of resource supply. These will be ever more pressing and urgent in the future. There is also the strong political voice with which the market system endows those who own or manage its productive apparatus. But we accept the system; there is no plausible alternative. Even the British Labour Party, long the custodian of a richly endowed dissent, has now rendered such acceptance.

And let us be fully aware of another circumstance: the survival of the modern market system was, in large measure, our accomplishment. It would not have so survived had it not been for the successful efforts of the social left. Capitalism in its original form was an insufferably cruel thing. Only with trade unions, pensions for the old, compensation for the unemployed, public health care, lower-cost housing, a safety net for the unfortunate and the deprived and public action to mitigate capitalism's commitment to boom and slump did it become socially and politically acceptable. Let us not be reticent: we are the custodians of a political tradition that saved classical capitalism from itself.

Let us also note that this salvation was over the entrenched and often vehement opposition of those so saved. That opposition remains to this day. The individuals and economic institutions most in the debt of both economic advance and social tranquillity are those that, now with money and voice, most oppose the action that serves those ends. Nothing on the political right is so certain as its opposition to what advances its own deeper, durable interest.

In recent years there has been a current of thought, or what is so described, which holds that all possible economic activity should be returned to the market. The market system having been accepted, it must now be universal; privatization has been made a public faith. This, needless to say, we reject. The question of private versus public action is a purely practical matter; the decision depends on the particular merits of the particular case. Conservatives need to be warned, as we warn ourselves: ideology can be a heavy blanket over thought. Our commitment is to thought. Thought also guides us on the flaws, inequities and cruelties in the market system, and on the needed social action. It is recognition of these flaws, inequities and cruelties that most effectively unites us in common purpose.

There is, first, the very evident fact that the market system is unreliable in its performance – that it moves from good times to bad, from boom to bust. In the process it brings deprivation to the most vulnerable of its participants. The only valid design is for an economy of steady well-being and reliable growth. This requires strong, intelligent public intervention to temper and arrest the speculative boom and to ensure against hardship and deprivation in the depressive aftermath.

There is no novelty as to what is required; the relevant action is the product of the best in economic thought over the past century. We must not be in fear of strong, productive economic performance. We must, however, have well in mind the danger of speculative excess. The public budget – taxes and expenditures – must be a restraining force. So also action against mergers and acquisitions and other manifestations of adverse corporate behaviour. Monetary restraint – higher interest rates – can be in order, a matter to which conservatives are often more than adequately agreeable. And there must also be general public recognition that the system is, by its nature, given to speculative excess. There is merit and possible caution in recognizing the inevitable.

In recession and against unemployment the course is better defined: there must be low interest rates to encourage borrowing for investment, an action also accepted by conservatives, who see in detached hygienic central-bank action a substitute for more effective anti-depressive policy. There must be further and effective employment policy. The social loss and human distress of unemployment must be directly addressed. This means there must be alternative public employment; the social waste of idleness cannot be accepted.

This Keynesian design, the main current of modern conservatism holds, has, it is held, gone out of fashion. Fashion should not be a controlling fact in economic policy. There is no substitute in recession for a policy of publicly insured employment and economic growth. That is our belief and our promise.

We also point out that one large and influential sector of conservative thought now accepts recurrent stagnation and recession, greatly preferring them to public action to counter their adverse effect. In this view unemployment is also the necessary counter to inflation. We cannot be casual about inflation; where wage and price restraints are relevant, we are willing to urge them. But we are also willing in the future, as in the past, to accept a modest increase in prices as a condition of steady economic growth. We do not seek the euthanasia of the rentier class; but we do not accept that an all-pervasive malignant fear of inflation should arrest all economic growth.

A reliably growing economy begins but does not end the agenda of the social left. There are specific flaws against which we must rally political strength and act. The market system distributes income in a highly unequal fashion – a matter on which the United States has, unquestionably, the adverse leadership. Strong and effective trade union organization, a humane minimum wage, social security, medical care, are a recognized part of the answer. So more directly is the progressive income tax. Few exercises in social argument are so obviously in defence of financial self-interest as those brought forward by the rich in argument against their taxes. It boils down to the slightly improbable case that the rich are not working because they have too little income, the poor because they have too much; that if you feed the horse enough oats, some will pass through to the road for the sparrows.

The social left does not seek equality in income distribution. People differ in ability and in aspiration in the pursuit of both financial reward and gain. There is also the inevitable role of initiative, luck and avarice. This must be accepted. There can be no retreat, however, from the goal of a socially defensible distribution of income. This, above all, the tax system must continue to address.

There must also be firm recognition of another major flaw of the market system. That is its allocation of income as between public and private services and functions. Private television, notably in the United States, is richly financed; urban public schools are seriously starved. Private dwellings are clean, tolerable and pleasant; public housing and public streets are in disrepair and filth. Libraries, public recreational facilities, basic social services – all more needed by the poor than the rich – are seen as a burden. The private living standard, in contrast, is good, even sacrosanct. This anomaly we do not tolerate.

More generally there must be an effective safety net – individual and family support – for all who live on the lower edge of the system or below. Nothing so limits the freedom of the citizen as a total absence of money.

In the United States there has just been a two-year, and for the time successful, attack on our welfare system – in plain language, a winning war of the affluent against the poor. Other countries have had a milder manifestation. In this conflict there is no question as to where we stand. There must be strong support for the social measures that protect the poorest of our people. A rich society can do no less.

We should also be aware of one important cause of this attack on public services and a safety net for the poor because it was also our accomplishment. Over the years we brought social programmes into existence – health care, social security, measures for a more reliably working economy, much else. In doing so, we made many people secure in their well-being and in consequence, as might be expected, more conservative in their public attitudes and expression. They now see help to the less fortunate as a threat to their own security. Let us again be aware of our political accomplishment. However, let us not be sorry; we were right.

I turn finally to the larger international scene. A closer association between the major economic powers is a fact of our times. Trade, international corporations, travel, technology, cultural activity and exchange have all had this effect. In contrast with the two wars that so darkened the first half of the twentieth century, this is a strongly favourable development for which there can be no regret. Blind nationalism has a cruel and depressing history. There are conditions, however, on which we must insist. The move towards closer international association should not be at cost to the welfare systems of the participating states. These must be protected. There must be effective co-ordination of social welfare policy, and of the larger and controlling fiscal and monetary policy. It is of this, not socially barren trade policy, that presidents and prime ministers increasingly must speak when they meet together, and for which there must be an effective international structure. There can be no case for the narrow commitment to the nation-state. But neither can there be one to a mindless course which sacrifices the social gains of the century just past and those for which there is still need.

There is another international obligation that we recognize: concern for human well-being does not stop at national frontiers – in particular, those of the fortunate countries. It must extend on to the poor of the planet; hunger, disease and death are equally a source of human suffering wherever and by whomever they are experienced. This all civilized people must accept.

The worst of suffering comes now from internal disorder and conflict. The people of the fortunate countries, on the whole, live peacefully together; this is one of the rewards of well-being. It is the poor who devastate and destroy each other. There must, accordingly, be a reliable commitment by the fortunate countries to end conflict, bring order when this is humanly essential. I do not see this as the special responsibility of any one country; I would like to see it as the effective and well-financed responsibility of the United Nations. The claims of national sovereignty do not protect against the slaughter of the poorest of the poor by the poor.

Beyond this, there must be an absolute obligation on the rich countries to give help. This is a matter with which I have long been concerned; we must not yield to the argument that because people are still poor, the help has been ineffective. In the early stages of development effort we were, indeed, too eager to transport the heavy industrial furniture of the developed lands to the new countries: steel mills, electric plants and dams. Human investment, that in health and education, we have now come to recognize as of central importance. Over the world we now recognize there is no literate population that is poor, no illiterate population that is other than poor.

Let us also be aware, a matter in the past not understood, that what is possible and right in social and economic action in the favoured countries cannot be transferred without thought to the poor. This too has been an error of past times.

Governments of sadly limited competence were given social and economic tasks beyond their capacity for effective action. All things, including social policy, must be in keeping with controlling circumstance. The early elementary role of government in the now advanced countries and that of relatively unhindered private enterprise were appropriate one to the other. Economic life and the social role of the state must be in keeping in the new countries. Failure to recognize this was a serious error of the social left as it first approached the problem of economic development.

I come to the end. Let our mood be good. The social attitude and action which I here urge are not of our invention. Perhaps we were not that resourceful, that innovative. They were given to us by history – by both the requirements and the opportunities of the highly developed economic and social structure. The elementary agrarian economy of past times did not suffer unemployment. Social security was not of high urgency. The young looked after the old. Health care was not important. Before the great modern advances in medicine and surgery the physician had little to sell. The choice between illness and health, death and life, was not controlled by ability to pay. It was urbanization that made necessary a great range of public services and a comprehensive structure of welfare support. Those who would reverse social action or even allow it to stagnate in the present are not in conflict with us; they are in conflict with the great force of history. We can even have a measure of sympathy for those who oppose us. We, not they, are in step with history.

JOHN KENNETH GALBRAITH

Acknowledgements

This book came about as a collaborative effort. The project began at the invitation of the Editors of *New Political Economy* – Tony Payne, Andrew Gamble and Ankie Hoogvelt – that I undertake to act as Editor of the journal's first special issue. After discussing the issues we could address we worked out a framework on globalization and political action. The result was 'Globalization and the Politics of Resistance', published in March 1997, as Vol. 2, No. 1 of *New Political Economy*. I would like to thank all of the people at *NPE* for the assistance they provided and particularly Tony Payne and Sylvia McColm for their help throughout the process. I would like to thank David Green for his assistance in the publishing of the special issue, and Lawrence Walton and Tracey Roberts at Carfax for all their help. Robert Latham and Jim Nolte are owed a great debt of gratitude for providing resources for a special symposium on 'The Politics of Globalization' held at the New School for Social Research in November 1996. I would like to thank John Kenneth Galbraith for consenting to speak at that symposium and for his interest in and contribution to the project. At Macmillan I would like to express my thanks to Tim Farmiloe, who originally commissioned the book version of the project, to Tim Shaw, as both series editor and contributor, to Aruna Vasudevan for all her assistance, and to Keith Povey for editorial advice. In the Department of Politics, University of Newcastle upon Tyne, my thanks go to Joan Davison, Morag Banning and Lesley Stanwix, all of whom have given so generously of their time. The members of the Newcastle Research Working Group on Globalization also played a valuable role in the work of this project and I would like to thank them again, including Louise Amoore, Richard Dodgson, Randall Germain, Paul Langley, Don Marshall, Elizabeth Pallister and Iain Watson. Finally, I would like to thank my family, especially my wife Dong- Sook Gills, and my children Shenandoah and Eugene, for all the love and support they have shown without which nothing would be possible.

BARRY K. GILLS

Some of the materials in this book were previously published in *New Political Economy*, Vol. 2, No. 1, March 1997, Special Issue *Globalization and the Politics of Resistance*, edited by Barry K. Gills. These materials are reproduced here (in revised form) with the permission of Carfax Publishing Company, PO Box 25, Abingdon, Oxfordshire OX14 3UE, UK.

List of Abbreviations

ACORN	Association of Community Organizations
ADV	Authoritarian Developmental Regime
AFL–CIO	American Federation of Labor–Congress of Industrial Organizations
AFSCME	American Federation of State, County and Municipal Employees
AIC	Advanced Industrialized Countries
AL	Awami League
BIS	Bank for International Settlements
BMA	Bangladesh Medical Association
BNP	Bangladesh Nationalist Party
BP	British Petroleum
BRAC	Bangladesh Rural Advancement Committee
CCRI	Clandestine Revolutionary Indigenous Committee
CEO	Chief Executive Officer
CEP	Canadian Communication, Energy, and Paperworkers Union
CETLAC	Centro de Estudios y Tables Laboral
CFDT	Confederation Française Democratique du Travail
CIOAC	Independent Confederation of Agricultural Workers and Peasants
CNC	National Peasant Confederation
CND	National Democratic Convention
CNOP	National Confederation of Popular Organizations
COB	Central Obrera Boliviana
CONAI	National Mediation Commission
COSATU	Congress of South African Trade Unions
CTJ	Citizens for Tax Justice
CTM	Confederation of Mexican Workers
CUT	Unified Workers Central of Brazil
CUT	Unitary Confederation of the Workers of Chile
CWA	Communication Workers of America
DFI	Development Financial Institutions
EFF	Extended Fund Facility
EOI	Export Orientated Industrialization
EPZ	Export Processing Zone

ESAP	Economic Structural Adjustment Programme
ETUC	European Trade Union Congress
EU	European Union
EWC	European Works Council
EZLN	Zapatista Army of National Liberation (Ejercito Zapatista de Liberacion Nacional)
FAT	Frente Autentico del Trabajo
FBCCI	Federation of Bangladesh Chambers of Commerce and Industries
FBUTA	Bangladesh Federation of University Teachers' Associations
FKTU	Korean Federation of Trade Unions
FLOC	Farm Labor Organizing Committee (AFL–CIO)
FNOC	National Federation of Organizations and Citizens
FOE	Friends of the Earth
FOWA	Federation of Ogoni Women's Associations
FZLN	Zapatista Front of National Liberation
G-7	Group of Seven Industrial Countries
GATT	General Agreement on Tariffs and Trade
GB	Grameen Bank
GDP	Gross Domestic Product
GK	Gonoshasthaya Kendra
GNP	Gross National Product
GSP	General System of Preferences
ICEF	International Federation of Chemical, Energy and General Workers' Unions
ICEM	International Federation of Chemical, Energy, Mine and General Workers' Unions
ICFTU	International Confederation of Free Trade Unions
IFI	International Financial Institutions
IGO	Intergovernmental Organization
ILO	International Labour Organization
IMF	International Monetary Fund
IMF (UNION)	International Metalworkers Federation
IPT	Industrial Policy Theory
IPTEP	Industrial Property Tax Exemption Programme
ITF	International Transport Workers Federation
ITS	International Trade Secretariat
IUF	International Union of Food (and Allied Workers Associations)
IWD	International Women's Day

JP	Jatiya Party
KCTU	Korean Confederation of Trade Unions
KMU	Kilusang Mayo Uno
LCD	Liquid Crystal Display
LCTJ	Louisiana Coalition for Tax Justice
MAPA	Minnesota Alliance for Progressive Action
MIF	Miners' International Federation
MNC	Multinational Corporation
MOSOP	Movement for the Survival of Ogoni People
MP	Member of Parliament
MPP	Market Promotion Programme
MTUC	Malaysian Trade Union Congress
MWENGO	Mwelekeo wa NGO
NAFTA	North America Free Trade Association
NANGO	National Association of Non-Governmental Organizations
NASA	National Aeronautic and Space Administration
NCG	Neutral Caretaker Government
NDC	Newly Democratized Country
NDP	New Democratic Party
NGO	Non-governmental Organization
NIC	Newly Industrializing Countries
NIE	Newly Industrializing Economy
NIEO	New International Economic Order
NIP	New Industrial Policy
NNPC	Nigerian National Petroleum Corporation
NTU	National Taxpayers' Union
NYCOP	National Youth Council Organization for Survival of Ogoni People
OCEZ	Emiliano Zapata Independent Peasant Alliance
ORIT	Regional Inter American Workers' Organization
PCM	Mexican Communist Party
PIRG	Public Interest Research Group
PNR	National Revolutionary Party
PPI	Progressive Policy Institute
PRD	Party of the Democratic Revolution
PRI	Institutional Revolutionary Party
PRM	Party of the Mexican Revolution
PSE	Pact for Economic Solidarity
PSUM	Unified Socialist Party of Mexico
PTTI	Postal, Telegraph, and Telephone International

RIP	Revised Investment Policy
SAP	Structural Adjustment Policy/Programme
SKOP	Sramic Karmachari Oikkya Parishal
SNTOAC	National Union of Farm Workers (CTM)
SOE	State-Owned Enterprise
STIP	Strategic Trade and Investment Policies
STRM	Sindicato de Telefonistas de la Republica Mexicana
STT	Strategic Trade Theory
TIE	Transnationals Information Exchange
TK	Taka
TNC	Transnational Corporation
UAW	United Autoworkers
UBINIG	Policy Research for Development Alternatives
UDU	Union of Ejido Unions and Peasant Organizations
UE	United Electrical, Radio and Machine Workers of America
UN	United Nations
UNPO	Unrepresented Nations and Peoples Organization
USSR	Union of Soviet Socialist Republics
W&D	Women and Development
WCC	World Company Councils
WCL	World Confederation of Labour
WFTU	World Federation of Trade Unions
ZANU–PF	Zimbabwe African National Union

Notes on the Contributors

Louise Amoore is a Lecturer in the Department of Government, University of Northumbria, UK, where she teaches international political economy. She is a member of the Newcastle Research Working Group on Globalization, Department of Politics, University of Newcastle upon Tyne. Her work has been published in *New Political Economy* and *Global Society*.

Terry Boswell is Professor of Sociology and Chair of the Department at Emory University, Atlanta, Georgia. His recent research interests include class solidarity versus racial conflict in US labor history, revolutions in Europe since 1500, and cross-national study of the relationship between class exploitation and income inequality.

Christine Chin is Assistant Professor of International Relations in the School of International Service at American University in Washington, DC. Her research and teaching interests are in the areas of Southeast Asia, international political economy, and cultural studies. She is the author of: *In Service and Servitude: Foreign Female Domestic Workers and the Malaysian 'Modernity Project'* (1998).

Richard Dodgson is a research fellow at the Health Policy Unit, London School of Hygiene and Tropical Medicine, University of London. He recently attained his PhD, written on the global women's health movement and the Cairo Conference on population, at the University of Newcastle upon Tyne. He is a member of the Newcastle Research Working Group on Globalization. He has taught at the Universities of Durham, Newcastle upon Tyne and Sunderland. His work has been published in *New Political Economy*. *Politics* and *Journal of Contemporary Health*.

Ian R. Douglas is a Visiting Scholar at the Watson Institute for International Studies, Brown University, where he teaches political philosophy. He is the general editor and director of the power foundation (www.power foundation.org). He is working on a project entitled, *On the Genealogy of Globalism*.

Richard Falk is Albert G. Milbank Professor of International Law and Practice at Princeton University, where he has been a member of faculty since 1961. He is the author of *On Humane Governance: Toward a New Global Politics* (1995); and *Law in the Emerging Global Village: A Post-Westphalian Perspective* (1998).

John Kenneth Galbraith is Professor Emeritus in Economics at Harvard University. Among his many works are: *The Great Crash* (1954); *The Affluent Society* (1962); *The New Industrial State* (1962); *The Culture of Contentment* (1992); and *The Good Society* (1997). He served in the administrations of Presidents Franklin D. Roosevelt and John F. Kennedy and has tirelessly continued to speak out for the values of a just society.

Barry K. Gills is Senior Lecturer in International Politics in the Department of Politics, University of Newcastle upon Tyne, UK, and Director of the Newcastle Research Working Group on Globalization. His works include *Low Intensity Democracy: Political Power in the New World Order* (edited with Joel Rocamora and Richard Wilson; 1993); *Transcending the State/Global Divide: A Neo-structuralist Agenda in International Relations* (edited with R. Palan, 1994); *The World System: Five Hundred Years or Five Thousand?* (edited with Andre Gunder Frank, 1993/6); *Regimes in Crisis: The Post-Soviet Era and the Implications for Development* (edited, with Shahid Qadir, 1995); and *Korea versus Korea: A Case of Contested Legitimacy* (1996).

Jeffrey A. Hart is Professor of Political Science at Indiana University, Bloomington, where he teaches international politics and international political economy. He taught at Princeton University from 1973 to 1980 and was visiting scholar at the Berkeley Roundtable on the International Economy from 1987–89. His publications include: *The New International Economic Order* (1983); *Interdependence in the Post Multilateral Era* (1985); *Rival Capitalists* (1992); *The Politics of International Economic Relations*, 5th edition (with Joan Spero, 1997); *Globalization and Governance* (edited with Aseem Prakash, 1999), *Coping with Globalization* (edited with Aseem Prakash, forthcoming) and *Responding to Globalization* (edited with Aseem Prakash, forthcoming), and numerous articles in journals including *International Organization*, and *World Politics*.

R. J. Barry Jones is Professor of International Relations at the University of Reading, UK. He was the founding secretary of the British International Studies Association and is the General Editor of the *Routledge Encyclopedia of International Political Economy*. His current research interests include globalization and the limits of state action. His recent work includes: *Globalization and Interdependence in the International Political Economy: Rhetoric and Reality* (1995).

Paul Langley is currently a research officer working for the City Council of Newcastle upon Tyne. He recently attained his PhD, written on world financial orders and world financial centers, from the University of Newcastle upon Tyne. He is a member of the Newcastle Research Working Group on Globalization. His work has been published in *New Political Economy*.

Robert Latham is the Director of the Social Science Research Council-MacArthur Foundation Program on International Peace and Security and an adjunct Assistant Professor at Columbia University, School of International Affairs. His book, *The Liberal Moment: Modernity, Security, and the Making of Postwar International Order* was published in 1997.

Don Marshall is a Research Fellow at the Sir Arthur Lewis Institute of Social and Economic Research, the University of the West Indies. His book, *The Caribbean, NAFTA and Regional Developmentalism* was published by Macmillan in 1998. He was a member of the Newcastle Research Working Group on Globalization from 1995–7. He is currently Managing Editor of the *Journal of Eastern Caribbean Studies*.

Sandra J. MacLean is an Assistant Professor of Political Science at Dalhousie University. She has published on civil society, peacebuilding and regionalism in the *Canadian Journal of Development Studies, Third World Quarterly*. Jeong (ed.) *The New Agenda for Peace Research* and van Walravan (ed.) *Early Warning and Conflict Prevention*.

James Mittelman is Professor in the School of International Service at American University, Washington, DC and has recently been a member at the Institute for Advanced Study in Princeton. His publications include *Innovation and Transformation in International Studies* (1997); *Out From Underdevelopment Revisited: Global Structures and the Remaking of the Third World* (with Mustapha Kamal Pasha;

1997); *Globalization: Critical Reflections* (edited, 1996); and *The Globalization Syndrome: Transformation and Resistance* (2000).

Adam David Morton is a doctoral candidate in the Department of International Politics, University of Wales, Aberystywth, completing his doctoral dissertation on 'Social Forces in the Making of Mexico: Hegemony and Neoliberalism in the International Political Economy'.

Cyril I. Obi is a Senior Research Fellow at the Nigerian Institute of International Affairs, Lagos, Nigeria and recently a visiting fellow at the African Studies Centre, Leiden, Netherlands. He is currently a Series Associate Member of St Antony's College, Oxford University. His research interests include international economic relations, globalization and the environment, and Nigerian politics, the petroleum sector and economic development. His publications include: *Structural Adjustment, Oil and Popular Struggles: The Deepening Crisis of State Legitimacy in Nigeria* (Dakar 1996–7).

Mustapha Kamal Pasha is Associate Professor of Comparative and International Political Economy in the School of International Service at American University in Washington, DC. He specializes in Third World political economy and culture, Islamic Studies, and South Asia, and he is the author of: *Colonial Political Economy: Recruitment and Underdevelopment in the Punjab* (1998); and *Out From Underdevelopment Revisited: Changing Global Structures and the Remaking of the Third World* (with James H. Mittelman, 1997).

Jan Nederveen Pieterse is Associate Professor in Sociology at the Institute of Social Studies in the Hague. He has taught in Ghana and the US and has been visiting professor in Japan and Indonesia. He is co-editor of *Review of International Political Economy* and an advisory editor to several journals. His books include: *White on Black: Images of Africa and Blacks in Western Popular Culture* (1992); *Empire and Emancipation* (1989); *Development – Deconstructions/Reconstructions* (forthcoming); and several edited volumes including: *Global Futures (forthcoming); World Orders in the Making: Humanitarian Intervention and Beyond* (1998); *The Decolonization of Imagination* (with Bhikhu Parekh, 1995); *Emancipations, Modern and Postmodern* (1992); and *Christianity and Hegemony* (1992).

Aseem Prakash is Assistant Professor of Strategic Management and Public Policy at the School of Business and Public Management, The George Washington University, Washington, DC. He is also a faculty member in the Department of Political Science and The Elliott School of International Affairs, The George Washington University. He is the author of *Greening the Firm: The Politics of Corporate Environmentalism* (Cambridge University Press, 2000) and the co-editor of *Globalization and Governance* (Routledge, 1999), *Coping with Globalization* (Routledge, 2000), and *Responding to Globalization* (Routledge, 2000). His research examines the impact of globalization of public policy and business strategy, and the political economy of environmental issues.

Fahimul Quadir is an Assistant Professor of Political Science at Queen's University in Kingston, Ontario and at the University of Chittagong, Bangladesh. He has published on issues of governance, democratization, economic liberalization and development in Thomas and Wilkin (eds), *Globalization and the South* and Poku and Pettiford (eds), *Redefining the Third World*.

Mark Rupert is Associate Professor of Political Science at Syracuse University's Maxwell School of Citizenship and Public Affairs, and teaches in the areas of international relations and political economy. He is the author of *Producing Hegemony: The Politics of Mass Production and American Global Power* (1995) and *Ideologies of Globalization: Contending Visions of a New World Order* (2000).

Johannes Dragsbaek Schmidt is Assistant Professor at the Research Center on Development and International Relations, Department of Development and Planning, Aalborg University, Denmark. He specializes in international political economy, social change, labor and South-East Asian development. His most recent work is *Globalization and Social Change* (edited with Jacques Hersh, 1999).

Timothy M. Shaw is Professor of Political Science and International Development Studies and Director of the Centre for Foreign Policy Studies at Dalhousie University. He is the Editor of the Macmillan International Political Economy series and has taught at universities in Nigeria, South Africa, Uganda, Zambia and Zimbabwe and has published widely on African affairs and development issues.

Dimitris Stevis is Associate Professor of Political Science at Colorado State University where he teaches international political economy and environmental politics. His recent work includes a comparative analysis of the impacts of regional and global economic integration on international labor and environmental politics and policy. He is co-editor of volume 12 of the International Political Economy Yearbook (International Studies Association/Lynne Rienner) on the environment. His work has appeared in journals including *New Political Economy, Work and Occupations*, and *Journal of World-Systems Research*.

Kenneth P. Thomas is Associate Professor of Political Science and Fellow, Center for International Studies, at the University of Missouri–St Louis. He is the author of: *Capital Beyond Borders: States and Firms in the Auto Industry, 1960–1994* (1997), and *Competing for Capital: European and North American Responses* (forthcoming)

Peter Waterman has recently retired from the Institute of Social Studies, The Hague, Netherlands, where he was resident for many years as both an activist and scholar. His most recent book is *Globalization, Social Movements and the New Internationalisms* (1998), which argues for a 'new global solidarity' that relates to a radicalized, globalized, informatized and complex capitalist modernity. He is co-editor (with Ronaldo Munck) of *Labour Worldwide in the Era of Globalization: Alternative Union Models in the New World Order* (1999).

Iain Watson is completing his PhD on postmodern considerations of social resistance, in the Department of Politics, University of Newcastle upon Tyne. He is a member of the Newcastle Research Working Group on Globalization. He has taught at the University of Newcastle upon Tyne and University of Northumbria. His work has been published in *New Political Economy*.

Part I

Globalization and Resistance: Thinking through Politics

1
Introduction: Globalization and the Politics of Resistance

Barry K. Gills

> 'rebellion is one of man's essential dimensions. It is our historical reality. Unless we ignore reality, we must find our values in it ... Man's solidarity is founded upon rebellion, and rebellion can only be justified by this solidarity ... In order to exist, man must rebel ... Rebellion is the common ground on which every man bases his first values. I *rebel* – therefore we *exist*.'
>
> Albert Camus, *The Rebel* (*L'Homme revolté*) 1951

The paradox of neoliberal economic globalization is that it both weakens and simultaneously activates the social forces of resistance. As the 'global crisis' of 1998–9 demonstrated to all of the world, the on-going debate on 'globalization' is strategic for the coming era. The shape of the future depends on its outcome. This book sets out to alter the intellectual and political terms of the globalization debate, and thus its strategic direction. Firstly, this goal is to be accomplished by asserting the centrality of 'the political' and repudiating narrow economic determinism and the 'teleology' of neoliberal economic globalization.

The key political tension in the coming era will be between the forces of neoliberal economic globalization, seeking to expand the freedom of capital, and the forces of social resistance, seeking to preserve and to redefine community and solidarity. It is by *acts of resistance* that we will establish our *solidarities* and our *identities* in the 'era' of globalization.

The analytical focus of the study of the globalization phenomena must therefore shift from the technical to the political. It is no longer sufficient for critics of globalization simply to 'document transnational neo-liberalism'.[1] There is a profound need for re-thinking the question of what social practices now constitute viable political strategies in the world economy.[2] This implies a direct relationship between new practice and new theory, which can be best accomplished in conscious alignment with the dissenting social forces of resistance.

A new 'politics of resistance' to neoliberal economic globalization invokes an analogy with the resistance movements of the Second World War.[3] While the world may currently seem to be dominated by an entrenched ideology there is yet the necessity (and the possibility) of purposeful resistance. Thus, the politics of resistance is not merely reactive or defensive, or representing a minority interest. Rather, it is a form of political action which should represent the general or societal interest and with the potential to transform the political situation and produce a real alternative.

What does the new politics of resistance seek to resist? 'Globalization' has become an extremely broad concept that can encompass everything, thus rendering the term either meaningless, confusing, or seductive to the unwary.[4] However, when the concept is expressed as 'neoliberal economic globalization' its meaning becomes clearer. I suggest that neoliberal economic globalization has four defining characteristics:

1 protection of the interests of capital and expansion of the process of capital accumulation on world scale;

2 a tendency towards homogenization of state policies and state forms to render them instrumental to the protection of capital and the process of capital accumulation on world scale, via a new 'market ideology';

3 the formation and expansion of a new tier of transnationalized institutional authority above the state's, which has the aim and purpose of re-articulating states to the purposes of facilitating global capital accumulation; and

4 the political exclusion of dissident social forces from the arena of state policy-making, in order to desocialize the subject and insulate the neoliberal state form against the societies over which they preside, thus facilitating the socialization of risk on behalf of capital.[5]

The main historical thrust of neoliberal economic globalization is to bring about a situation in which private capital and 'the market' alone determine the restructuring of economic, political and cultural life, making alternative values or institutions subordinate. Rather than capital and 'the economy' being embedded in society and harnessed to serve social ends, 'the economy' becomes the master of society and of all within it, and society exists to serve the ends of capital and its need for self-expansion.[6] It is a necessary aspect of this process that 'politics' itself, and 'democracy' in particular, should become increasingly formalistic, stripped of substantive radical, revolutionary, or even reformist content, any of which might challenge the consolidation of the hegemony of capital over society.

Rather than a historical triumph of democracy and capitalist market ideology via globalization,[7] we face a danger of slipping ever deeper into a 'historic malaise' of capitalism engendered by globalization.[8] Existing democracies, and the complex social compromises on which they rest, confront a lingering death accompanied by growing social polarization and conflict, while new or 'low intensity democracies' are marked by the limited degree of progressive change they allow, rather than by their transformative capacity.[9] The democratic gains of the past, and potential gains of the future, are re-interpreted as being 'fetters' on the capital accumulation process, which the economy, we are told, can no longer afford. The claims of social justice are submerged beneath claims for 'natural justice' via the marketplace. Compete or die! Competition is life! These are the new slogans of ascendant capital over moribund society. However, it is obvious that wherever there is competition, only a few will be winners, and many will be losers.

Thus, the real impetus of neoliberal economic globalization is more likely to be socially and politically retrogressive than progressive. An historical retrogression of capitalist civilization would be a period characterized by greater social polarization between rich and poor, increasing inequality, growing concentration of wealth, intensified competition for market shares, crippling debt service payments for weaker economies, and an unstable political order both domestically and internationally. Many are so mesmerized by the idea of linear progress and the putative role of scientific rationality and technology within it, that they may be unaware even of the possibility of historical retrogression, though many societies have suffered such processes in the past.

By advocating a doctrine of the inescapable technological determination of the future, neoliberal economic globalization defines a single mode of reorganization of social practices. This teleology of capital, being both ahistorical and above all apolitical, attempts to inculcate the mythological notion that the political process is now merely a 'transmission mechanism' from 'capital logic' to society. Globalization discourse invalidates its critics as 'unrealistic' because they recognize neither the validity nor the inevitability of this single and 'mythological' mode of thought. But we must begin our critique of globalization precisely by challenging its 'myth' , and by recognizing that it is an abstraction deliberately cast in the mythological mode. As such, it is wielded as a power concept over society, endowed with emotive resonance drawing upon a heightening of the sense of compulsion, fear, and the imperative of speed.[10]

I begin our critique, therefore, by challenging the idea that neoliberal economic globalization is either historically necessary or inevitable. Globalization is a contested concept, not a received theory. There is no single determinant economic logic external to society, to the state, and to political processes. Methodologically, it is necessary to insist upon the socially contested and historically open nature of all forms of political economy, 'globalization' foremost among them. Having made a 'historicist turn' we must begin by making the effort to 'bring people back in' to international political economy as the agents at the centre of historical change.[11] Otherwise, we are left with socially barren formulations that strip people and agency from history, leaving only 'structure' as the over-determining 'reality'. When 'globalization' implies 'the death of politics', it feeds on political cynicism, defeatism, and immobilism.

But 'wild capitalism' or 'savage capitalism' is as unacceptable as the boom and bust cycle and the extremes of exploitation and conflict with which it is so clearly historically associated. As the pendulum of history is urged to swing back to the norms and forms of pre-unionized, pre-welfare state, and pre-democratic capitalism, history teaches us that people *will resist*. They will not passively accept 'an open ended and long term challenge to the majority's quality of life'. Indeed, 'Once that majority also understands that the obstacles standing in the way of a reversal of these trends are not immutable historical laws or technological inevitabilities, but political choices imposed on them by a venal and short-sighted minority, the time will be ripe for change.'[12]

To begin to reconstruct the politics of resistance in the 'era of globalization' we must first insist on the right to rebel, that is on the inalienable right of society and social forces to protect themselves from the destructive vagaries of the unregulated (or 'self-regulating') market and to choose their own meaningful ways

of constituting their solidarities, their collectivities, and
ities to this end. Among the 'manifesto of social rights' *vis-u* .
'globalization', I would suggest the following:

1 the right of individuals, families and communities to employment, welfare, social stability and social justice;
2 the right of labour, whether in the formal or informal sectors,
   unionized or non-unionized, to resist unemployment, austerity
   measures, reduced life chances, increased insecurity, atomization,
   alienation, dislocation and immiseration;
3 the right of the poor, dispossessed and marginalized, wherever
   they exist, to resist the imposition of poverty and the intensification of social polarization;
4 the right of the people to reclaim and deploy government (state
   power) in their own self-defence, at all levels from local, national,
   and regional to global, and whether through radical, revolutionary
   or reformist forms;
5 the right of all people to establish social solidarities and autonomous forms of social organization outside the state and the
   market; and finally
6 the right to imagine 'post-globalization' and realize alternative
   modes of human development.

The contributors to this volume address the 'politics of resistance'
from a wide variety of perspectives. As John Kenneth Galbraith argues,
in the present era many elites seem increasingly preoccupied by
the pursuit of 'socially barren trade policy'.[13] The weakening of society
and the state in terms of their organizational capacity to resist globalization threatens national welfare systems, privileging tighter
international economic integration at the expense of some of the
social gains of the past century. This 'mindless course' marches
under the banner of the new market ideology.[14] As states compete
for the favours of transnationally mobile capital, the 'race to the
bottom' threatens to increase the rate of exploitation of labour at
global scale. The deregulation of finance and decentering of production contribute to the destabilization of national societies and
their political frameworks. As state capacity decreases the structural
power of capital increases, as do social and class conflicts. All states
and societies seem under pressure to make ever greater concessions
to capital, including greater capital mobility, flexibilization of labour,
lower social burdens and higher (indirect) social subsidies for capital., the upshot of which is a redistribution of wealth from labour
to capital. All states are potentially vulnerable to sudden capital

movement, whether by productive or 'speculative' capital. The recent Asian/global crisis of 1997–9 clearly demonstrated the power of mobile capital to destabilize economies, societies, and states.

What is needed is the political will to develop an alternative global political agenda of social and economic restructuring. This agenda should involve the building of new coalitions of social forces working directly with each other and where possible through governments to bring about a new diplomacy of co-ordination. This co-ordination should encompass improving social, welfare, and employment standards, aligning fiscal and monetary policies, international labour standards (especially in transnational firms), universal and binding corporate 'codes of conduct', and tighter controls on cross-border capital movement, especially short-term speculative capital movement.

As Richard Falk argues, elitist 'globalization-from-above' must be met by an assertive and effective 'globalization-from-below'.[15] The countervailing forces include labour, social movements, and the state. All three forces are needed, but with the necessity to transcend exclusionist practices of the past and avoid retreat into narrow localism or traditional nationalism. 'Globalization-from-below' should also mean establishing new roles for leadership from the global 'South', and by labour and women from the South in particular, in constructing the new practices of global civil society. As Jan Nederveen Pieterse and Peter Waterman point out, the re-articulation of 'global solidarity' requires networking and new communicative and organizational modes of practice linking local, national, regional, and global level strategies for reform.[16] The internal flaws of past movements, including racism, sexism, xenophobia and 'protectionism' *vis-à-vis* other groups, imply the need for a significant attitudinal change among the social forces of resistance in order to enhance the effectiveness of new attempts to achieve broader social and international solidarity.[17] In the labour movement, a legacy of exclusionist practices, native prejudice, bureaucratic organization and corporatist structures still hampers international solidarity efforts, but the possibility of overcoming some of these problems does exist and is made imperative by the new conditions of the world economy.[18] Cultural prejudices that stereotype rather than illuminate the nature of social movements must be transcended, and this is particularly the case at present in the attitude of Western observers to Islamic social movements.[19] It is only by seizing the opportunities of global communication that emancipatory movements can create via new practice a new human consciousness, aimed directly at the civilizing of global society.[20] It is thus that by *acts of resistance* that the necessary connection between new practice and new theory is to be established, from which may flow an alternative global civilization.

There is a need for 'unifying strategies' by resistance and emancipatory movements in order to confront globalizing capitalism with commensurate organizational capacity. However, this should certainly not take the form of the homogenizing imperialist modernization which constituted the dominant universalism of the past era. What is needed is perhaps an 'indigenization' of universalism, by which I mean that any new form of universalism must flow, in the first instance, from the 'bottom' upward, that is from the people to their organizations and not the other way around. It is by confronting common experiences, derived from the common impetus of neoliberal economic globalization and its effects on the majority, that such a common consciousness can emerge. 'Global solidarity' may not replace local and national society, nor the privileging of these sites of social action, but it will become an ever more necessary and useful supplement to them. We seem to be moving beyond the era of the religious universalist, the liberal cosmopolitan, and even the socialist internationalist. Nor can we make a universal prescription to return to either the Keynesian welfare state or to the 'national' social democratic state of the past era. Both have been criticized for having done much to disarm civil society, thus preparing the way for the onset of neoliberal economic globalization.[21]

The issues on which the new resistance movements campaign may seem diverse, ranging from indigenous peoples' land rights, national land reform and social justice, resistance to structural adjustment programmes, opposition to 'corporate welfare' subsidies, women's empowerment, environmental protection, to the struggle for national and international labour rights,[22] but all are part of a societal response to market-driven globalization. There can be no new grand strategy or grand narrative across such a diversity of struggles, nor need there be such. These movements and the new practices of global solidarity will form new sources of democratic and progressive change at local, national and global scales, as well as constituting new sources of knowledge and epistemology for 'global civilization.'

The 'guiding ideology' of these new global practices of solidarity need not entail the grand strategies of the past. It can consist of a small core of values, which can be interpreted through a variety of cultural understandings. I would suggest the following credo:

> Neither the market nor capital logic ever create equality or social justice automatically. The creation of a just and prosperous society always requires conscious normatively committed human action, recognizing our moral duty to fellow humanity. Wealth and prosperity are socially determined outcomes and are achieved through a fair distribution of resources and social product. Human progress is measured by the achievement of social justice and the elimination of poverty and oppression, not by the unbridled accumulation of private wealth or the naked exercise of power.

It is time to *overturn* neoliberal economic globalization, and by doing so to create a new world.

Notes

1 The original version of this argument was made in my editorial introduction to 'Globalization and the Politics of Resistance', a special issue of *New Political Economy* (Vol. 2, No. 1, March 1997). See also: André C. Drainville, 'International Political Economy in the Age of Open Marxsim', *Review of International Political Economy*, Vol. 1, No. 1 (1994), pp. 105–32, 425.

2 See the chapter by James Mittleman and Christine Chin in this volume.

3 I am indebted to Susan George for this analogy, made at a Fellows meeting of the Transnational Institute, Amsterdam.

4 For discussion of the exaggerated claims of 'globalization' and the comparison to other concepts, such as 'interdependence' see the chapter by R. J. Barry Jones in this volume.

5 See the chapter by Louise Amoore, Richard Dodgson, Barry K. Gills, Paul Langley, Don Marshall, and Iain Watson in this volume.

6 For further discussion of the Polanyian perspective on the relations between society, the state and the market see the chapter by Robert Latham in this volume.

7 Examples of the triumphalist perspectives on globalization can be found in *Foreign Policy* (Summer 1997), 'The Globalization Debate'. For a discussion of populist interpretation in North America see the chapter by Mark Rupert in this volume.

8 See: Barry Gills, 'Whither Democracy? Globalization and the "New Hellenism"', in Caroline Thomas and Peter Wilkin (eds), *Globalization and the South* (Macmillan, 1996).

9 See: Barry Gills, Joel Rocamora and Richard Wilson (eds), *Low Intensity Democracy: Political Power in the New World Order* (Pluto, 1993); and Steve Smith, 'US Democracy Promotion: Theoretical Reflections', in Michael Cox, Takashi Inoguchi and John Ikenberry (eds), *US Democracy*

Promotion (Oxford University Press, 1999); and Barry Gills 'American Power, Neoliberal Globalization, and Low Intensity Democracy: An Unstable Trinity?', in Michael Cox, Takashi Inoguchi and John Ikenberry (eds), *US Democracy Promotion* (Oxford University Press, 1999).

10 See the chapter by Ian Douglas in this volume.

11 See: 'The Call to Historicize International Political Economy', by Louise Amoore, Richard Dodgson, Randall Germain, Barry Gills, Paul Langley, and Iain Watson, in *Review of International Political Economy* Vol. 7, No. 1 (2000).

12 Manfred Bienefeld, 'Capitalism and the Nation State in the Dog Days of the Twentieth Century', in Ralph Miliband and Leo Panitch (eds), *The Socialist Register* (Merlin Press, 1995), p. 103.

13 See the foreword by John Kenneth Galbraith in this volume and his 'Preface' to the special issue on 'Globalisation and the Politics of Resistance', *New Political Economy*, Vol. 2, No. 1 (March 1997), pp. 5–9.

14 *Ibid.*

15 See the chapter by Richard Falk in this volume.

16 See the chapters by Peter Waterman and Jan Nederveen Pieterse in this volume.

17 See the chapter by Adam David Morten on the Zapatista movement in this volume. For an example of the consequences of failure to build sufficient social alliances at national and regional level see the chapter by Cyril I. Obi in this volume.

18 See the chapters by Dimitris Stevis and Terry Boswell, and Johannes D. Schmidt in this volume.

19 See the chapter by Mustapha Kemal Pasha in this volume.

20 See the chapters by Peter Waterman and Jan Nederveen Pieterse in this volume.

21 See the chapters by Jeffrey A. Hart and Aseem Prakash, by Robert Latham, and by R. J. Barry Jones in this volume.

22 See the chapters by Sandra J. Maclean, Fahimul Quadir and Timothy Shaw; Kenneth Thomas; Dimitris Stevis and Terry Boswell; Johannes D. Schmidt; Cyril I. Obi; Adam David Morten; and Mustapha Kemal Pasha; and Louise Amoore *et al.* in this volume.

2
Overturning 'Globalization': Resisting Teleology, Reclaiming Politics

Louise Amoore, Richard Dodgson, Barry Gills,
Paul Langley, Don Marshall and Iain Watson

First order questions: do we accept 'globalization'?

The term 'globalization' has served as an arresting metaphor to provide explanation, meaning, and understanding of the nature of contemporary capitalism, though not all of the processes that currently come under the rubric of globalization are new.[1] It is meant to suggest a number of analytically distinct phenomena and developments within the international system, while combining them into a single overarching process of change. Considerable attention centres on the application of new (often information based) technologies to the production process, and parallel changes in management, organization, and communications at corporate, societal, and state levels.

Moreover, the current vogue has been to establish globalization as both epoch and epistemology. Its ideational foundation is rooted in notions of 'progress' and perpetual change. Neoliberalism seemingly triumphs in the intellectual firmament, as modernization theory is resuscitated to forecast convergence of economic and political systems across the globe due to the inexorable processes of capitalization/capital accumulation. In the words of one recent critical commentator, however, 'In reality, globalization is to the world economy what monetarism is to the domestic economy. It represents the final triumph of capital over labour...'.[2] The OECD promotes a Panglossian view of globalization as a liberal utopia giving 'all countries the possibility of participating in world development and all consumers the assurance of benefiting from increasingly vigorous competition between producers'.[3] On the other side of the

12

debate, as eminent a figure as J. K. Galbraith sums up the trends of the past fifteen years as 'The Uncertain Miracle' and warns of 'the possibility of a depressive equilibrium as regards unemployment.'[4] Ralf Dahrendorf worries 'How can the affluent societies of the world retain their wealth, freedom, and social cohesion in the face of the destructive pressures of economic globalization?'[5] Other economists worry that the trade liberalization and financial deregulation of the market dominated 1980s and 1990s have been associated with deflationary economic outcomes, while countries importing huge amounts of footloose capital can be destabilized rather than developed. The upshot is that rampant neoliberal economic globalization may not result in a new global utopia, but rather in a global dystopia. The threat of severe economic destabilization of many countries ranging from Russia, East Asia, and Brazil during the 'global crisis' of 1997/9 and a stream of commentary on global crisis that accompanied these events testify to the now common concern for the ability of the 'market system' to provide stability and welfare.

Even though a number of scholars critique the triumphalist strain within globalization discourse[6] they nevertheless seem to accept the basic assertion that contemporary capitalism has entered a new phase; i.e. globalization as epistemology leads to globalization as epoch. Thus a tendency to a univocal discourse (in this respect) has become a problem, and should be re-examined. For example, neo-classicists take the view that finance, culture, markets, and production are now so sufficiently interlinked as to constitute a change in global capitalism of abiding significance, making the retreat of the state inevitable and irreversible. Post-modernists and post-industrialists tend to mark the epochal shift in capitalism as occurring in the wake of significant 1970s adjustments. Neo-Schumpeterians echo these views by emphasizing the impact of technological change on the industrial base of core economies and thus on global capitalism. Regulationists and post-Fordists place emphasis on changes occurring in core firms, i.e. 'leaner' organization and management and 'flexible' production techniques. Neo-Gramscian scholars establish a changing order by referring to the transnational policy influence of an epistemic community of business elites, imbricated with a network of officials in governments and in various multilateral institutions.

The effect of all this analysis is too often, in our view, to create and sustain an assumption that globalization is manifestly obvious and inexorable. It is precisely this fundamental assumption that we wish to challenge. Globalization is a contested concept, not a received theory. In our view, it is a serious analytical, as well as political mistake to begin from the assumption 'Globalization *is*.' This raises the question of whether there is some 'single logic' at work in the processes of globalization, and our attitude to such a concept. The answer to this question depends on what is meant by 'logic'. If the logic of globalization is taken to mean something external to society and the state and inexorable, then we firmly reject this notion of a single logic. If on the other hand, a single logic is conceptualized as a set of common pressures or trends that we are all becoming increasingly bound up in, even though the patterns of responses are uneven, then we can provisionally accept such a concept.[7] However, it may be clarifying to talk about logic in terms of processes of capital accumulation, for example, as opposed to *the* logic of capital accumulation.

We arrive at a formulation of the problem whereby globalization as over-determined 'reality', i.e. as something 'external', has to be rejected, yet certain processes which currently come under the rubric of globalization and have real and felt damaging effects on people must be recognized and 'resisted', a process which begins by 'demystifying' them. Therefore, we insist that it is necessary to ask where these realities come from, i.e. does globalization originate from the ideological sphere? Thus, globalization has to be resisted both as ideology[8] and therefore in a struggle against intellectual opponents through elaboration of an alternative political economy, as well as at the level of the practical and political, i.e. via 'concrete strategies of resistance'.

We seek in the remainder of this research note to highlight some of the problems associated with deploying the concept globalization to our research agenda. This is done by questioning assumptions made about the presumed definition of globalization and its relationship with the state; civil society; and social movements (old and new).

What is globalization? The definitional problem

Most scholars seem to agree that globalization encompasses a broad range of material and non-material aspects of production, distribution, management, finance, information and communications technologies, and capital accumulation. The most visible effects or processes of globalization seem to be:

1 the increase in the speed and flow/flight of capital in money form;
2 the expansion of offshore financial markets;
3 the advance of computer-driven technologies;
4 the renewed impetus towards regionalization.

The choice of the root 'global' (implying a totality) and its transformation into an action-process verb form (-ization), seems to imbue the concept with a special meaning and social power.

When globalization is narrowed to the neoliberal project of economic globalization, then the outlines of a definition become clearer. In essence, we would contend that neoliberal economic globalization has four defining characteristics:

1 protection of the interests of capital and expansion of the process of capital accumulation (if this is viewed as occurring within and because of a structural crisis in capitalism or a long term economic stagnation, then neoliberal economic globalization is essentially a strategy of 'crisis management' or 'stabilization');
2 the tendency towards homogenization of state policies and even state forms towards the end of protecting capital and expanding the process of capital accumulation, via a new economic orthodoxy, i.e. 'market ideology' (wherein even the state itself becomes subject to marketization while simultaneously being deployed instrumentally on behalf of capital);
3 the addition and expansion of a layer of transnationalized institutional authority 'above the states' (which has the aim and purpose of penetrating states and re-articulating them to the purposes of global capital accumulation);
4 the exclusion of dissident social forces from the arena of state policy-making (in order to insulate the new neoliberal state form against the societies over which they preside and in order to facilitate the 'socialization of risk' on behalf of the interests of capital).

Nevertheless, the debate on globalization is obscured by a pervasive conceptual fuzziness surrounding the term itself. The definition of globalization exists in a wide range of permutations, with little consensus between the different approaches. There is certainly a set of 'clusters' of definition, according to the perspective or issue area from which the definition emanates. A crude typology of such definitional clusters might include the following categories: economic processes; political processes; world culture processes; and global civil society processes. As a discussant in the IPE debate on 'globalization' on the internet commented: 'Within each cluster, there is a substantial degree of variation in the degree of theoretical self-consciousness of usage of the term, the facts of globalization emphasized in the definition, and the degree to which "globalization" is considered to be a multidimensional process.'[9]

If we are to identify a common element across most of the prevailing approaches, then the notion of an 'epochal shift' does appear to be key. This idea consists of the notion that all societies, stimulated by the forces of global change, are taking on 'new' forms. These new configurations are characterized variously as, for example, 'post-Fordism',[10] post-modernity[11] post-industrialism.[12] There is, then, a general notion of reorganization 'after' something, though little agreement exists on exactly what the important crisis-ridden event(s) was or were. Nevertheless, the idea of profound discontinuity seems to prevail over the idea of fundamental continuity.

Although there is a certain attractiveness in avoiding precise definition, and of staking out a 'break' in history and declaring a 'crossroads' in historical capitalism, these are problematic from a 'social science' point of view. The reification of a 'new phase' and according it iconic status is a device which opens the gates to a conflation of theories. Misshapen fragments of ideas become integrated into a generalized overarching explanation. Thus, 'globalization' becomes a 'horse for every course'. Diverse perspectives are conflated in order to provide evidence of wholesale change. 'Globalization' tends to become a 'totalizing notion', and at the very least there is a strong tendency to eclecticism. For example, Castells and Hall[13] seek to explain changes in cities and regions through combining the dynamics of technological revolution, the formation of a global economy, and the emergence of the 'information age'. Bob Jessop uses an eclectic mix of post-Fordist thought, combining elements from the regulation school and the neo-Schumpeterians.[14] The problem of conflation of theories, which is a more serious matter than mere eclecticism, also manifests itself in terms of the empirical evidence deployed in analyses of globalization processes. Empirical evidence is commonly drawn from specific cases or 'ideal type' models which are then 'generalized up' to explain the whole picture; a kind of positivistic holism. For example, the 'industrial districts' of Third Italy and Baden Wurrtemburg are offered as models for the post-industrial production system.[15] The result of conceptual conflation is broadly twofold; on the one hand for those seeking to manage the contemporary situation, the conceptual incoherence breeds simplicity in a complex world.[16] A new grand narrative may be emerging from disparate fragments of global analysis. On the other hand, for those unable to untangle the conflated strands of the debate, it breeds genuine confusion.

The teleology of 'globalization'

In seeking to unravel some of these ideational strands, it is useful to draw out what we consider to be the flawed assumptions underlying the dominant discourse of globalization. The five points we briefly review below are all aspects of the teleology of globalization and make clear its apolitical impetus. Social agency in the form of the state, social movements, and organized labour are all basic to forms of politics we currently understand and practice, yet the teleology of globalization tends to produce the idea of the 'death of politics' as well as the demise of the nation-state.

1 **Technological change is presented as the driving force of globalization**, i.e. changes in science, technology and production methods essentially determine the future for workers, managers, the state, and their inter-relationships. The introduction of new technologies heralds a transitional crisis as social and political institutions strive to 'catch-up,' but via a pre-determined set of forms. Globalization, then, is conceived in a teleological manner. Technological change is an 'iron cage', and 'everyone is doing it'. These processes are presumably beyond our control.

2 **Globalization is framed in the essentialistic.** Changes in economics, events such as the oil crises, the break-up of Bretton Woods, and other macro-structural causes are variously interpreted as compelling societies to 'make the leap' to 'globalization' as if there were no other alternative. The precise contours are unclear, however. Are we jumping form Fordism to post-Fordism, from modernity to post-modernity, from the industrial to the post-industrial, or all three perhaps? What is omitted in the essentialistic reading of globalization is the notion of the historically and socially embedded conditions and relations, which themselves condition the outcome of complex socially constructed 'events' such as 'globalization'.

3 **There is a strong emphasis, from many perspectives, on the notion of convergence**, which is the idea that from divergent starting points and diverse institutional bases, societies become increasingly alike. For example, there is supposedly convergence

at the level of the nation-state as its borders are transcended by the globalization of finance, production and trade.[17] Technological advances in financial systems are said to herald the arrival of 'quicksilver capital',[18] and new structural forces in the world economy.[19] The rapid maturation of technologies is equated with the absolute necessity for firms to 'go global'.[20] Culture is said to be undergoing homogenization as technology breaks down traditional cultural territories.[21] The global competition imperative is overwhelmingly adopted as a business mantra, provoking debates regarding the 'right' path for the twenty-first century organization of the production and labour processes,[22] and indeed the right path for 'nations' (i.e. states) to follow.[23] But is this ahistorical abstraction any more than (Almondian) modernization theory 'gone berserk'? We have moved from the earlier idea of convergence between East and West towards a state-managed social democracy, to a presumed convergence between North, South, East and West, towards a post-statist neoliberal market society wherein the state and labour have lost power to corporations.

4 **Globalization is presented instrumentally.** There is a tendency to simplify the description of change in order to prescribe a set of formulae to manage change. Debate surrounding global change finds academic analysis cutting across business management guides and political campaigns. Academic commentary, policy discourse, and corporate strategy become ever more closely intertwined.[24] The result is a preoccupation with both political 'strategic' crisis management, and 'strategic' business management. However, there is a political deception at the root of this instrumentality. The political choice to liberalize and lower barriers to trade and international money in the late 1970s and during the 1980s involved a choice by governments of how to present this change to the public. Governments normally choose not to argue that the presumed benefits of liberalization (higher aggregate wealth) would outweigh the costs (lower wages and higher unemployment in industries facing new competition) since, 'To argue that way would only have drawn attention to the costs. Better to say that changes in the world economy left no choice but to liberalize.'[25] At the corporate/media level the concept is instrumentally presented to society in the advertising campaigns for everything from credit cards to soft drinks. We are encouraged to equip ourselves with these essential products and services for life in the 'global village'.

5 **Globalization is presented as a benign process.** Social conflict

is posited as being confined to the adjustment phase, with new practices promising 'worker empowerment', the formation of 'new solidarities', and even the return of a craft-based 'yeoman democracy'.[26] As the institutions of the old order give way to new structures, conflict is viewed as a temporary by-product of restructuring. Globalization becomes a harmless automatic process that transcends 'the political', perhaps once and for all. As the Director of the OECD implied in an interview in *Le Monde* published in 1992, entitled 'globalization is here to stay',[27] our task is to accept and adjust. Even on the left of the academic spectrum, a number of authors make the mistake of assuming that 'globalization is here to stay', even if endorsing a variety of presumed national or regional regulatory responses. Such 'tinkering at the margins' of globalization, however, has the unintended effect of helping the globalization project to consolidate itself. This approach is therefore conservative (with a small c), in the sense of conserving the main theses of globalization, instead of making a determined effort to 'overturn globalization'.

So far the questions posed contra globalization have still on the whole not been sufficiently framed in the explicitly *political*. Nevertheless, globalization is now being challenged by a more critical question-raising and empirical research agenda. The clarification of the definition of globalization and the 'testing' of the concept has recently become a first order issue in research in this field. To what extent is globalization distinguishable from interdependence?[28] How important is the distinction between multi-national corporation and trans-national corporation?[29] We are now seeing a rise in academic interest in persistent elements of diversity, divergence, conflict and difference. The 'new institutional' economics and economic sociology of recent years raises pertinent questions as to the 'embeddedness' of social practices and the social and historical nature of change.[30] Simultaneously we are seeing an increased emphasis on the study of 'national trajectories' in, for example, welfare and industrial restructuring.[31] Rigorous testing in terms of empirical examination and the study of 'bearers of change' has become more visible in recent years.[32] The rise in critiques based around the use of 'myth' and ideology support the general trend towards questioning, stripping the concept to its bare essence to expose its political dangers.[33] Attempts to expose the dangers of the concept have also been presented to the public through the media.[34]

Globalization and the state: retreat or return?

Many globalization theorists suggest a profound disjuncture between the persistence of territorial sovereignty as the organizing principal of international politics and the increasingly global structure of finance, production, society and culture. This position has two fundamental consequences. First, traditional paradigms which have taken the territorially bounded nation-state as the central unit of analysis are rendered redundant. Globalization becomes epistemology as the study of human action and interaction is perceived to require a transnational mode of enquiry.[35] Second, the presumed erosion of national economies and societies raises a question mark over the potential political power of the state in the coming global era. Both 'inside' and 'outside' territorial borders, the power of governments and institutions to shape the economic and social environment in which they find themselves appears to have waned. Such consequences demand that the relationship between the state and the processes of global restructuring be central to the globalization debate. To this end, it is possible to identify the emergence of three broad schools of thought.

The currently dominant conceptualization of the relationship between globalization and the state views transnationalization as seriously undermining the basis of the nation-state as a territorially bounded economic, political and social unit. The structure of the wholesale financial system is held to have been transformed, from primarily national with some transnational linkages to largely global with some national differences.[36] Similarly, national corporations that in the past firmly associated themselves with their 'home' economy are believed to have been replaced by genuinely transnational corporations (TNCs).[37] Once relatively cohesive national societies are now held to be undermined by global cultural flows carried across borders by technological and media infrastructures.[38]

Consequently, state authority over economy and society is viewed as undergoing a period of diffusion; leaking 'upwards' to inter-state institutions, global social movements, and TNCs; shifting 'sideways' to global financial markets and the more powerful states; and descending 'downwards' to quasi-public regional and local institutions.[39] Further, it is suggested that state structures, institutions and policies converge around a complex and contrary melding of neoliberal rhetoric and the competitive provision of incentives for transnationally operating capital. States lose their economic policy-making sovereignty, becoming locked into the financially orthodox policies of low inflation and 'strong' and 'sound' public finance by the power of global financial markets.[40] The nature of the competitive struggle between states has shifted from conflict for control of territory and wealth-creating resources to the competitive provision of human and physical infrastructures in order to attract transnationally operating capital,[41] with the concomitant decline in the significance of defence and foreign policy and increase in the importance of industrial and trade policy.[42] Fundamentally, the result of this, the dominant conceptualization, is an understanding of the processes of global restructuring in which the state is viewed as merely responding to market, cultural and technological changes occurring above and beyond the state itself.

A direct challenge to this commanding orthodoxy is the claim that the 'decline of the state' in the face of the forces of globalization has been exaggerated. The basis for this view is the recognition that the foundations of the global economy remain largely national in character.[43] National capitalisms do not converge around a single form but persist, particularly with reference to alternative state–finance–industry relations.[44] Nationally specific state structures and institutions continue to interact with the international political economy ensuring that national development trajectories are sustained.[45] Analysis of key wholesale financial indicators such as interest rates, securities trading, and savings and investment illustrates that contrary to the popular vision of 'seamless' global markets, most economic variables remain firmly national in orientation.[46] Similarly, examination of the ownership, management and organization of the world's largest corporations suggests that they maintain established associations with their national bases, and therefore are best characterized as 'multinational'.[47] As a consequence, states are held to continue to exercise considerable authority in the management of the national economy.[48] Similarly, for the 'regulation school' the system of national monetary management persists as it is a crucial component of the 'mode of regulation', that is the institutional milieu which underpins capital accumulation.[49] Ultimately, this understanding of the relationship between the state and globalization suggests that the processes of global restructuring have been driven by the interaction between contending national capitalisms. As Zysman asserts,

> National developments have, then, driven changes in the global economy; even more than a so-called 'globalization' has driven

national evolution. It is the success of particular countries, rather than some unfolding of a singular global market logic based on more and faster transactions, that has forced adaptations.[50]

The argument that the restructuring of the contemporary era has and continues to be determined by the distribution of power within and between the major nation-states and their rival capitalisms leads to changes being characterized as 'internationalization' and not globalization.[51]

A third position suggests that the usual understanding of a dichotomy between the state and globalization is an illusion, as the processes of global restructuring are largely embedded within state structures and institutions, politically contingent on state policies and actions, and primarily about the reorganization of the state.[52] The nature of state intervention may have changed, but the state has not necessarily diminished in its significance to contemporary capitalism. Some parallels can be drawn here to Polanyi's approach to the so-called laissez-faire state associated with the rise of industrial capitalism, in that the separation of economy from polity is recognized to require the exercise of state power.[53] In its minimalist form, this view identifies the continuing role of the state as the ultimate guarantor of the rights of capital whether national or foreign.[54] More broadly, however, the 'internal' restructuring of the relationship between the state and national economy/society and the 'transnationalization' of the state itself, as national systems of regulation are replaced by global systems of regulation, are both identified as fundamental to globalization.[55] A new layer of politics above the state is highlighted, based around increased national regulatory co-operation and new institutional forums.[56] In essence, this interpretation places the state at the centre of analysis of globalization, viewing the processes of change as shaped by the restructuring of political power.

Taken together, the alternative schools of thought outlined above suggest that, contrary to the dominant view, globalization is a set of multi-dimensional processes in which the state is not transcended, but rather is of fundamental significance. In short, the immediate sources of globalization are to be found precisely in the 'political' domain. The research agenda which follows from this suggests the need to challenge the dominant techno-rational interpretation by asking how and why state institutions and policies came to be at the heart of globalization. We are able to move beyond the domi-

nant discourse which suggests that there is no alternative to the
neoliberal state form to show that the processes of restructuring
are politically contingent on the predominance of neoliberal forces
and policies at the level of state politics.

The position that the national state is still the most important
site of social change or still capable of controlling a national economic
development trajectory is necessary, but not sufficient to 'overturn
globalization'.[57] Likewise, reclaiming the 'national economy' and
state manoeuvrability are positive steps towards recognizing social
contestation and the centrality of the *political* process, but insofar
as they remain bound in these statist frameworks they remain limited.
We must move beyond 'technicist' arguments on the continued role
and efficacy of the state. They do not yet constitute an unambiguous
progressive counter-position to neoliberal economic globalization.
Once it has been shown that globalization and the immediate responses to it are indeed squarely in the realm of 'the political', this
can form the basis of expanding the domain of the political further
to press for *social* as opposed to narrowly economic concerns.

Such a counter-hegemonic position must concentrate on the question of *social reform* and the changing relationship between 'civil
society' and the state or between 'social forces' and 'state power'.
Civil society has recently become the subject of much academic
interest. This new interest has concentrated around the idea of civil
society being seen as the source of a socio-political challenge to
the state, capitalism, and the inter-state system.[58] Civil society therefore can no longer simply be seen as an agglomeration of institutions
and social relations which are separate from the state. Indeed,
following Gramsci on this point, it is our view that:

> civil society is the sphere of class struggles and of popular demo-
> cratic struggles. Thus, civil society is the sphere in which a
> dominant social group organizes consent and hegemony. It is
> also the sphere where the subordinate social groups may organize
> their opposition and construct an alternative hegemony – counter-
> hegemony.[59]

The caution over the uncritical use of statist frameworks is particularly the case when evidence from East Asian developmental states
is deployed in defence of the national economy/state manoeuvrability position, given that most of these 'models' were authoritarian.
The 'return of the state' position, though a welcome antidote to

the 'retreat of the state' position, is incomplete without further analysis of and focus upon the recomposition of social forces and their need and capacity to alter or channel the political direction of the state and the economy or, in Polanyian terms of the 'double movement', the prospect of society regaining control in response to the destabilizing effects of the unregulated market.

Conclusion: globalization, social agency and resistance

The forms of resistance which are emerging are diverse, and this implies a need for critical differentiation between forms of resistance, since not all are moving in the same direction or could be categorized as necessarily 'progressive' in their 'resistance'. However, what is clear is that the new politics of social resistance to neoliberal economic globalization is not confined to the traditional framework of national politics. Among the new and old sites of resistance are: local (urban and rural) communities; indigenous peoples' communities; organized labour; and an ever-growing range of national, regional and global social movements. The emerging forms of resistance act in and across different spatial scales, encompassing the local, national, regional, and global. Movements like the Zapatistas, the global women's health movement, Jubilee 2000, or the campaign to establish international labour standards, each illustrate how the new politics of resistance seeks to operate across all of these scales. More and more individuals in many movements recognize the need for new strategies of resistance which include stronger regional or international alliances and broader social coalitions.

However, both scholarly and activist opinion tends to be divided on the real political possibilities of the new types of international or global resistance, and we acknowledge the pessimists concern that difficulties must be admitted and openly confronted. However, we are convinced that such movements are not illusory or merely transitory. They are a representation of changing popular forces and a necessary and inevitable social response to the forces of neoliberal economic globalization. The source of their effectiveness resides precisely in their broad social appeal and their ability to transcend traditionally confining political spaces and attitudes. Their validity rests in their continued roots in civil society and their ability to construct transnational networks of solidarity based on coordination and linkages in a common struggle for social rights and human dignity.

What then is the future for political resistance against neoliberal globalization? One thing is clear, the close relationship between the state and economic restructuring means that resistance to globalization will continue to come from within national civil society and national social movements, including organized labour. The future success of resistance movements to neoliberal globalization may be brought a step closer if resistance organizations themselves highlight the close relationship between the state and globalization. Resistance groups should act to break down the myth, which is often perpetrated by governments themselves, that the state is helpless in the face of globalization. Resistance movements need to continue to stress the links between global restructuring and other issues of public discontent, such as unemployment, environmental degradation, malnutrition and decline of health care services. A better understanding of the linkages between the state and economic restructuring and the breakdown in the social fabric needs to be popularized, as does the centrality of the role of social forces in resisting neoliberal globalization.

To be successful, resistance to neoliberal globalization must be conducted in a more co-ordinated manner on local, national, regional, and global levels. Economic restructuring is occurring on all levels, therefore resistance movements cannot defeat it by concentrating on one level alone; capital can always side-step such opposition. Although civil society continues to be primarily a national phenomenon, an incipient 'global civil society' exists and represents a potent new force for progressive and democratic change. Resistance movements must re-invent the state–society relationship and the political process by transcending traditional national boundaries, through establishing new networks of solidarity, building regional and international resistance movements.

In the past social movements and organized labour have been more confined to the local and national level, sustained as they are by the popular myths of the nation-state (for example that each state creates its own 'national' society), than capital, which has always been more capable of escaping the 'national' to promote its interests. Given the extension of capital's 'flight' from the nation-state, it is necessary and urgent that resistance movements attempt to achieve a similar scale of operation. Paradoxically, the current discourse on globalization and the 'end of the nation-state', the new ideology of expanding capital, actually provides an opportunity for popular resistance movements to escape the myths of the nation-state and build new popular transnational movements.

Notes

1 For further discussion see Craig N. Murphy, *International Organization and Industrial Change: Global Governance since 1850* (Polity Press, 1994).
2 Larry Elliott, 'Putting trade in its place', *Guardian*, 27 May 1996.
3 Ibid., citing OECD statement in May 1996.
4 J. K. Galbraith, *The World Economy Since the Wars* (Sinclair Stevenson, 1994), pp. 247–8.
5 Ralf Dahrendorf, 'Preserving Prosperity', *New Statesman and Society*, December, 1995.
6 See, for example the special issue by *Millennium*, Vol. 24, No. 3 (1995) on neoliberal economic globalization, including S. Gill 'Globalization, market civilization and disciplinary neoliberalism', pp. 399–423.
7 We are indebted to Hugo Radice for bringing this point to our attention.
8 See Robert W. Cox, 'A perspective on globalization', in James H. Mittleman (ed.), *Globalization: Critical Reflections* (Lynne Rienner, 1996) pp. 21–32.
9 Mark Beatty, IPE Discussion, Internet: 'Globalization: What does it mean and is it good or bad?' 8 Oct. 1996; ipe@csf.colorado.edu; Beatty.4@osu.edu.
10 See, for example, M. Aglietta, *A Theory of Capitalist Regulation* (New Left Books, 1979); Alain Lipietz, *Mirages and Miracles: The Crises of Global Fordism* (Verso, 1985); Robert Boyer, *La théorie de la regulation: une analyse critique* (La Decouverte, 1986); Bob Jessop, 'Fordism and Post-Fordism: Critique and Reformulation', in M. Storper and A. J. Scott (eds), *Pathways to Industrialization and Regional Development* (Routledge, 1992).
11 David Harvey, *The Condition of Postmodernity* (Basil Blackwell, 1989). J. F. Lyotard, *The Postmodern Condition* (Manchester University Press, 1986).
12 M. Castells, *The Information City: Information Technology, Economic Restructuring, and the Urban Regional Process* (Basil Blackwell, 1989).
13 M. Castells and P. G. Hall, *Technopoles of the World: The Making of 21st Century Industrial Complexes* (Routledge, 1994), p. 3.
14 Jessop, 'Fordism and Post-Fordism.'
15 M. Piore and C. Sabel, *The Second Industrial Divide: Possibilities for Prosperity* (Basic Books, 1984).
16 R. J. Barry Jones, *Globalization and Interdependence in the International Political Economy: Rhetoric and Reality* (Pinter, 1995).
17 Kenichi Ohmae, *The Borderless World: Power and Strategy in the Interlinked Economy* (Collins, 1990).
18 R. B. McKenzie and D. R. Lee, *Quicksilver Capital: How the Rapid Movement of Wealth has Changed the World* (Free Press, 1991).
19 Susan Strange, *States and Markets: An Introduction to International Political Economy* (Pinter, 1988).
20 S. Gill and D. Law, *The Global Political Economy* (Harvester Wheatsheaf, 1988).
21 Roland Robertson, *Globalization: Social Theory and Global Culture* (Sage, 1992).
22 Michael Porter, *The Competitive Advantage of Nations* (Macmillan, 1992).
23 Robert Reich, *The Work of Nations: Preparing Ourselves for 21st Century Capitalism* (Knopf, 1992); Philip. G. Gerny, *The Changing Architecture of Politics: Structure, Agency and the Future of the State* (Sage, 1990).

24 Anna Pollert, *Farewell to Flexibility* (Basil Blackwell, 1991).
25 'The Myth of the Powerless State', *The Economist*, 7 October 1995, pp. 15–16.
26 Piore and Sabel, *The Second Industrial Divide*.
27 See 'La technologie et l'économie, les relations determinantes' sur les facteurs techniques de la globalisation' OECD, Paris, 1992.
28 Jones, *Globalization and Interdependence*.
29 Razeen Sally, 'Multinational Enterprises, Political Economy and Institutional Theory: Domestic Embeddedness in the Context of Internationalization', *Review of International Political Economy*, Vol. 1, No. 1 (1994), pp. 161–92.
30 Geoffrey Hodgson, *The Economics of Institutions* (Edward Elgar, 1994), Neil J. Smelser and Richard Swedberg (eds), *Handbook of Economic Sociology* (Princeton, 1994).
31 John Zysman, 'The Myth of "Global" Economy: Enduring National Foundations and Emerging Regional Realities'. *New Political Economy*, Vol. 1, No. 2 (1996), pp. 157–84. See also: Gøsta Esping-Andersen (ed.), *Welfare States in Transition: National Adaptations in Global Economies* (Sage, 1996).
32 James H. Mittelman (ed.), *Globalization: Critical Reflections* (Lynne Rienner, 1996); Winifried Ruigrok and Rob van Tulder, *The Logic of International Restructuring: The Management of Dependencies in Rival Industrial Complexes* (Routledge, 1995); Jones, *Globalization and Interdependence*.
33 Mittelman, *Globalization: Critical Reflections*. P. Hirst and G. Thompson, *Globalization in Question* (Polity Press, 1996).
34 Will Hutton, *The State We're In* (Jonathan Cape, 1995).
35 Roland Robertson, 'Mapping the Global Condition: Globalization as the Central Concept', *Theory, Culture and Society*, Vol. 7, No. 1 (1990), pp. 15–30. For a discussion and critique of the 'transnational model' in the study of the globalization of finance, see Benjamin Cohen, 'Phoenix Risen: The Resurrection of Global Finance', *World Politics*, Vol. 48, (1996), pp. 268–96.
36 Susan Strange, 'Finance, Information and Power', *Review of International Studies*, Vol. 16, No. 2 (1990), pp. 259–74; Philip Cerny, 'The Infrastructure of the Infrastructure? Towards 'Embedded Financial Orthodoxy' in the International Political Economy', in R. Palan and B. Gills (eds), *Transcending the State–Global Divide: A Neostructuralist Agenda in International Relations* (Lynne Rienner, 1994), pp. 223–50.
37 Robert Reich, *The Work of Nations: A Blueprint for the Future* (Simon & Schuster, 1991).
38 Robertson, 'Mapping the Global Condition'.
39 Susan Strange, 'The Defective State', *Daedalus*, Vol. 124, No. 2 (1995), pp. 55–74.
40 Cerny, 'The Infrastructure of the Infrastructure?'.
41 Reich, *The Work of Nations*.
42 Strange, 'The Defective State', pp. 55–7.
43 J. Zysman, 'The Myth of a 'Global' Economy: Enduring National Foundations and Emerging Regional Realities', *New Political Economy*, Vol. 1, No. 2 (1996), pp. 157–84.
44 Andrew Cox, 'The State–Finance–Industry Relationship in Comparative

Perspective', in Andrew Cox (ed.), *The State, Finance and Industry* (Wheatsheaf, 1986), pp. 1–59.

45   Zysman, 'The Myth of a "Global: Economy'.

46   P. Hirst and G. Thompson, *Globalization in Question* (Polity Press, 1996), Ch. 2; R. J. Barry Jones, *Globalization and Interdependence in the International Political Economy: Rhetoric and Reality* (Pinter, 1995), Ch. 6.

47   W. Ruigrok and R. Van Tulder, *The Logic of International Restructuring* (Routledge, 1995).

48   G. Garret and P. Lange, 'Political Responses to Interdependence: What's "Left" for the Left?' *International Organization*, Vol. 45, No. 4 (1991), pp. 539–64.

49   Alain Lipietz, *Mirages and Miracles: The Crisis in Global Fordism* (Verso, 1987).

50   Zysman, 'The Myth of a "Global" Economy', p. 164.

51   Hirst and Thompson, *Globalization in Question.*

52   Leo Panitch, 'Globalization and the State', *Socialist Register: Between Globalism and Nationalism* (1994), pp. 60–93.

53   Karl Polanyi, *The Great Transformation: The Political and Economic Origins of Our Time* (Beacon Press, 1944).

54   S. Sassen, 'The State and the Global City: Notes Towards a Conception of Place Centred Governance', *Competition and Change: The Journal of Global Business and Political Economy*, Vol. 1, No. 1 (1995), pp. 31–50.

55   S. Pooley, 'The State Rules, OK? The Continuing Political Economy of Nation-States', *Capital and Class*, Vol. 43, No.1 (1991), 65–82.

56   Philip Cerny, *The Changing Architecture of Politics: Structure, Agency and the Future of the State* (Sage, 1990), Ch. 8.

57   André C. Drainville, 'International Political Economy in the Age of Open Marxism', *Review of International Political Economy*, Vol. 1, No. 1; Zysman, 'The Myth of a Global Economy'; Robert Boyer and Daniel Drache, *States against Markets: The Limits of Globalization* (Routledge, 1996); Suzanne Berger and Ronald Dore, *National Diversity and Global Capitalism* (Cornell University Press, Ithaca and London, 1996).

58   Much of this academic interest has come from scholars within the disciplines of International Relations and International Political Economy. For example: Robert Cox, *Production, Power and World Order: Social Forces in the Making of History* (Columbia University Press, 1987); Martin Shaw, 'Civil Society and Global Politics: Beyond a Social Movement Approach', *Millennium: Journal of International Studies*, Vol. 23, No. 3 (1994), pp. 647–76; and Ronnie D. Lipshutz, 'Reconstructing World Politics: The Emergence of Global Civil Society', *Millennium: Journal of International Studies*, Vol. 21, No. 3 (1992), pp. 389–420.

59   Roger Simon, *Gramsci's Political Thought: An Introduction* (Lawrence & Wishart, 1991), p. 27.

3
Conceptualizing Resistance to Globalization

Christine B.N. Chin and James H. Mittelman

Assessments of resistance to globalization are necessarily influenced by the manner in which one conceptualizes these processes. Too often, both of the terms ('resistance' and 'globalization') are used promiscuously, the latter as a buzzword or catchall and the former in many different ways, sometimes as a synonym for challenges, protests, intransigence, or even evasions. Hence, we seek to juxtapose alternative explanations of resistance and highlight the complexities of conceptualizing it. The purpose of this chapter, then, is to explore the question, what is the meaning of resistance in the context of globalization?

Perhaps the most potent force restructuring world order at the turn of the millennium, globalization encompasses multiple changes in the economy, politics, and culture. Among the main features of economic globalization are a fundamental shift toward an integrated and co-ordinated division of labour in production and trade. The global division of labour consists of new technologies, especially in communications and transportation; a reorientation in emphasis from the old Fordist production systems toward post-Fordism, with pressures for greater flexibility in the work force and heightened patterns of specialization; and distinctive regional divisions of labour tethered to the growth mechanisms of the world economy. Today, cross-border flows – undocumented workers, finance, knowledge, and information – take on new proportions and transcend territorial states. What is new as well is the reduction of effective regulatory control over this activity.[1]

Concurrent to these accelerations and decelerations in different zones of the global economy are political responses to economic globalization. To delimit the politics of globalization, one must first come to terms with the concept of globalization itself. Broadly speaking, there are two interpretations. The strong thesis advanced by some of the purveyors of globalization holds that it is a totalizing or homogenizing force washing across all shores and battering down the barriers that stand in its way.[2] In fact, much of the discomfort with the literature on globalization focuses on this strong argument about a 'borderless world.'[3] Whereas the enthusiasts of globalization overwork the category and engage in economic overdetermination, some critically minded scholars embrace a less demanding and, in our view, a more compelling claim: globalization is not only about a series of intensifications in the dynamics of capitalism (i.e., competition and accumulation), but also fundamentally about interactions – changes in different spheres of social activity, the ways that they compress time and space, and their varied impact on strata in zones of the world economy. In this sense, globalization may be construed as a partial, incomplete, and contradictory process – an uneasy correlation of economic forces, power relations, and social structures.

A major asymmetry in the globalization trend is between its economic and political levels. Although it would be wrong to concede the neoclassical premise that economics and politics are separable realms, it is clear, at least in analytical terms, that globalization's hegemonic project is neoliberalism and that liberal democracy has not kept pace with its spread. In the space opened by this disjuncture, resistance movements are on the rise. But they cannot solely be understood as a political reaction to globalization. Rather, in the teeth of globalizing tendencies, resistance movements shape and are constitutive of cultural processes. Such is the main thesis to be developed in this Chapter.

For us, and in brief, culture may be regarded as interest-constituted social processes that create specific and different whole ways of life, of which material social life is an inextricable part.[4] There is no dearth of culturally laden manifestations of resistance to globalization. Culminating in the election of a Government of National Unity, led by the African National Congress, in South Africa in 1994, the worldwide anti-apartheid movement against a racial monopoly of the means of production, buttressed by substantial flows of foreign capital, may be the foremost example of a movement against globalization from above. There are numerous illustrations of more localized resistance, such as the Zapatista armed uprising among the Maya Indians against the Mexican government's neoliberal reforms, symbolically launched on 1 January 1994, the day of the inauguration of the North American Free Trade Agreement. But it would be facile to conceptualize resistance only as declared organized opposition to institutionalized economic and military power. One must dig deep to excavate the everyday individual and collective activities that fall short of open opposition. To grasp resistance to globalization, one must also examine the subtexts of political and cultural life, the possibilities and potential for structural transformation.

We begin to delve the constitutive role of power in shaping cultural critiques of economic globalization as well as patterns of struggle by revisiting the works of three master theorists of resistance, even if their writing was not explicitly directed at the contemporary phase of globalization: Antonio Gramsci's concept of counterhegemony, Karl Polanyi's notion of countermovements, and James C. Scott's idea of infrapolitics. For the sake of brevity, our compass is limited to these authors; other conceptualizations and systematic empirical referents cannot be provided within the space allotted to us. We hold that the trialectic of Gramsci–Polanyi–Scott, set forth through a critical evaluation of each author's work in the next three sections of this Chapter, offers a sound basis for reconceptualizing resistance. The conclusion then probes the convergence and contrasting emphases within the triad, and also suggests directions for further study and exploratory research.

Resistance as counterhegemony

Ostensibly, Gramsci's analysis of social change as explicated in *Selections from the Prison Notebooks* neither could have anticipated nor accounted for globalization.[5] The notes were written between 1929 and 1935 while Gramsci, a member of parliament and the general secretary of the Communist Party, was imprisoned by the fascist regime in Italy. In his discussions of state–society relations, Gramsci was concerned particularly with orthodox Marxist and bourgeois liberal theoretical frameworks that privileged 'economism' by reducing transformations in all aspects of social life to economic determinants.

Gramsci's theoretical efforts to transcend economism are applicable to conceptualizing resistance at the turn of the millennium. In place of economism, he developed the concept of hegemony. Hegemony encompasses whole ways of life: it is a dynamic lived process in which social identities, relations, organizations, and structures based on asymmetrical distributions of power and influence are constituted by the dominant classes. Hegemony, then, is as much economic as it is 'ethico-political' in shaping relations of domination and subordination.

The institutions of civil society such as the church, family, schools, media, and trade associations give meaning and organize everyday life so that the need for the application of force is reduced. Hegemony is established when power and control over social life are perceived as emanating from 'self-government' (i.e., self-government of individuals embedded in communities) as opposed to an external source(s) such as the state or the dominant strata.[6] Since hegemony is a lived process, different historical contexts will produce different forms of hegemony with different sets of actors, such as the nineteenth-century 'passive revolution' of the Risorgimento, in which the bourgeoisie in Italy attained power without fundamental restructuring from below, and the early twentieth-century proletarian revolutionary leadership in Russia.

The processes of establishing hegemony, however, can never be complete because the hegemonic project presumes and requires the participation of subordinate groups. While hegemony is being implemented, maintained, and/or defended, it can be challenged and resisted in the interlocking realms of civil society, political society, and the state.

Different forms and dimensions of resistance to hegemony are subsumed under the rubric of counterhegemony. Implicit in the counterhegemonic project are 'wars of movement' and 'wars of position', in which people engage in openly declared collective action against the state. Wars of movement are frontal assaults against the state (e.g., labour strikes or even military action), whereas wars of position can be read as nonviolent resistance, e.g. boycotts, that are designed to impede everyday functions of the state.[7] The objective of both types of war is to seize control of the state.

Wars of movement and position are expressions of counterhegemonic consciousness at the collective level. They represent moments in history when individuals come together in violent and nonviolent confrontations with the state. The question remains, how and why does counterhegemonic consciousness emerge in everyday life, leading to openly declared collective action?

Gramsci's discussion of common sense in the development of counterhegemonic consciousness is crucial to explaining historical and/or contemporary forms of resistance. Common sense that is held and practised in everyday life is neither linear nor unitary; it is the product of an individual's relationship to and position in a variety of social groups. Importantly, the coexistence of conformity and resistance in common sense can give rise to inconsistencies between thought and action, which help explain contradictory behaviour on the part of a subaltern group which may embrace its 'own conception of the world' while still adopting conceptions borrowed from dominant classes.[8] By arguing that individuals and groups possess critical consciousness – albeit 'in flashes' – of their subordinate positions in society, Gramsci acknowledged the ambiguity of resistance and dismissed the overly deterministic and unidimensional explanation of false consciousness.

Nevertheless, in the discussion of thought and action, Gramsci was careful not to suggest that submission in the face of domination is the simple product of the subaltern's rational calculation of costs and benefits (in the sense that resistance would be futile at best, or would elicit retaliatory action, at worst). The fragmentation of social identity which characterizes and is characterized by simultaneous membership in different groups means that it is possible, if not probable, that the subaltern can be progressive on certain issues and reactionary on others in the same instance.

A Gramscian reading of resistance would have to explicate the development of counterhegemonic consciousness that informs wars of movement and position, as well as national-popular actions led by organic intellectuals from all walks of life who can meld theory and praxis to construct and embed a new common sense that binds disparate voices and consciousness into a coherent program of change. In his time, Gramsci called for organic intellectuals to infuse common sense with a philosophy of praxis that encourages subaltern groups' critical understanding of their subordination in society. The objective is a 'national–popular' movement constituted by alliances between the leaders (in league with their organic intellectuals) and the led (subaltern). Whereas wars of movement and position capture the state, the national–popular movement provides the new basis for whole ways of life.

Gramsci did not offer programmatic ways that a philosophy of praxis could transcend the fragmentation of identity and interests. With contemporary globalization, the interpenetration of forces at the local, national, regional, and world levels implies that different peoples enter into alliances that can be and are ever more contradictory: e.g. low-wage female factory workers in Free Trade Zones who also are members or supporters of Islamist movements in Southeast Asia. A new common sense has to address effectively or make coherent women's critical understanding of the tensions, limitations, and opportunities inherent in their identities as daughters or wives in the household, as low wage workers on the factory floor, as citizens, and as Muslims in the local, national, and transnational Islamic communities.

Moreover, globalization begets openly declared forms of resistance that may or may not have the state as a target. In a context in which liberal, authoritarian, and ex-communist states-in-transition alike are becoming facilitators for transnational capital, if and when it occurs the driving force(s) of openly declared resistance against the state must be analysed within a larger framework. At issue are the contradictory ways in which state structures and policies assume 'educative' functions that nurture a new kind of citizenry and civilization commensurate with the requirements of transnational capital, while trying to maintain the legitimacy with which to govern.[9] In this connection, one can profitably invoke Gramsci's insights into civil society and resistance, about which he offered many pointers, although they were not always congruent with one another.

Although wars of movement and position may still be discerned, sometimes in nascent form, the compression of time and space has created new venues of and for collective resistance transcending national borders. Contemporary social movements simultaneously occupy local, national, transnational and/or global space as a result of innovations in, and applications of, technologies that produce instantaneous communication across borders (e.g. the Internet, facsimile machines, cellular mobile phones, and globalized media). The Gramscian framework of resistance must be stretched to encompass new actors and spaces from which counterhegemonic consciousness is expressed. In the following section, we discuss the possibility of further considering social movements as a form of resistance.

Resistance as countermovements

In *The Great Transformation: The Political and Economic Origins of Our Time*, Karl Polanyi argued that the causes of global political, economic and social crises of the 1930s leading to World War Two may be traced to state-supported implementation of the 'self-regulating' market system during the eighteenth and nineteenth centuries.[10] The movement to install and expand the self-regulating market sparked protective measures or countermovements to re-exert social control over the market – hence, the notion of a double movement.

Polanyi understood resistance in the form of countermovements as having arisen from, and affecting, different and whole ways of life. Protecting workers from the commodification process implies defending the social relations and institutions of which they are a part:

> *In disposing of a man's labor power the system would, incidentally, dispose of the physical, psychological, and moral entity 'man' attached to that tag. Robbed of the protective covering of cultural institutions, human beings would perish from the effects of social exposure* [emphasis added]; they would die as victims of acute social dislocation through vice, perversion ... No society could stand the effects of such a system of crude fiction even for the shortest stretch of time unless its human and natural substance as well as its business organization was protected against the ravages of this satanic mill.[11]

The movement-countermovement framework thus allows one to conceptualize contemporary social movements as a form of resistance since the latter are, in the main, defined as 'a form of collective action (a) based on solidarity, (b) carrying on a conflict, (c) breaking the limits of the system in which action occurs.'[12] The level of analysis would have to be extended from the national to the transnational and/or global levels since some contemporary social movements, e.g. those that concern environmental destruction, women's rights, and indigenous peoples' rights, appear to bypass the state in search of transnational or global solutions.

There are two implicit problems in the counter/social movement framework. Collectivity is assumed in the notion 'movement' and this has the effect of constructing counter/social movements as united fronts in and of themselves. In the past decade or so, the fragmented nature of the feminist movement is evidenced in the internal conflict and domination generated from differences of race, religion, class, and nationality, in spite of, and because of, attempts to address national and global patriarchy.[13]

Also imputed in counter/social movements is the presence of organizational structure. This may be the case with some social movements (e.g. Greenpeace and Friends of the Earth in the environmental movement), but 'submerged networks' with no clearly defined organizational structure too have formed in an era of globalization. Participants in submerged networks live their everyday lives mostly without engaging in openly declared contestations:

> They question definition of codes, nomination of reality. They don't ask, they offer. They offer by their own existence other ways of defining the meaning of individual and collective action. They act as new media: they enlighten what every system doesn't say of itself, the amount of silence, violence, irrationality which is always hidden in dominant codes.[14]

The presence of submerged networks gives new meaning to resistance. Even though participants can mobilize to protest state policies, open engagement or confrontation with the state or even transnational corporations is not the immediate or even ultimate objective. In the absence of openly declared collective action, resistance has to be read as the ways in which peoples live their everyday lives. Submerged networks affirm that even though resistance can be manifestly political and/or economic, it is shaped by and shapes whole ways of life. In advanced industrialized societies, examples of submerged networks are those in which families and their friends make it a point – in their consumption habits – to refuse to buy tuna fish caught using methods that destroy entire dolphin populations, or to purchase only consumer products from companies that actively practice environmental conservationism. Such acts have economic consequences in the corporate world, and political consequences for policy-makers. Significantly, submerged networks are sites of emerging alternative values and lifestyles.

In Egypt, for example, submerged networks exist in the popular quarters and among the common people, known as the *sha'b*. Networks radiate from the family – the basic unit of social organization in the *sha'b* – to include ties that transcend class, occupation, and kin. The 'familial ethos' governs the allocation and distribution of material and symbolic resources in the *sha'b*.[15] In the present unspoken pact between the Egyptian state and the *sha'b*, state legitimacy is maintained by the distribution of basic goods and services to the *sha'b* in return for political acquiescence. Participants of the *sha'b* acquiesce to, as much as they engage in, resistance against the state. Members of the Islamist movement, who also are members of the *sha'b*, have been known to and can draw on submerged network ties to smuggle arms, and on occasion, to mobilize and organize mass protests against the state.

The notion of the Polanyian double movement thus has a distinct advantage of neatly encapsulating openly declared demands on the national, transnational, and/or global levels, for protective measures against various dimensions in the implementation and expansion of the self-regulating market. As discussed, however, the movement–countermovement framework neither advances analysis of differences within countermovements nor anticipates undeclared forms of resistance, both of which have emerged and must be addressed in conceptualizing collective resistance to globalization.

Resistance as infrapolitics

In 1990, James C. Scott introduced the idea of 'infrapolitics' as everyday forms of resistance conducted singularly and/or collectively, but which fall short of openly declared contestations. What began as his attempt to understand the conditions for peasant rebellions in Southeast Asia and the absence of openly declared resistance in a village in rapidly industrializing Malaysia gradually led to the conceptualization of 'infrapolitics' to explain the changing meaning of politics and resistance in most forms of day-to-day dominant–subordinate relations.[16]

Scott warned that in the context of increasingly complex societies, the absence of openly declared contestations should not be mistaken for acquiescence. It is in the realm of informal assemblages such as the parallel market, workplace, household, and local community, when people negotiate resources and values on an everyday basis, that 'counterhegemonic consciousness is elaborated.'[17] These are the sites of infrapolitical activities that range from footdragging, squatting, and gossip to the development of dissident subcultures.

Taken at face value, such activities cannot tell us anything about counterhegemonic discourse until we account for the conditions from which they emerge. Infrapolitics is identified by juxtaposing what Scott calls the 'public' and 'hidden transcripts'. Public transcripts are verbal and nonverbal acts carried out by the dominant party or, 'to put it crudely, the *self*-portrait of dominant elites as they would have themselves seen'.[18] They are the public record of superior–subordinate relations in which the latter appears to willingly acquiesce in the stated and unstated expectations of the former. Hidden transcripts, on the other hand, consist of what subordinate parties say and do beyond the realm of the public transcript or the

observation of the dominant. In the context of surveillance structures set up by the dominant class(es) or the state, hidden transcripts
record infrapolitical activities that surreptitiously challenge practices
of economic, status, and ideological domination.

The study of infrapolitics, we believe, is premised on what sociol-
ogists call ontological narratives.[19] Ontological narrativity does not
refer to the mode of representation or the traditional 'story-telling'
method of historians (i.e. a method of presenting historical knowledge) considered nonexplanatory and atheoretical by mainstream
social scientists. Rather, ontological narratives are the stories that
social actors tell, and in the process come to define themselves or
to construct their identities and perceive conditions that promote
and/or mitigate the possibility for change.[20]

Even though hidden transcripts record contestations over material
and symbolic resources and values in everyday life, they do not
occur in a localized vacuum. Infrapolitical activities are the product
of interactions between structure and agency: the ways that real
and perceived constraints and opportunities affect the behaviour of
subordinate groups. Scott's analysis of infrapolitical activities thus
falls short of capturing the complexities inherent in undeclared forms
of everyday resistance. In his study of landlord–peasant relations
in a rural Malay village, Scott asserted that analysis of state structures and policies were important *only* to the extent that they
impinged on local class relations.[21] Especially during the 1980s and
in the context of national agricultural development policies and
fluctuating global prices of commodities, landlord–peasant relations
were shaped by impingements on, and interactions among, the rural
community, state structures and policies, as well as the transformations marking a globalizing economic system.

Superior–subordinate relations, such as those of the landlord–peasant, manager–worker, husband–wife, and state official–squatter, are
embedded in the whole ways of life, of which state structures and
policies play an important part. Take for instance, policies designed
to normalize the patriarchal nuclear family form as most natural
in and for the expansion and maintenance of capitalist free markets,
and/or that privilege scientific/technical education at the expense
of the humanities. Such policies enframe worldviews insofar as they
directly and indirectly affect all aspects of social life from the rate
of urbanization, housing development, and employment opportunities, to the control and distribution of resources in the household.

In increasingly complex social contexts, subalterns do not have an unproblematic unitary identity. Nor can their behaviour be explained by implicit reference to the economic model of the self-interested utility-maximizer. Put simply, infrapolitical activities are not the mere product of subaltern decisions to conduct undeclared resistance in the face of surveillance structures set up by the dominant strata.

Class is but one (albeit important) modality of identity in landlord–peasant or other forms of dominant–subordinate relations. The different and possibly conflicting modalities of subaltern identity can be as real, and under certain conditions, as constraining on behaviour as the actual or perceived futility and fear of openly declared resistance in the face of domination. By putting a unidimensional face on resistance, Scott inadvertently assigns a similar unidimensional face to domination, even though he analytically distinguishes economic, status, and ideological domination.

In this connection, Gramsci reminded us that subaltern identities are embedded in complex overlapping social networks in which individuals simultaneously assume positions of domination and subordination (perhaps as a husband or wife, an elder or junior, a manager or office clerk, and a donor or recipient of aid). Analysis of the manner in which particular combinations of identity are expressed in the context of structural constraints can help explain why, given systems of surveillance (in which rewards and punishments inhere), some conform while others engage in infrapolitical activities of different types. Conversely, this approach also deepens analysis of the changing nature of domination.

Hidden transcripts have the potential to facilitate understanding of the *internal politics* of subaltern groups. The phenomenon of 'domination within domination' occurs in cases in which contradictory alliances are formed between the dominant and the subordinate that, in turn, dominate others. Although Scott acknowledges this point, his emphasis on class without sufficient attention to the interactions between class and non-class forces undermines the efficacy of the infrapolitical framework. The immediate focus on class presumes that the development of class consciousness stands apart exclusively from other modalities of identity.

It is, indeed, possible to argue that class contests in the context of surveillance can and do lead to infrapolitical activities that are grounded in material life. This argument is made possible *only* after having considered how and why the class dimension comes to be privileged and expressed over other modalities of identity. To do otherwise would reaffirm what Gramsci called 'economism', and subsequently relegate non-economic considerations to the ambit of superstructure.

Infrapolitics is embedded in whole ways of life, part of which is the material dimension. They embody contestations over the processes of grounded identity construction, maintenance, and transformation, of which the symbolic and material dimensions of class are intertwined with other modalities of identity, such as age, gender, race-ethnicity, religion, nationality, and/or sexuality. The identification, juxtaposition, and analyses of public and hidden transcripts can highlight the conditions in which certain dimensions of counterhegemonic consciousness develop, and how different or even conflicting perspectives within hidden transcripts are negotiated and/or (not) resolved in everyday life.

Resistance conceptualized as infrapolitical activities offers a viable avenue for generating theoretically grounded studies of everyday responses to globalizing structures and processes. If conducted with sensitivity to the complex interplay between or among multiple identities in the context of structural constraints, the study of public and hidden transcripts may reveal changing notions and practices of work, family, and politics, for example, as peoples seek to negotiate a semblance of social control over the expansion of market forces in diverse spheres of their lives. At the same time, one should not overwork the broad category of infrapolitics by imagining that every sort of response to globalizing structures is resistance. Whereas Scott carefully argues that diverse modes of resistance may or may not coalesce to oppose authority structures, it is important to avoid treating resistance as an omnibus category.

An emerging framework

The conduct and meaning of resistance are culturally embedded. This foundational proposition is no less applicable or relevant in conceptualizing contemporary resistance to globalization, as it was to Gramsci, Polanyi, and Scott's analyses of social change in different historical periods. The three master theorists acknowledged, implicitly and explicitly, that resistance arises from and is constitutive of specific and whole ways of life.

From this elemental proposition, however, the theorists diverged in their respective discussions of the forms and dimensions of resistance. Gramsci and Polanyi focused on the collective level, whereas Scott drew attention more to the level of the individual, as well as class, in everyday life. As delineated by the grid below, the main targets and modes of resistance differ from one theorist to another: Gramscian wars of movement and position against the state (though not to the neglect of change within civil society short of toppling the state), Polanyian counter-movements against market forces, and Scott's infrapolitical activities in the face of everyday domination.

	Main target	*Mode of resistance*
Gramsci	state apparatuses (understood as an instrument of education)	wars of movement and position
Polanyi	market forces (and their legitimation)	countermovements aimed at self-protection
Scott	ideologies (public transcripts)	counterdiscourses

Differences in levels of analysis, main targets and modes of resistance should not be reasoned only by way of the intellectual proclivities of each theorist per se. Rather, the conceptual tensions among the theorists correspond to, and reflect, the changing conditions of social life: from Gramsci to Polanyi to Scott, as societies became more complex, so too did the targets and modes of resistance. Contemporary transformations in social life in general, and state–society relations in particular, imply that all three major targets and modes of resistance coexist and are modified in the globalizing process.

The important conversation and debate among theorists forms a framework that may be profitably fastened to neoliberal globalization. The emerging framework points to possibilities of identifying and contesting forms of domination, expanding political space, and opening new venues – hence redefinitions of politics. Seen from the observation points of this triad, a conceptualization of contemporary resistance to globalization sensitizes one to the following shift in ontology, suggested below.

Forms of resistance

As political and economic power becomes more diffuse and less institutionalized, so too will forms of resistance. Undeclared forms of resistance conducted individually and collectively in submerged networks parallel openly declared forms of resistance embodied in wars of movement and position, and countermovements. Depending on the context, everyday activities such as what one wears (e.g. the veil in Muslim societies or the 'dashiki' in the African-American community), buys, or consumes may qualify as resistance – as much as that of organized strikes, boycotts, and even armed insurgencies against states and transnational corporations throughout the world. One of the key challenges here is to problematize the absence of openly declared forms of resistance. Doing so can explicate the changing meaning of politics as a result of interactions between forces of change on the local, national, regional, and global levels.

Agents of resistance

In the past, agents of resistance were synonymous mostly with union workers, armed rebel/peasants, and political dissidents, including students and certain intellectuals, as class contestations assumed overt political and, in some cases, military dimensions. At present, agents of resistance are not restricted to such actors. They range from blue collar and white collar workers, and to clerics, home-makers, and middle managers. It is important to note that even state functionaries can resist the wholesale implementation of neoliberal development paths, e.g. those who insist on 'Asian-style democracy' in the midst of establishing open markets and free trade. It is the complex ways in which symbolic resources and values articulate with the material conditions of life in different societies that produce a variety of organic intellectuals, a more encompassing group in the current phase of globalization. Class contest only partly form the basis of resistance. Instead, agents of resistance emerge from interactions between structure and agency that lead to the contextual privileging of particular intersections of different modalities of identity, i.e. class–nationality–gender–race/ethnicity–religion–sexuality. Implicit in the designation of different peoples as agents of resistance is an expansion of the boundaries associated with the traditional sites of political life.

Sites of resistance

Resistance is localized, regionalized, and globalized at the same time that economic globalization slices across geopolitical borders. What this means, in part, is that the 'public-private' dichotomy no longer holds, for most (albeit not all) dimensions of social life are affected, in varying and interconnected ways by globalizing forces. Everyday life in the household and the informal market can facilitate, as well as resist, such forces in distinctly material and symbolic ways. Another closely related phenomenon is the development of cyberspace, a site in which resistance finds its instantaneous audience via the Internet or World Wide Web. Counterdiscourse is a mode of globalized resistance in cyberspace. One has to bear in mind, however, that although states in general are incapable of effectively monitoring and censoring cyberspatial counterdiscourse, this particular mode of resistance is open mainly to those who have access to computers, modems, and the Internet.

Strategies of resistance

By strategies, we refer to the actual ways that people, whose modes of existence are threatened by globalization (e.g. through job loss, encroachment on community lands, or undermining of cultural integrity) respond in a sustained manner toward achieving certain objectives. While forms of struggle differ, groups may adopt varied means to contest, scale up or down, and link objectively and subjectively to their counterparts in other countries or regions. Local movements become transnational or global with sustained access to communication technologies that construct and maintain communities of like-minded individuals. For example, community activists and scholars meet at different forums for the exchange of information and plans. An emerging strategy of 'borderless solidarity' is to link single issues such as environmental degradation, women's rights, and racism, and to highlight the interconnectedness of varied dimensions of social life. Analyses of this may bring to bear the conditions and methods by which commonality can be achieved in spite of, and because of, the fragmentation of identities and interests as political life is being globalized. Nonetheless, evolving global strategies of resistance do not necessarily sidetrack the state. Under certain circumstances, strategies of resistance can and do pit state agencies against one another (e.g. in the case of shipping toxic waste to the developing world, state agencies in charge of environmental protection may join in protests, while their counterparts responsible for industrial development continue to encourage the kind and methods of industrialization that cause environmental destruction). Studies of global, transnational, and local resistance must then take into account transformations in state structures, whether or not strategies of resistance manifestly engage the state.

Quite clearly, an ontology of resistance to globalization requires grounding. When contextualized, the elements of *forms, agents, sites, and strategies* may be viewed in terms of their interactions so as to delimit durable patterns and the potential for structural transformation. The Gramsci–Polanyi–Scott triad calls for conceptual frameworks that link different levels of analysis. Integration of the local with the global can bring to the fore the conditions in which different *forms, agents, sites, and strategies* of resistance emerge from the conjunctures and disjunctures in the global political economy.

Notes

1 See, especially, Gary Gereffi, 'The Elusive Last Lap in the Quest for Developed-Country Status', in James H. Mittelman (ed.), *Globalization: Critical Reflections* (Lynne Rienner, 1996); and James H. Mittelman, 'Rethinking the International Division of Labour in the Context of Globalisation', *Third World Quarterly*, Vol. 16 (1995), pp. 273–94, and 'Global Restructuring of Production and Migration', in Yoshikazu Sakamoto (ed.), *Global Transformation: Challenges to the State System* (United Nations University Press, 1994).

2 See, especially, Kenichi Ohmae, *The Borderless World: Power and Strategy in the Interlinked Economy* (HarperCollins, 1990).

3 See, especially, Paul Q. Hirst and Grahame Thompson, *Globalization in Question: The International Economy and the Possibilities of Governance* (Basil Blackwell, 1996).

4 Our definition of culture is borrowed from Raymond Williams. For a more detailed conceptualization of culture, see Williams' book, *Marxism and Literature* (Oxford University Press, 1977).

5 Antonio Gramsci, *Selections from the Prison Notebooks*, trans. and ed. Quintin Hoare and Geoffrey Nowell Smith (Lawrence & Wishart, International Publishers, 1971).

6 Gramsci, *Prison Notebooks*, p. 268.

7 Gramsci, *Prison Notebooks*, pp. 229–30. Gramsci also linked wars of position to 'passive revolution' of the dominant classes – i.e. revolution from above – that sidesteps the need for fundamental restructuring from below. See, pp. 106–20.

8 Gramsci, *Prison Notebooks*, p. 326–7.

9 See, for example, Christine B.N. Chin, *In Service and Servitude: Foreign Female Domestic Workers and the Malaysian 'Modernity Project'* (Columbia University Press, 1998).

10 Karl Polanyi, *The Great Transformation: The Political and Economic Origins of Our Time* (Beacon Press, 1944). For a discussion of different forms of the state and of the ways they relate to the market as well as world order, see Robert W. Cox, *Production, Power, and World Order* (Columbia University Press, 1986).

11 Polanyi, *Great Transformation*, p. 73.

12 Alberto Melucci, 'The Symbolic Challenge of Contemporary Social Movements', *Social Research*, Vol. 52 (1985), p. 795.

13 See, especially, bell hooks, *Feminist Theory: From Margin to Center* (South End Press, 1984), and *Ain't I a Woman: Black Women and Feminism* (South

End Press, 1981); and Chandra Mohanty, Ann Russo and Lourdes Torres (eds), *Third World Women and the Politics of Feminism* (Indiana University Press, 1991).

14 Melucci, 'Symbolic Challenge', p. 812.

15 'While the noun *sha'b* refers to a collective people, populace, or folk and has an implicit collective connotation to it, as an adjective *sha'bi* demarcates a wide range of indigenous practices, tastes, and patterns in everyday life', (Diane Singerman, *Avenues of Participation: Family, Politics and Networks in Urban Quarters of Cairo* (Princeton University Press, 1995), pp. 10–11.

16 James C. Scott, *The Moral Economy of the Peasant: Rebellion and Subsistence in Southeast Asia* (Yale University Press, 1976); *Weapons of the Weak: Everyday Forms of Peasant Resistance* (Yale University Press, 1985); and *Domination and the Arts of Resistance: Hidden Transcripts* (Yale University Press, 1990).

17 Scott, *Domination*, p. 200, emphasis in the original.

18 Scott, *Domination*, p. 18.

19 Margaret R. Somers, 'The Narrative Constitution of Identity: A Relational and Network Approach', *Theory and Society*, Vol. 23 (1994), pp. 605–49.

20 See, especially, Judith Butler and Joan Scott (eds), *Feminists Theorize the Political* (Routledge, 1992); Clifford Geertz (ed.), *Local Knowledge: Further Essays in Interpretive Anthropology* (Basic Books, 1983); and Charles Taylor, *Sources of the Self: The Making of the Modern Identity* (Harvard University Press, 1987).

21 Scott, *Weapons of the Weak*, p. xix.

4
Resisting 'Globalization-from-Above' through 'Globalization-from-Below'

Richard Falk

A normative assessment of globalization

Globalization, with all of its uncertainties and inadequacies as a term, does usefully call attention to a series of developments associated with the ongoing dynamic of economic restructuring at the global level. The negative essence of this dynamic, as unfolding within the present historical time frame, is to impose on governments the discipline of global capital in a manner that promotes economistic policy making in national arenas of decision, subjugating the outlook of governments, political parties, leaders and élites and often accentuating distress to vulnerable and disadvantaged regions and peoples.

Among the consequences is a one-sided depoliticizing of the state as neoliberalism becomes 'the only game in town', according to widely accepted perceptions that are dutifully disseminated by the mainstream media to all corners of the planet. Such a neoliberal mindset is deeply opposed to social public sector expenditures devoted to welfare, job creation, environmental protection, health care, education, and even the alleviation of poverty. To a great extent, these expenditures are entrenched, and difficult to diminish directly because of legal obstacles and citizen backlash, as well as varying degrees of electoral accountability in constitutional democracies. Nevertheless, the political tide is definitely running in the neoliberal direction, and will continue to do so as long as the public can be induced to ingest the pill of social austerity without reacting too vigorously. To date, the mainstream has been generally pacified, especially as represented by principal political parties, and what reaction has occurred has too often been expressed by a surge of support for nativist, right-wing extremism that indicts global capital and blames immigrants for high unemployment and stagnant wages.

This set of circumstances, if not properly modified, presages a generally grim future for human society, including a tendency to make alternative orientations towards economic policy appear irrelevant; to the extent believed, this induces a climate of resignation and despair. To the extent that normative goals continue to be affirmed within political arenas, as is the case to varying degrees with human rights and environmental protection, their substantive claims on resources are treated either as an unfortunate, if necessary, burden on the grand objectives of growth and competitiveness or as a humanitarian luxury that is becoming less affordable and acceptable in an integrated market-driven world economy.

Indeed, one of the obvious spillover effects of the mindset induced by globalization is to exert strong downward pressure on public goods expenditures, especially those with an external or global dimension. The financial strains being experienced by the United Nations, despite the savings associated with the absence of strategic rivalry of the sort that fuelled the Cold War arms race, is emblematic of declining political support for global public goods, and runs counter to the widespread realization that the growing complexity of international life requires increasing global capabilities for coordination and governance, at minimum for the sake of efficiency.[1]

In the context of international trade, both domestic labour and minority groups in rich countries of the North mount pressure to attach human rights and environmental conditionalities to trade considerations, whereas business and financial élites resist such advocacy (unless they happen to be operating outside the global marketplace, and hence have an anachronistic territorial, statist outlook on sales and profits) as it diminishes their 'out-sourcing' opportunities to take advantage of dramatically lower labour costs and weaker regulatory standards in most of the South.

Economic globalization has also had some major positive benefits, including a partial levelling-up impact on North–South relations and a rising standard of living for several hundred million people in Asia, which has included rescuing many millions from poverty. Indeed, according to recent UNDP figures the proportion of the poor globally, but not their absolute number, has been declining during the past several years. There are some indications that after

countries reach a certain level of development, especially in response to the demands of an expanding urban middle class, pressures
mount to improve workplace and environmental conditions. Such
governments also become more confident actors on the global stage,
challenging inequities and biases of geopolitical structures; Malaysia typifies such a pattern. There is nothing inherently wrong with
encouraging economies of scale and the pursuit of comparative
advantage so long as the social, environmental, political and cultural effects are mainly beneficial. What is objectionable is to indulge
a kind of market mysticism that accords policy hegemony to the
promotion of economic growth, disregarding adverse social effects
and shaping economic policy on the basis of ideological certitudes
that are not attentive to the realities of human suffering.

Globalization is also historically influenced by several contingent
factors that intensify these adverse human effects, that is, the social
costs of the process. First of all, in the current period globalization
is proceeding in an ideological atmosphere in which neoliberal
thinking and priorities go virtually unchallenged, especially in the
leading market economies; the collapse of the social 'other' has
encouraged capitalism to pursue its market logic with a relentless-
ness that has not been evident since the first decades of the industrial
revolution. Second, this neoliberal climate of opinion is reinforced
by an anti-government societal mood that is composed of many
elements, including a consumerist reluctance to pay taxes; an alleged failure by government to be successful when promoting social
objectives; a 'third wave' set of decentralizing technological moves
that emphasize the transformative civilizational role of computers
and electronic information; and a declining capacity of political
parties to provide their own citizenry with forward-looking policy
proposals. Third, the policy orientation of government has also grown
steadily more business-focused, reflecting the decline of organized
labour as a social force, resulting in the serious erosion of the perceived threat of revolutionary opposition from what Immanuel
Wallerstein usefully identifies as 'the dangerous classes'.[2] In addition, the mobility of capital is increasing in a world economy that
is much more shaped by financial flows and the acquisition of intellectual property rights than it is by manufacturing and trade in
tangible goods and services. Fourth, the fiscal imperatives of debt
and deficit reduction in the interests of transnational monetary
stability reinforce other aspects of globalization. Fifth, this unfolding of globalization as a historical process is occurring within an

international order that exhibits gross inequalities of every variety, thereby concentrating the benefits of growth upon already advantaged sectors within and among societies and worsening the relative and absolute condition of those already most disadvantaged. The experience of sub-Saharan Africa is strongly confirmatory of this generalization.[3]

Thus it is that globalization in *this* historical setting poses a particular form of normative challenge that is distinctive and different from what it would be in other globalizing circumstances. The challenge being posed is directed, above all, at the survival of, and maybe the very possibility of sustaining, the compassionate state, as typified by the humane achievements of the Scandinavian countries up through the 1980s and by the optimistic gradualism of social democratic approaches to politics.[4] The impacts attributed to globalization have been strongly reinforced by the most influential readings given to the ending of the Cold War, discrediting not only utopian socialism, but any self-conscious societal project aimed at the betterment of living conditions for the poor or regarding the minimizing of social disparities as generally desirable.

These ideological and operational aspects of globalization are associated with the way transnational market forces dominate the policy scene, including the significant cooptation of state power. This pattern of development is identified here as 'globalization-from-above', a set of forces and legitimating ideas that is in many respects located beyond the effective reach of territorial authority and that has enlisted most governments as tacit partners. But globalization, so conceived, has generated criticism and resistance, both of a local, grassroots variety, based on the concreteness of the specifics of time and place – e.g. the siting of a dam or nuclear power plant or the destruction of a forest – and on a transnational basis, involving the linking of knowledge and political action in hundreds of civil initiatives. It is this latter aggregate of phenomena that is described here under the rubric of 'globalization-from-below'.[5]

Given this understanding it is useful to ask the question – what is the normative potential of globalization-from-below? The idea of normative potential is to conceptualize widely shared world order values: minimizing violence, maximizing economic well-being, realizing social and political justice, and upholding environmental quality.[6] These values often interact inconsistently, but are normatively coherent in the sense of depicting the main dimensions of a widely shared consensus as to the promotion of benevolent forms world order, and seem at odds in crucial respects with part of the orientation and some of the main impacts of globalization-from-above in its current historical phase. In all probability, globalization-from-above would have different and generally more positive normative impacts if the prevailing ideological climate was conditioned by social democracy rather than by neoliberalism or if the adaptation of the state was subject to stronger countervailing societal or transnational pressures of a character that accorded more fully with world order values. This historical setting of globalization exhibits various tendencies of unequal significance, the identification of which helps us assess whether globalization-from-below is capable of neutralizing some of the detrimental impacts of globalization-from-above. A further caveat is in order. The dichotomizing distinction between above and below is only a first approximation of the main social formations attributable to globalization. Closer scrutiny suggests numerous cross-cutting diagonal alignments that bring grassroots forces into various positive and negative relationships with governmental and neoliberal policies. Coalition possibilities vary also in relation to issue area. For instance, transnational social initiatives with respect to economic and social rights may be affirmed by some governments, while comparable initiatives directed at environmental protection or disarmament would appeal to other governments.

The new politics of resistance in an era of globalization

Political oppositional forms in relation to globalization-from-above have been shaped by several specific conditions. First, there is the virtual futility of concentrating upon conventional electoral politics, given the extent to which principal political parties in constitutional democracies have subscribed to a program and orientation that accepts the essential features of the discipline of global capital. This development may not persist if social forces can be mobilized in such a way as to press social democratic leaderships effectively to resume their commitment to the establishment of a compassionate state, and such an outlook proves to be generally viable in the context of governing. To succeed, except under special circumstances, would imply that globalization-from-above was not structurally powerful enough to prevent defections at the unit level of the state. Of course, variations of constraining influence arise from many factors, including the ideological stance of the leadership, efficiency in handling the social agenda, disparities in wealth and income, and the overall growth rates of the national, regional and global economies. The main conclusion remains. Resistance to economic globalization is not likely to be effective if it relies on matters of political economy.

Second, criticism of economic globalization at the level of societal politics is unlikely to have a major impact on public and élite opinion until a credible alternative economic approach is fashioned intellectually, and such an alternative approach has enough mobilizing effect on people that a new perception of the 'dangerous classes' – which this time is not likely to be the industrial working class – re-enters discourse, again making economic and political élites nervous enough about their managerial ability to contain opposition to begin seriously entertaining more progressive policy options. In such an altered atmosphere it is easy to imagine the negotiation of social contracts that restore balance to the interests of people and those of markets.

Third, aside from the re-emergence of dangerous classes, there are prospects that ecological constraints of various sorts will induce the market to send a variety of signals calling for a negotiated transition to managed economic growth in the interest of sustainability. Under these circumstances, with limits on growth being required for both environmental reasons and middle-term business profitability, it may be possible at some now unforeseen point in the future to reach a series of agreements on a regional basis, and perhaps even globally, that amount to a global social contract. The objective of such an instrument, which would not need to be formally agreed upon, would be to balance anxieties about the carrying capacity of the earth against a range of social demands about securing the basic needs of individuals and communities, quite possibly on a regional level.

Fourth, globalization-from-above is definitely encouraging a resurgence of support for right-wing extremism, a varied and evolving array of political movements that may scare governments dominated by moderate outlooks into rethinking their degree of acquiescence to the discipline of global capital. Electoral results in several European countries, including Austria and France, revealed both growing support for the political right and a turn to the far right by citizens faced with the fiscal symptoms of economic globalization, including cutbacks in social services, high interest rates, capital outflows and instability in employment and prospects. Will national political parties and governments be able to recover their legitimacy and authority by responding effectively to this challenge without successfully modifying the global setting and its current impact on the policy-making process?

Fifth, will labour militancy become somewhat more effective and socially visible as it shifts its focus from industrial age priorities of wages and workplace conditions to such emerging concerns as downsizing, out-sourcing, and job security? There are also possibilities of engaging wider constituencies than organized labour in this struggle, individuals, and groups that are feeling some of the negative effects of globalizing tendencies. Jacques Chirac seemed sufficiently shaken by the December 1995 large-scale work-stoppages and demonstrations that he partially reversed ideological course, at least rhetorically, and suddenly called for the creation of 'a social Europe', which was a retreat from a basic tenet of neoliberalism and thus provided a psychological victory for the perspectives favouring globalization-from-below. Subsequent demonstrations and strikes in France appear to have been generalized societal, especially urban, reactions against the austerity budget being implemented by the government so as to qualify the country for participation in plans to establish currency and monetary union within the framework of the European Union. But rhetorical victories do not necessarily produce adjustments in policy, particularly if the structures that underpin the neoliberal approach are strong and elusive, as is the case with the world economy. In retrospect, Chirac's conversion to the cause of a social Europe seems like little more than a tactical manoeuvre designed to gain more operating room, comparable perhaps to George Bush, the arch realist, momentarily extolling the virtues of the United Nations during the Gulf crisis and proclaiming a new world order. After the crisis passed, so did the opportunistic embrace Bush had made of a more law-oriented system of security for international society.

Another indicative development with respect to labour is a renewed recourse to the strike weapon as a means for working people to resist globalization. Organized labour, despite economic growth in the North, has not been able to share in the material benefits of a larger economic pie because of the impinging effects of competitiveness and fiscal austerity, and in numerous economic sectors it has been losing jobs and facing a continuous threat of industrial relocation. The General Motors strike of October 1996 in Canada was a harbinger of both a new wave of labour militancy and a new agenda of grievances. The strike focused on precisely these issues, involving a direct challenge to the approach of the managers of economic globalization. It was symbolically, as well as intrinsically, important, suggesting a new direction of emphasis in the labour movement that has all sorts of potential for transnational cooperative activities across societies whose workers have benefited from globalization, but whose working conditions are miserable in a variety of respects.

Sixth, and informing the whole process of globalization, whether from above or below, is the weakening of control by the state over identity politics, with a variety of positive and negative consequences. Transnational networks of affiliation in relation to gender, race, and class have become more tenable, although confusingly they coexist with an ultra-nationalist backlash politics that seeks to reappropriate the state for the benefit of traditional ethnic identities. In important respects, backlash politics represents the inversion of globalization-from-below, that is, a repudiation of globalization-from-above by a reliance on the protectionist capabilities of the state, a tactic that has generally been an economic failure, most spectacularly in relation to the experience of the Soviet bloc countries in the latter stages of the Cold War. In contrast, China, with its opening to the forces of globalization-from-above, while suppressing those associated with globalization-from-below, has enjoyed spectacular economic success, although at high human costs. The main point, however, is that the democratic spaces available to resist globalization-from-above tend to be mainly situated at either local levels of engagement or transnationally. One very invisible siting has been in relation to global conferences under the auspices of the United Nations on a variety of policy issues, including environment, development, human rights, the role of women, the social responsibilities of government, population pressures and problems of urban life and habitat. What has been impressive has been the creative tactics used by transnational participating groups, denied formal access because of their lack of statist credentials, yet exerting a considerable impact on the agenda and substantive outcomes of intergovernmental activities, and at the same time strengthening transnational links. Starting with the Rio Conference on Environment and Development in 1992, through the 1993 Vienna Conference on Human Rights and Development, the 1994 Cairo Conference on Population and Development, the 1995 Social Summit in Copenhagen, and the Beijing Conference on Women and Development, to the 1996 Istanbul Conference on

Habitat and Development, there has been a flow of gatherings that acknowledged to varying degrees the emergent role of globalization-from-below. These events were early experiments in a new sort of participatory politics that had little connection with the traditional practices of politics within states, and could be regarded as fledgling attempts to constitute 'global democracy'.

Such developments, representing a definite effort to engage directly both statist and market forces, produced their own kind of backlash politics. At first, at Rio and Vienna, the effort was a cooptive one, acknowledging the participation of globalization-from-below as legitimate and significant, yet controlling outcomes. But later on, at Cairo, Copenhagen, and Beijing, the more radical potentialities of these democratizing forces were perceived as adversaries of the neoliberal conception of political economy, and the format of a global conference open to both types of globalization began to be perceived as risky, possibly an early sighting of the next wave of revolutionary challenge, the rebirth of dangerous classes in the sense earlier reserved for the labour movement.

If this assessment of action and reaction is generally accurate it suggests the probability of several adjustments. To begin with, there may emerge a reluctance to finance and organize global conferences under the banner of the United Nations that address non-technical matters of human concern. There will be a search for new formats by forces associated with globalization-from-below, possibly increasing the oppositional character of participation, creating a hostile presence at meetings of the Group of Seven or at the annual meetings of the Board of Governors of the IMF or World Bank, possibly organizing tribunals of the people to consider allegations against globalization-from-above. In effect, if the challenge of globalization-from-below is to become dangerous enough to tempt those representing globalization-from-above to seek accommodation, new tactics will have to be developed. One direction of activity that is easier to organize is to concentrate energies of resistance at the regional levels of encounter, especially in Europe and Asia-Pacific, at intergovernmental gatherings devoted to expanding relative and absolute growth for the region *vis-à-vis* the global economy. The Third World Network, based in Penang, has been very effective in educating the cadres of resistance to globalization-from-above about adverse effects and encouraging various types of opposition. Otherwise, resistance to globalization-from-above and the ascendancy of market forces is likely to be ignored.

Seventh, it has become necessary to formulate a programmatic response to this pattern of action and reaction between those political tendencies seeking to embody the logic of the market in structures of global economic governance, such as the World Trade Organization and the Bretton Woods institutions, and the transnational political forces seeking to realize the vision of cosmopolitan democracy.[7] More directly, militant tactics may also be selectively employed to supplement the regulatory efforts, feeble at best, of national governments. Such a dynamic was initiated successfully by Greenpeace several years ago to reverse a decision by Shell Oil, approved by the British government, to sink a large oil rig named Brent Spar in the North Sea. The issue here was one of environmental protection, but the tactic of consumer leverage is potentially deployable in relation to any issue that finds its way onto the transnational social agenda. What induced the Shell turnaround – although it never conceded the possible environmental dangers of its planned disposal of the oil rig – was the focus of the boycott on Shell service stations, especially those located in Germany. Indeed, the impact of this initiative was so great that both the *Wall Street Journal* and the *Financial Times* editorialized against Greenpeace, complaining that it had become 'an environmental superpower'.

At this stage, the politics of resistance in this emergent era of globalization are in formation. Because of the global scope, combined with the unevenness of economic and political conditions, the tactics and priorities will be diverse, adapted to the local, national, and regional circumstances. Just as globalization-from-above tends towards homogeneity and unity, so globalization-from-below tends towards heterogeneity and diversity, even tension and contradiction. This contrast highlights the fundamental difference between top-down hierarchical politics and bottom-up participatory politics. It is not a zero-sum rivalry, but rather one in which the transnational democratic goals are designed to reconcile global market operations with the well-being of peoples and with the carrying capacity of the earth. Whether such a reconciliation is possible is likely to be the most salient political challenge at the dawn of a new millennium.

Notes

1 See two reports of global commissions of eminent persons, published as *Our Global Neighbourhood* by the Commission on Global Governance (Oxford; New York: Oxford University Press, 1995); and *Caring for the*

Future by the Independent Commission on Population and the Quality of Life (Oxford University Press, 1996).

2   I. Wallerstein, *After Liberalism* (New Press, 1995), pp. 1–8, 93–107.

3   Effectively argued in S. Kothari, 'Where are the People? The United Nations, Global Economic Institutions and Governance,' in C. Reus-Smit, A. Jarvis and A. Paolini (eds), *The United Nations: Between Sovereignty and Global Governance* (Macmillan, 1997).

4   This position is elaborated in R. Falk, 'An Inquiry into the Political Economy of World Order', *New Political Economy* 1 (1996), 13–26.

5   For initial reliance on this terminology with respect to globalization, see R. Falk, 'The Making of Global Citizenship', in J. Brecher, J. B. Childs and J. Cutler (eds), *Global Visions: Beyond the New World Order* (South End Press, 1993), pp. 39–50. For a useful and sophisticated overview of globalization-from-below in the context of transnational environmentalism, see P. Wapner, *Environmental Activism and World Civic Politics* (SUNY Press, 1996).

6   For an attempted clarification of world order values and their interrelations, see R. Falk, *A Study of Future Worlds* (Free Press, 1975), pp. 11–43.

7   A comprehensive and important effort to formulate such a perspective is to be found in the writings of D. Held, *Democracy and the Global Order: From the Modern State to Cosmopolitan Democracy* (Polity Press, 1995), pp. 267–86.

5
Globalization versus Community: Stakeholding, Communitarianism and the Challenge of Globalization

R. J. Barry Jones

Globalization, as a condition or a set of processes, now attracts considerable attention from academics, journalists and politicians. A similar level of attention has also been directed to a set of critical issues concerning economic vitality, employment and social cohesion within many of the established industrialized societies and is reflected in the work of stakeholding theorists and social communitarians. These two areas of concern are intimately interrelated, but often treated separately in popular debate and discussion.[1]

The first purpose of this chapter is to argue that a significant number of the problems addressed by stakeholder theorists and communitarian thinkers are connected with structural changes in the international political economy, signalled by the popular idea of globalization. The second purpose is to highlight the dangers inherent in the tension between the 'realities' of a globalizing world economy and stakeholding and communitarian impulses.

The problem with much of the globalization debate is that it has tended to be a 'top-down' approach to contemporary developments, while the stakeholding agenda for economic revitalization and the communitarian project for social regeneration have usually been developed from a 'bottom-up' perspective. This difference of origin has inhibited systematic cross-fertilization, while encouraging the kind of peremptory dismissal of the need to relate policy proposals to a clear political economy with which Peter Mandelson and Roger Liddle met criticisms[2] of their co-authored political tract *The Blair Revolution*.[3]

Not only have the new proponents of stakeholding political

economy, and of communitarian social and political theory, tended to neglect the role and implications of globalization, they have also evaded the wider ethical implications of community-based approaches to politics and political economy. Such issues are, however, of critical significance to the orderly development of the international system and have, accordingly, been at the heart of the pivotal debates between *cosmopolitan* and *communitarian* international political theorists. The relative absence of debate amongst international political theorists and the theorists of domestic communitarianism and stakeholding political economy constitutes a second major hiatus in contemporary theory and analysis.

The problems of interrelating the globalization debates with the communitarian and stakeholding debates, and with the cosmopolitan-communitarian debate, is that each embraces internal complexities that compound the problems of relating the one to the other. The initial problems concern the ambiguity of the term globalization and the contested character of its current level and durability. These complexities are linked to the problems of differentiating the analytically distinct roles of globalization processes and pressures, technological advances, and 'local' political, economic and social polices, upon economic vitality, unemployment and social cohesion.

Globalization

Globalization has become a popular shibboleth of much contemporary discussion of global economics and politics. Unfortunately, its employment has been marked more by imprecision than by care and discrimination. The concept of globalization requires far greater precision in definition and usage if it is to clarify more than it obscures. The sources, implications, management, and even restraint, of advancing globalization demand detailed investigation.[4]

The core of contemporary globalization has been summarized by Paul Hirst and Grahame Thompson, albeit from a sceptical perspective, as resting upon a global economy in which ' . . . distinct national economies and, therefore, domestic strategies of national economic management are increasingly irrelevant . . . (as the world is) . . . dominated by uncontrollable market forces' and the uncontrolled influence of transnational corporations.[5] Such a supposed transformation of the economic dimension of life leads, thence, to a range of changed social conditions, and subjectivities, in which, in the view of Malcolm Waters 'the constraints of geography on social and cultural arrangements recede and in which people become increasingly aware that they are receding.'[6]

However, many theorists of globalization (Hirst and Thompson excepted), are unclear as to whether the phenomenon to which they aver has materialized, is approaching, or is merely a set of processes which might, under certain circumstances, generate a truly globalized world: an ambiguity which the globalization literature shares with much of that on integration, both international and regional. However, the core characteristics attributed to a globalized world are rarely novel features. Contemporary globalization, therefore, may be primarily a matter of the acceleration and intensification of the interrelated effects of a number of established conditions and processes. Transformations of quantitative changes into fundamental qualitative change are a complex and controversial matter.[7]

The variability of contemporary empirical evidence on the current level of economic globalization suggests a highly uneven situation. There is widespread agreement that a high level of integration has developed within the world's financial sector, with world-wide mergers of financial firms, international alliances and twenty-four hour systems for financial transfers and trading.[8] However, diversity within the world's capital and financial markets has not yet been entirely eliminated.[9] Moreover, such integration has not been an exclusively market-led process, for the influence of state governments has been central to the emergence of the international financial system in its present form[10] and could still be the source of major changes, and even retrenchment, albeit at a substantial cost.

Beyond the financial sector, the situation remains complex and uneven.[11] Hirst and Thompson's study of the activities of leading multinational corporations indicates that few, if any, contemporary multinational corporations conform to the ideal-type of a fully globalized company.[12] Patterns of trade and economic 'dependence' are also highly varied: with the preponderance of the trade of the Advanced Industrialized Countries (AICs) being undertaken with other AICs; with most Less Developed Countries being involved in highly asymmetrical trade relations primarily with a small number of AICs; and with some evidence of regionalization within the world economy.[13]

As with the case of financial integration, patterns of activity by multinational companies and international trade relations are all open to change, and even to reversal, under the influence of a range of economic, social and political influences. The complex sources and patterns of change within the international political economy thus require not merely an effective theoretical perspective upon political economy, but also an analytical approach to change that can accommodate the complex interactions between structures and agents in human affairs.[14]

Globalization and community: the stakeholding and communitarian agendas

The further advance of globalization is generally held to have a number of important implications for activity at the level of extant communities (however defined and identified), including the reduced effectiveness of the policy instruments that remain available to state authorities. Levels of employment, and associated remuneration within local communities may also have been significantly affected by aspects of globalization. With depressive effects on wage levels within some AICs, and disruptive impacts upon the stability of families and local communities, concerns about the pressures of globalization dovetail with anxieties about the well-being of the social fabric of many mature industrialized societies.

Stakeholding has been dubbed a vague, if not old-fashioned, concept by its political and theoretical critics.[15] What is clear in the stakeholding agenda, however, is its emphasis upon the principle that 'a firm's activity affects many parties: shareholders, customers, employees, suppliers, the local community and the natural environment.'[16] The programme resulting from such a perception is intended 'to design institutions, systems and a wider architecture which creates a better economic and social balance, and with it a culture in which common humanity and the instinct to collaborate are allowed to flower'[17] and emphasizes the potential role of such instruments as regional banks and tax incentives for communally-sensitive activities, including training and measures of environmental protection.[18]

The concern of such a stakeholding approach with the immediate well-being of the community of the business enterprise and the community within which it operates, is clear. Stakeholding is also, however, mooted as a major plank in a wider strategy for the economic revitalization of those societies that have entered the economic and industrial Doldrums. Such recovery would, in turn, reduce unemployment and increase the security of those in jobs, thereby contributing to communal well-being. Stakeholding is thus offered as a contribution to the problems of the community through the general process of economic revival.

The communitarian project, particularly in policy-orientated social theory[19] is focused primarily at the local, or communal level. Such a programme links with the stakeholding agenda through the way in which changes in patterns of employment and economic well-being may influence the ethical and behavioural foundations of local societies. Widespread unemployment is widely acknowledged to be socially corrosive. Increased insecurity amongst, and pressures upon, those still in work has also been identified as a significant source of stress, of tension within families, and of a wider failure to participate actively in the local community.

The communitarian/stakeholding fusion thus provides an attractive basis for revivalist policy. Here, exaggerations of the extent and impact of contemporary globalization may be as misleading as the prognostications of theoreticians of stakeholding who ignore the international economic context (within which local economic and industrial policy has to be implemented) or those communitarians who focus exclusively on the level of the local community.

Globalization processes are considerably encouraged by, and often rely upon, the facilities provided by the latest information technology. However, globalization, to the extent that it develops, exerts its own pressures upon firms and governments to acquire and deploy the latest information technologies in their pursuit of competitiveness and/or control. Globalization is now held to be conditioning state policies, in extent and kind. However, many of the more advanced forms of globalization have arisen from the past actions and decisions of governments, both intentional, or unintentional, as the evolution of the contemporary international financial system demonstrates.[20] Technological innovation has, finally, been as much a matter of governmental initiative, particularly in the case of the modern computer 'revolution',[21] as it has been a factor and an influence purely exogenous to the political system.

Governmental policies may also act as an independent influence upon developments. However, official policies might be so constrained by external developments, and fundamental pressures, as to be little more than reflections of forces in the wider world economy. Finally, policy-makers might invoke globalization, and its supposed effects and constraints, merely as sources of apparent justification for policies that they wish to implement for quite other reasons.

Stakeholding economic communities in a globalized world economy

Stakeholding is not the only arrow in the quiver of those who seek radical solutions to the economic revitalization of those industrial economies that are now suffering increased competition from abroad and high levels of unemployment at home. A range of policies embracing new tax incentives for industrial investment, new relationships between financial and industrial sectors, encouragement for industrial innovation, and measures to enhance levels of education and training have all been mooted as paths to a better future for struggling economies. Such practices are not entirely new and have been identified as significant sources of the economic success of Germany and Japan.

The core of the stakeholding agenda turns upon the business enterprise's enhanced sense of responsibility and responsiveness towards those with whom it interacts. The stakeholders in such a vision include employees, members of the immediate community within which the firm operates its facilities, suppliers of the components and services that it 'consumes' in its productive activities and those who receive or are affected by the production and distribution of its output. The primary responsibilities of the firm are thus expanded beyond the more traditional concern for its shareholders. Financial institutions, and institutional investors in industry, are enjoined to accommodate this wider agenda in their attitudes towards the general management of industry and, if necessary, to the short-term gains that can be derived from their investments. The well-being of the entire range of stakeholders, in both the short and longer-term, thus becomes the active concern of the firm and also becomes central to the legislative and regulative activities of the wider political system.[22]

The difficulties of the stakeholder project become clear, however, when the pressures generated by a globalizing international political economy are considered and the problems of time and inherent analytical uncertainty are incorporated. If, as has been argued, the contemporary problems of faltering economic competitiveness and unemployment reflect, in part at least, that dynamic fusion of industrial mobility, international competition and technological innovation that is the substance of much that passes for globalization, then continued globalization will place the stakeholding agenda under considerable pressure. Most of the core elements of the stakeholding agenda involve costs, at least in the short term. Greater sensitivity to the local community will entail the direct costs of environmental restraint and aesthetic sensibility, and the indirect costs of increased levels of consultation. Greater concern for suppliers will involve the loss of short-term opportunities for cheaper supplies of inputs and services. Greater concern for the longer-term well-being of consumers will involve increased research and development to produce safer and more satisfactory products and may, as in the case of tobacco products, entail withdrawal from entire areas of production and distribution.

Enhanced concern for employees is central to the stakeholding agenda, but highlights its inherent difficulties. The retention of employees during times of reduced demand entails clear short-term costs for a company. Foregoing opportunities to shed labour when introducing new labour-saving equipment and systems might entail costs, unless output can be increased (and sold successfully) in proportion to the increase in productivity. The introduction of higher wage rates, which would enhance the well-being of workers, enrich the local community and possibly reduce the burden of supplementary benefits paid by the wider community to low-paid workers, would also be costly in the short-term.

All such innovations encounter the dilemmas common to discussions of minimum wage policies within societies. Within short-term, static analysis, the introduction of a minimum wage, or the increase of an existing minimum wage, threatens to generate a reduction in employment. Workers whom it is only marginally profitable to employ at an initial, relatively low wage, might become less attractive at a higher rate of pay. The encouragement to introduce labour saving technology increases with any increase in wage rates. Most significantly, in a world of intensifying international competition, the introduction of a minimum wage, or an increase in the level of an existing minimum wage, might encourage companies to relocate to lower wage economies. Companies which do not move and which seek to maintain employment levels, might find themselves under intensifying price competition from lower wage-cost producers abroad. It is, moreover, this last danger that might prove decisive in encouraging a company to invest in labour-saving, and hence employment-reducing, technology before it is overwhelmed by lower-cost, lower-price foreign competition.

In a world of increasing competition, therefore, the effects on employment within one economy will not be evidenced simply, or even primarily, through increased levels of domestic-production-displacing imports from low-wage-cost economies. The environment of intensifying price competition may prove sufficient as to counter well-intentioned stakeholder policies, as well as the related policy of a minimum wage.

Such an argument, however, rests upon the kind of static analysis that has been all too common in conventional economics.[23] The proponents of minimum wage policies, and other stakeholding proposals, may well adopt a more dynamic perspective. A minimum wage might prove to be a positive spur to innovations in industry and the upgrading of worker competencies and capabilities. This would increase competitiveness, both quantitative and qualitative and thus enhance longer-term employment prospects.

New industrial policies might, however, have differential effects: some industries might move forward with speed and good effective under the stimulus; others might falter and fail, or relocate to less demanding parts of the world. In some industries the net longer-term effect might be an increase in employment and/or an improved contribution to the wider community, in others it might mean reduced employment and a diminished local contribution.

Time also enters the equation here, for the speed with which different industries and individual firms will respond to a new policy context will vary considerably. Some large firms may be able to adopt positively and rapidly; others might be far slower. Some firms, especially in the small- to medium-size band, might be extinguished by the pressures created by the new climate; others might be re-stimulated to press ahead with innovation and expansion. However, the short run may be decisive for it is there that unsuccessful firms die and in which business leaders make the critical decisions that will determine their performance in the longer term.

Communitarianism in a globalized world economy

The problems confronting stakeholding and minimum wage proposals in a world of international competition, international industrial mobility and technological change, are also reflected in the challenges faced by the communitarian programme for social and political regeneration. Again, a primarily 'local' perspective threatens to condemn such a programme to the parochial and confronts it with serious obstacles.

A frontal challenge to the individualistic and rights-oriented character of contemporary forms[24] of political and philosophical liberalism is a central part of the communitarians' critical response to much of the supposed social fragmentation and ethical dissolution of contemporary Western societies.[25] The explicit rejection of liberalism's excesses within domestic polity and society also hints at an implicitly critical view of the ethical universalism that has underpinned the liberal approach to economic life.

The agenda emerging from a diversity of thinkers is devoted to social and moral reconstruction at the level of the community, often local but sometimes 'national'. The components of this agenda embrace the revival of a popular sense of community amongst people who have become separated from one another;[26] the redirection of the school curriculum towards the fostering of socially constructive attitudes and behavioural dispositions;[27] the restoration of a sense of responsibility, and capability, for effective parenting of children;[28] and the development of the institutions of governance and social action to reflect more fully, and to foster more effectively, the impulses for common action revealed by the myriad social movements and interest groups that arise within contemporary societies.[29]

A central theme of communitarian discourse is a re-assertion of individual responsibilities as a counter to the over-emphasis of rights within many modern societies. Some social communitarians also criticize a growing over-reliance upon the provision of a range of goods and services to individuals and groups by state-level authorities.

Where individual responsibility relates to effective parenting or participation in valuable communal activities, such a social-communitarian agenda relates only obliquely to the deeper currents of the political economy. Where the assertion of individual responsibility embraces the economic life of the individual or the local community, however, matters become a little more complex. Differences clearly exist between the manner in which individuals and local communities have responded to economic adversity at different times and in different places. Changes in culture, expectation and outlook are complicit in these variations. However, the problems facing those who are dispossessed or seriously disadvantaged economically remain substantial, irrespective of time and place. Moreover, the capacity to respond effectively to economic problems that arise from developments beyond the direct control of the individual or the local community will necessarily be limited. The impact of structural economic changes may not only discard the competencies of many individuals but may also leave whole communities shell-shocked and chronically demoralized. It is unsurprising, therefore, that the advent of endemic unemployment has encouraged, if not precipitated, accelerating social dissolution and decay in many of the major cities of the industrialized world.

Intensifying international competition for industrial goods, industrial relocation by multinational corporations and the acceleration of changes in goods and their technologies of production, have combined to generate much of the contemporary epidemic of unemployment and associated social crisis. Globalization, then, is reinforcing technological sources of unemployment, de-skilling in a wide range of industries, and general downward pressures upon wage levels and conditions of employment in many economies.

Recognition of the implications of advancing globalization is therefore central to a sound diagnosis of the contemporary ailment of many societies and to the effective prescriptions of appropriate cures. Unfortunately, many of the community-focused proposals of stakeholding theorists for economic reconstruction and the prescriptions of community-oriented policies for economic revitalization and reorganization encounter substantial obstacles. These obstacles emanate from the complex of competition, relocation, and technological innovation that is contemporary 'globalization'.

In the absence of a clear recognition of the 'external' economic sources of many contemporary social difficulties, and without acknowledgement of the obstacles that the 'external' domain will continue to place before more communally-responsive economic and industrial policies, and their social corollaries, a good part of the communitarian project will be doomed to frustration. Worse, it might sink into a vindictiveness of spirit and punitive impulses in practice. The long-term unemployed might be pilloried for a condition that is, in large part, a function of structural changes in the world economy and forced into demeaning 'jobs' to justify a paucity of public financial support. Single parents whose families have been sundered by the pressures of unemployment and/or chronic poverty might be condemned for a lack of moral worth, while facing insuperable obstacles to personal economic salvation. Such a response by communitarians to the local casualties of structural changes in the global economy heralds an even more complex set of reactions, and potentialities, when their attention does finally turn towards the international economy within which their own communities are located.

Cosmopolitanism versus communitarianism in a global system

Revivalist communitarianism at the local level dovetails with the communitarianism of international political theorists when attention turns to the wider world within which 'communities' are located. The tension is between ascribing ethical priority to extant communities and entertaining an ethical cosmopolitanism of one of two types: either a global cosmopolitanism that envisages a truly global community, with many of the ethical and empirical properties of geographically more specific communities; or a cosmopolitanism of rational, self-interested individuals for whom, and from amongst whom, a viable (essentially 'liberal') ethic can be expected.

Theorists of a communitarian disposition, explicitly or implicitly, doubt the viability of cosmopolitan perspectives, of either variant. David Miller argues that 'thick' ties of common identity and relationship are necessary foundations of those communities that can provide and sustain significant levels of welfare for their members. The sense of nationality that arises within such communities is more robust than any mere 'constitutional patriotism', in which common identity is confined to participation in some common institutions of public governance.[30] Danilo Zolo, concludes that global governance based upon cosmopolitan ethics and presumptions is a vain expectation and that state-level societies have to maintain modest and cautious expectations in their international conduct.[31]

Strong hints of a communitarian approach to international and transnational issues and an implicit rejection of cosmopolitan ethics and dispositions of both types frequently surface in discussions of the question of the treatment of potential immigrants. For example, the tension between the claims of existing members of established communities and those of potential new entrants is discussed by Daniel J. Tichenor.[32]

Such self-regarding ethical impulses hint at a general repudiation of the special kind of cosmopolitan ethic upon which liberal free-trade theory and practice has long rested. Free trade is often defended by its advocates on the grounds not only of efficiency but also of equity. By such arguments, free trade encourages the optimal employment of the world's productive resources and, hence, the highest possible level of consumer satisfaction globally. Free trade also provides all the peoples of the world with the best opportunities to deploy their aptitudes and energies optimally and, thence, to achieve the highest possible levels of production and standards of living.

The ethical implications of this latter proposition reinforces the efficiency arguments inherent in the first set of propositions and may, in extreme cases, be deemed to counter arguments for restraint of trade, where the simple efficiency argument in favour of free trade at all times and under all conditions is qualified by such empirical complications as the excessive costs of adjustment.

If cosmopolitanism founders in the face of a more communitarian view of the ethics of economic behaviour, then the issue of free trade, or its restraint, becomes simply a matter of assumptions and calculations about relative efficiencies. Moreover, general disposition towards the moral primacy of the local, or 'national' community may well be reinforced if programmes of economic reconstruction of communal renewal are frustrated by external constraints. The subordination of the interests of potential immigrants is at one with the denial of the claims of foreign workers abroad for access for their products to domestic markets. This, in turn, shades into the larger-scale issue of the prioritization of domestic economic well-being, where there is a perceived or actual clash over the development of other societies. International aid programmes may thus be vulnerable to a communitarian critique. When communitarians turn from condemnation of their less fortunate fellow citizens, they may well turn to condemnation of those abroad who can be identified (rightly or wrongly) as the source of persistent domestic economic ills. The idea of globalization fits well with such dispositions through its embrace of many of the major sources of contemporary economic and industrial changes. The complex and controversial character of globalization is no deterrent to communitarians turned economic nationalists. The complexity of the issues involved in technological change, of foreign direct investment, and of the picture with regard to the scale and impact of competition from low-production-cost economies,[33] is, again, no obstacle to the elevation of the globalization thesis to the status of gospel. Rightly or wrongly, then, the complex of conditions and forces that are summarized by the popular notion of globalization may well induce a critical reaction amongst the communitarian-minded that could fuel challenges to the further advance of the phenomenon.

The weakness of the cosmopolitan impulse in the contemporary world in practice encourages a communitarian challenge that is likely, in turn, to further undermine cosmopolitan dispositions. There is, however, a body of observers who identify signs of an emergent global society that promises to match any growth of economic globalization.

Global society, cosmopolitanism, global governance and the communitarian challenge

The idea of a global society rests upon the observation of a number of recent conditions and issues. Global 'social' relations are believed to have been encouraged by the arrival of modern communications technologies, particularly those supporting the internet, and by the availability of relatively cheap and rapid international transport. Acknowledgement of a range of apparently pressing problems that require worldwide responses has further encouraged the notion that a new sense of global community, and capacity for effective action on a global level, has arisen, or will shortly emerge.[34] Community might thus be developing at a global level, thereby transcending traditional communitarianism and fusing it with cosmopolitanism, to generate a form of universal communitarianism.

The auguries are not encouraging for such a vision of a global society, however. Genuine transnational, or inter-societal, communications are relatively rare and remain largely the province of such unrepresentative individuals and groups as statesmen, financiers, leaders of business and academics. The travel undertaken by the great majority of holiday-makers involves little real contact with the societies nominally visited. The limited extent of a global culture rests upon the mass export of Western cultural products, particularly popular music and the moving image, and, to a lesser extent, modes of dress. The arrival of new consumer goods clearly impacts upon the recipients but does not, in itself, generate cultural homogeneity. Indeed, the experience of such cultural and material imports may merely drive a dynamic reaction, ultimately generating a dialectic of difference rather than convergence.

The acknowledgement of common problems and the need for common responses is also insufficient, on its own, to generate a new global society, with appropriate capacities for collective response and communal governance. Indeed, the functionalist mode of thought upon which such expectations are based has a poor predictive record historically, and may encourage unduly optimistic expectations about the future. Major changes in human affairs in the past have been driven by a far more complex set of factors and forces than can be accommodated by simple functionalist interpretations and, moreover, have often been precipitated by dysfunctional conditions rather than clear-sighted visions of desirable futures.

Patterns of change and development in human affairs are highly constrained by extant conditions. Such a path-dependent view of change suggests that problems of a domestic or an international origin are more likely to prompt a re-emphasis of traditional institutions and behavioural patterns, rather than experiments with novel patterns of affiliation and response.[35] Indeed, the very economic processes and pressures that lie behind many contemporary tendencies towards globalization, and that are at the root of many of the problems being experiences at the level of the local community, will be destructive of dispositions towards the global conviviality, (in Fred Hirsch terms)[36] that may be essential for an effective response at the global level.

A central problem, then, is that economic globalization may conflict with, rather than complement, the emergence of genuine global society and the cosmopolitan sentiments upon which it must rest. Unfortunately, such a situation will, in turn, hinder the emergence of effective global governance and thus leave the established global operators – multinational corporations, international financial agencies, transnational terrorist groups and international criminal syndicates – insufficiently regulated and restrained. However, a communitarian revolt against globalization might offer an alternative path to restored popular governance on a local, 'national', or even regional basis.

Conclusion: globalization versus community; community versus globalization

Considerable controversy and uncertainty persist over the general development of the International Political Economy. There are contrary indications of greater globalization and of increased regionalization. Possibilities exist of a measure of re-'nationalization' of the focus of activity in some areas of economic life. Such complex, and sometimes contrary, tendencies may, indeed, reflect common influences or be causally interrelated.

The contested concept and uncertain reality of contemporary globalization continue to command the most serious, critical examination, given the range and significance of its supposed effects upon the lives and prospects of states and communities. In any investigation of levels of unemployment, and linked conditions of social stability and instability within local communities, the varied influences of global pressures, technological change and local (i.e. state level) policies, have to be carefully and clearly differentiated.

The delicate fusion of lightly regulated market economics with the social provision of services in health, welfare and educational realms, which John Ruggie has dubbed 'embedded liberalism', may be frontally threatened by many of the pressures and problems generated by a globalizing world.[37] Such exogenous constraints may also have an equally serious effect upon the viability of the stakeholding and communitarian projects. Should such exogenous constraints, particularly those emanating from an unsympathetic international economy, prove overwhelming, then stakeholding policies might prove to be vain, or even counterproductive, and the communitarian project may be still-born or distorted.

Persistent communitarianism in a hostile international economic climate may assume little more than a punitive complexion domestically and/or a highly neo-mercantilist face externally. The extent to which the problems addressed by the communitarian project are exogenous to the communities in question, and the degree to which the success of that project requires a sympathetic external environment, remain central questions.

The cosmopolitan and communitarian approaches to international relations provide two diametrically opposed views of how the 'good life' may be pursued and preserved. The cosmopolitan contends that an acceptance of the basic commonality of mankind must provide the central foundation for all the principles governing conduct amongst human beings, whether they are acting as individuals or as collectivities. The communitarian contends that well being and 'good' conduct can only be ensured within, and hence by, well-ordered and cohesive collectivities, of which the modern state is a prominent, if not the prime, example.

The debate between cosmopolitans and communitarians is conventionally the domain of those concerned primarily with the principles and practices of political interaction amongst currently separated peoples. It also bears upon the moral arguments over the international provision of economic and humanitarian aid. The cosmopolitan–communitarian debate has, however, substantial echoes on the ethical wing of the arguments between the proponents of free trade and the advocates of more self-regarding economic policies at the state or community level. Those who would seek protection for their communities from the winds of intensifying international competition are accused by free-traders of damaging the moral right of foreign producers to supply and trade competitive goods and services and hence advance their much desired well-being. Should the progress of globalization entail, or reflect, the intensification of such competitive pressures, then cosmopolitan free-traders would insist that the costs must be accepted by the communities upon whom those pressures fall.

Communitarians, in direct contrast to cosmopolitans, would reject such ethical argument for accepting unconstrained free trade and attendant competition. The acceptance of new or intensified competitive pressures rests upon practical considerations: how far will the community be aided or damaged by such developments and, if damaged, how far will this damage weaken the community's (or state's) capacity to ensure the wider well-being of its members.

The analytical landscape displayed by Chris Brown in his *International Relations Theory: New Normative Approaches*[38] thus extends into the economic domain; into the contemporary concern with globalization; and into the domestic agenda of communitarian theory, with its concern for communal experiences of disruptive pressures and communal capacities to promote and preserve the 'good life'.

The growth of interest in stakeholding ideas and in communitarian theory reflects a growing concern with the contemporary condition, particularly within a number of the more mature industrial societies. Wider involvement in economic and industrial decision-making is central to the response of stakeholding theorists, while greater individual responsibility, and reinvigorated communal action, is a core theme of much communitarian thinking. Both programmes, however, echo a background concern with the threat to the viability of community and communitarian projects posed by globalization.

The salience of globalization to communitarian theory has to be exposed to critical examination. It is important to distinguish, at least analytically, between the exogenous and endogenous problems of economic systems and of communities. Thus attention must be directed to the varied sources of economic performance, to the degree to which evidence of social and family breakdown reflects rapidly changed employment conditions, and the extent to which these changed conditions reflect wider pressures and processes, linked to globalization. These must then be differentiated clearly from endogenous influences in the realms of national policies, local economic practices, popular ethics and cultural values.

In summary, contemporary concerns with globalization engage with a range of conceptual and empirical issues that are central to the general development of the world economic and political system, and its component communities. The concern of international political theorists with the schism between cosmopolitan and communitarian dispositions highlights the division of potential responses, both ethical and practical, to the growth of pressures from the international system. The stakeholder programme and the communitarian social and political project both implicitly embrace the problem of exogenous pressures upon communities, and upon the capacity of local communities and individuals to operate effectively in such a world and to sustain communal values and expectations. Benign and malign views of globalization and its central processes thus contend as analysis confronts the constraints that the international and global context exerts upon the vitality and well-being of communities.

Notes

1　A notable exception being John Gray in 'Hollowing out the Core', *Guardian*, 26 March 1995, p. 26.

2　Peter Mandelson and Roger Liddle, 'Come the Revolution . . .' *Guardian*, 27 March 1996, p. 17.

3　Peter Mandelson and Roger Liddle, *The Blair Revolution – Can New Labour Deliver?* (Faber, 1996).

4　For examples of which see R. J. Barry Jones, *Globalization and Interdependence in the International Political Economy: Rhetoric and Reality*, (Pinter, 1995); Randall Germain (ed.), *Globalization and its Critics* (Macmillan, 1999).

5　Paul Hirst and Grahame Thompson, *Globalization in Question: The International Economy and the Possibilities of Governance* (Polity Press, 1996), p. 1.

6　Malcolm Waters, *Globalization* (Routledge, 1995), p. 3.

7　For a further discussion of these issues see: Barry Jones, *Globalization and Interdependence* (op. cit.), esp. pp. 11–15.

8　For example, Hirst and Thompson, *Globalization in Question*, pp. 34–40; Barry Jones, *Globalization and Interdependence*, pp. 104–9; and Richard O'Brien, *Global Financial Integration: The End of Geography* (Pinter/RIIA, 1992).

9　Barry Jones, *Globalization and Interdependence*, esp. pp. 105–9.

10　Hirst and Thompson, *Globalization in Question*, esp. pp. 33–4.

11　For a succinct, recent survey see: John Zysman, 'The Myth of a "Global" Economy: Enduring National Foundations and Emerging Regional Realities', *New Political Economy*, Vol. 1, No. 2 (1996), pp. 157–84.

12　*Ibid.*, Ch. 4.

13　See, especially, Barry Jones, *Globalization and Interdependence*, pp. 118–63.

14　On which, see R. J. Barry Jones, 'The Globalization Debate in Perspective: Purposes and Practices in a Polymorphous World', in R. Germain (ed.), *Globalization and its Critics* (Macmillan, 1999).

15　See 'Stakeholder Capitalism', *The Economist*, 10 February 1996, pp. 23–5.

16   Paul Ekins, *A New World Order: Grassroots Movements for Global Change* (Routledge, 1992), p. 128.

17   Will Hutton, *The State to Come* (Vintage, 1997), pp. 64–5.

18   *Ibid.*, p. 73.

19   Social theorists like Amitai Etzioni have focused more upon the policy dimensions of a communitarian agenda than have the political theorists of a 'communitarian' persuasion, who have instead concentrated upon the contrast between holistic and atomistic views of human activity, while often retaining broadly 'liberal' policy dispositions. See: Charles Taylor, 'Cross-purposes: the Liberal–Communitarian Debate', in N. L. Rosenblum, *Liberalism and the Moral Life* (Harvard University Press, 1989), pp. 159–82.

20   See, in particular, Susan Strange, *Casino Capitalism* (Basil Blackwell, 1986).

21   For a succinct account of which see: R. J. Barry Jones, *Conflict and Control in the World Economy: Contemporary Economic Realism and Neo-Mercantilism* (Harvester/Wheatsheaf, 1986), pp. 230–51.

22   For a wider discussion see: Will Hutton, *The State We're In* (Jonathan Cape, 1995), esp. Ch. 12.

23   For a critical discussion of which, see: R. J. Barry Jones, *Conflict and Control*, esp. Ch. 2.

24   On the distinction between contemporary liberalism and its earlier forms, in this respect, see: Thomas A. Spragens, Jr, 'Communitarian Liberalism', in Amitai Etzioni (ed.), *New Communitarian Thinking: Persons, Virtues, Institutions, and Communities* (University of Virginia Press, 1995), pp. 37–51.

25   See, in particular, Philip Selznick, 'Personhood and Moral Obligation', in Etzioni, New Communitarian Thinking, pp. 100–125; also Philip Selznick, *The Moral Commonwealth: Social Theory and the Promise of Community* (University of California Press, 1992), esp. Chs 13, 14 and 15.

26   See: Jean Bethke Elshtain, 'The Communitarian Individual', in Etzioni, *New Communitarian Thinking*, pp. 99–109.

27   Amitai Etzioni, *The Spirit of Community: Rights, Responsibilities and the Communitarian Agenda* (Fontana, 1995), Ch. 3.

28   *Ibid.*, Ch. 2.

29   *Ibid.*, Ch. 9; and William M. Sullivan, 'Institutions as the Infrastructure of Democracy', in Etzioni, *New Communitarian Thinking*, pp. 170–80.

30   David Miller, *On Nationality* (Oxford University Press, 1995), esp. pp. 72–9 and 187–9.

31   Danilo Zolo, *Cosmopolis: Prospects for World Government* (Polity Press, 1997).

32   Daniel J. Tichenor, 'Immigration and Political Community in the United States', in Etzioni, *New Communitarian Thinking*, pp. 259–79.

33   On the modest impact of imports from low-labour-cost economies see: 'First among equals', *The Economist*, 15 January 1995, p. 77.

34   For a succinct summary of such views see: Martin Shaw, *Global Society and International Relations: Sociological Concepts and Political Perspectives* (Polity Press, 1994).

35   For a further discussion see: Barry Jones, 'The Globalization Debate in Perspective'.

36 Fred Hirsch, *Social Limits to Growth* (Routledge & Kegan Paul, 1977).
37 See, in particular, John Gerrard Ruggie, 'At Home Abroad, Abroad at Home: International Liberalization and Domestic Stability in the New World Economy', *Millennium*, Vol. 24, No. 3 (Winter, 1995), pp. 507–26.
38 C. J. Brown, *International Relations Theory: New Normative Approaches* (Harvester/Wheatsheaf, 1992).

6
Globalization and the Transformation of Economic Rights

Robert Latham

In one of best of the many recent manifestos on the virtues and opportunities inherent in globalization, Richard O'Brien distinguishes between the terms 'international' ('activities taking place between nations'); 'multinational' ('activities taking place in more than one nation'); and 'global' ('operations within an integrated whole').[1] O'Brien, an employee of American Express Bank and perhaps abstracting from corporate goals and strategy, went on to claim:

> A truly global service knows no internal boundaries, can be offered throughout the globe, and pays scant attention to national aspects. The closer we get to a global, integral whole, the closer we get to the end of geography.

Ultimately, he writes the 'end of geography is all about the reduction of barriers'.[2]

At first sight O'Brien appears to offer a version of the long-standing story – made famous by Marx and Engels – of the emergence of a 'world market'. All things, everywhere, are subject to sale and capitalists are able to purchase, trade, produce, and market in any feasible locale around the world. Over the last decades, so the typical story goes, this market has become increasingly integrated or globalized as flows of capital, goods, information, and identities have smashed old limits and barriers, even in the face of sometimes resurgent protectionism. But O'Brien is different. He argues there is a world full of barriers, despite the potential for some global market integration based on global level regulation and coordination. For him,

Kenichi Ohmae's notion of a 'borderless world' unrealistically assumes that states will 'not interfere' as this world forms.[3] Despite the recent strides of liberalization easing market transactions across boundaries, there remain over 180 separate regulatory regimes (i.e. states). The intricacies of European integration underscore how formidable the construction of anything like a global common market would be. Yet O'Brien speaks the language of the end of geography. How can 'a global, integral whole' form in a world of barriers? O'Brien unwittingly avoids contradicting himself because for him it is not the single world market per se that is forming into 'a global, integral whole'. What he describes is the emergence of separate networks around foreign exchange, securities, debt, investment, and financial services.[4] These networks constitute distinct markets. In O'Brien's own words:

> [W]hat we can observe here is the development of global networks as links between markets [that] develop even where barriers still exist. A global network in effect seeks to offer a global service but does not depend on integration of markets. Advancing technology is offering more ways of developing global networks in addition to the base of a physical presence in each market.[5]

Rather than look to one giant world market space being formed, we are to see multiple networks of enormous proportions forming distinct market spaces, integrating as wholes across the globe. Readers experienced in the Internet will instantly grasp the analogy with the formation of a cyberspace that essentially transcends traditional national communication system barriers. A worldwide integration of global communications and information is not necessary for the continued expansion and consolidation of cyberspace across the globe. The market network for foreign exchange likewise does not depend on the integration of national currency systems.

O'Brien, like many other observers of globalization, adopts the stance that states are the source of current and future barriers. Whereas he sees risks that state intervention might cook the golden goose of emerging global markets, critics of the social costs of globalization – such as unemployment, impoverishment, economic insecurity, or food price shocks – fear that states are unable to shield their citizens from these costs. My sympathy is with the fearful critics. But I want to argue in this Chapter that contending with the social effects of O'Brien's global markets should not rest on the faith that states, if they could, would guard against the forces of globalization in the interest of their citizens. We need to go deeper into the very terms by which material life is organized across the planet. The simple notion that the state should be (re)empowered as a guardian does not get us there. The question is, upon what political and ideological basis would it be (re)empowered? The task is to place the possibilities of state action in a broad normative context that incorporates a diverse range of practices, actors, and strategies on a global rather than a national basis.

Whose state, for what?

Increasingly commentators are looking back to Karl Polanyi's *The Great Transformation* to frame their understanding of how the effects of globalization can be responded to or resisted politically.[6] Polanyi made clear that, in the face of the dislocations and insecurities generated by both global and domestic markets, states, alone or collaboratively, are likely sooner or later to act on behalf of their national societies to counter these effects. Polanyi continues to resonate for critics of unbridled globalization not only because of his analysis of countermeasures on behalf of communities, but also because he sharply denounced the ways that markets took on a self-regulating aura, operating in a fashion that was 'disembedded' from the societies they often ravaged. Disembedded markets make societies conform to the logic of commercialization; embedded markets or economies, in contrast, would conform to the needs of societies. O'Brien's market networks, as integral wholes coming into being, have taken on this self-regulating aura. They increasingly draw capital and resources that once were part of a public sector or national wealth into their nets through extensive trading that has no connection to social needs, or through privatization programs that place infrastructure and enterprises on the world investment market. The construction of new social spaces – markets or otherwise – is never innocent and without powerful implications. They displace, change, challenge, and reconfigure practices, principles, institutions, and resources.

Writing at the end of the Second World War, Polanyi was guardedly optimistic that states, organized as liberal democracies, could discipline national and global economies so that they would meet the needs of individuals in societies to ensure their economic well-being. He thought this was possible because – although markets and market economies were generally taken to be natural to material existence and capable of a kind of spontaneous generation – they depended profoundly for their construction on state action. If markets could be made by states, then they could be, if not unmade, at least contained or redirected to the advancement of social well-being and security by states. Why should states undo their handy-work? Polanyi, of course, had the history of protective measures undertaken throughout the life of capitalism, most recently during the depression years (ending in some very undemocratic regimes). However, protection from market forces is one thing, challenging the basic organization of material life around markets is another. Throughout his book, Polanyi shows how protective measures, rather than undoing market power, have made it even more feasible by softening its ravages and avoiding its total delegitimation among affected populations. Short of socialist revolution, nowhere does Polanyi identify or think through the range of modern state actions necessary to contest the organization of material life around markets, however much he desired them.[7]

Eric Helleiner has recently shown how post-World War II planners were able to fashion a Bretton Woods system that allowed western states to use international markets to advance the well-being of their western societies, yielding the traditional welfare state.[8] Polanyi had hinted at the attraction of this type of reconciliation of society and international market. But as Helleiner continues his argument he demonstrates how the successors to those same planners, in a fit of liberalization, undid the Bretton Woods system, allowing finance and investment to begin to form into the 'floating' market net-works described by O'Brien. The notion that international financial markets should contribute to the protection of most individuals in developed states and societies was all but abandoned a generation later. What survived, however, as legitimate was the operation of global markets.

We should not forget, however, that the Bretton Woods system was hardly experienced by developing states and societies as con-ducive to well-being. The reasons for the contests in the 1960s and '70s between the developed and developing states over unfair terms of trade, burdens of debt, and patterns of investment are for many too quickly forgotten in the current rush to critique a contempor-ary globalization in which the security of westerners is often of primary concern.

The basic lesson for me is that we ought to be suspicious of both the depth and scope of commitment to truly institutionalizing protection by states. After all, Polanyi identified protection as typically taking form as ad hoc or makeshift measures established in response to the better planned formation of markets. Thus, the measures can undone in a similar, ad hoc fashion. Moreover, the international bureaucracies advancing the liberalization of markets and privatization such as the IMF are directed by states, albeit only the powerful Western states, most of all the US.

There are two related reasons for being suspicious of a direct recourse to the state to resist globalization. One, just pointed to, is its profound western bias. The implicit assumption is often that, given the incapacities of non-western states, it will be the great powers that will do the protecting, at least internationally. Yet why should we assume they will look out for the interests of non-western societies? History is no comfort here, since the postwar protection of western welfare states was constructed in part on the backs of those non-western societies.

Second, although critics of the costs of globalization are often astutely observant regarding the dynamics of global market forces, they, in their focus on global phenomena, tend to forget what was taken for granted by the New Left in the 1960s and 1970s. Important segments of state and national elites may not only ideologically assume markets are supreme, they may be unduly influenced by the power and interests of the very corporations that have so much to gain from the operation and development of global market networks.[9] In turn, these forces and the state officials responsive to them can incapacitate the state as a force of protection or countermovement. It is a mistake to assume that a resurrected European welfare state of the sixties can be a spearhead for countermovement. The turn to the right in the 1980s, symbolized by the Thatcher and Reagan revolutions, is sadly only part of a story of change that makes that vision specious.[10]

Unfortunately, one of the paradoxes of globalization is that, on the one hand, the making of market networks rests on constructing relatively barrier-free global spaces within which to operate. On the other hand, that very construction requires that powerful boundaries – ideological or otherwise – be placed around the action and capacities of states to interfere in those spaces. In the developing world, the impact of these new boundaries, imposed most visibly through structural adjustment programmes, is far greater since most states, facing a sometimes hostile international economic environment and rampant internal corruption, have only had historically limited capacities to order the material life of their societies.

Polanyi was writing in the midst of what I have elsewhere called a 'liberal moment'.[11] Self-determination, democratic governance, and individual and group rights became particularly salient as the terror of world war slowly lifted. States were understood to be central to the realization of these liberal principles. Indeed, if not the state then what? When Polanyi looked beyond the state he saw the international market interests that had helped pave the way for two world wars by ignoring the needs of societies for protection. Today, of course, there is a growing faith that grassroots organizations, self-help cooperatives, local enterprises, and new social movements can fill some of the gaps of protection left lying open. But, again, if global market networks are integrating wholes increasingly detached from the needs of communities, then it is difficult to envision how local forces of limited authority could harness them, especially if the most – and many of the less – powerful states are complicit in that detachment.

Democratic provisionism

I believe if we read Polanyi only from the perspective of formal political institutions we are likely to overlook a far more basic approach to the relationship between markets and social life. This alternative has the advantage of directly speaking to the crucial issue of the formation of political will within and across societies not only to contest and resist globalizing forces, but to rethink how we approach the organization of material life on a global basis, through states or other political forms.

To get at this alternative we need to go back to a basic, unifying concern in Polanyi's work that moves beyond the formal understanding of economics associated with the analysis and application of rational distribution systems, scientific laws, and means–ends calculus. Polanyi wanted to reestablish that economics – or economic life more broadly – is about 'man's [sic] dependence for his living upon nature and his fellows . . . [and] refers to the interchange with his natural and social environment, insofar as this results in supplying him with the means of material want-satisfaction.'[12] Without this understanding, the notion that economic practices and institutions should and could be embedded in the needs of society makes little sense. He would have us remember what some might now take as a kind of primeval question: *What are economies for?* Much of *The Great Transformation* is dedicated to showing how, in the organization of material life around market systems, the liberal utopia of a harmonious match of supply and demand across divisions of labour overlooked the possibility that market systems would form their own logic, laws, and interests separate from the rest of society. Thereby, they would become sundered from the more basic social purpose of supplying all of humankind, the impoverished as well as the privileged, 'with the means of material want-satisfaction'.[13]

Polanyi in answering the question 'What are economies for?' wanted to redirect attention to the activity basic to all societies: provision of the means of existence. Looking across history, cultures, and civilizations, he saw that this ubiquitous activity need not be treated as the exclusive purview of the market.[14] But this was exactly what he observed in the middle of the twentieth century. Markets increasingly monopolized provision. Even more, provision came to be seen as a function of the operation of market economies. In other words, provision became one of the benefits of markets (along with profits and freedom), rather than markets being one among a number of mechanisms or logics of provision. Despite the history of alternative modes of provision in the many so-called primitive and archaic societies that Polanyi studied, in his time socialist command economies were taken as the only working alternative.

The post-World War II period opened up the possibility of a less extreme partial alternative, the modern welfare state. It was characterized by varying levels of nationalized industry, workers' rights and security, industrial democracy, and income redistribution. While markets, in practice, are increasingly monopolizing provision, symbolically, the function of provision is strongly associated with the welfare state. This symbolic association allows the attackers of the public provision to displace basic concerns with provision, as applied to both states and markets, with a focus regarding the latter on consumption and the accumulation of wealth. While welfare functions will continue into the future, to the extent that defenders of the welfare state treat it as *the* answer to global forces, they play into a rhetorically deadly game. It is indeed promising that some progressive scholars and activists from the western social democratic tradition have begun to ask questions and formulate political agendas that are global in scope and are cognizant of the limitations of old models.[15]

I believe this questioning needs to join up with, or at least pay special attention to, the efforts to fashion effective mechanisms for provision mentioned above, such as cooperatives that are increasingly a part of life in the developing world. Typically, these are understood as part of 'coping strategies' constructed or employed in the face of adjustment programmes, price shocks, and the erosion of already weak or near nonexistent public sectors. Any progressive westerner who has traveled in places like Latin America or South Asia should be impressed not only with the knowledge of activists, but their strong political commitment to provisionist action. Whether or not this activist strength stems from the lack of public provision in the developing world, western progressives should not derive their notions of what communities or 'civil societies' are capable of based solely on their observations about the west, where apathy if not also clearly nonprogressive ideologies appear prevalent among all classes.

But just as we should be sceptical that developing world alternatives can counter global market forces, we also should not idealize developing world efforts to cope with dislocations as the route to post-market provision, especially since large segments of the most impoverished of the world have not been able to organize as such, sometimes because they are painfully uprooted from their communities and forced to migrate regionally or globally. But rather than be pessimistic, we can come back to Polanyi and read his entire corpus, not just *The Great Transformation*, as suggesting that there is no one strategy, mechanism, or schema like socialism or localism for contending with the social costs of markets. Thus, we need an approach that is self-consciously heterogeneous, but which also takes provision as a central and unifying task. We might call such an approach provisionism or, more specifically and for reasons I will consider shortly, *democratic provisionism*.

Provisionism begins from the basic proposition that the purpose of institutions and activities that shape material life is to provide communities with goods, services, and other values necessary to sustain community or group life, free of deprivation. Any economic institution and activity should benefit directly in goods, services, or other defined values all the communities or groups that are directly affected by it. From one perspective, provisionism can be taken to mean that all communities and their constituents have rights of provision and thereby claims on economic transactions and exchanges that draw from, occur within, or simply impact them. From another, provisionism can mean that a community's own economic systems and institutions should be providing for all.

In addition, I have purposefully included the phrase 'other defined values' to make clear that it is not only goods and services as typically understood that answer the question 'provision of what?' If the sustenance of community or group life is taken seriously, those values might include the viability of what Polanyi called 'habitat', and which today we can translate as meaning the conditions, environmental and infrastructural, that are essential for a healthy existence in a given locale or national space and that have been stressed by greens and those committed to sustainable development.[16] Other values might include social security, human services, and education. Which values are stressed depends on the nature of the society or community in question.

I believe the attempt to reinject social purpose into economic life would directly challenge the kind of developing network market spaces written about by O'Brien and others. Transactions within them approach a kind of abstract profit-taking that has little connection with provision. It is one thing when these transactions involve foreign exchange, damaging enough as it erodes already weakened governments or forces enterprises to throw workers out of work. But it is another thing when whole industries, often times constituting basic infrastructure, become drawn up into global investment networks within which foreign investors or purchasers pay little attention to how these industries became essential to the basic provision of a national or local community.

Polanyi showed how trade became an important dimension of provision for a society. Goods that were not available or too costly to produce in a locale could be traded for with others. At the end of the twentieth century trade continues to be essential to provision. Despite the unfortunate history of unfair trade practices between the developed and developing worlds – where the latter as suppliers of primary goods and now cheap labour could have perhaps done better in terms of provision to their national communities – trade does bring in goods and services to developing societies that otherwise would not be present. However, even trade becomes problematic from the perspective of provisionism to the extent that new networks of intra- and inter-firm trade are developing that not only have no direct provisionary benefit to affected communities, but actually may undermine other benefits. Moreover, trade can become concentrated in luxury items that exclude poorer constituents and help precipitate the trade imbalances that further erode the capacity for national economic provision.

Despite these limitations, the world's economies and economic systems are generally in the business of provision. Provision is taking place everywhere, locally, nationally, regionally, and internationally. And on the whole many people, except the most extremely deprived, are arguably better provided for than in any time in history. The point is rather that millions of people in every region are facing deprivation or increasing social insecurity and there is every reason to believe that, in the face of the global forces described above, things will be getting worse for them and others who will be joining them.

To some, democratic provisionism will sound like a version of green economic philosophy. However, if we take Polanyi's eclectic and broad historical perspective seriously, democratic provisionism can be understood to be quite different. As observers of the greens have made clear, they emphasize local initiatives and distrust 'large-scale institutions'.[17] But not only is small often not powerful as pointed out above, it sometimes is not beautiful. The history of corruption and abuse in local contexts is long and bloody, involving traditional landlords, opportunistic functionaries, or maquiladora enforcers. Democratic provisionism begins from the assumption that large-scale institutions like states, markets, or trade and communications systems can be extremely valuable politically and economically as mechanisms of provision. When it comes to provision we need it all: global, local, state, regional, market, collectivist, industrial, capitalist, socialist, and modes not yet imagined. The point is that populations would need to hold it all accountable to the basic tenets of democratic provisionism. As a result, the old boundaries between public and private provision would be less relevant. Provisionism would provide a normative basis to contest and discipline state policies as well as market outcomes, serving as a sort of common moral denominator across the myriad modes of authority and allocation operating globally. Rather than simply bemoan the exploitation of markets and thereupon call for their abolition or severe containment, democratic provisionists would seek to organize the political capacity to develop strategies for the exploitation of markets for the ends of provision. Such an approach would recognize the proliferation of material goods, capital, and services to which industrialism and market economies have contributed.[18] While the state-led development associated with the NICs of east Asia is likely to stand as an attractive path, these countries developed in very different historical circumstances than are faced today, especially *vis-à-vis* the market networks described above. Market exploitation may rest on far more collaborative projects between societies, from regional Tobin taxes on foreign exchange transactions, to collective renegotiation of terms of resource extraction and export commodity pricing.

The eclectic nature of democratic provisionism rests on the understanding that provision constitutes a distinct dimension of social existence that can take different forms in the different practices and institutions that bear on it, as manifested in various local, national, and regional contexts, from cooperatives in Mexico to development zones in east Asia. When viewed from a global perspective, these specific practices and institutions can show great variation not only across social spaces, but across time as well. One could imagine writing the history of provision as a distinct domain of practices, principles, and institutions. Perhaps Polanyi had something like this in mind when he became engaged in the comparison of ancient, archaic, and modern systems of provision. Among the advantages of viewing provision as a domain is that it underscores that a wide array of actors are involved in provision, from states and corporations, to self-help, grassroots organizations. In addition, it allows for differences in the principles of provision emphasized by communities and societies. Quite different things can be meant by the terms that constitute the basic tenets of provisionism, such as 'benefit', 'values', 'directly affected', and 'sustenance of community life'. Where equality of income might be crucial for one community, it might be less so for another.

Viewing provision as a domain allows for the commitment to provisionism to be global in reach, while at the same time locally specific. As a result, holding global market networks accountable to the principles of provisionism, through perhaps new forms of collaborative regulations between states and societies at the global level, can be connected with provisionist political and ideological projects implemented in local contexts as well. It is exactly this type of linkage that has been critical to the neoliberal project of adjustment and liberalization executed through international organizations such as the World Bank, states, local authorities, and corporations in global, regional, and local contexts.

The politics of provision

Provision is a domain whose universal, global reach rests on a diversity of approaches and principles. Democracy in this context cannot mean, in the face of this diversity, the governing of that domain on a global basis according to classic principles of representation. If democracy means, literally, rule by the people (demos), we need not limit how we might understand what 'to rule' means. Rather than direct, authoritative control over some realm, we can understand rule to mean a prevalence of something that shapes outcomes and relations (as when we say something 'rules supreme'). When this sense of rule is joined with demos in the context of the domain of provision, democracy denotes exactly a diversity of approaches proposed or in practice, that can compete for adherence by groups and communities.[19] Through competing organizations – from political parties to NGOs – individuals and groups could chose alternative approaches to realizing provision. The lack of alternatives – in the face of the growing market monopolization – currently plagues the domain of provision. This outcome surely reflects the uneven power of actors within and across societies. Any proposals to democratize provision would therefore have to account for ways of redressing these imbalances, in the least through the popular mobilization of sometimes desperate populations. In this sense, democratic provisionism is profoundly dependent on the broader processes of political democratization occurring in places such as Indonesia, even as I write. New parties, such as political democracy movements, already have or would need to add an emphasis on alternatives for provision to their political programmes. To avoid replaying the tragic history of third world political movements in the 1960s and '70s that did make provision central to their programmes, parties would need to take the other meaning of provision seriously and treat their proposals as flexible, makeshift (provisional) efforts that are subject to spontaneous revision, most of all from below as conditions change, approaches fail, and better ones emerge.[20] This will hardly lead to harmonious societies and communities since conflict over provisionist approaches as interests is inevitable.

Obviously, the advancement of a democratic provisionism will rest ultimately on the capturing of state power, the one institution that has the kind of political history and authority – however compromised – to advance provisionist measures rapidly. States may be down as forces of provision, but they are hardly out. Notwithstanding western apathy, I believe popular power has never been greater in human history. It would be tragic if that power and provision became trapped only in the narrow models of how to organize liberal democratic regimes. But in looking beyond the state, especially at local alternatives it should be recognized that unless states, rather than just international NGOs, can facilitate those alternatives – in the ways they have historically facilitated the emergence of markets and private corporate power – those alternatives are likely to contribute to change but not in decisive ways.

Also likely to be important is the potential for cooperative efforts between different states and societies, advancing provisionist concerns across different local and regional spaces. The incentive for that cooperation will likely at first be negative: as an effort to thwart globalizing market power. Much thinking about international relations has been geared to showing how cooperation is not possible (even in the old NIEO-world of developing states), except in exceptional circumstances like war or its preparation or around narrow sets of issues that rest on thin agendas and institutions. In looking to reinforce the incentives for cooperation, some might be tempted to treat the threats of market power as analogous to war. Alternatively, it should not be overlooked that provisionist states and societies might not operate with the same logics and incentives as the classic war- and economy-making state, upon which existing models of international cooperation rest. Overcoming the 'cooperation gap' might become in itself central to the strategies of democratic provision.

The greatest gap to be bridged, however, is that between communities in the developed and developing worlds. It is just as difficult as ever to imagine even increasingly insecure western labour forces or those relatively impoverished by western standards as easily identifying with their counterparts in non-western societies. Hopes of finding linkages have occupied twentieth-century progressives for decades and hopeful signs have ebbed and flowed with each new epoch. Perhaps the latest glimmer of hope emerges from the renewed effort of western unions to reach out to labour in the developing world. Far more of this type of exchange is necessary. Democratic provisionism in the least offers the basis for some common language around basic tenets bearing on material life. The alternative is to close ranks in a series of communitarian nightmares, the hints of which were articulated by US presidential candidate Patrick Buchanan.

As this chapter attests, thinking about democratic provisionism is above all an ideological gesture. Its manifestations are everywhere and at the same nowhere. Its putative founder, Karl Polanyi, in his attempt to reground economic life, left us one of the most challenging

intellectual as well as political legacies for attempting to
wards, as he put it, 'freedom in complex societies'. It i.
known fact that the original 1944 edition of *The Great Tra*
tion ended quite pessimistically about the coming post-war period.
He changed that provisional conclusion, making it far more optimistic, and we at the end of the twentieth century need likewise to
change our own.

Notes

1 R. O'Brien, *Global Financial Integration: The End of Geography* (Pinter/ RIAA, 1992), p. 5.
2 *Ibid.*, p. 70.
3 *Ibid.*, p. 100. See K. Ohmae, *The Borderless World: Power and Strategy in the Interlinked Economy* (Harper, 1990).
4 We might also include emerging networks of production – subsuming both intra- and inter-firm trade – where maximum flexibility of location and staffing are central.
5 O'Brien, *Financial Integration*, p. 32.
6 The place they look is K. Polanyi, *The Great Transformation: The Political and Economic Origins of Our Time* (Beacon Press, 1944).
7 He, in his inspiring conclusion, is assuredly aware of their need.
8 E. Helleiner, *States and the Reemergence of Global Finance* (Cornell University Press, 1994).
9 It is important to not treat the west as monolithic. The balance between popular and corporate power ranges across a spectrum.
10 For a sense of the depth of that story of change see R. Wade, 'Japan, the World Bank, and the Art of Paradigm Maintenance: The East Asian Miracle in Political Perspective', *New Left Review*, No. 217 (1996), pp. 5–36.
11 R. Latham, *The Liberal Moment: Modernity, Security, and the Making of Postwar International Order* (Columbia University Press, 1997).
12 K. Polanyi, C. M. Arensberg, and H. W. Pearson (eds), *Trade and Market in the Early Empires* (Free Press, 1957), p. 243.
13 Polanyi's European focus, which made sense before World War II, would likely, if he were to write today, be replaced by a far more global one that accounted for the extreme impoverishment in the developing world.
14 Few read any of Polanyi's work outside of *The Great Transformation*. His corpus was broadly non-western and even more deeply historical than is typically thought. For a good survey of that corpus see his essays in G. Dalton (ed.), *Primitive, Archaic, and Modern Economies* (Beacon Press, 1968).
15 The Greens stand out as an example and are discussed in the context of the western scholarly tradition of international political economy in E. Helleiner, 'International Political Economy and the Greens', *New Political Economy*, Vol. 1 (1996), pp. 59–78.
16 I use the word group in order to insure that those aggregates of indi- viduals who do not necessary qualify as a 'community', because of dislocations are included. I have in mind particularly migrants.

17 Helleiner, 'The Greens', p. 67.
18 The attractiveness of exploiting capitalism was essential to the thinking of Marx. Socialist revolution could only be successful if it was preceded by the full development of bourgeois capitalism.
19 This notion of democracy was forcefully advocated by the American political scientist, E. E. Schattschneider, *The Semi-Sovereign People* (Holt, Rinehart & Winston, 1960), who thought direct and representational democratic models were unrealistic. For him democracy 'is a political system in which the people have a choice among alternatives created by competing political organizations and leaders' (141).
20 This would be consistent with Polanyi's emphasis, *The Great Transformation*, pp. 41, 86, on the 'makeshift' character of counter-movements.

7
Rearticulation of the State in a Globalizing World Economy[1]

Jeffrey A. Hart and Aseem Prakash

Introduction

In this Chapter we discuss the implications of globalization for the post World War II order based on 'embedded liberalism' – the marriage of free trade with domestic demand-side intervention.[2] We suggest that the increasingly oligopolistic nature of world markets, and the scramble among states for attracting and retaining high-technology industries, is creating incentives for state interventions in forms of strategic trade and investment policies (STIPs). STIPs enable countries to develop architectures of supply[3] that are major pull-factors in attracting investment from multinational corporations (MNCs). Thus STIPs are an important element of state strategy to resist the de-nationalizing impact of globalization and to preserve the industrial base of the country.

However, a widespread use of STIPs undermines free trade, and at the domestic level, it refocuses allocations of state resources from demand-side social interventions to supply-side initiatives. For these reasons, STIPs undermine the postwar order based on embedded liberalism. Since the new order offers little except by way of trickle-down prosperity to the losers in globalizing economies, it is resisted by both the political left and the political right.[4] There is a need to reconsider arguments for the whole-scale scrapping of demand-side interventions, hallmarks of the Keynesian welfare state, and to retain mechanisms or create new ones that offer losers from a globalization a stake in the well-being of the system. Such compromises have been a defining feature of modern capitalism.[5]

Globalization: financial integration, MNCs and technologized production

The Great Depression of the 1930s is often viewed as an important contributor to the rise of Fascism and to World War II. The post-war Bretton Woods institutions were created to prevent a repeat of the mistakes that led to the Great Depression. These institutions were predicated upon what Ruggie calls embedded liberalism. Globalization is viewed as undermining embedded liberalism.[6] In this Chapter we focus on economic globalization, paying particular attention to evidence that important economic actors increasingly treat the globe, and not any particular country or region, as the unit of analysis for key economic decisions. We assume that promoters of economic globalization are primarily multinational corporations, although the actions of states to take advantage of or cope with globalization certainly affect the direction and rate of globalization processes.[7] Economic globalization is not making the state irrelevant. Rather, we believe, it is creating conditions for its rearticulation, particularly with respect to influencing market processes. States are not capitulating to de-nationalizing processes of globalization; rather states are employing a variety of strategies to protect their domestic industrial base and national well-being. As Boyer and Drache observe, even though specific Keynesian policies may not be useful in a globalized economy, his larger vision that markets are not self-organizing and state interventions may be necessary to pursue national goals, remains valid.[8]

The three hallmarks of economic globalization are financial integration, an increased importance of MNCs in global economic activity, and the technologization of economic activity, that is, the increasing salience of high technology products in global trade and investment. Let us briefly examine data on these variables. Increasing levels of financial integration are evidenced in the following:[9]

1 The stock of international bank lending (cross-border lending plus domestic lending denominated in foreign currency) has increased from 4 per cent of the combined Gross National Product (GDP) of the OECD countries in 1980 to 44 per cent in 1990.

2 In 1992, the daily turnover of currency markets was around $900 billion.

3 In 1994, the market capitalization of stock markets all over the world totaled about $15 trillion, more than 2.5 times the Gross National Product of the USA, the world's largest national economy.

Indicators on the activity of MNCs are equally dramatic:

1 By 1995, the internationalization of production had reached un-precedented levels with foreign direct investment (FDI) stocks at $2.6 trillion.
2 In 1992, the global sales of foreign affiliates of MNCs stood at $5.2 trillion exceeding arm's length trade of $3 trillion.
3 About one-third of the arm's length trade takes place on an intra-firm basis.[10]

Economic activity has also increasingly become technology-intensive and firms are allocating ever higher sums to research and development. High technology could be embodied in final products, inter-mediate products, or capital goods. Consider the following trends: (1) Between 1975 and 1990, the share of technologically-intensive industries in total FDI devoted to manufacturing increased from 27 per cent to 40 per cent;[11] (2) MNCs have significantly increased their spending on research and development. For example, the research and development expenditures of US-based MNCs (in constant 1987 dollars) grew by 43 per cent during 1982–91.[12]

In this Chapter we focus on implications of technologization of economic activity and the resulting incentives for states to use STIPs to develop domestic architectures of supply in critical technologies. By employing such policies, states attempt to maintain their dom-estic manufacturing base, high labour productivity levels, and the concomitant high standards of living of the domestic workforce. One could therefore interpret STIPs a policy response of states to resist the homogenizing and de-nationalizing pressure of economic globalization.

The performance of political leaders in advanced industrial countries is increasingly judged on the basis of economic indicators such as economic growth, unemployment, inflation rate, etc. To deliver on these indicators, policy-makers need to attract and retain capital investments. To do this successfully, they are required by globalized financial markets to control government expenditures and to reduce budgetary deficits so that public borrowing will not crowd out private investments in the capital market. Consequently, states are adopting two kinds of strategy. First, they are undertaking supply-side initia-tives such as creating physical infrastructure, lowering transaction costs, protecting intellectual and other property rights, investing in human capital, etc.[13] States may also indulge in beggar-thy-neighbour policies ('regulation arbitrage', as Cerny puts it),[14] for example, by competitively lowering economic, social, and environmental regulations.[15] In addition, we suggest that states have incentives to employ STIPs to create and maintain domestic architectures of supply in critical technologies.

Along with undertaking supply-side initiatives, states are downsizing their demand-side interventions. The presumable reason is to rein in the fiscal crisis that has resulted from the expanded scope of welfare policies and the 'agency costs'[16] of administering them.[17] State interventions can be conceptualized as collective goods. Unlike Cerny, we do not consider all outputs of state interventions to be public goods.[18] Public goods are a specific category of collective goods in that they are non-rival and non-excludable. Other collective goods such as common pool-resources and club/toll goods are associated with different category of governance issues.[19] One can classify welfare support to individuals in distress as some sort of common-pool resource which is rival but non-excludable. Such common-pool resources are bound to be 'over-grazed', resulting in the degradation of the resource (fiscal crisis in this context). In contrast, since corporate welfare in the form of direct support for enterprises from the budget is often an excludable club-good or private good, its beneficiaries have incentives to organize themselves and safeguard their privileges. Though globalization is leading to a downsizing of corporate welfare for the state enterprises (as in Europe), there is little clamor for downsizing corporate welfare for private actors. This probably reflects the politics of globalization since its main champions are private corporations.

Globalized financial infrastructure and the increased economic power of the MNCs is perceived to have limited the efficacy of traditional economic interventions. The globalized financial infrastructure is marked by internationally mobile capital, especially short-term capital. International capital mobility makes it more difficult for domestic monetary authorities to control inflation by manipulating the money supply. When credit is tightened in order to stem inflation, foreign capital will flow in to take advantage of higher interest rates. When credit is loosened to promote economic growth and reduce unemployment, foreign capital will flow out. In theory at least, financial globalization takes away two degrees of freedom (the control over money supply and exchange rates) from the menu of policy instruments available to the state. As Tinbergen argued, the number of policy objectives can never exceed the number of policy instruments,[20] the state is presumably forced to shed some policy objectives just to grapple with internationally mobile capital.

We observe simply that it is tempting to deal with this problem by removing social safety nets because the beneficiaries of such programmes are actors who cannot 'vote with their feet'.[21] The expanded cost and scope of supply-side interventions, particularly those justified in terms of theories of strategic trade and investment, crowd out demand-side interventions. In sum, globalization erodes the political support among financially powerful and mobile economic actors for Keynesian demand-side interventions and at the same time as it creates new demands for supply-side spending.

States vary in their willingness and capability to engage in supply-side interventions or to downsize demand-side interventions. Willingness and ability to intervene critically depends on the history of state–society relationships (Waltz's second image) as well as the state's place in the international system (the third image). For example, under the Structural Adjustment Programmes of the International Monetary Fund (IMF) and World Bank requiring domestic deflation, states have mixed success in reducing domestic absorption. Especially in democratic societies, states face considerable domestic opposition to downsizing welfare policies. It is difficult, however, to predict *a priori* which type of state–societal arrangement (corporatist, pluralist, statist, etc.) will best equip a country to cope with globalization. A number of scholars argue that there are different forms of capitalism and that only some forms are consistent with supply-side interventions.[22] For example, the United States has rarely engaged in active supply-side interventions, partly because of the ideational and institutional grip of neo-classical economics, but also because of its key role in setting up the postwar multilateral system (based on Keynesian embedded liberalism). On the other hand, since both neoclassical and Keynesian ideas are less influential in Japan than in the United States, the Japanese government faces less political opposition to its supply-side interventionist role. In this paper we will not be able analyse the various categories of state–society arrangements and their impact on a state's capacity to confront economic globalization. We also will not be able to analyse how a nation's position in the international system may impede or facilitate its willingness or ability to cope with economic globalization. Instead, we will focus on how globalization creates incentives for states to adopt STIPs and how a widespread adoption of STIPs can undermine the political and economic order based on embedded liberalism.

Strategic trade and investment policies

Trade policies are supposed to encourage or inhibit exports and imports. Tariffs and non-tariff barriers (of which they are hundreds of different kinds) are examples of trade policy instruments. Two questions that have been hotly debated since the time of Adam Smith are: should there be a trade policy at all and what kinds of trade policies can benefit a specific country?

Smith made a case for free trade based on absolute advantage. The Ricardian trade theory, also known as the classical trade theory, argued for free trade based on comparative and not absolute advantage.[23] The neoclassical trade theory, pioneered by Eli Hecksher and Bertil Ohlin, also identified comparative advantage as the basis of international trade.[24] The Hecksher–Ohlin (H–O) model assumes declining or constant returns to scale (growth of output can never grow faster than the growth of inputs), perfect competition in product and factor markets (there are many producers and few barriers to entry for new producers), and perfectly mobile technology. Since, in Smithian, Ricardian, and H–O models free trade benefits all the participants, states are advised not to have trade policies but should simply open their economies to free trade.

New Trade Theories or Strategic Trade Theories (STTs) relax the assumptions of the H–O model.[25] STTs assume imperfectly competitive markets and increasing returns to scale. They then deduce that domestic firms can benefit asymmetrically from international trade if the state intervenes on their behalf. By doing so, the state can shift the supernormal profits, and eventually jobs, associated with industries in imperfectly competitive markets from one country to another. Given the importance of economic issues on political agendas, states are tempted to adopt strategic trade policies that STTs suggest will do this.

Industrial policies, state intervention in domestic economy to promote critical industries, also have a long history of intellectual discourse – starting with the earliest defenses of infant-industry policies[26] and including the vigorous defense of import-substitution policies by Latin American economists like Raul Prebisch.[27] Industrial policies differ from macroeconomic policies in that they target only a subset of the economy. Whereas macroeconomic policies (such as tax rates, level of government spending, interest-rate policies, etc.) generally do not discriminate among types of firms or industries, industrial policies (such as R&D subsidies, tax subsidies, preferential loans, preferential credit allocations, etc.) can be granted to some firms or industries and not others.

Industrial policy theories (IPTs) fall in three broad categories: technological trajectory theories,[28] structuralist theories,[29] and institutionalist theories.[30] Though these categories overlap, they provide different rationales for industrial policies.

The technological trajectory theories argue that technological flows across national boundaries are imperfect even when capital is highly mobile. State intervention may be needed to secure 'first-mover advantages'[31] for domestic firms in high-technology industries for which initial investments are large, learning curves are steep, and architectures of supply are difficult to reproduce. In this case, it is extremely risky for firms to make the necessary investments without governmental support of some kind. However, if they fail to do so, the country loses the chance to earn revenues and generate employment in that particular industry for a reasonably long time. Such industries are often designated as 'strategic' for this reason and have a larger claim on governmental resources than other industries. It helps, of course, if they involve technologies which also have military applications. Examples in recent years would include the computer, semiconductor, and aerospace industries.

The structuralists argue that industrial policies are one way that non-hegemonic countries can challenge the power of the hegemon, primarily through free riding on the liberal trade and monetary institutions established by a hegemon by promoting exports of domestically-produced goods and capital to the rest of the world while protecting their domestic economies from international competition in the form of imports and capital inflows.

Institutionalist theorists focus on the historically-rooted differences in state–societal arrangements and their impact on competitiveness of domestic firms. Some institutional configurations systematically create barriers to imports and inward investments and thereby shelter domestic firms from international competition. For example, contrast the relatively open nature of the US system, marked by low government–industry collaboration, with the relatively closed Japanese system marked by significant business–government collaboration. Institutionalists argue that these differences create advantages for Japanese firms to compete in global markets.[32]

In this Chapter, we focus on the technological trajectory version of industrial policy theorizing and link it to theories of strategic trade. As suggested earlier, we identify three distinguishing characteristics of globalization – financial integration, increasing economic clout of MNCs, and the technologization of economic activity. To be globally competitive in high-technology products, firms must have adequate and timely access to related technologies (e.g. for materials, components, and manufacturing equipment). This can only be ensured by a well developed architecture-of-supply in those products and technologies. In high technology industries, it is very important for suppliers to be located near producers because suppliers and producers often must collaborate on designing both products and production processes. Even if the suppliers are not locally owned, they must have a local presence for this sort of collaboration to be practical.[33] According to Borrus and Hart, architectures of supply refers to:

> [T]he structure of markets and of other organized interactions through which component, materials, and equipment technologies reach producers... Technology diffusion, like technology development, is a path-dependent process of learning in which today's ability to exploit technology grows out of yesterday's experience ad practices... The speed and degree to which technical know-how flows across national boundaries thus depends crucially upon the character of local capabilities... In this context, 'effective access' exists when technological capabilities are available in the required amount and quality, in a timely fashion, and at a competitive cost.[34]

A good example of this can be found in the relationship between semiconductor producers and the makers of tools used in semiconductor manufacturing – e.g. photolithography equipment, chemical vapour deposition devices, steppers, etc. It is often difficult for US semiconductor manufacturers to obtain access to state-of-the-art tools from Japanese equipment manufacturers because the main customers of the latter are in Japan and the tool-makers do not have sufficient resources to locate a subsidiary near their potential US customers. A similar problem exists currently for US liquid crystal display (LCD) firms, since most of the suppliers are currently in Japan servicing Japanese customers (even if they are not Japanese firms). The Japanese semiconductor industry faced the same problem when it tried to compete with the US industry in the 1960s and early 1970s. It succeeded only after it received fairly substantial assistance from the Japanese government during the mid and late 1970s to create its own set of suppliers.

This suggests that countries having appropriate architectures of supply will have an easier time than those without them in keeping domestic firms internationally competitive and in attracting inward investments by foreign multinational corporations interested in participating in the global market for a particular high technology product. An example of this would be IBM's decision in 1986 to work with Toshiba in a joint venture in Japan to manufacture active matrix LCDs. Similarly, Hewlett-Packard works with Canon in Japan via its Japanese subsidiary to manufacture engines for its laser printers. The technological trajectory version of industrial policy theorizing, in our view, best frames the challenge globalization poses to embedded liberalism.

Erosion of the distinction between trade and industrial policies

How are industrial policies related to trade policies? Trade and industrial policies overlap if promoting exports or restricting imports affects the international competitiveness of domestic firms. Economic globalization blurs the boundaries between domestic and international markets. Domestic firms can tap international markets either through exports, foreign direct investment,[35] or through international cooperative arrangements with foreign firms.

The essence of industrial policy – as supported by strategic trade and industrial policy theories, is to keep foreign competition at bay for a period of time while government subsidies combined with private sector investments can create an internationally competitive domestic industry and, by implication, a viable local architecture-of-supply. Keeping the foreign competition at bay may require a combination of import restrictions and restrictions on inflows of foreign investment, while at the same time encouraging foreign firms to share needed technologies at the lowest possible price.

So it is clear that at least one key component of industrial policy, especially as it has been practised in Asia, is trade policy in the form of FDI restrictions.[36] What are the implication of restricting inward FDI? First, at a general level, impediments to inward FDI are similar to tariffs in that they reduce the amount of competition that domestic firms face in servicing the domestic market.[37] Unlike tariffs, such impediments do not generate revenues for the state in the form of customs receipts, but like tariffs they generally increase the prices of goods that might have been imported or produced locally by foreign investors in the absence of FDI restrictions.

Second, restrictions on inflows of FDI can be used to bar foreign supplier firms from participating in local architectures of supply. This is what happened, for example, after the Japanese government and semiconductor industry were successful in fostering the growth of a domestic semiconductor tool-making industry. It became much more difficult for US suppliers of lithography equipment, for example, to sell machines to Japanese semiconductor firms. It is important to note that often the technologically-advanced sectors are most vociferous in demanding such kinds of techno-nationalism.

Third, the combination of import and inward investment barriers encourages foreign firms to set up joint ventures or licensing arrangements with domestic firms as a last resort for getting some foothold in the domestic market. This tends to give domestic firms greater bargaining power to obtain access to needed foreign technology without paying exorbitant prices. This only occurs, it should be noted, if the combination of public and private resources actually creates an internationally competitive industry. Otherwise, foreign firms will not be so desperate to get a piece of the market by sharing or licensing technology.

Fourth, MNCs often invest in each other's home markets because they do not want their competitors to have safe-havens.[38] This is to deny competitors the opportunities to earn super-normal profits in their home market and use these profits to subsidize their operations in foreign markets. Japanese firms, in particular, are often accused of employing such dumping strategies. Such tit-for-tat strategies adopted by MNCs get impeded if there are impediments to FDI flows.

STIPs and embedded liberalism

Ruggie's notion of embedded liberalism links the rise of the Keynesian welfare state to an agreement among the major industrialized nations to keep the global trading system as open as possible. Keynesian states frequently employs two categories of demand-side interventions. First, are the social safety-net interventions, such as unemployment benefits, medical benefits, and old age pensions, to compensate the losers from free trade as well to provide for the vulnerable sections of society. Second, are the macroeconomic interventions to stabilize the economy. Of course, social safety nets also stabilize aggregate demand. Similarly, counter-cyclical policies also have a social multiplier in addition to the economic multiplier. The Keynesian state is under attack for undertaking both these categories of interventions.

The logic of embedded liberalism depends on a broad social consensus on the value of preserving free trade. Maintaining this broad consensus on free trade was always somewhat problematic, but since end of the 1970s that task has become substantially more difficult. There are at least three ontological strategies of conceptualizing opposition to free trade. First, the Stolper–Samuelson theorem explains why foreign trade creates asymmetrical benefits across domestic factors of production: greater foreign trade tends to benefit the relatively abundant factor of production disproportionately.[39] Second, the Ricardo–Viner approach uses industries as the unit of analysis. It predicts that free trade will be opposed by import-competing industries.[40] Third, when preferences for free trade are observed at the firm level, it is suggested that domestic firms with substantial exports as well as MNCs having substantial intra-subsidiary trade will favour free trade since any form of protectionism disrupts their established business arrangements.[41]

Free trade increases a country's exports as well as its imports. A country has comparative advantages in products which use its relatively abundant factor intensively. Since the relatively abundant factor is intensively used in exports, free trade increases its earnings. On the other hand, since the relatively scarce factor is intensively used in products which compete with the imports, its earnings fall. Then why should the scarce factor accept free trade? Clearly, some sort of side-payments to the scarce factor are required to make free-trade Hicks–Kaldor superior for all the factors of production.[42] Similarly, sectors and firms hurt by free trade have incentives to oppose it and lobby for protectionism.

Keynesian social interventions therefore can be interpreted as side-payments to domestic actors hurt by the multilateral trade regime established at Bretton Woods. The popular perception is that imports into industrialized countries typically consist of low-technology products produced in low-wage countries which hurt the domestic sunset industries. Some sort of side-payments are therefore made to the constituencies dependent on such industries. Since the fiscal crisis confronting most of the industrialized countries is downsizing such side-payments, actors hurt by free trade are demanding protection from imports. Thus, globalization and free trade is being opposed by organized labour in sunset industries as well as other constituencies which hitherto were beneficiaries of the embedded-liberalism compromise.

Social interventions may also be justified as tools of counter-cyclical demand management. Keynesians view such payments as built-in stabilizers – they reflate the economy during recessions and deflate it during booms. However, such side-payments have exhibited a kind of ratchet effect and have kept on increasing without regard to the willingness of taxpayers to be taxed further. As long as there is some faith in the efficacy of Keynesian demand-management policies to smooth out economic cycles, Keynesian free traders can justify social interventions on purely economic grounds. The assumption is that taxpayers will go along with changes in spending and tax levels that are designed to reduce economic cyclicality. As the Keynesian demand management becomes more difficult because of economic globalization, however, the advocates of counter cyclical macroeconomic and social policies find it more and more difficult to justify them politically.

We have argued that STIPs are attractive to cope with economic globalization, particularly the technologization of traded products. Because access to critical technologies has become one of the primary considerations for locating new investments by multinational corporations (see Porter (1990) and Dunning (1993)), robust architectures of supply are vital to international economic success. Firms with access to such architectures of supply are more likely to be able to develop and commercialize high technology products and to be 'first-movers' in global markets. Since first-movers earn super-normal profits, a substantial portion of which can be transferred to subsequent research and development to preserve first-mover advantages, countries with more such firms will be better able to create jobs and prosperity in the domestic economy. The resemblance with the Schumpeterian idea of monopoly profits financing the 'perennial gales of creative destruction' is not coincidental.[43]

As the technologization of traded products proceeds, market imperfections (particularly the rise of giant firms capable of enjoying a monopoly or quasi-monopoly status) may be accentuated. Since technology development and commercialization is very expensive, markets cannot support a large number of players in high technology sectors. Hence, the technologized global markets will tend to be oligopolistic or monopolistic. The resulting growth in super-normal profits will create further incentives for state interventions leading to a further undermining of the international regimes that were established under 'embedded liberalism'.

We have argued above that a separation of trade and industrial policy in international regimes has become increasingly difficult. The General Agreement on Tariffs and Trade (GATT), with its emphasis on reducing trade barriers, was useful when manufacturing industries dominated world trade. The compartmentalization of trade policy and industrial policies was also legitimate at that time. However, with the rising share of the service industries in world trade, the technologization of trade, and the growing subsidies and restrictions on foreign investment flows in high technology industries, the premises under which the GATT (now the World Trade Organization) operated have changed. The failure of the GATT to address investment issues along with trade issues has become, in the age of strategic trade and industrial policies, a major deficiency. The same can be said for the Bretton Woods regime's failures to adequately address trade in services, intellectual property protection, and R&D subsidies.

In sum, we see STIPs as challenging the order based on embedded liberalism on two grounds. At the domestic level, they crowd out demand-side social interventions. At the international level, STIPs undermine free trade. STIPs are attractive for two reasons. First, they help to create internationally competitive domestic firms with local architectures of supply, a key factor for attracting the investment of MNCs in a globalized world economy. Second, they become a bargaining chip to ensure that domestic firms are not discriminated against in foreign markets, especially in foreign markets where STIPs are already being used to discriminate against foreign firms. In this way, globalization is undermining the multilateralism that was based on the embedded-liberalism compromise by encouraging the wider adoption of STIPs.

Conclusions: coping with globalization; resisting de-nationalizing tendencies

STIPs can be viewed as policy instruments to harmonize national political economy to the demands of the globalized economy; as strategies of states to resist the de-nationalization tendencies of globalization by emphasizing the space coordinates of technology generation and diffusion. Though both STIPs and Keynesian economics recommend state interventions in the economy, they provide different rationales and distinctive visions for them. STIPs are selective supply-side sectoral interventions to enhance the competitiveness of specific domestic industries by facilitating the emergence of local architectures of supply. Keynesian interventions are macroeconomic in focus and operate mainly from the demand side.

Economic globalization is increasingly marked by a high degree of technologization of traded products leading to market imperfections. Market imperfections create a potential for super-normal profits. STIPs are instruments to transfer such super-normal profits from foreign to domestic firms. Thus, it not surprising that in the US, technologically-intensive industries such as semiconductor, telecommunication, and aircraft manufacturing have been in the forefront of demanding some kind of technological policy to better equip them to safeguard their home turf as well as remain competitive in global markets.

In an increasingly globalized economy, there is a significant overlap between trade and industrial policies. Hence any interventions to enhance the competitiveness of domestic firms or to enhance the attraction of one's country for foreign capital can be subsumed under STIPs. To cope with globalization, states adopt supply-side interventions which tend to crowd-out previous demand-side interventions because of budgetary constraints.

However, the free trade and internationalization of production is causing massive domestic dislocation. As a result, a large constituency is emerging that is feeling threatened by the pace and extent of globalization. They link globalization with the shrinking of the welfare state and the various entitlement programmes. This constituency extends well beyond blue-collar labour; it includes important groups such as retirees who are numerically significant in rapidly aging populations across industrialized countries. This opposition creates electoral incentives for politicians to continue with demand-side interventions. Since globalization challenges embedded liberalism, it is also resisted by the constituencies which benefited from the embedded-liberalism compromise.

Further, the use of STIPs to gain national advantage has been criticized (mainly by economists) because of the problems inherent in measuring externalities, differentiating normal from super-normal profits, differentiating domestic from foreign firms in a globalizing world economy, and preventing public officials and/or private interest groups using STIPs for rent seeking. Even though these criticisms are quite reasonable, STIPs remain attractive for governments trying to cope with the increasing technologization of traded products in an increasingly global world economy. The political power of the idea of emulating the success stories of Asia is difficult to resist. It is also clear that a widespread adoption of STIPs may lead to increasing allocative inefficiencies in the world economy, if not massive trade wars, by undermining the multilateral norms of the GATT/WTO and other postwar international economic regimes. Thus, the debate on STIPs provides a powerful stimulus to rethink how the institutions linking states and markets within and across countries may be restructured. Further, they challenge us to work through the implications of economic globalization and state policies to resist certain aspects. Globalization is clearly forcing a reorganization of existing politico-economic arrangements. However, states and societies still retain considerable leeway in resisting the de-nationalizing tendencies of globalization and protecting the domestic technological and industrial base.

Notes

1 This is a revised version of our article: 'The Decline of "Embedded Liberalism" and the Rearticulation of the Keynesian Welfare State', *New Political Economy*, Vol. 2, No. 1 (1997), pp. 65–78. We thank Barry Gills, Brenda Bushouse and Larry Schroeder for their comments.

2 John G. Ruggie, 'International Regimes, Transactions, and Change: Embedded Liberalism in the Postwar Economic Order', *International Organization*, Vol. 36 (1982), pp. 379–415.

3 Michael Borrus and Jeffrey A. Hart, 'Display's the Thing: The Real Stakes in the Conflict over High-Resolution Displays,' *Journal of Policy Analysis and Management*, Vol. 13 (1994), pp. 21–54.

4 Krugman argues that domestic economic problems cannot be attributed to international trade. This is disputed by many on both theoretical and empirical grounds. For a review of this debate, see *Foreign Affairs*, March/April (1994) for Krugman's piece: 'Competitiveness: A Dangerous Obsession,' and *Foreign Affairs*, July/August 1994, for rebuttals to it.

5 Peter J. Katzenstein, *Small States in World Markets* (Cornell University Press, 1985); and Jeffrey A. Hart, *Rival Capitalists* (Cornell University Press, 1992).

6 For a discussion on various notions of globalization and the implications of globalization on governance, see Aseem Prakash and Jeffrey A. Hart, 'Introduction', *Globalization and Governance* (forthcoming).

7 Philip G. Cerny, 'Globalization and the Changing Logic of Collective Action', *International Organization*, Vol. 49, No. 4 (1995), pp. 595–625.

8 Robert Boyer and Daniel Drache, 'Introduction', in Robert Boyer and Daniel Drache, *States Against Markets: The Limits of Globalization* (Routledge, 1996), pp. 1–30.

9 The data are from Robert Wade, 'Globalization and its Limits', in *National*

Diversity and Global Capitalism, ed. Suzanne Berger and Ronald Dore (Cornell University Press, 1996, 60–88); International Finance Corporation, *Emerging Stock Markets Factbook 1995* (International Finance Corporations, 1995); and Livingston Douglas, *The Bond Market* (Probus, 1995).

10 United Nations Conference on Trade and Development, *World Investment Report 1995* (United Nations).

11 Sylvia Ostry and Richard R. Nelson, *Technonationalism and Techno-Globalism: Conflict and Cooperation* (Brookings Institution, 1995).

12 United Nations Conference on Trade and Development, *World Investment Report 1995* (New York: United Nations). This report also notes MNCs account for nearly 75–80 per cent of civilian research and development expenditures.

13 For example, the works of Michael E. Porter, *The Competitive Advantage of Nations* (Free Press, 1990); Robert Reich, *The Works of Nations* (Vintage, 1992); and John H. Dunning, *The Globalization of Business* (Routledge, 1993).

14 *Op. cit.*

15 Herman E. Daly, 'Problems with Free Trade: Neoclassical and Steady State Perspectives', in Durwood Zaekle, Paul Orbuch and Robert F. Housman (eds), *Trade and Environment: Law, Economics, and Public Policy* (Center for Study of International Environmental Law, 1993), pp. 147–57.

16 Charles Wolf, Jr, 'A Theory of Non Market Failures', *Public Interest* (Spring, 1979), pp. 114–133.

17 This is often operationalized as the budget deficit as a proportion of the GDP. For example, one of the eligibility conditions for joining the Euro is that the country's budget deficit must not exceed 3 per cent of its GNP.

18 *Op. cit.*

19 For an extended discussion see, Elinor Ostrom, Roy Gardner and James Walker, *Rules, Games and Common-Pool Resources* (University of Michigan Press, 1994).

20 Jan Tinbergen, *On the Theory of Economic Policy*, 2nd edn (North Holland, 1966 [1952]).

21 Charles M. Tiebout, 'A Pure Theory of Local Expenditures,' *Journal of Political Economy*, Vol. 64 (1956), pp. 416–24.

22 Alexander Gerschenkron, *Economic Backwardness in Historical Perspective* (Harvard University Press, 1962); Stephen D. Krasner, 'US Commercial and Monetary Policy: Unravelling the Paradox of External Strength and Internal Weakness', *International Organization*, Vol. 31 (1978), pp. 635–71; Peter J. Katzenstein, 'Conclusions', in Peter J. Katzenstein (ed.), *Between Power and Plenty* (University of Wisconsin Press, 1978), pp. 295–336; Philippe Schmitter, 'Still a Century of Corporatism', in Philippe Schmitter and Gerhard Lehmbruch (eds) *Trends Towards Corporatist Intermediation* (California: Sage, 1979), pp. 7–52; Chalmers Johnson, *MITI and the Japanese Miracle* (Stanford University Press, 1982); John Zysman, *Government, Markets, and Growth* (Cornell University Press, 1983); Peter A. Hall, *Governing the Economy* (Oxford University Press, 1986); Peter A. Hall, 'Conclusions: The Politics of Keynesian Ideas', in Peter A. Hall (ed.),

The Political Power of Economic Ideas: Keynesianism across Nations (Princeton University Press, 1989); David Vogel, *National Styles of Regulations* (Cornell University Press, 1986); George C. Lodge and Ezra Vogel (eds), *Ideology and National Competitiveness* (Harvard Business School Press, 1987); and Jeffrey A. Hart, *Rival Capitalists* (Cornell University Press, 1992).

23 David Ricardo, *Principles of Political Economy and Taxation* (Dutton, 1973 [1819]).

24 Bertil Ohlin, *Interregional and International Trade* (Harvard University Press, 1993).

25 For examples of this work, see Barbara J. Spencer and James A. Brander, 'International R&D Rivalry and Industrial Strategy,' *Review of Economic Studies*, Vol. 50 (October, 1983), pp. 707–22; James A. Brander and Barbara J. Spencer, 'Export Subsidies and International Market Share Rivalry', *Journal of International Economics* (February, 1985), pp. 85–100; Avinash Dixit, 'International Trade Policy for Oligopolistic Industries,' *Economic Journal*, Vol. 94, Supplement (1983), pp. 1–16; Elhanan Helpman, 'Increasing Returns, Imperfect Markets, and Trade Theory', in *Handbook of International Economics*, edited by Ronald W. Jones, Peter B. Kenen (Amsterdam: North Holland, 1984); Paul R. Krugman, 'Introduction: New Thinking About Trade Policy', in *Strategic Trade Policy and the New International Economics*, edited by Paul R. Krugman (MIT Press, 1986), pp. 1–22; Paul R. Krugman, 'The Myth of Asia's Miracle', *Foreign Affairs*, Vol. 73, No. 6 (1994), pp. 62–78; and Klaus Stegemann, 'Policy Rivalry among Industrial States: What Can We Learn from Models of Strategic Trade Policy?' *International Organization*, Vol. 43, No. 4 (1989), pp. 73–100.

26 Some prominent eighteenth and nineteenth century nationalists such as Hamilton, List, and Schmoller argued for state support and temporary tariff protection for 'infant industries'. See *The Reports of Alexander Hamilton*, edited by Jacob E. Cooke (Harper & Row, 1964 [1791]); Friedreich List, 'Political and Cosmopolitan Economy', reprinted in *The National Systems of Political Economy* (Augustus M. Kelly, 1966 [1885]); and Gustav Schmoller, *The Mercantile System and its Historical Significance* (Peter Smith, 1931 [1895]). In spite of these challenges from the non-British nationalist thinkers, the minimalist view of the state inherent in Smithian economics retained dominance within political economy until the publication of *The General Theory* in 1936. See, John Maynard Keynes, *The General Theory of Employment, Interest, and Money* (Harcourt, Brace & World, 1936).

27 Raul Prebisch, *The Economic Development in Latin America and its Principal Problems* (New York: United Nation Economic Commission for Latin America, 1950); and Raul Prebisch, 'Commercial Policy in the Underdeveloped Countries,' *American Economic Review: Papers and Proceedings* (May, 1959), pp. 251–73. See also Albert O. Hirschman, *National Power and the Structure of Foreign Trade* (California University Press, 1945); Albert O. Hirschman, *A Bias for Hope: Essays in Development and Latin America* (Yale University Press, 1971); H. W. Singer, 'Economic Progress in Underdeveloped Countries', *Social Research*, Vol. 16 (March, 1949), pp. 1–11; and H. W. Singer, 'The Distribution of Gains Between Investing and Borrowing Countries', *American Economic Review: Papers and Proceedings* (May, 1950), pp. 473–85.

28   Michael Borrus, *Competing for Control* (Ballinger, 1988); Laura D'Andrea Tyson, *Who's Bashing Whom? Trade Conflict in High Technology Industries?* (Institute of International Economics, 1992); and Steve Weber and John Zysman, 'The Risk that Mercantilism Will Define the Next Security System', in *The Highest Stakes*, edited by Wayne Sandholtz *et al.* (Oxford University Press, 1992), pp. 167–96.

29   Jean Jacques Servan-Schreiber, *The American Challenge*, transl. by Ronald Steel (Atheneum, 1968); Christian Stoffaes, *Fins des mondes: déclin et renouveau de l'économie* (Odile Jacob, 1987); Robert Gilpin, *The Political Economy of International Relations* (Princeton University Press, 1987); and David A. Lake, *Power, Protection, and Free Trade: International Sources of US Commercial Strategy, 1887–1939* (Cornell University Press, 1988).

30   J. Dennis Encarnation, *Rivals Beyond Trade: America versus Japan in Global Competition* (Cornell University Press, 1992).

31   Oliver E. Williamson, *Market and Hierarchies: Analysis and Antitrust and Implications* (Free Press, 1975), p. 34.

32   For a review of Japan's industrial policies, see Ronald Dore, *Structural Rigidities* (Stanford University Press, 1986); David Friedman, *The Misunderstood Miracle* (Cornell University Press, 1988); Daniel Okimoto, *MITI and the Japanese Miracle* (Stanford University Press, 1989); Chalmers Johnson, Laura D'Andrea Tyson and John Zysman (eds), *Politics and Productivity* (Ballinger, 1989); Ito Takatoshi, *The Japanese Economy* (MIT Press, 1992); Shigeto Tsuru, *Japanese Capitalism* (Cambridge University Press, 1993); and Kent Calder, *Strategic Capitalism* (Princeton University Press, 1993).

33   Boyer and Drache also note that 'The very process of internationalization reveals the persistence of national systems of innovation which are deeply embedded in a web of interrelated political, education and financial institutions which cannot be copied or adapted' (*op. cit.*, p. 14).

34   *Op. cit.*, pp. 22–3.

35   DeAnne Julius, *Global Companies and Public Policy: The Growing Challenge of Foreign Direct Investment* (Council on Foreign Relations Press, 1990); James R. Markusen, 'The Boundaries of Multinational Enterprises and the Theory of International Trade,' *Journal of Economic Perspectives*, Vol. 9 (1995), pp. 169–89.

36   This is not to say that the role of non-governmental arrangements, especially the *Keiretsu* in Japan, was trivial. This is the reason why the Structural Impediment Initiative talks between the US and Japan during 1989–90 focused on institutional obstacles, as opposed to specific government policies, to foreign economic activity in Japan.

37   However, the US government has not made active use of FDI restrictions to shield domestic firms. For a discussion on trade restrictions and their impact on inward FDI flows, see, Dennis J. Encarnation, *op. cit.*; and John B. Goodman, Debra Spar and David B. Yoffie, 'Foreign Direct Investment and the Demand for Protection in the United States,' *International Organization*, 50 (1996), pp. 565–91.

38   David Yoffie, 'Conclusions and Implications', in David Yoffie (ed.) *Beyond Free Trade: Firms, Governments, and Global Competition* (Harvard Business School Press, 1993), pp. 429–50.

39 W. F. Stolper and Paul A. Samuelson, 'Protection and Real Wages', *Review of Economic Studies* (1941); and Ronald Rogowski, *Commerce and Coalitions: How Trade Affects Domestic Political Alignments* (Princeton University Press, 1989).

40 This argument is associated with the works of scholars such as Magee and Frieden. See, Stephen Magee, 'Three Simple Tests of the Stolper-Samuelson Theorem', in Peter Oppenheimer, (ed.), *Issues in International Economics* (London: Oriel Press), pp. 138–53; and Jeffry A. Frieden, 'Invested Interests: The Politics of National Economic Policies in a World of Global Finance', *International Organization*, Vol. 45, No. 4, autumn 1991, pp. 426–51.

41 Gerald K. Helleiner, 1977 'Transnational Enterprises and the New Political Economy of US Trade Policy', *Oxford Economic Papers*, Vol. 29 (1977), pp. 102–16; and Helen V. Milner, *Resisting Protectionism: Global Industries and the Politics of International Trade* (Princeton University Press, 1988).

42 A change is pareto superior if no actor is worse off in the new situation versus the status quo. However, if some actors lose and some others gain, then new situation is pareto non-comparable. If the aggregate gains of the winners exceed the aggregate loses of the losers (the net benefit is positive), then the change is Hicks-Kaldor superior in that the winners can potentially compensate the losers and still be left with a surplus.

43 Joseph A. Schumpeter, *Capitalism, Socialism, and Democracy* (George Allen & Unwin, 1976 [1943]).

8
Globalization and the Retreat of the State[1]

Ian R. Douglas

Throughout the human sciences 'globalization' has become *the* explanatory concept of social change in the 1990s. In the study of political economy a rich combination of interconnected characteristics are conventionally identified as constituents of the larger dynamic: the ascendance of the 'stateless corporation'; the emergence of the trillion dollar '24–hour, integrated global financial market-place'; the sharpening of competition under capital mobility and the 'law of one price'; the proliferation of foreign direct investment; the increase in intercontinental migration; and the emergence of a 'global information society'. Everything from the rise of neoliberal transnational technocracy to crises of governance, ecology and citizenship, from the fragmentation of institutions and institutional boundaries, to decolonization, democratization, pluralism and sub-nationalism, have been explained in relation to the 'globalization process'.

Equally important, though less studied, are the social imperatives established on the back of the rise to hegemony of the concept of globalization. Exposed on all sides, the proto-typical citizen of this *fin de siècle* has to be 'agile', 'rapid', 'mobile' and 'adaptive'; 'inventive', 'competitive', 'self-reliant' and 'self-motivated'; 'self-monitoring', 'self-governing', 'efficient', and 'effective'. Indeed, a whole new lexicon has emerged – an ensemble of icons and slogans which of themselves resemble a new civic and political rationality. While all-too-keen to proclaim the 'logic' and unshakeable corporeality of 'globalization', few commentators have interrogated the politics of its attendant *practices* or attempted a sustained analysis of this discourse itself.

Globalization has been seen to be driven by markets and independent actors, entailing the transcendence of state-authorial structures. So diffused is the phenomena that the notion of there being a location of political intent appears somewhat absurd. This thesis has implications for a 'politics of resistance' to globalization. The critique of globalization as a form of *political ordering* is foreclosed. The hegemony of market, technological, accidental and developmental explanations of its ascendance leave no room for critical reflection.[2] In each, the forces deemed to be constitutive of globalization are seen to have come from the *outside*. Globalization becomes inexorable and inevitable, setting forth both the conditions of its possibility and the telos of its projected future. 'There is no alternative.' Questions of power, politics and accountability are eliminated from the discussion.

In the attempt to open up new spaces for critique, indeed existence, we may usefully begin by questioning this depoliticization. In this Chapter I suggest that many of the most important constituent themes of our contemporary epoch come from *within*, not without, the realm of political in(ter)vention. But we need first to address the thesis that has done most to convince us of the obverse.

The retreat of the state

The most conspicuous proponents of the externality of globalization remain Theodore Levitt, Robert Reich, Kenichi Ohmae, Susan Strange and Phil Cerny. The primary evidence suggested for this is the decline of state authority in general. Strange writes: 'state authority has leaked away, upwards, sideways, and downwards. In some matters, it seems even to have gone nowhere, just evaporated. The realm of anarchy in society and economy has become more extensive as that of all kinds of authority has diminished.' The state – it seems – is increasingly 'hollowing out'; 'accelerating technological change . . . inevitably, relaxes the authority of the state over enterprises based and directed from inside their territorial borders.' 'Authority' we are told 'over society and economy' has become diffused in a neomedieval fashion, and that some necessary authority once exercised by states is now exercised by no one.' Governments are the 'victims' of accelerating technological change, and the integration of all parts of the globe into a single market economy.[3] Technology, for Strange, is the great 'neglected factor', and 'prime cause', of the shift in the 'state–market balance of power'.

This externality of technology is the ghost in the machine of many a contemporary analysis of globalization. In the writings of Cerny, the theme of exterior technological advance is never far from view in his account of the changing nature of the state and states-system. 'The essence of the state – and the main practical condition for its viability' Cerny writes:

> lies in the fact that sovereign and autonomous political institutions are capable of deriving legitimacy from a distinct citizenry located in a defined territory. The international system did not present a fundamental challenge ... [indeed it] constituted a bulwark of the state and the ultimate proof of its sovereignty and autonomy. However, increasing transnational interpenetration has the potential to transform the international system from a true states system into one in which this external bulwark is eroded and eventually undermined.[4]

This 'process', though not 'homogenous', is 'at the heart of globalization'. This one-step removal allows Cerny to refer almost uniformly to globalization as an external force to which states have to react. Having challenged the integrity of the international system, globalization – it seems – constitutes a challenge to the state itself.

Via his notion of 'autonomous structural dynamic', and its effect on traditional governmental authority, Cerny traces the emergence of the 'competition state' to the effects of a series of external events: the collapse of the Bretton Woods agreement; the subsequent explosion of transnational financial flows; the decompartmentalization of financial services; the deregulation of markets; and the proliferation of forms of disintermediation. While the exact balance between 'reactiveness' and 'proactiveness' on the part of the state remains unclear, Cerny holds that states found their capacity to make policy increasingly constrained, and their actions challenged. 'Deregulation' writes Cerny, 'was the reaction of the American state to the problems it was experiencing in maintaining its financial – and therefore its political – hegemony, but deregulation, by its very nature, entailed the next turn of the screw.'[5] An 'autonomous dynamic' emerged, limiting further the parameters of governmental decision-making. A growth in financial innovation and 'arbitrage' enabled the transnational financial structure to act largely independently of the regulatory constraints of the states system. For Cerny, an 'embedded financial orthodoxy' has emerged via which the state is rationalized and subordinated. Though the state still has a role (it is the 'agent of its own transformation'), it clearly follows rather than leads the market. Similar themes are developed by Levitt. 'Cosmopolitanism' he writes:

is no longer the monopoly of the intellectual and leisure classes; it is becoming the established property and defining characteristic of all sectors everywhere in the world. Gradually and irresistibly it breaks down the walls of economic insularity, nationalism, and chauvinism. What we see today as escalating commercial nationalism is simply the last violent death rattle of an obsolete institution.[6]

Again, the metaphor is one of penetration from outside. The hold of the ship of state (its homology) has been fractured. Lest they sink, governments are fast in retreat.

However (in)accurate an assessment of reality these statements may be, they have been backed up by a whole wave of commentators and pundits who for innumerable reasons have sought to foretell the decline of the state and traditional authority. A number of subthemes have emerged. First, free and unregulated global finance has outrun the ability of economists and ministers alike to keep up. 'It is virtually impossible' writes Vincent Cable, 'to go back to exchange controls as an economic regulator.'[7] *Inevitability is established.* Second, the hypermobility of the 'stateless corporation' is deemed to challenge the legislative and taxing capacities of governmental institutions.[8] 'Governments are forced back onto indirect taxes.'[9] *Further privatization and marketization is validated.* Third, the rise of new market actors have rendered 'national' projects inept. 'The Nation State' writes Ohmae, 'has become an unnatural, even dysfunctional unit for organizing human activity and managing economic endeavour in a borderless world.'[10] *Globalism is naturalized within the popular unconscious.* Fourth, in creating a 'global society' globalization has fragmented centralized authority.[11] In the words of Mathew Horsman and Andrew Marshall:

Effortless communications across boundaries undermine the nation-state's control; increased mobility, and the increased willingness of people to migrate, undermine its cohesiveness. Business abhors borders, and seeks to circumvent them. Information travels across borders and nation-states are hard pressed to control the flow . . . The nation-state . . . is increasingly powerless to withstand these pressures.[12]

Political agency is de-centered. As Peter Riddell has argued: 'politics has entered an age of increasing limits'.[13]

Some scholars have already questioned the globalization thesis on its own terms, for example Eric Helleiner on the historical reversal of the Bretton Woods agreement, and the ways in which this was mediated and initiated by governments;[14] Bob Jessop on the transition to post-Fordism, and how the 'Schumpeterian Workfare State' entails not an outright rejection but the reformulation of the principles of the Keynesian Welfare State;[15] and the conceptual and empirical work of R. J. Barry Jones, Paul Hirst and Grahame Thompson on internationalization, transnationalization, interdependence and globalization, and the distinctions between them.[16] This work allows us to re-think the concept of globalization and the place of governments in its processes. However, it needs to be supplemented. A deeper historical reading is necessary in support of the more overtly political readings of Stephen Gill, Michael McKinley and Michael Shapiro.[17]

Analysis of the historical development of modern political order raises important questions as to the validity of the popular correspondence between globalization and the retreat of the state. In my view, we are not witnessing an 'evaporation of authority' but its reverse: the deeper embedding of a particular *modality of government* through acceleration, the rise of neoliberal orthodoxy, and the imminent collapse of 'expanse' in a world increasingly regarded as a 'single place'. Globalization (shorthand for each of these) must be questioned as a 'rationality of government', as a *method* of conducting, organizing, and regularizing politics.

However, we should be aware of the political consequences of reification – of locating this 'rationality' in history. The aim is not to evoke attitudes of fatalism, quietism and paralysis in the face of a falsely projected transhistorical law. To do so would merely mirror the discourse I aim to disempower. On the contrary, though I argue that globalization has a deep history, beyond perhaps even the birth of modernity, its preconditions are *politically* specific, its *genealogy* open, yet traceable. In highlighting the parameters of a new critical approach, the aim is to begin the task – which is simultaneously the first responsibility of a 'politics of resistance' – of knowing not only the *terrain* within which we are situated, but also how we got here.[18] In the words of Lewis Mumford: 'Without a long running start in history, we shall not have the momentum needed, in our consciousness, to take a sufficiently bold leap into the future.'[19]

Globalization and the development of modern political order

Diverse though they are, the broad ensemble of discourses and practices that pundits refer to as 'globalization' share at least one common theme: the displacement of *space* through the command of *time*. It is this theme, above all others, that underpins the discourse of the 'stateless corporation', the 'global migrant', the birth of an 'informational society' and the linking of all parts of the globe to virtual markets. It also acts to support the thesis of the externality of globalization to politics, and the challenge of all of the above to traditional authority.

Yet contrary to popular belief, this theme (or constitutive principle) is hardly new. Viewed in this way – the displacement of space through the command of time – the genealogy of globalism and globalization can be seen as essentially the history of man's technical *movement*, reaching its zenith with the collapse of all boundaries. And in that genealogy of *transit*, as described by Mumford it is the sixteenth century which marks the emergence of a new era of generalized mobility. The 'new spirit of society', he argues: 'was on the side of rapid transportation. The hastening of movement and the conquest of space, the feverish desire to 'get somewhere' ... Mass, velocity, and time were categories of social effort before Newton's law was formulated.'[20] For Mumford – unlike our contemporary gurus of globalization – this 'new spirit' could not be explained only in terms of technology or accident, but had to be seen within the context of 'biotechnics': the ways in which man consciously establishes mastery over the realm of 'men and things'. The genealogy of motion, or *man-in-movement*, was for Mumford, a *political* history that finds a particular hold in that epoch in which modern man was formed.

Michel Foucault also identified the 'problem of movement' as one defining the 'political imagination' of the early-modern epoch.[21] Like Mumford, Foucault sought to explain this problem in relation to the development of certain forms of political order (the social structures through which populations have been organized and combined, multiplied, made knowable and effective). Analysing the birth of the modern 'citizenry' as the precondition to the birth of capitalist modernity as a whole, Foucault's 'genealogies' are an essential contribution to the history of modern political order and, I would argue, to globalization.

What Foucault sought to explain was what he saw as the central dilemma of modern political rationality: how to mobilize society, making each citizen an essential cog in the general machine, without making each and all more difficult to govern. The way in which he did this was to trace the coming together of a certain mentality of government (or 'governmentality'), which precisely aimed to make movements regular, though seemingly unrestricted by the intervention of power. For Foucault, this positive moulding marked the advent of 'an age of biopower': an investment in bodies, in populations, in rhythms; in constituting the parameters within which 'life' would become regular. It is this 'mentality' that I take to be the unspoken rationality of neoliberal globalization. Indeed, globalization is the final stage in the 'governmentalization of the state' that Foucault suggested was perhaps the most 'fundamental phenomenon in Western history'.[22]

This 'governmentalization' was, for Foucault:

1 The ensemble formed by institutions, procedures, analyses and reflections, the calculations and tactics that allow the exercise of this very specific albeit complex form of power, which has as its target population, as its principal form of knowledge political economy, and its essential technical means apparatuses of security.

2 The tendency which, over a long period and throughout the West, has steadily led towards the pre-eminence over all other forms (sovereignty, discipline, etc.) of this type of power which may be termed government, resulting, on the one hand in the formation of a whole series of specific governmental apparatuses, and, on the other, in the development of a whole complex of *savoirs*.

3 The process, or rather the result of the process, through which the state of justice of the Middle Ages, transformed into the administrative state during the fifteenth and sixteenth century, gradually becomes 'governmentalized'.[23]

This history – the history of the regularization of bodies – begins, for Foucault, in the classical period with the emergence of a new form of political knowledge referred to as the 'theory of police'.

Epitomized in the 'cameralist' writings of Seckendorff, Dithmar and Darjes, among others, the aim of this new political knowledge – *polizeiwissenschaft*, or 'police science' – was to make individuals 'useful for the world', while preventing – as far as was possible – the new powers afforded to bodies becoming in any way a 'problem' for the state.[24] Power, therefore, had to reach into the very grain of individuals: their tastes, perceptions and desires, but also their *movements*. The central themes of ordering and securitization ran parallel to the mastery of the 'rhythmics' of the populace. In the words of cameralist von Justi: 'The domestic security of a state consists in such a well-ordered constitution of the same that all parts of the civic body are held in their appropriate correlation, and in the consequent repose . . .'

For cameralist (and later also, physiocratic) thinkers the objective of the art of government was: 'to develop those elements constitutive of individuals' lives in such a way that their development also fosters the strength of the state'.[25] This 'strength' of the state was conceived in two ways: as the harnessing of civil kinetics in the making of a productive economy, which in and of itself – augments the overall stability and sedateness of the populace as a collective whole. In the words of von Rohr, 'The best means of enriching a land is to take care that many people are drawn into the land, and also that all the subjects through diligent labour may have their support and means of gain.'[26] Enrichment meant not only material welfare, but the welfare of the state as defined by its tranquillity (social order) and security (strength). Productivity, diligence and 'happiness' emerged as the objectives of the cameralist mode of government, simultaneously individualized and totalized. As described by Foucault, the three co-ordinates of 'freedom', 'inner strength' and 'security' increasingly came to dominate the positive constitution of civic order, conditioning the historical development of 'politi1cal government' from the eighteenth century onward.

Does globalization and the 'retreat of the state' have a place within this history? How – if at all – is globalization conditioned by this development of political order, or what Foucault would call 'Western governmentality'? Obviously much has changed since 'police science' was practised in continental Europe. In revisiting this history *vis-à-vis* the question of globalization my aim is not to suggest a perfect match, or unbroken thread. Cameralism remained collectivist, globalization is clearly individualist. One might argue – as many have – that the concern for 'popular security' and 'happiness' (police theory's justification for intervention) reached its zenith, and died, with the welfare state. Our age of neoliberalism is the less one of 'tranquillity' and 'appropriate correlation', than 'insecurity', 'paranoia' and 'disorganization'. Yet a number of cameralist themes remain at the heart of contemporary 'governmentality'. Moreover, globalization is making these themes more visible, less escapable.

Keeping ahead

Foremost is the dual aim of *mobilizing* and *ordering* described by Foucault as the basic aim of modern political rationality. In the remarkable words of von Justi: 'A properly constituted state must be exactly analogous to a machine, in which all the wheels and gears are precisely adjusted to one another; and the ruler must be the foreman, and the mainspring, or the soul . . . which sets every-thing in motion.'[27] It is this form of political channelling that I argue has survived, becoming more visible the more we look at the hidden practices of globalization: a *political technology* that at once reaches into the very grain of the individual and touches society as a whole, making each and both useful and docile, productive yet predictable, mobile yet regular. In its contemporary manifestation this technology of power can be seen best in the discourse of globalism.

Two principles dominate this discourse: spatial annihilation and what we may call the *obligation-to-mobility*. The former can be regarded as the 'modality of becoming' of globalism. The latter corresponds to the channelling of energies, the passing of life into history, both individualized and collective.[28] An example of the former: 'We believe', runs a promotion for Kawasaki, 'that to fulfil our potential as a global corporation, we have to continually push back frontiers of space'.[29] Fast becoming a *fatal necessity*: 'For US Corporations, the Modern-Day Byword Is "Globalize or Die".'[30] To conquer the world one first has to obliterate it! Here globalism not only consumes distance, but will bring everything to hand that *is* distant. 'You wanted to travel?', asks BSkyB. 'No need to bother.' The dream of the 'terminal-citizen' – equivalent to the 'virtual corporation' – is achieved when arrival occurs without ever having to *leave*.[31]

Parallel to globalism emerges the principle of 'immediacy' as the technical achievement making the destruction of distance possible. Ironically, given its principle effect (immobilism), it is this immediacy that creates and drives a new kind of *hyper-motion*, emerging not so much from *history* as from an endless and inescapable *present*. In 1989 Jack Welch, chairman and CEO of General Electric talks of the 'global moment', of 'lightening speed', 'fast action', and 'act-ing with speed': 'The world moves much faster today.'[32] In 1991, in an interview on the 'logic of global business', President and CEO of Asea Brown Boveri, asked: 'Why emphasize speed over precision? Because the costs of delay exceed the costs of mistakes.'[33] In 1994, Vice President Al Gore talks of a 'planetary information network that transmits messages and images at the speed of light', allowing 'families and friends' to 'transcend the barriers of time and distance'.[34] In 1995 a special issue of *Time* on technology and the 'global agenda' begins the cover story article with one word, followed by a full stop. The word is 'acceleration'.

Here immediacy (globalism) not so much consumes distance, as the *necessities of immediacy* create the imperative of consuming distance. Yet this 'endless and inescapable present' *in itself* emerges from history. From Mumford's desire to 'get somewhere' to cameralism's investment in motion, it is the sixteenth century that lies behind the new vernacular of global-neoliberal capitalism! This longer genealogy is reflected nowhere better than in the astounding words that accompanied one of the first advertisements to use a picture of the globe as seen from 'deep space':

> Who can fail to be moved by the photographs of our earth – this great globe upon whose surface we dwell – taken from outer space? We gaze downward through the lens and from the vehicles of technology, seeing our planet from the perspectives provided by science. Uncounted centuries of thought and work preceded this moment; the contributions of generations went into its preparation.[35]

Note the equally astonishing words of an advertisement for Daimler Benz published widely during 1995. Under a double-page spread of the 'NASA earthrise', the dialogue ran as follows:

> Making dreams come true is both a poetic and an accurate definition of progress. Consider man's ancient dream of 'automotion', fulfilled at last by the automobile a century ago. But mankind's dreams have always refused to remain earthbound. They have enabled him to soar like a bird, to explore distant planets . . .[36]

The automobile is linked to progress, progress to poetics, automotion to the dreams of the ancients, and each and all to our own endless (kinetic) possibilities. There is a significance in the selection of the image of the globe. The very fact that the earth can be seen from a planetary vantage is testament both to the ability of man to reach beyond the threshold of escape velocity (28,000 kilometres per hour, orbital speed, the 'speed of liberation'), and obliterate the 239,000 miles that separates the earth from the moon in a single snapshot.[37] The effects of acceleration are in the aesthetic as the eye captures in a moment the expanse and the smallness of the world, and reduces to zero the distance necessary to gain that very perspective.

Above all, in that single image, we witness the collision from which globalism and motion would become synonymous (orbital speed that obliterates distance, entirely remaking our relation to the world). It is this collision, this threshold which also establishes an *obligation-to-mobility*. In terms of the implications of the discourse, aesthetics and practices of globalism for the art of government, foremost has been the historical reversal of 'motivational crises'.[38] This has been achieved through an intensification of anxiety allied perfectly with the discourse of the retreat of the state: the spectre of 'global competition', the rise of the 'risk society', 'new smartness' ('Work smarter, not just harder'),[39] outsourcing and 'just-in-time'. 'You have no choice': there is, in the words of Walter Wriston, 'no place to hide'.[40] As Norman Ornstein of the American Enterprise Institute has argued, in the face of global competition: 'people are going round with guillotines over their heads.'[41] 'Companies that do not adapt to the new global realities', writes Theodore Levitt, 'will become *victims* of those that do.'[42] 'Create a sense of urgency', 'involve everyone in everything', 'Man is', write Peters and Waterman, 'waiting for motivation'.[43] As the 'promotion' confirms: who can fail to be *moved* by the photographs of our earth? Is it any surprise to find out that Martin Heidegger – perhaps our century's greatest philosopher of technology – feared the image of the earth as seen from space more than he did the atomic bomb? The 'uprooting of man', he wrote,[6] 'has already taken place'.[44]

How can we fail to see that these transformations point the way to a new form of governance: one based on a radical displacement of people and space – a radical uprooting that at one and the same time keeps people where they are in that *everything arrives*? The discourse itself seems often to be so innocent. No one seems to question the violence of the speeding up of the world, or the immobilizing effect of the collapse of all barriers. For example, take the words of Jack Welch: '[I]f you're not flexible enough to handle rapid change and make quick decisions, you won't win.'[45] Such a simple formula confirming something quite incredible: the omnipotence and omnivoyance of acceleration. In every word spoken, in every word written, can we not hear the distant echo of those political commanders, those specific technicians of government, who so dominated the horizon of the early-modern period, constituting the parameters within which bodies would assemble, become regular, productive and secure? Their first concern was spatial (the hospital, the workhouse, the prison, the city), but increasingly this has given way to a form of regulation based upon *duration* and *sequence* (chronopolitics). It is in mistaking this shift that so many have rallied to the discourse of the 'retreat of the state'. They have mistaken the crisis of geography for a crisis of the state itself.

Revisiting 'the retreat of the state'

It is not the retreat of a state whose authority and power rests in the homology of *space*, but the further embedding of an art of 'political anatomy' that takes as its point of intervention *time* itself. The power of command over bodies *is itself displaced* as these bodies are multiplied and put into motion, so that increasingly power is concerned not only to command the *environments* that bodies will transform (in production, consumption, reproduction), but the very *processes* of bodies themselves in such a way that: 'they may operate as one wishes, with the techniques, the speed and the efficiency that one determines.'[46] We move from the constitution of spaces to 'the regulation of time [as] the primary attribute of all government.'[47] With globalism – wherein beyond all else it is *time* which is the key factor of winning and losing – we find the realization of the strategic dream of the founders of the early modern police state: a civilian population at once occupied yet attentive, self-regulated yet disciplined, under pressure yet unquestioning. All through the governing of its rhythms, the moulding of its habits, the channelling of its energies and consciousness. What does this say about the authority of the state?

'Time and Space', wrote Marinetti, 'died yesterday. We already live in the absolute, because we have created eternal, omnipresent speed . . .'[48] The usual response is that such contemporary transformations are indicative of (and follow from) a generalized shift in the locus of command from the state to the market. Understood as such it would be quite wrong to view the consequences of such changes as anything other than the accidental outcome of technological

and market forces (as Al Gore was keen to point out: 'Governments
didn't do this. People did.'),[49] or as the logic of these forces played
out over the *longue durée*. In both approaches there is no consideration of the ways in which *political security* has been upheld, indeed deepened, by the social imperatives of the global age. One
clear reason why such an explanation has been shy in coming forward is the residual insistence to view state and market (politics
and economics) as separate entities with differing, if not contradictory, interests. Such a view cannot survive even a cursory reading
of the genealogy of modern political order. The state can not, nor
ever could, be defined *merely* as the institutions of government.
Nor can it – nor could it ever – be regarded in isolation from the
market. The Western liberal tradition of 'political economy' insisted
on this isolation for political and moral reasons (it was never a
'natural' division, but it was a convenient one). Once normalized
within the liberal imagination it clearly worked to shield the political interventions necessary to establish and uphold the 'social
market-economy'.[50]

In the light of this, the question of 'authority' has not only to
be viewed in its broader setting (of the state–society matrix), but
must also be placed in its historical setting (and its developmental
transformations). As this historical setting quickly highlights, 'society'
itself – in Polanyi's terms – was 'discovered'. Therefore the issue of
'authority' has to be supplemented by the issue of *political tech-
nique*: of how populations are ordered, regularized and governed.
That genealogy (beginning, for the modern era, in the classical age)
reveals that for 300 years at least the implicit objective of political
reason has been to pass the responsibilities of government on to
the shoulders of individuals. Formulated best in the words of von
Justi, modern political reason was to be: 'concerned chiefly with
the conduct and sustenance of the subjects, and its great purpose
is to put both in such equilibrium and correlation that the subjects
of the republic will be useful, and in a position easily to support
themselves.'[51] The contemporary dissolution of the face of government (institutional fragmentation, dispersion of state authority,
diminishing policy autonomy, and so on), says nothing of this longer
history of diffusion that lies at the heart of the modern rational
order called forth by the founders of the modern state.

What Justi was describing 250 years ago was the desire of the
state to decentralize its functions and pass them on to the populace as a whole. The aim was to create individuals in the mould of

the state itself (the citizen-soldier).[52] Cumulatively, as he himself imagined, over the long-term, 'government' would give way to *governance*. This was not in any way in contradiction with the principles of the state. If anything, this paring down was simply the logic of the pursuit of 'efficiency'. As this efficiency is reached, the state reaches it's 'ideal form'. As Paul Virilio has described, in Occidental history this ideal form corresponds with the move from the age of visibility (institutions, governments) to the age of disappearance (endocolonization, the obligation-to-mobility).[53] When all of this was imagined 300 years ago why do so many express such a sense of surprise that the state is eclipsing its own image?

To return to the terminal state thesis, ironically, we can agree with the assessment of Susan Strange: the state *is* increasingly hollow! The differences between the assessment I suggest and that of Strange (among others) is that on the one hand, I dispute that our contemporary epoch is a 'return to medievalism'. There are indeed remarkable continuities in the principle of 'diffusion' running through the modern period as a whole. However, this hollowing out is actually the *extension* rather than the fragmentation of state-ordered power. Since the transformation of Machiavellianism and the ascendance of 'reason of state', the rise of social contractarianism and the birth of market society, state authority has followed its own path to diffusion, finding ever new means by which to become its own 'ghost in the machine'. This form of 'government' cannot be reduced instrumentally to the actions of institutions. As Colin Gordon suggests, 'the state has no essence'.[54] 'Authority', then – at least over the modern period – has also to be defined *beyond the state*, into what Foucault termed the 'positive unconscious': 'The fundamental codes of a culture – those governing its language, its schemas of perception, its exchanges, its techniques, its values, the hierarchy of its practices ... the *space* of knowledge.'[55] 'The question of power', he writes:

> is greatly impoverished if posed solely in terms of legislation, or the constitution, or the state, the state apparatus. Power is much more complicated, much more dense and diffuse than a set of laws or a state apparatus. One cannot understand the development of the productive forces of capitalism, nor even conceive of their technological development, if the apparatuses of power are not taken into consideration.[56]

In setting up a simple distinction between diffusion (anarchy) and centralization (authority), Strange, Cerny, Ohmae, Reich and others simply misread the history of the modern state, and the genealogy of modern power. Because of this they cannot fail to misread the significance and nature of globalism and globalization. Cerny, for example, is quite wrong in his suggestion that: 'Until the last few years, the long-term development of the "modern" world order has been characterized by a process of *centralization* and *hierachization* of power.'[57] The reverse is the case. The contemporary acceleration of our social lives under the necessities of global competitiveness actually produces the polar opposite! The modern world order which has been characterized over the long term by a political project of *decentralization* and *equalization* has only recently given way to *hierachization* based upon *individualization* (the passing – in the words of Ulrich Beck – of each person's biography into his or her own hands[58]), and *centralization* based upon *homogenization* (the ascendance of a new global vernacular, the moulding of societies *en masse* under the 'universal dromos' of the logic of speed).

If Cerny misreads the genealogy, he is not wrong, however, about the result: the stabilization of a whole world order by the 'immanent differentiation' of power. As Cerny has described, there is a dimension to social reality that he terms 'functional conflict', operating to make the contemporary era *dynamically and structurally stable*.[59] '[A]n international plurilateral system', he writes, 'being a "complex" structure, characterized by cross-cutting division of labour, and bonded through "organic solidarity" – can be stabilized through the very cross-cutting nature of conflict within it. It, in effect, may become a self-regulatory system.'[60] What Cerny fails to see is that plurilaterialism when extended over the world becomes a hollow kind of difference. If everyone holds a torch there is so much light in the world that no one has a shadow. Individuality is 'whitewashed', and otherness dissolves into 'the same'. What in effect he describes is a kind of 'order out of chaos', or 'anarchical society', which, of course, is anything but differential.

In addition to the failure to fully consider the historical development of the state, this confusion lies also in the inconsistency with which the term 'the state' is employed and defined. Strange, for example, in *The Retreat of the State*, qualified her use of the concept of 'state authority' to refer to the 'state as a public good'.[61] This qualification is crucial, changing the whole impact and meaning of her argument. From the 'end of the state' we now have 'news' (belatedly one has to add) of the end of a particular *form* of state. What Strange ends up saying is that we have witnessed a progressive rolling back of the *functions* of the (welfare) state. In other terms, though certain *functions* may have been discarded, power itself may not have diminished, nor be 'defective'.

Yet all of this (despite the qualification) is not the picture that one finds in the *nuance* of *The Retreat of the State*. Strange – for the most part – is consistent with her earlier theme: the retreat of the state is a *forced* retreat. Several phrases set the tone of the book ('overall decline in state power', the 'hollowness of state authority', 'diffusion of authority'), without precisely outlining the specifics of each and their implications. The state, it would seem, has been blown over by the hurricane of 'impersonal forces' that constitute world markets. Why the historical transformation of a particular form of state (the Keynesian welfare state) should be taken to be equivalent to the historical transcendence of the state itself is left unexplained. Moreover, for someone who has advocated the dissolution of the scholarly division between politics and economics, the zero-sum discussion of 'markets win, governments lose' seems additionally 'strange'.[62]

In part Strange makes the same mistake as the celebratory Marxist treatments of state crisis in the early to mid-1970s. An overstatement then (as Robert Cox has argued, most theorists were: 'less concerned with the synchronic conditions reinforcing stability than with the diachronic developments explaining structural transformations.'),[63] and a confusion between the *functions* and the *structures* of the state, was a crucial component in the intellectual 'triumph' of the neoliberal hegemonic project. In the context of a generalized discourse of 'crisis' neoliberal political technicians appropriated the 'end of the state' thesis both as a vindication of their economic beliefs and a pre-emptive counter-movement against the as-then socialist agenda of national ownership. This is a complex discursive history into which Strange's 'retreat of the state' thesis accords suitably with the interests of 'disciplinary neoliberalism'.[64] In the positive light of the 'retreat of the state', the historical withdrawal of the state can once again be presented as a logic of 'global capital' and global capital can be presented as the logic of the withdrawal of the state. It is a discourse that has served efficiently to mask the historical defeat of the worker collectivities apt to unrest and the accelerating intensification of everyday pressures under the tyrannies of information-capitalism.

By remaining blind to the genealogy of modern political rationality, research on the issue of globalization is unable to highlight
the political interests that profit from the forces of contemporary
governmentality that have progressively replaced visible (and accountable) authority in the ordering of men and things.

Globalization, j'accuse

I began this chapter by identifying several themes that underpin
the rise to hegemony of the concept of globalization. These themes
– which have become in important ways, social imperatives – have,
I argued, gone largely unquestioned as a result of the thesis of the
'retreat of the state'. In my view this thesis is suspect for two reasons.
First, it presents a one-sided history. Alternative contemporary
accounts (Helleiner, Jessop, Jones *et al.*) highlight not only that the
division between state and market is artificial, but moreover, that
'the state' (as defined by the 'declinists' themselves) was (and still
is) *fundamentally involved* in the policy decisions that spawned
'globalization' *as they describe it*.

My second challenge to the retreat of the state thesis is that it
ignores the broader constitution and genealogy of power over modern
world history. This genealogy attests to diffusion rather than centralization running hand-in-hand with the history of modern
liberalism. In that case, to focus *now* upon the rise of individualism, and to inflate that somehow with a crisis of the state in general,
is narrow and ahistorical. Moreover, in conceiving 'the state' only
in terms of its instrumental functions (legislature, taxation, border
controls, etc.), and in assuming a positive relationship between 'state
power' and visibility, we are prevented from recognizing a whole
series of discourses and practices running coterminous with globalization that have worked to stabilize the world economy, and the
individuals working within it. I suggested here that in contemporary discourses of globalism the themes of 'spatial annihilation' and
the 'obligation-to-mobility' work precisely as ordering and assem-
bling practices, suggesting less the 'retreat of the state' than its
disappearance into its *ideal form* (integral, automatic, the 'society
of control').[65]

Globalization in this sense is both a 'strategy' and an 'imperative'. The former explains the ways in which individuals have, in a
process of self-constitution, *globalized*. The latter points – at least
implicitly – to the benefits afforded to civic authority of them doing

so (ordered, motivated, mobile masses). In jumping to the cause of the 'end of the state', too many have misunderstood the genealogy of modern political order, and its transformations. Such a misunderstanding is itself *political*. On the back of the thesis of the terminal state, globalization is viewed as a means to liberation in the age of limited government. The discourse of the 'defective', 'dysfunctional', and 'retreating' state has effectively served as the perfect alibi to a near perfect crime: the wholesale disciplining of world labour through the social extension of the discourses of globalism, acceleration, informatization, risk, doubt, and state debilitation. Seen to be external to the historical processes of political struggle, globalization has been afforded a particular exemption from critique. Forms of possible resistance have been artificially delimited. The most radical statement that can be made is to call for a nationally regulated, socialized market. Yet globalization is neither inevitable nor inexorable. We must forget the fatal link suggested between globalization and state decline. There is no paradigm shift without power. By internalizing the discourse of 'the global', and its associate myths, we all become 'vectors' ensuring the transmission of the new normalcy. We must find a way out of that labyrinth of mirrors.

In the hope of reclaiming political space, it is time to move beyond the critique of globalization *on its own terms* and begin to place it within a broader context of the rationality of modern order in all of its elements. We must re-politicize the regularization of modern societies. We must re-politicize capital and our relation to space and time. We must begin to politicize the 'disappearance' of the state that legitimates the intensification of pressures while shielding their source. And we must politicize the logic of speed that dominates our culture, thrusting us into the global epoch, individualizing and fragmenting, reducing to zero all forms of resistance while simultaneously reproducing and imposing its apparatus of violence on individuals and whole societies alike. Against these silent practices that demark globalization as a domain of power we should reserve the right to say no.

In this way we may break open the discursive limits of contemporary governance, and globalization as a form of that political reason. Clearly this entails the rethinking of many of the themes basic to the contemporary study of political economy and international relations. So be it. Under any other illusion we're missing the fact that globalization is itself a form of power: not so much a bonfire of controls as a *re-coding of the politics of order.*[66] The recognition of our current dangers is not an abstract nihilism, it is not the admission of defeat, but the only possible beginning in the task of thinking anew about the attractions and possibilities of an alternative future.

Notes

1 A version of this chapter was published in 'Globalization and the Politics of Resistance', the special issue of *New Political Economy* edited by Barry Gills, 'Globalization and the End of the State?', *New Political Economy*, Vol. 2, No. 1 (1997), pp. 165–77.

2 The 'market' approach is best epitomized in the writings of Theodore Levitt, Richard Barnet, Kenichi Ohmae and Michael Porter. The 'technological' catalyst is central in the writings of Susan Strange, Walter Wriston, Manuel Castells, and François Chesnais. An 'accidental' theme can be found in the writings of Phil Cerny and Walter Wriston. The 'developmental' approach is best outlined in the works of Roland Robertson, Anthony Giddens and Immanuel Wallerstein.

3 Susan Strange, 'The Defective State', *Dædalus: Journal of the American Academy of Arts*, Vol. 124, No. 2 (1995), p. 56., p. 59, p. 71; Susan, Strange, *The Retreat of the State: The Diffusion of Power in the World Economy* (Cambridge University Press, 1996), pp. 7–14.

4 Philip G. Cerny, 'What Next for the State?', in Eleonore Kofman and Gillian Youngs (eds), *Globalization: Theory and Practice* (Pinter, 1996), p. 123.

5 Philip G. Cerny, 'The Infrastructure of the Infrastructure? Toward "Embedded Financial Orthodoxy" in the International Political Economy', in Ronen Palan and Barry Gills (eds), *Transcending the State–Global Divide: A Neostructuralist Agenda in International Relations* (Lynne Rienner, 1993), p. 239.

6 Theodore Levitt, 'The Globalization of Markets', *Harvard Business Review* (May–June, 1983), p. 101.

7 Vincent Cable, 'The Diminished Nation-State: A Study in the Loss of Economic Power', *Dædalus: Journal of the American Academy of Arts*, Vol. 124, No. 2 (1995), p. 27.

8 William J. Holstein, 'The Stateless Corporation', *Business Week* (14 May, 1990), pp. 98–100.

9 Cable, 'The Diminished Nation-State', p. 42.

10 Kenichi Ohmae, 'The Rise of the Region State', *Foreign Affairs* (Spring, 1993), p. 78.

11 Mathew Horsman and Andrew Marshall, *After the Nation State: Citizens, Tribalism and the New World Disorder* (HarperCollins, 1994), pp. 234–5, J. A. Camilleri and J. Falk, *The End of Sovereignty: The Politics of a Shrinking and Fragmented World* (Edward Elgar, 1992), and Kenichi Ohmae, *The End of the Nation State* (Free Press, 1995).

12 Horsman and Marshall, *After the Nation State*, p. 60.

13 Peter Riddell, 'Leaders in Cloud Cuckoo Land', *The Times* (28 August, 1995), p. 14.

14 Eric Helleiner, *States and the Re-emergence of Global Finance* (Ithaca, 1994). See also: Ron Martin, 'Stateless Monies, Global Financial Integration and National Economic Autonomy: The End of Geography?' in Stuart Corbridge, Nigel Thrift and Ron Martin (eds), *Money, Power and Space* (Basil Blackwell, 1994).

15 Bob Jessop, 'Post-Fordism and the State', in Ash Amin (ed.), *Post-Fordism: A Reader* (Blackwell, 1995).

16 R. J. Barry Jones *Globalisation and Interdependence in the International Political Economy: Rhetoric and Reality* (Pinter, 1995), Paul Hirst and Grahame Thompson, *Globalization in Question* (Polity, 1996).

17 See: Stephen Gill, 'Globalization, Market Civilization, and Disciplinary Neoliberalism', *Millennium: Journal of International Studies*, Vol. 24, No. 3 (1995), pp. 399–423; Michael McKinley, 'Globalism as Clausewitzian Strategy: Annihilation, War Equivalence, and Insecurity in the New World Order', paper presented to the 37th Annual Convention of the International Studies Association, San Diego, April 16–20, 1996; Michael J. Shapiro, 'The Spectre of Globalization', paper presented to the 38th Annual Convention of the International Studies Association, Toronto, March 18–22, 1997.

18 See: Ian R. Douglas, *On the Genealogy of Globalism: The Birth of Biokinetic Society*, manuscript in preparation.

19 Lewis Mumford, *The City in History: Its Origins, Its Transformations and Its Prospects* (Harvester, 1961), p. 3.

20 *Ibid.*, p. 368. Michel Serres argues a similar point, analysing the transition from the 'clockwork age' to the 'motor age'. See: Michel Serres, 'It was before the (World) Exhibition', in Jean Clair and Harold Szeeman (eds), *Junggesellenmaschinen; les machines célibataires* (Venice: Alfieri, 1975).

21 The prevalence of the metaphor of 'immobility' in early modern medical research of the causes of melancholia (and 'perpetual flux' as the cause of mania) is highlighted in Michel Foucault's, *Madness and Civilization: A History of Insanity in the Age of Reason* (Tavistock, 1967), pp. 123–34. On the importance of 'mobility' to nineteenth-century economic thought, see: Timothy L. Alborn, 'Economic Man, Economic Machine: Images of Circulation in the Victorian Money Market', in Philip Mirowski (ed.), *Natural Images in Economic Thought: 'Markets read in tooth and claw'* (Cambridge, 1994), pp. 173–96. On the principle of circulation (and its government), in urban planning, see: Paul Virilio, *Speed and Politics: An Essay on Dromology* (Semiotext(e), 1986), *Popular Defense and Ecological Struggles* (Semiotext(e), 1990), and *The Lost Dimension* (Semiotext(e), 1991). On the metaphor of 'exchange', see: Michel Foucault, *The Order of Things: An Archaeology of the Human Sciences* (Tavistock, 1970), pp. 166–214.

22 Michel Foucault, 'Governmentality', in Graham Burchell, Colin Gordon and Peter Miller (eds), *The Foucault Effect: Studies in Governmentality* (Harvester Wheatsheaf, 1991), p. 104.

23 *Ibid.*, pp. 102–3.

24 Viet Ludwig von Seckendorff, *Der Teutsch Fürstenstaat* (1656), *Der Christen Staat* (1685), Justus Christoph Dithmar, *Oeconomie, Polizei- und Cameralwissenchaft* (1755), Joachim Georg Darjes, *Elementa metaphysica*

(1743), *Institutiones juriprudentiae universalis* (1745), *Discurs uber Natur-und Volkerrecht* (1762). See: Pasquale Pasquino, 'Theatrum politicum: The Genealogy of Capital-police and the State of Prosperity', in Burchell *et al.* (eds), *The Foucault Effect.*

25 Michel Foucault, 'Omnes et Singulatim: Towards a Criticism of "Political Reason"', in Sterling M. McMurrin (ed.), *The Tanner Lectures on Human Values*, Vol. 2 (University of Utah Press: 1981), p. 252.

26 Julius Bernhard von Rohr, *Haushaltungsbibliothek* (1716), quoted in Small, *The Cameralists*, p. 189. Giovanni Botero had already recognized the importance of economic security in the late sixteenth century: 'interest in the state can be secured by compelling [citizens] to undertake some work, such as agriculture or any trade which will give them a sufficient income to live on.' Giovanni Botero, *The Reason of State* (Routledge & Kegan Paul, 1956), p. 92.

27 Johann Heinrich Gottlob von Justi, quoted in Geraint Parry, 'Enlightened Government and its Critics in Eighteenth-Century Germany', *Historical Journal*, Vol. 7, No. 2 (1963) p. 182.

28 Michel Foucault, *The History of Sexuality*, Volume 1 (Allen Lane, 1979), pp. 139–41.

29 *The Economist*, 'Japan Survey' (9–15 July 1994), p. 8.

30 *International Herald Tribune* (3–4 September 1994), p. 15.

31 Paul Virilio, *Open Sky* (Verso, 1997), p. 19; William H. Davidow and Michael Malone, 'The Virtual Corporation', *Business Week*, 8 February 1993.

32 Jack Welch, quoted in Noel Tichy and Ram Charan, 'Speed, Simplicity, Self-Confidence: An Interview with Jack Welch', *Harvard Business Review* (September–October 1989), p. 115.

33 Percy Barnevik, in William Taylor, 'The Logic of Global Business: An Interview with ABB's Percy Barnevik', *Harvard Business Review* (March–April, 1991), p. 104.

34 Al Gore, speech to the International Telecommunications Union, 21 March 1994. Available on the Internet at: http://www.freedonia.com/ctheory/

35 Ashland Oil and Refining Company, *Harvard Business Review*, July–August 1969, p. 17.

36 Daimler Benz marketing campaign, 1995–6.

37 Virilio, *Open Sky*, pp. 1–3, and Paul Virilio, *The Vision Machine* (Indiana University Press, 1994), p. 4.

38 Jürgen Habermas, *Legitimation Crisis* (Beacon Press, 1975).

39 British Telecom marketing campaign, 1995–6. See Andrew Ross, 'The New Smartness', *Science as Culture*, Vol. 4, No. 1 (1993), pp. 94–109.

40 Tom Peters, *Thriving on Chaos: Handbook for a Management Revolution* (Pan Books, 1987), p. 189; Walter Wriston, 'Technology and Sovereignty', *Foreign Affairs*, Vol. 67 (1988), p. 71; and see Thomas J. Peters and Robert H. Waterman, *In Search of Excellence: Lessons from America's Best-Run Companies* (Harper & Row, 1982).

41 Norman Ornstein, quoted in Reginald Dale, 'Toward the Millennium: the economic revolution has begun', Special Report: Global Agenda, *Time, International* (13 March, 1995), pp. 45–6.

42 Levitt, 'The Globalization of Markets', p. 93–112 (emphasis added).
43 Peters, *Thriving on Chaos*, pp. 471–7, pp. 285–94; Peters and Waterman, *In Search of Excellence*, pp. 55–86.
44 Martin Heidegger, '"Only a God Can Save Us": *Der Spiegel*'s Interview with Martin Heidegger', in Richard Wolin (ed.), *The Heidegger Controversy: A Critical Reader* (MIT Press, 1993), pp. 105–6.
45 Tichy and Charan, 'Speed, Simplicity, Self-Confidence', p. 114.
46 Foucault, *Discipline and Punish*, p. 138.
47 Elias Canetti, *Crowds and Power* (Penguin, 1973), p. 462.
48 Filippo Tommaso Marinetti, *Selected Writings* (London, 1972), p. 41.
49 Al Gore, speech to the International Telecommunications Union.
50 Karl Polanyi, *The Great Transformation* (Beacon Press, 1957 edn), pp. 56–77, pp. 111–29.
51 Johann Heinrich Gottlob von Justi, *Staatswirthschaft* (1758), quoted in Albion M. Small, *The Cameralists: Pioneers of German Social Polity* (University of Chicago Press, 1909), p. 328.
52 Foucault, *Discipline and Punish*, p. 135.
53 'Until the Second World War – until the concentration camps – societies were societies of incarceration, of imprisonment in the Foucauldian sense. The great transparency of the world, whether through satellites or simply through tourists, brought about an overexposure of these places to observation, to the press and public opinion which now ban concentration camps. You can't isolate anything in the world of ubiquity and instantaneousness . . . This required the promotion of another kind of repression, which is disappearance . . .' Paul Virilio and Sylvère Lotringer, *Pure War* (Semiotext(e), 1983) p. 88. See also Paul Virilio, *The Aesthetics of Disappearance* (Semiotext(e), 1991).
54 Colin Gordon, 'Introduction' in Burchell *et al.* (eds), *The Foucault Effect*, p. 4.
55 Foucault, *The Order of Things*, p. xx–xxii.
56 Michel Foucault, *Foucault Live* (Semiotext(e), 1996), p. 235.
57 Philip G. Cerny, 'Globalization and Structural Differentiation: Between Plurilateralism and the New Middle Ages', paper presented in Indianapolis, October 12–13, 1996.
58 Ulrich Beck, *Risk Society: Towards a New Modernity* (Sage, 1992), p. 135.
59 Philip G. Cerny, 'Plurilateralism: Structural Differentiation and Functional Conflict in the Post-Cold War World Order', *Millennium: Journal of International Studies*, Vol. 22, No. 1 (1993), pp. 27–51.
60 *Ibid.*, p. 45.
61 Strange, *The Retreat of the State*, p. xii.
62 Strange goes so far as to term this transition a 'reversal'; Strange, *The Retreat of the State*, p. 4.
63 Robert W. Cox, *Production, Power and World Order: Social Forces in the Making of History* (Columbia University, 1987), p. 396.
64 Gill, 'Globalization, Market Civilization, and Disciplinary Neoliberalism'.
65 Virilio, *Popular Defense and Ecological Struggles*, pp. 33, 66; Gilles Deleuze, 'Postscript on the Societies of Control', *October*, Vol. 59 (1992), pp. 3–7.
66 I borrow this phrase from Colin Gordon's introduction to: Burchell *et al.* (eds), *The Foucault Effect*, p. 26.

Part II

Strategies of Resistance: From the Local to the Global

9
Social Movements, Local Places and Globalized Spaces: Implications for 'Globalization from Below'

Peter Waterman

Introduction: thinking and acting in a globalized world[1]

[T]he capacity of most social movements to command place better than space puts a strong emphasis upon the potential
connection between place and social identity. This is manifest
in political action . . . The consequent dilemmas of social or working-class movements in the face of a universalising capitalism
are shared by other oppositional groups – racial minorities, colonized peoples, women, etc. – who are relatively empowered to
organise in place but disempowered when it comes to organizing over space. In clinging, often of necessity, to a place-bound
identity, however, such oppositional movements become a part
of the very fragmentation which a mobile capitalism and flexible
accumulation can feed upon. 'Think globally and act locally' was
the revolutionary slogan of the 1960s. It bears repeating.[2]

The condition of globality – simultaneously level, process, epoch
and episteme – provides an increasingly central terrain for social
movements. This flies in the face of much social-movement experience
and not a little social-movement theory. These suggest that locality
is the privileged site for movements, and that what flows upwards
or outwards from here is 'resistance' and/or 'reform'. Theoretically-
critical and socially-committed understandings of globalization suggest
that the local and the global are increasingly and inextricably inter-
penetrated. That the global provides an increasingly central space

135

for social movements does not mean that it is unproblematic or uncontested. The global/ization process implies for popular forces and social movements threats, promises – and seductions. Success here requires not only a new worldview (in both senses of this potent term), but a new understanding of global citizenship, of global solidarity, and of global communication/culture. Out of new political experiences and theoretical understandings flow the beginnings of an alternative global civilizational project. This requires recognition that what we have so far witnessed, in answer to globalization from above, is 'globalization from the middle' and that the articulation of this with 'globalization from below' has to be continually worked for.

Globalization, its discontents and alternatives

Previous worldviews – Christian, Liberal, Marxist, Developmentalist, Third Worldist, World Systemic – have been in different ways people-blind. They have suggested that relations-across-borders (to put this as blandly and broadly as possible) are those of or between belief-systems, nations, economies, states, cultures, blocs. Even when inspired or energized by ideals of peace, emancipation, plenty, justice and democracy, they have delivered advances incorporating old barbarisms and resulting in new contradictions and conflicts, on ever-increasing scales and with ever-more-dangerous consequences.

Globalization, however, makes it possible, for the first time in human history, for emancipatory forces to at least begin to see the world both whole and holistically, to understand the interlocking of civilization/barbarism and to propose understandings and strategies aimed directly at the civilizing of global society. The worldview offered below is just one of a number of attempts to do this.

Firstly, then, our present period is one of a complex, globalized, high-risk, information and service capitalism – a condition or moment not of post-modernity but of a high or radicalized modernity. Old social, economic, political, military, cultural and other conflicts are raised to higher levels (in terms of both intensity and sites), these being supplemented by new and truly global ones. The decentering of capitalist and statist power implies a dramatic increase in the number, type, complexity, sites and levels of social tension, conflict and negotiation. An informatized capitalism is one in which society – or societies – are subjected simultaneously to increased scope or stretch and to increased intensity or deepening.

This in turn implies increased interdependency, globalized localities and localized globalities, subjected to the simultaneous, complex and uneven effects of homogenization and heterogenization. This is, consequently, a world in which we are increasingly condemned to think both dialectically and ethically: dialectically because of the complexity and contradictions; ethically because our choices have sharply increasing socio-geographic and historical stretch and effect.

Secondly, globalization and globalism, particularly in their neoliberal form, provoke new political, social and cultural responses that are increasingly globalized. We can here identify three ideal-type responses: that of celebration (accepting the role of serialized global consumer, individualized voter), that of rejection (on particularistic, essentialist or fundamentalist grounds, whether religious, national, socialist or cultural) and that of critique/surpassal (coming primarily from the new alternative, or radical–democratic, social movements). This is represented in Figure 9.1. Figure 9.1a also suggests how the 'alternative', local-to-global, response overlaps with/is penetrated by celebratory or rejectionist elements. Figure 9.1b reveals the tension between engagement and autonomy in alternative social movements/ spaces, suggesting the necessity to move or balance between an excess of engagement with capital/state (incorporation) or of autonomy in civil society (self-isolation). Any 'alternative' social movement, or related non-governmental organization (NGO), can thus find itself in multiple positions, in local-to-global space, or at particular times. It is, for example, possible for a feminist movement, organization or tendency (local-to-global) to be simultaneously self-isolated (within civil society, from other feminists or women, from men) and incorporated (into reform strategies or intermediating roles promoted by capital or state). A complex, interdependent, yet uneven and unbalanced global order, requires complex, interdependent global alternatives, which the alternative movements are beginning to offer. In so far as it is globalized, moreover, contemporary capitalism promotes communication and culture to increasing pre-eminence, this providing an eminently disputable terrain for such new emancipatory movements. Cultural globalization makes an alternative global solidarity culture both necessary and possible. The form of the new global solidarity movements is, thus, increasingly that of 'information internationalisms'.

Thirdly, globalization implies the increasing centrality of the trans-, supra- or non-territorial terrain, as well as of global institutions, processes and instances, and therefore the possibility and necessity

Fig. 9.1a   Responses to globalization: local, national, regional, global

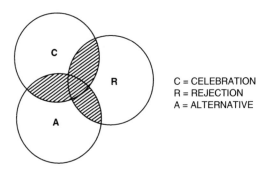

C = CELEBRATION
R = REJECTION
A = ALTERNATIVE

Fig. 9.1b   Social movement engagement/autonomy: local, national, regional, global

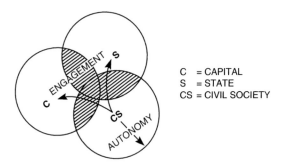

C = CAPITAL
S = STATE
CS = CIVIL SOCIETY

for the civilizing of global society. Global civil society, understood as one created out of conflict with the capitalist and (inter-)state spheres, is a privileged terrain (not the sole one) for the construction of liberty, equality, solidarity, ecological care and cultural tolerance/creation. This is, however, not a paradise to be announced, discovered or inhabited, it is a habitat to be jointly constructed by autonomous, democratic and pluralist forces. This requires engagement with/in existing inter-state and transnational capitalist instances and processes. It also requires engagement with/in churches, religions, and within and between NGOs/social movements that often reproduce the structures and behaviours they claim to surpass. NGOs, as earlier suggested, can be found in any autonomous or ambiguous position within the 'alternative' circle of Figure 9.1a and the 'civil society' one of Figure 9.1b. The development of a global civil society both depends on and stimulates the democratization, deconcentration and decentralization of inter-state organizations, transnational capitalist companies and religious institutions. A new concept of world citizenship is required to simultaneously synthesize and surpass those of the past. This would have as its utopian imaginary a citizenship without borders, classes or genders.

Fourthly, globalization raises the question of transforming internationalism (etymologically and historically a relation between nations, nationals and nationalities) into global solidarity. The latter is a movement and ethic identifying and addressing global social issues, identities and movements – including the national and ethnic. This means replacing the rhetorical internationalism of the nation-state period (when mass real-life experience was not universal and the universal was therefore unreal to masses) by one addressable and addressed to a world increasingly experienced by such masses of people – though differentially and unevenly – as both real and universal. A new universalism, both recognising and promoting plurality, must be based on a relational ontology, in which relating to others is not so much what we do as who we are. A monological ethic – in which universalistic principles dominate procedures – requires surpassing with a dialogical ethic, in which procedures allow for the possibility of developing a common discourse between different and unequal partners.

Fifthly, globalization, and the related collapse of both Communist and Radical-Nationalist alternatives to capitalism, helps us to understand that history does not consist of evolutionary stages (the higher, or later, the better), even less of binarily-opposed phases (civilized v. barbaric, modern v. traditional, post-modern v. modern). It is becoming increasingly possible to recognize that we are living mixed times (for those who prefer this language: simultaneously pre-modern, modern, and post-modern). It is this that allows the 'primitive', 'traditional', 'barbarian', 'pre-modern' Huarani indigenes of Amazonian Ecuador to pass messages to 'modern' Netherlanders about a 'post-modern' future.

The rest of this chapter considers the implications of such an understanding for global solidarity, communications/culture, citizenship, and the inter-relationship of the local and global, the middle class and popular classes, in the era of globalization.

A complex solidarity for a complex globality

Globalization creates a world that can increasingly be experienced as both real and universal, thus allowing for a universalism that is more than faith or obligation, a global solidarity that is more than a merely imagined community. The new global solidarity projects descend from, selectively re-articulate, allow for, but surpass, religious, liberal and socialist universalisms; proposing neither a return to an unchanging golden past nor a leap into a perfect future – here or hereafter – they allow for and require a dialogue of civilizations and ages, a solidarity with both past and future.

Here I will suggest an understanding of international solidarity that goes beyond both poetic and philosophical discourses, and any attempt at a one-word qualifier ('reciprocal', 'reflexive'), but by building on rather than dismissing such. The understanding offered is a more political and a more complex one. It is also, I think, one that could aid research. Solidarity is here assumed to be: (1) informed by and positively articulated with equality, liberty, peace, tolerance, and more-recent emancipatory/life-protective ideals; (2) primarily a relationship between people and peoples, even where mediated by state, market and bureaucratic/hierarchical organizations; (3) an active process of negotiating differences, or creating identity (as distinguished from traditional notions of 'solidarity as community' which may *assume* identity).

International solidarity – old or new, local or global, is here understood in terms of the acronym ISCRAR (an ironic semi-mnemonic: *Iskra* was Lenin's newspaper). This spells out as Identity, Substitution, Complementarity, Reciprocity, Affinity and Restitution.

Identity or identity creation is what commonly underlies socialist calls for international solidarity, usually in reference to oppressed and divided classes or categories in opposition to powerful and united oppressors (capitalists, imperialists). By itself, however, an Identity Solidarity can be reductionist and self-isolating, excluding unalikes. In so far as the identity is oppositional, it is a negative quality, often determined by the nature and project of the enemy or opponent (as with much traditional socialist internationalism).

Substitution implies standing up, or in, for a weaker or poorer other. This is how international solidarity has been usually understood amongst Development Co-operators and 'First-World Third-Worldists'. By itself, however, a Substitution Solidarity can lead to substitutionism (acting and speaking for the other), and it can permit the reproduction of existing inequalities. This is a criticism of Development Co-operation, which may function to create a single community of guilt and moral superiority within 'donor countries', whilst creating or reproducing further feelings of dependency and/or resentment in countries where social crises have evidently been worsening.

Complementarity suggests the provision of that which is missing, and therefore an exchange of different desired qualities. A Complementary Solidarity would mean that what was moving in each direction could differ but be equally valued by participants in the transaction. In so far as it meant that some kind of physical goods (cash, equipment, political support) were mostly moving in one direction and that some kind of moral or emotional goods (expressions of appreciation and gratitude) were mostly being received, we could be involved in an 'unequal exchange' of a problematic character.

Reciprocity suggests mutual interchange, care, protection and support. It could be taken as *the* definition of the new global solidarity. Global Reciprocity Solidarity, however, could be understood as a principle of equal exchange, in which (as with states) one is exchanging political equivalents, or (as with capitalists) on the basis of calculated economic advantage. And it could therefore imply that one would defend the rights of others only if, or in expectation of, reciprocation by the other.

Affinity suggests mutual appreciation or attraction, and therefore a relationship of mutual respect and support, in which what is sought, appreciated or valued by each party is shared. Affinity would seem to have more to do with values, feelings and friendship. An Affinity Solidarity would seem to allow for global linkages within or between ideologies or movements, including between people without contact but acting in the same spirit. In so far as it approximates friendship, it would seem to be inevitably particular, if not particularistic.

Restitution suggests the putting right of a past wrong, the recognition of historical responsibility, a 'solidarity with the past', a solidarity across time rather than space. This comes close to intergovernmental war reparations, with the consequent danger of buying off guilt.

The value of such an understanding would seem to be the following: (1) that it is multi-faceted and complex; (2) that each type holds part of the meaning and that each is only part of the meaning;

(3) that it is subversive of simple binary or (r)evolutionary oppositions between bad and good, old and new, material and moral
solidarity; (4) that it enables critique of partial or one-sided solidarities; (5) that it could be developed into a research instrument,
permitting, for example, surveys of the meaning(s) of solidarity for
those involved.

From aspect to essence: global solidarity as communication

An exemplar – or at least an example – of alternative social movements operating under the conditions of an informatized and
globalized capitalism, that of women is, at least implicitly, a communications internationalism. This has several different but
interconnected meanings. The first is that it operates in the sphere
of ideas, information and images, revealing that which is globally
concealed, suggesting new meanings for that which is revealed. The
second and consequent one is that, like other such, it is particularly active and effective on the terrain of communication, media,
culture. The third is that, again like other such, its basic relational
principle is that of the network rather than the organization. The
fourth, and consequent, one is that the movement needs to be
primarily understood in communicational/cultural rather than in
the traditional political/organizational terms.

The global sphere of ideas, information and images

There is nothing immaterial, superstructural or derivative about this
sphere, although in the industrial phase of capitalism it may have
appeared as all three. We do not, at the other extreme, need to
become discourse-determinists to recognize both the increasing centrality of this sphere and the potential for emancipatory movement
and radical democracy it contains. That this sphere is created and
dominated by the logic of capital cannot conceal its contradictory
nature: capital, capitalists, capitalisms, cannot simply control this
sphere in the way they did the factory, the family, the state, the
school and the gun. This is also a non-territorial sphere, meaning
one increasingly capable of that expanding growth, flexibility and
democratization that the capitalism of industry and the state-nation
has promised/denied. It is growth here that will make an ecological steady-state possible globally, without such 'conservatism' implying
stagnation or reaction. The problem to be overcome is that of the

invisibility of this sphere: that it is either transparent to emancipatory movements, or else handled with concepts and understandings borrowed from, for example, politics.

The global terrain of communication, media, culture

At national level, or within a nation-state-dominated discourse, we can recognize as distinct, overlapping and mutually-informing cultural spheres, the Dominant, the Popular and the Alternative. But, the Popular (in so far as this implies places actively and intensively lived in and culturally shaped by poorer population sectors) can hardly be said to have a place or space at global level. The Popular is here carried, shaped and articulated by either the immensely powerful Dominant global means or the still tiny and marginal Alternative ones – which are in mutual dispute for hegemony over the Popular. The marginality of the Alternative is less important for social movements than recognition of: (1) the creative freedom permitted by such marginality; (2) the name and increasing centrality of this terrain; (3) the necessity and possibility of disputing it. It has been argued, in relation to its democratic potential, that cyberspace is less like a hammer (a means, a tool, for doing something to something) than Germany (a place, space, culture). It is, actually, a hammer *and* Germany *and* Utopia ('nowhere', 'a good place', a community yet to be imagined and created). Globally it is a space of increasingly public dispute, as radical-democratic social movements mobilize for a People's Communication Charter and related political transformations. These, and other such projects, both require and are creating democratic and pluralist global communication networks that are increasingly specialized and professional.

Networking as a principle of global inter-relationship[3]

Networking is both the oldest and the most common form of human social relationship. It was only with the development of industrial and state-national capitalism that the formal, hierarchical organization (authoritarian, representative-democratic, participatory-democratic) came to impose itself, to suck power and meaning out of such networks, to concentrate all decision-making power within itself, to project itself as both the real and ideal relational form. The transformation to a globalized and informatized capitalism brings back the networking principle with a vengeance – primarily vengeance against those subaltern strata now locked into and dependent on the traditional hierarchical organization! There is, thus, nothing essentially virtuous about networking either now or in the recent (or, for that matter, pre-capitalist) past.

In talking of networking however, we are considering human inter-relationships, including those within and between organizations, in *communication* terms. In so far as networks are conceived of as horizontal, flexible, incorporating participation and feedback, we can also value these over the rigid hierarchical organization, and attempt to thus distinguish 'our' networks from 'their' networks. We have, however, also to recognize that within any particular political domain – geographical, social, professional – networking does not only mean an informal and flexible horizontal relation-ship between equals and alike, but also informal vertical relationships between such, and informal horizontal relations between unequals and unalikes.

Networks also have different architectures, such as the star, the wheel and the web (including a World Wide Web increasingly used by social movements and activist academics) implying differential influence and control. Network-babble therefore needs, today, to be replaced by network analysis, including consideration of roles within, or in relation to, them, of the cost of individual/group in-volvement, of the extent of their connectivity, of their density, and of the role of opinion leaders (who can evidently convert a net-work into a 'following').

All these complexities and qualifications notwithstanding, the idea, value and practice of networking opens wide perspectives to emancipatory global movements, previously (self-)condemned to reproduce the pyramidal and hierarchical structure of the corpora-tion, factory, state, army, prison, church or (Goddess forbid!) university. Indeed, the archetypal political party of liberal democ-racy was invented by the German labour and socialist movement, in its early, emancipatory moment: it was criticized almost one century ago for its creation and reproduction of oligarchy. If the extreme form of emancipatory internationalism was at one time represented by the Comintern (combining characteristics of an early Christian sect, the Jesuit order, the Islamic jihad, and the state foreign intel-ligence or spy ring), the new ideal must be the Italian one of the 'biodegradable organization' (an ideal activists are more likely to welcome in general theory than in particular effect or as promoted practice).

From national subjects to global citizens: insiders without outsiders

The notion of global citizenship has at least two inter-related problems attached to it. The first is that of the social, territorial inclusion/exclusion anchored historically in the concept of rights/responsibilities within a city (later state-nation). The second is its relationship to a sovereign power, whether aristocratic, monarchical or republican. A global citizenship would be one without outsiders, unless we are thinking of extra-terrestrial territories or beings. It would also be one recognizing that, today more than ever, 'sovereign power' at global level is complex and dispersed. Yet, given globalization, some such notion seems not only inescapable but also attractive.

The idea of global citizenship is a logical implication of theoretical and political discussion of multi-tiered citizenship, itself a result of the creation of such regional polities as the European Union, and of a relativization of state-nation centrality. It is attractive for numerous reasons. One is shown by the way in which women have been able to successfully appeal to the European Court of Justice against the state-nation. Another attraction is that of embodying universal rights and responsibilities in people and peoples rather than the state-nation.

The non-existence of a recognizable global sovereign is less an obstacle than a challenge to emancipatory global movements. That there is no single address for the People's Communication Charter or the Cultural Environment Movement, does not prevent them from seeking for and identifying the places where power is concentrated, nor from pressing for citizen-like rights – and responsibilities – in this sphere. In this case, perhaps, global-citizens-in-the-making might be also *creating* a global sovereignty (subject to both *perestroika* and *glasnost*) over an increasingly privatized sphere that is monopolistic in tendency, individualizing, intrusive and destructive of human sociality and creativity.

The concept of the world citizen appropriate to the era of globalization can no longer be that of the religious universalist, the liberal cosmopolitan or the socialist internationalist. Ecological theory has already begun to conceptualize the matter, identifying as hypothetical global citizens (1) the global capitalist; (2) the global reformer; (3) the environmental manager; and (4) the earth citizen.

Notions of 'cosmopolitan democracy', and extensive related discussion, sensitizes us to the growing importance of international institutions – and the impact that these have on notions of democracy that assume the sovereign nation-state. They may, however, be based on an over-optimistic projection forward from the 1990s wave of UN activity, and of the NGO/civil society role in global conferences. We do not know, at this uncertain moment, what US or other major state/bloc interest there is in anything more than a slimmed-down set of such institutions, with serious global decision-making confined to smaller and more-secretive clubs – with carefully-selected, purely-decorative, NGO 'consultative committees' as a cheap but decorative fringe.

Discussion around global institutions in terms of democracy has nonetheless extended the notion of 'double democratization' – of both state and civil society – to the global level. If this kind of discussion often makes a simple identification of the latter with the new alternative social movements or NGOs, critical reflection on the latter suggests the necessity for a third democratization – of full citizenship within a sphere that often reproduces the hierarchy, secrecy and competitivity of capital, state, and of those old bureaucratized labour or socialist movements over which superiority is claimed.

Conclusion: 'One evil empire down; one to go'[4]

This paper is about the increasing possibility of, and necessity for, virtuous spirals in a globalizing world. I have, I hope, also suggested that these can become vicious circles or even downward spirals. So this is a plea for working on virtuous spirals between the global and local – however these are conceived – and for virtuous circles within globalized space.

If, at the beginning of the century, it was more or less clear which space was national and which international, which local and which global, at the end this is no longer so. If I reflect on International Women's Day (IWD) 1997 at my own institute, it is difficult, if not impossible, to distinguish the global and the local. Women students, from the Women and Development Programme (W&D), brought this into the institute with the local version of a global campaign against sexual harassment. A public meeting made apparent that the institute was, in its procedures, failing to recognize the structured inequality between harasser (male) and harassed (female). Further revealed was a locally-, nationally- or regionally-specific combination of liberal-patriarchal assumption and liberal-democratic intention. This institute is a Dutch, state-dependent, internationally-staffed and Third-World-oriented institute of Westernized development studies. The students are primarily from the Third World (i.e. two-thirds of our globalized whole). A number of them are feminists, formed not only by local struggles and feminists but also by First-World and even First-World*ist* feminisms – as well as by such global feminism as was articulated at the 4th World Conference on Women in Beijing (where 30–40 past W&D graduates met each other and present staff). Where, in this case, is the global and where the local? Which is influencing which? And, in this struggle for a citizenship recognizing and allowing for difference, where does feminist power and initiative originate, lie or accumulate?

The institute is not, of course, local in the way of . . . where? Chiapas in the Deep South of Mexico? Its inhabitants are not lo-calized like . . . who? The white male dockers of Liverpool in the north-west of England? Both communities are involved in conflicts caused by neoliberal globalization, and one can learn about and support the struggles of their men and women through internationally accessible alternative media and the Internet. Through the World Wide Web they are not only part of but contributing to a world-wide web of solidarity. It therefore occurs to me that, as global and local movements increasingly interpenetrate and inform each other, we possibly need to concentrate less on places or levels than processes and flows.

Another thought. What we have been talking about here is 'globalization from below' only in a rhetorical sense (although one could ask, rhetorically, and with an eye to the sub-title above: do we not need a new radical-democratic global rhetoric?). The active agents of the new global solidarity are mostly – like those actually accessing, entering and downloading from the Internet – tertiary-educated middle-class professionals, academics and technicians. This is not a matter for concealment or even embarrassment. Most nine-teenth-and early twentieth-century bearers of labour and socialist internationalism were either middle class or – through their activity as (semi-)professional internationalists – became so. It is worth re-membering that in 1914 it was not so much the 'labour bureaucracy' or 'labour aristocracy' that betrayed the working class but the na-tional and nationalist working classes that 'betrayed' their commonly internationalist leaders! This was a traumatic and formative experi-ence in international social movement history that does not bear repetition. The new internationalists need to unite not only with each other but with their respective publics, constituencies, masses.

Yet another thought. There is a belief, or at least a wish, in the international labour and socialist movement, as well as amongst some left social theorists, that it might be possible to return to, or revive, the liberal-democratic national welfare state of the post-1945 era, or its socialist-nationalist opposite number, or their international projection in the UN institutions. This is to ignore the historical evidence: anti-capitalist and anti-imperialist revolutions can be reversed, or at least vitiated; the revolutions of or inside capitalism – industrial, informational – cannot, or have not. It is also to fail to consider how the Keynesian national(ist) welfare model, in curious duplication of its national-communist competitor, disarmed social movements and civil society, thus permitting, if not preparing the way, for national and global neoliberalism.

The fate of the reports of successive international commissions of the great and the good, Brandt, Brundtland and Our Global Neighbourhood[5] (I may have missed one or two) do not augur well for such attempts to regain the Paradigm Lost. They have been joined, in the dustbin of global reformist utopianism, by the 1970s–80s projects (promoted by leftist politicians and academics, and endorsed by authoritarian Third World and Communist states) for the New World This That and The Other Order. Yet it seems impossible that some convincing statist and reformist project for taming or civilizing global casino capitalism will *not* develop over the next decade! The new alternative global social movements should support such but not identify with them. What, it seems to me, they should be doing is thinking about the kind of world, the kind of state, the kind of nation, the kind of welfare desirable, necessary and possible under conditions of globalization.[6]

David Harvey was actually right about modern social movements having their strength in local places rather than globalized spaces, at least up till – say – the 1970s. But his conclusion would be a disastrous guide to the present or future. 'Think globally and act locally'? How the world, and perceptions of it, have changed! We cannot today repeat the slogans of the 1960s, when globalization was a problem without a name and global solidarity was still called internationalism.

The revolutionary slogan for the next century has already been invented: 'Think globally, act locally; think locally, act globally.' To which I would like to add: 'Think dialectically: act self-reflexively.'

This is, in other words, an epoch in which survival demands (1) the replacement of binary by dialectical thinking; (2) a recognition that relating to (distant) others is not what we do but who we are; (3) that, particularly when speaking of the universal, we make ourselves and our 'subject position' visible and ourselves available to the reader, inviting and encouraging her/him to see us as part of an inevitably partial and particular contribution to a new kind of internationalism.

Notes

1 This chapter has been much stimulated by 'Globalization and the Politics of Resistance', the special issue of *New Political Economy* Vol. 2, No. 1. (1997), edited by Barry Gills, particularly the contributions to this of Christine Chin and James Mittelman, and the concluding essay by the Newcastle Research Working Group on Globalization.

2 David Harvey, *The Condition of Postmodernity* (Basil Blackwell, 1989), pp. 302–3.

3 This section was written before I became aware of even the first of three volumes on 'the information age' by Manuel Castells: *The Information Age: Economy, Society and Culture*, Vol. I: *The Rise of the Network Society*, 556 pp.; Vol. II: *The Power of Identity*, 461 pp.; Vol. III: *End of Millennium*, 418pp. (Blackwell, 1996, 1997, 1998). He adds a crucial new angle on our emerging world to those of us whose image of it has consisted of a synthesis of the one-word understandings of other thinkers – 'complex', 'high-modern', 'risk', 'informatized'. But crucial to his understanding is the notion of our globalized and informatized world as one of networking. For my review of the work as a whole, see Peter Waterman, 'The Brave New World of Manuel Castells: What on Earth (or in the Ether) is Going On?', *Development and Change* (Vol. 30, No. 2, 1999). See also Peter Waterman, 'Review Article: A New Global Solidarity Praxis for a World in Which "The Future is Not What it Used to Be"', *Transnational Associations*, No. 3 (1996), 163–80; Peter Waterman, *Globalization, Social Movements and the New Internationalisms* (London: Cassell, 1998).

4 The words of Michael Moore, American social critic, comedian and filmmaker, in his programme, *The Big One*, BBC 2 TV, 6 April 1997. Moore, from Flint, Michigan (de-industrialized and deserted by General Motors), is one of my local and working-class heroes. He makes films about the working-class and popular condition in the US with, I believe, universal appeal.

5 Commission on Global Governance, *Our Global Neighbourhood: The Report of the Commission on Global Governance* (Oxford University Press, 1995).

6 Relevant literature is reviewed, and many crucial issues raised, in a review article by Jan Nederveen Pieterse, 'Going Global: Futures of Capitalism (A Review Article)', *Development and Change*, Vol. 28, No. 2 (1997), pp. 367–82.

10
From National Resistance to International Labour Politics

Dimitris Stevis and Terry Boswell

> 'Beyond the built-in agenda, issues which have been pro-
> posed by some countries include *trade and labour standards*
> (the most potentially controversial of all these subjects).'
> Renato Ruggiero, Director-General World Trade Organiza-
> tion (WTO), 28 May 1996.[1]

Neoliberal integration presents labour with momentous challenges.[2]
Neoliberal ideology defines the world as one where expanding free
trade and investment are the only true sources of economic development and prosperity. Policies that regulate competition, restrict
capital mobility, transfer income, protect the disadvantaged, or in
any other way interfere with global market expansion and corporate discretion are defined as inimical to progress. Thus, labour and
other subordinate social forces are called upon to contest the ideology
and practice of neoliberal integration, including the political institutions that promote and manage it. While national acts of resistance
are unavoidable and necessary, they are not sufficient.

The current historical conjuncture presents labour with an opening for international collaboration, the main ingredients of which
are formalized international integration, decline of labour union
power in core countries, and the end of the Cold War. Formalized
integration legitimates cross-border cooperation while the decline
of labour unions, particularly in some countries and sectors, motivates
them to look abroad for allies.[3] Finally, the end of the Cold War
has removed a major source of misplaced energy and an obstacle
to autonomous labour politics. International labour politics, however, will not be the mechanistic byproduct of these factors. Nor

will it emerge from the radicalization and growth of individual national or sectoral movements, no matter how militant. A proactive labour politics will require reciprocal commitments to practical programmes of action, inclusive politics, and efficacious international connections in order to deal with challenges both external and internal to labour. Thus, while there is no guarantee that international labour politics will be successful, it will not happen unless intended.

In what follows we provide evidence that diverse workers' organizations are responding to these challenges and briefly highlight positive lessons and plausible improvements. Our evidence is focused in four ways. First, it draws upon global, North American, and Western European labour politics.[4] Second, we have chosen examples that involve workers more than their allies. Among those, we highlight reciprocal connections rather than one-way acts of solidarity or foreign policy. Finally, space requires that we choose examples that are both significant in themselves and representative of the different levels and tendencies in international labour politics.

The economics and politics of neoliberal integration

World economic transactions and movements have expanded phenomenally in the post-war era, especially in the last decade. The extent of expansion, and with it the deepening, if uneven, integration of the world economy, has been so profound as to usher in the term 'globalization' to describe the result.[5] Most significantly, however, global and regional integrations have become increasingly neoliberal, shedding the domestic social constraints that characterized capitalism for much of the post WWII era.[6]

A great success of neoliberal discourse has been in imparting the impression that its hegemony is a quasi-natural development, independent of political action and state intervention. Yet, the power and authority of domestic institutions is central to the initiation and continuation of the neoliberal capitalism, domestically and abroad. The Thatcher and Reagan administrations vigorously used state power for promoting their particular domestic and international agendas. Similar heavy-handed uses of state power have been evident wherever neoliberal alliances have come into power. Examples include Mexico, Brazil, India, and Russia.

But, state institutions and rules are also necessary to govern regional and global integration. Herein is a contradiction in neoliberal ideology. For mobility and trade, capital requires common standards and contract enforcement by third-party authorities. It also requires the mechanisms that will prevent the permanent and potentially destabilizing marginalization of countries and groups. That is, a world market requires global governance, irrespective of neoliberal diatribes against the intrusive state. In order to explain the emergence and resilience of globalization, and of the forms that it has been taking, we cannot look to some invisible hand or to the discursive success of an intellectual avant guarde. Gaining state power and transforming state institutions domestically and internationally have been central to the neoliberal project since Bretton Woods. As such, the US hegemony succeeded in two ways. First, it reintegrated the world economy to its pre-WWI heights. Secondly, it has managed to institutionalize neoliberalism in international governmental organizations (IGOs) that allowed multilateral agreement and thus enforcement against individual averse members.

The World Bank and the International Monetary Fund (IMF) can deeply affect the politics of countries undergoing structural adjustments and economic difficulties. The 1995 Mexican crisis, and subsequent crises, have enhanced the crisis management role of the IMF.[7] The WTO's supranational capacities are particularly important for enforcing the new trade regime and for establishing global standards for business (but not for contentious labour). To again quote Ruggiero, 'The system needs to be understood. It is not simply about "free trade."... opening markets is one thing, keeping them open for an investment to be a success is another and requires conditions to be both predictable and secure. That means credible and enforceable rules...'[8] This trend is further underscored by the draft Multilateral Agreement on Investment that gives corporations unprecedented global legal standing and rights.

The significance of state institutions is also evident at the regional level. European integration continues to be driven by trade, standardization, and monetary priorities, while social policies do not carry the same weight as economic priorities. Labour rights are below most domestic levels.[9] Integration has also been formalized in North America. The North American Free Trade Agreement (NAFTA) does not possess the supranationalism of the EU but its rules regarding origin, intellectual property, and dispute resolution, are quite intrusive. And while the participants have negotiated labour and environmental side-agreements, their provisions may actually encourage lower domestic standards.[10]

From national resistance to international politics

Faced with declining membership, weakening rights, and a threatened social welfare system, labour's typical resistance has been *national* and, sometimes, *nativist* in character. Workers seeking to defend and restore national protection have occasionally made Faustian alliances with xenophobic conservatives in bashing Mexico or Japan, as has been the case in the USA, or North Africa, as has been the case in France.

Nativism, however, is only the exception and may be fading among labour unions. During the last few years there have been widespread strikes against austerity measures and attacks on labour rights.[11] The increased level of protests in various European countries has kept the Social Charter on the agenda, against the brutal exigencies of monetary unification and the determination of neoliberal alliances.[12] Strikes in Spain, Italy, France, Greece, Belgium, and Germany have made the point that 'societies can say no' to uneven integration and still remain in favour of a unified Europe.[13] Even the 'New Labour' government in Britain has given formal notice of its accession to the Social Charter.

Important mobilizations have also taken place in Asia and Latin America. Determined strikes by the Korean Confederation of Trade Unions (KCTU) before the crisis slowed down the efforts of the government to enhance managerial discretion in hiring and firing.[14] Throughout Latin America, from Panama to Argentina, massive strikes have brought these countries to a standstill and have generated violent governmental reactions.[15] The recent successes of the Teamsters, against United Parcel Service, and of the Communications Workers of America, against US Airways, may herald a turning point in US labour politics, as well.

National mobilizations, however, have gone beyond simply resisting the initiatives of neoliberal alliances. Independent labour movements have grown in countries such as South Korea and France,[16] while labour's historic attachment to particular parties has been undermined in countries such as Bolivia, Argentina, and France.[17] In Mexico[18] and the USA,[19] traditional labour politics is contested from within the labour movement.

Global organizations, both governmental and non-governmental, have taken notice of the social unrest.[20] These organizations, however, generally see labour unions only as an instrument for increasing productivity and preserving industrial peace. What can labour learn from their reactions? One lesson is that militant protests have forced neoliberal leaders to address social issues, and to temper social welfare cuts. A second lesson is that in the absence of long-term, organized international labour politics, they can get away with such limited responses.

Towards an international labour politics

The ideology that paints transnational capital as par excellence supranationalist and anti-statist also paints labour with the colours of nativism, isolationism, and parochialism. In a number of cases these colours are deserved. Yet, from the very beginning of the current resurgence of liberal internationalism, during the late 1950s and early 1960s, a number of national and international labour organizations sought to counteract transnational capital by promoting transnational collective bargaining. Throughout the 1970s, international labour organizations promoted the adoption of Codes of Conduct for transnational corporations at IGOs such as the International Labour Organization, the United Nations, and the Organization for Economic Cooperation and Development.[21]

Faced with resolute corporate opposition and considered suspect by Cold Warriors, international organizers had few chances to establish successes on which to build and few authorities on which to call to enforce any success. With the end of the Cold War, and ironically, the development of strong regional and global IGOs designed to enforce neoliberal standards and contracts, international labour movements have a new set of conditions that offer real possibilities of enforceable world labour standards. Global and regional labour organizations could play an important role in promoting transnational rules and standards that are mutually reinforcing, something that national organizations cannot easily do.

Global labour politics

What is the role for global labour organizations? The end of the Cold War erases a major obstacle to collaboration.[22] Even in the absence of the Cold War, however, there exist strong centrifugal pressures.[23] The recent debates over whether the World Trade Organization should include a labour clause clearly highlight both the possibilities of global labour cleavages and the potentially positive role that global federations can play – a role for which they are not well prepared, however.[24]

The ICFTU has developed a 'social clause', to be included in international economic policies, that meets the approval of unions from all over the world. While its clause is a good starting point it is also evident that goals that have been central to the labour movement for over one hundred years, such as the eight-hour day, are not included.[25] In addition, it has also been working to secure formal status, similar to that which labour has in the International Labour Organization, in global fora, such as the annual meetings of the G-7, and IGOs, such as the WTO. Its failure, so far, further recommends that merely lobbying IGOs is a lost cause.

Nonetheless, in recent years the ICFTU has become more active in international fora, more even-handed in identifying labour violations and offering its moral support, and has expanded its membership to include more radical unions, such as the Brazilian CUT.[26] These developments have had a positive impact on its activities, as has been the case with ICFTU's Regional Inter American Workers Organization (ORIT, Spanish acronym). ORIT has been historically controlled by the AFL–CIO and has served the purposes of the Cold War. In recent years, however, more activist national federations, such as the Canadian Labour Congress, the Brazilian CUT, as well as the Unitary Confederation of the Workers of Chile (CUT) have been trying to activate ORIT in advance of Pan-American integration.[27]

On balance, however, in order for the ICFTU to play a positive and proactive role it does require brave political and organizational reforms. At the very least, it must be granted specific supranational capacities to negotiate programs of action and political agendas or, at least, resolve disagreements. Better representation of the interests of the less industrial and industrializing world is also long overdue. Finally, more resources and more operational activities, such as training and assistance, will greatly enhance its efficacy. Loose confederalism may avoid some disputes among unions, but it also perpetuates their marginal role.

A second group of global labour organizations are the International Trade Secretariats (ITSs).[28] Throughout their history some have been more active than others, reflecting priorities of leading unions within the Secretariats as well as the abilities of certain leaders. In the 1960s and 1970s three Secretariats sought to organize World Company Councils (WCC).[29] Although imaginative, the Councils were too bureaucratic and focused on already unionized labour, and were immobilized by disagreements amongst leading unions. These problems, combined with resolute opposition by capital, led to their practical abandonment.

In recent years, a number of ITSs have again become more active. Some have been involved in 'corporate campaigns'. In their broadest sense, corporate campaigns focus organizing around a specific transnational company trying to involve multiple stakeholders. Thus, they provide the ITSs with opportunities for organizational, operational and programmatic rejuvenation.[30] In their narrower senses they focus on collaboration among existing unions.

The Postal, Telegraph and Telephone International (PTTI), for instance, has facilitated coordination among the unions of the Canadian Northern Telecom from eight different countries. The PTTI ensured that they were widely publicized and that unions in Europe and Asia responded positively.[31] The newly merged ICEM sees itself as consciously working to create a 'progressive trade union voice' that goes beyond narrow trade-unionism, and is more responsive to regional and sectoral specificities. Motivated by the experience with the US strike against Bridgestone it is also seeking to create company networks that will allow national unions at various levels to network and coordinate across boundaries.[32]

Like the ICFTU, the Secretariats have limited resources and authority. With more resources and some supranational authority they could play a more active operational role, whether with respect to coordinating organizing or bargaining or, at the very least, establishing and maintaining networks amongst unionists. In addition, Secretariats can also play an important self-governance role at the sectoral level, complementing that of global and regional organizations. ITSs without some horizontal connections could well aggravate the ever-present potential for sectoral divisions.

Both the ICFTU and the ITSs bring together national organizations at the very top. Their organizational structures and their ideological trajectories have led them to cautious and lowest-common-denominator politics, as well as hostility to non-official activism.[33] We believe, however, that they are worth contesting, reforming and revitalizing. Given their organizational characteristics, this is most likely to come through member unions or federations.[34] Parallel to any 'official' initiatives, however, a number of activists have sought to revitalize international labour practices by building alternative communications, networks, and agendas.

The formation of the WCCs signified that labour leaders recognized the value of information and communication. But while a few workers had access to information and communications they were not participants, leading to new efforts at horizontal worker communications. The growth of the Internet has offered labour activists – in conjunction with environmentalists, human rights activists, and feminists – an important medium.[35] Currently, there are a number of networks that provide both information and opportunities for direct communications.[36]

Electronic media are an important instrument but their speed and abundance should not obscure some quite serious problems. First, the majority of the world's workers do not have access to electronic media, and communication that depends on gates can easily be controlled by gate-keepers. Second, widespread access to media does not guarantee participation and common action. In general, however, improving access to electronic and other appropriate means of communication is a key component to building and maintaining horizontal relations within labour and between workers and other movements.

One organization that has consciously sought to create horizontal networks is the Transnationals Information Exchange (TIE). Formed in 1979 with the support of non-labour groups,[37] its original aim was to provide service to workers by drawing upon a network of researchers. During most of the 1980s it operated along the lines of a service organization. By the early 1990s it had clearly recast itself as an activist organization seeking to identify, work with, and bring together activists, locals and movements. In becoming a more activist organization, it has also adopted a more explicit politics, centred around a critique of 'Toyotism' and lean production. Thus, its activities are now driven by a practical and political agenda.[38]

From its initial base in Amsterdam, and after overcoming a number of growth pains, it has expanded to a network that centres around offices in Brazil, North America, the Netherlands, Germany, Russia and Thailand. In addition to its early focus on the auto and cocoa/chocolate production industries, it has expanded to include textiles, education and telecommunications. Organizationally, the TIE can best be thought of as a tight network. The various regional components have operational autonomy but their activities are reviewed and evaluated by the whole network. In addition, the TIE's grounding in a shared theoretical approach and its commitment to building alternative cross-border networks provide the sinews that give it focus and resilience.

European labour politics

National European unions and federations have been cautious participants in the project of European integration, mostly because states and capital were unwilling to commit to a European system of industrial relations. With the institutionalization of the 'social dialogue' during the late 1980s, the European Trade Union Confederation (ETUC) has become formally engaged in European affairs.[39] Some European labour policies, such as the European Works Councils (EWC) Directive, although limited to informing and consulting workers, provide unions with the opportunity to collaborate across boundaries, and many have risen to the challenge.[40] During the recent dispute over Renault's closing of one of its Belgian plants, the ETUC and national unions cast their reaction as a violation of the Directive and argued for its broadening and deepening. The Directive has also generated an opportunity for transatlantic coordination. Because a number of US multinationals have formed EWCs, the AFL–CIO and the ETUC have decided to pursue some collaborative activities on the subject of works councils.[41]

Around the ETUC there now exists a comprehensive network of sectoral organizations. It has managed to bring together almost all of the national federations of twenty-eight European countries, bridging significant ideological or organizational preferences. Most importantly, the Confederation has facilitated the development of a European level labour agenda. Nonetheless, it still remains a weak inter-societal organization.[42] Most of its work centres around the 'social dialogue' perpetuating its dependence on the Commission and further delaying the creation of horizontal networks and deep trans-societal connections.

As a result, a number of individual European unions and groups of activists continue their efforts to establish cross-border connections. Going back to the 1980s, dock-workers have sought to establish autonomous networks while the TIE's European branches have been bringing together workers and unions at the local and subnational levels. A German and a British union formed the first transnational union in modern times.[43] Renault's decision to close its plant at Vilvoorde, Belgium, was met with wide condemnation and the first 'euro-strike',[44] defeating the company's efforts to externalize the costs of its policy onto the Belgian workers.

One final example of growing pan-European activism is the European March Against Unemployment. This series of marches was conceived in June of 1996 and converged on Amsterdam on

14 June 1997, just before the Intergovernmental Conference met there. A number of things make the event interesting. First, it involved representatives of the unemployed from a number of countries, many associated with major unions. Second, the marches were coordinated through networks, with a French organization playing the nodal role. Finally, there was a planned follow-up evaluation to prepare for further European initiatives and for the consolidation of networks.[45]

North American labour politics

The North American labour movements are nowhere close to forming an umbrella organization like the ETUC, nor is there any significant collaboration of all three national federations, except for the case of ORIT, discussed previously. There is, however, increasing collaboration among unions, locals and activists.[46] We focus on cases that involve the USA and Mexico because labour internationalism between the two is even more difficult, yet necessary, than it is between the USA and Canada.[47]

One example of such collaboration between large unions which are in the mainstream of national labour politics is the alliance of the Sindicato de Telefonistas de la Republica Mexicana (STRM) and the Communications Workers of America (CWA). In 1992 the two unions, along with the Canadian Communications, Energy, and Paperworkers Union (CEP), signed a strategic alliance. One prominent result of their collaboration has been the skilfull use of the North American Agreement on Labour Cooperation by the STRM and the CWA. As part of their overall organizing strategies, the two unions have lodged two complaints. The first was lodged by STRM on behalf of the CWA while the CWA lodged the second on behalf of the STRM. The tactic is brilliant in that few expected that such complaints would be directed against the USA. Moreover, it establishes the two unions as equal partners – an important accomplishment given the sense of superiority that permeates the attitude of many USA unions *vis-à-vis* Mexican unions.[48]

A unique example of collaboration that involves members of national federations is that between the AFL–CIO's Farm Labour Organizing Committee (FLOC) and the CTM's National Union of Farm Workers (SNTOAC).[49] Their collaboration deals with migrant farmers, traditionally among the least protected in the USA. The FLOC has been organizing farmworkers in the Midwest since 1967. Threatened with relocation of agricultural activities to Western Mexico, it moved to establish contacts with SNTOAC. This strategy was further facilitated by its joining the AFL–CIO in 1993. The two unions have utilized corporate campaigns against specific products (tomatoes and pickles) of specific companies (Campbell, Vlasic and Heinz). In organizing, they reach out to communities and in bargaining they have sought to raise the wages of Mexican farm workers.

Two independent unions that have engaged in a long-term strategic alliance are the United Electrical, Radio and Machine Workers of America (UE) and the Frente Autentico del Trabajo (FAT).[50] In 1992 they initiated a strategic organizing alliance centering around FAT's efforts to unionize *maquiladoras* in Ciudad Juarez and Ciudad Chihuahua. UE's decline in membership due to the relocation of USA companies to Mexico was a motivating factor in establishing new forms of international solidarity. During 1994, along with the Teamsters, they lodged the first two cases that highlighted limitations of the North American Agreement on Labour Cooperation. That same year, FAT assisted a UE organizing campaign in Milwaukee. These experiences have led the two unions to deepen their relationship beyond plant-based organizing and to seek alliances with other unions. One result is an organizational initiative that brings together various unions from the Echlin corporation's plants throughout North America. Another result has been a more systematic approach to worker visits, particularly by women, who constitute the main labour force in the *maquiladoras*. A third result has been the opening of the Centro de Estudios y Taller Laboral (CETLAC) in Ciudad Juarez, in collaboration with the Teamsters. The CETLAC responds to the realization that organizing should have roots in the community and will serve as a focal point for practical collaboration, including education on labour rights and the development of a pro-labour culture. Finally the two unions are sponsoring a Cross-Border Community/Labour Mural Project at the FAT's headquarters in Mexico City and one in Chicago. In short, the connections between the two organizations are becoming richer than a limited organizing drive.

Both unions are well known for their social unionism. In addition, even though small, they are both well developed and democratic organizations with some, if limited, resources. Finally the UE plays an important role within the US Labour Party and the FAT in the *Foro* group of dissident labour unions. For all of these reasons their collaboration can have a broader impact and merits the attention of progressive activists.

A third type of long-term collaboration involves networks of workers and locals. A primary example of such collaboration centres around Ford's Cuautitlan plant, near Mexico City.[51] For over fifteen years the Ford Workers' Democratic Movement has sought to form an independent union and has contested a number of elections. Throughout the years, UAW locals have established contacts with the Movement in the form of visits, material support, solidarity actions, and observation of union elections. Both the Canadian Auto Workers and the Canadian Labour Congress have also shown their strong support. In addition, the TIE/North America has facilitated the formation of a network of auto workers in North America. The automobile industry is a leading force of continental integration and the struggles at the plant exposed the undemocratic practices of the CTM, as well as the timidity of the UAW. The Ford workers' struggle provided an opportunity for creating a cross-border a network with deep roots in all three countries.

While North American labour unions have yet to formulate common agendas, cross-border collaboration has progressed well beyond exploratory meetings. It is too early to evaluate the impacts of the changes in the AFL–CIO's international department.[52] We are hopeful, however, that there will continue to be important democratic voices in North American labour politics, particularly with the increased involvement of the more democratic and militant Canadian unions, such as the Canadian Auto Workers and Steel Workers.

Conclusions: the challenges of international labour politics

Neoliberal globalization is not an opportunity for labour; it is a challenge and an incentive. Its dire and uneven impacts, along with the end of the Cold War, have led a number of unions to reconsider their strategies. More importantly, its formalization through tangible global and regional governmental organizations adds urgency and legitimacy to a global labour agenda. But, we believe, these conditions are not sufficient to produce an international labour politics but could well lead to divisions along regional blocs or sectoral lines. A proactive international labour politics must confront both external and internal challenges and must do so through practical action, inclusive politics and efficacious organizations. In conclusion, we outline ten important challenges.

1 Whatever their specific views, most unions would agree that they should at least contest politically the nature and rules of

state power at the domestic level. Now, they must also contest the rules and organization of regional and international governance. While they should not limit their strategy to lobbying IGOs, contract standards and market regulation are clearly shifting to the international level.

2 All over the world, workers are continuously pitted against each other, often in words that proffer concern for their plight. Neoliberals attack the inflexibility of labour laws, turning the unemployed and underemployed against unionized workers. Fascists and racists blame immigrants and foreigners. While these discourses breed insecurity, systems of industrial relations that put a premium on industrial peace without commensurate decision-making powers, further disempower workers and unions. In the most immediate sense, these developments are motivated by, and breed social forces that, are deeply inimical to the rights of working people.

3 Unions must frequently and critically reconsider whom they represent. Unskilled workers, some categories of white-collar workers, migrants, subordinate ethnic or racial groups, informal sector workers, women, children and older people have received little attention.[53] Not only do their large numbers make it necessary to organize them but, their special circumstances will force unions to confront issues of gender relations, xenophobia, and the very nature of work.

4 Unions are only one of many social forces maligned by predatory liberalism. Migrants, unskilled workers, retirees, women, and whole communities are also its victims, while political parties, human rights and religious groups, some state agencies, and environmentalists may object on a variety of practical and moral grounds. Labour will be well served by initiating and participating in social movement campaigns, organized around related and mutually reinforcing topics of broad appeal. Successful participation in such alliances will reinvigorate labour unions and will keep the question of social equity on the agendas of other movements.[54]

5 Participatory communications and networks are necessary and, frequently, the only desirable connections. There are often compelling reasons to avoid institutionalization. Sooner rather than later, however, international labour politics will have to confront organizational questions. Commitment to international politics will require important shifts of resources and priorities

inside national, regional, and global organizations. International confederations and jealously guarded domestic unions may be the paths of least resistance but they will also perpetuate labour's marginal international role. In our view, a multi-tiered system of directly representative and democratic organizations is a desirable, but not exhaustive, ingredient of international labour politics for both operational and self-governance reasons. While various operational and agenda building activities are better handled at different spatial and sectoral levels, umbrella organizations are necessary to temper centrifugal tendencies.

6 The evidence suggests that much pressure for international politics is coming from intra-union networks, as well as from alternative networks that bring together labour activists. Most of these activists have a vision of a labour politics that is participatory and inclusive of other social movements. Alternative networks and tendencies, therefore, are valuable, we contend, both because they may lead existing organizations to reform and because they are necessary ingredients of a vital and democratic labour movement.

7 Engaging in practical international collaboration is the necessary springboard of international labour politics. In the course of action, participants learn and create. The world political economy allows innumerable opportunities for non-redundant activities at various spatial and sectoral levels. How to find collaborators, how to establish fair and productive relations, how to move from being national to being trans-societal – these are the practical problems that groups and unions engaged in international politics must routinely face.

8 Practical action is often adequate to the task at hand. Is it adequate, however, as a response to the broad and deep priorities of neoliberalism? We believe that it is not. Cross-border collaborations require ideological and theoretical foundations that give them meaning and direction. Yet we also do not think that it is possible, or desirable, for international labour politics to be driven by a single ideology or theory. In our view, labour's most successful responses in the future will be those that are based on explicit goal-oriented agendas and common political discourse.

9 Labour agendas should be appropriate to the spatial or sectoral characteristics of the issue at hand and should facilitate cross-border and cross-movement alliances. Building such agendas

requires commitment to cross-cultural understanding and will-ingness to engage in productive negotiations. Issues that enjoy broad appeal, such as child labour, can produce deep resent-ment if they seem to be directed from one group of workers against another. If properly negotiated, however, the regulation of child labour can be a key ingredient of a global labour agenda and the foundation of fruitful alliances with other movements.

10 As neoliberal hegemony suggests, it would be wrong to deny the power of political discourse. A common discourse that will appeal to a critical mass of workers, labour activists, and acti-vists from other issue areas is a necessary precondition for identification, communication and the fruitful negotiation of ideological and practical preferences.[55] Such a discourse could centre around a 'global bill of rights' that emphasizes both in-dividual and social democracy. During the past century unions were at the forefront of the struggle for democracy at the dom-estic level. To raise the question of global democracy in the next century is a task that the labour movement can ignore only at the risk of its own historical relevance.

Acknowledgements

We would like to thank the following people for their assistance: Robin Alexander, Julio Cesar Guerrero, Eduardo Diaz, Jeffrey Harrod, Alex Hicks, Jens Huhn, Sheila Katz, Benedicto Martinez, Eric Myers, Marsha Niemeijer, Martha Ojeda, Jorge Robles, Peter Waterman.

Notes

1 Renato, Ruggiero 'The Road Ahead: International Trade Policy in the Era of the World Trade Organization', report by the Director-General of the WTO, 28 May 1996. At http://www.unicc.org:80/wto/welcome.html; wto/whats_new/press49.html (emphasis added).

2 Our use of neoliberalism is similar to what Robert Cox calls 'hyperliberalism'. See *Production, Power and World Order: Social Forces in the Making of History* (Columbia University Press, 1987), Ch.8.

3 John Logue, *Toward a Theory of Trade Union Internationalism* (Kent Popular Press, 1980).

4 Labour movements in the North do not have the answers but, because of their strategic position and history, some are very much part of the problem. While it may not revolutionize, the integration into inter-national labour politics of more politicized unions from countries such as S. Korea, the Philippines, South Africa and Brazil, will only have a positive role. For background see Iram Jacome Rodrigues, 'The CUT [Unified Workers Central of Brazil]: New Unionism at a Crossroads', *NACLA Report on the Americas*, Vol. 28, No. 6 (1995), pp. 30–4; Kim Scipes, 'Under-

standing the New Labour Movements in the 'Third World': The Emergence of Social Movement Unionism', *Critical Sociology*, Vol. 19, No. 2 (1992), pp. 81–101; Peter Waterman, *From Labor Internationalism to Global Solidarity* (Manuscript, 1997), Ch. 5.

5 The Group of Lisbon, *Limits to Competition* (MIT Press, 1995).

6 John Gerard Ruggie, 'At Home Abroad, Abroad at Home: International Liberalization and Domestic Stability in the New World Economy', *Millennium*, Vol. 24, No. 3 (1994), pp. 507–26.

7 Eric Leser, 'Les pays du G7 jugent "essentielle" une meillure surveillance des risques de marché', *Le Monde*, 2 July 1996, p. 21.

8 Ruggiero (1996), p. 1.

9 Michael Gold, 'An Overview of the Social Dimension', in Michael Gold (ed.), *The Social Dimension: Employment Policy in the European Community* (Macmillan Press, 1993), Ch. 1.

10 Ian Robinson, *North American Trade as if Democracy Mattered: What's Wrong With NAFTA and What are the Alternatives?* (Canadian Centre for Policy Alternatives and International Labour Rights Education and Research Fund, 1993).

11 For a brief overview see Kim Moody, 'Austerity Fuels Mass Strikes Around the World', *Labor Notes*, No. 217 (1997), pp. 1, 14. For current information see postings at http://www.labournet.org.uk and http://www.igc.org/labornet.

12 Philippe Lemaitre, 'Bruxelles a réuni une table ronde pour mobilizer les partenaires sociaux sur un "pacte européen pour l'emploi"' *Le Monde*, 30 April 1996, p. 2; 'Insecure or Jobless, Europeans Renew Protests', *New York Times*, national edition, 25 March 1997, p. C4.

13 For Germany see Lucas Delattre, 'Les syndicats rassemblent 250,000 personnes contre le plan gouvernemental allemand d'austérité', *Le Monde*, 10 September 1996, p. 3. On December 1995 French strikes see articles under 'La grande révolte Française contre l'Europe libérale', *Le Monde Diplomatique*, No. 502, (January 1996). On the Fall 1996 truckers' strikes see Pascal Galinter, 'Les syndicats jugent insuffisantes les concessions des transporteurs', *Le Monde*, 26 November 1996, p. 6.

14 Nicholas D. Kristoff, 'Clashes in Seoul as Strike Widens its Grip', *New York Times*, national edition, 29 December 1996, p. A10. Current postings at http://www.labournet.org.uk/

15 'La COB [Central Obrera Boliviana] quiere unidad originaria, obrera y popular', *Presencia* (Bolivia), 27 June 1996, p. 3. On recent deadly suppression of miners' strike see *NACLA*, Vol. 30, No. 5 (March/April 1997), p. 1. Calvin Sims, 'Argentina Stops for a Day as Millions Strike', *New York Times*, national edition, 28 September 1996, p. 5. New national strikes took place in August of 1997.

16 The national strike in S. Korea in early 1997 gave the KCTU a more prominent role and forced the formerly government-controlled Korean Federation of Trade Unions to support the strike. In France, the Confédération Française Democratique du Travail's (CFDT) lukewarm approach to the mobilizations of 1995 and 1996 has led a tendency within its ranks (CFDT en Lutte) to go public.

17 For Bolivia and Argentina see note no. 15. For relations between the French Confédération General du Travail and the Communist Party see Alain Beuve-Mery, 'Louis Viannet va quitter le bureau national du Parti Communiste', *Le Monde*, 19 December 1996, p. 6.

18 A number of mainstream and progressive unions have formed the *Foro* alliance to contest the hegemony of the Confederación des Trabajadores Mexicanos. For current and dependable information on Mexican labour politics see biweekly *Mexican Labor News and Analysis* at http://www.igc.apc.org/unitedelect/, a product of the collaboration between the United Electrical and Machine Workers of America (UE) and the Frente Autentico del Trabajo (FAT). The *Foro* is now a federation.

19 Long before John Sweeney's election to the presidency of the AFL–CIO in the Fall of 1995, a number of smaller AFL–CIO unions, locals, and activists had embarked upon the development of an independent labour party, whose founding convention took place in the Summer of 1996. While it is not clear what its electoral fate will be, its membership is evidence that the AFL–CIO is not ideologically monolithic. On priorities and composition of Labour Party, see http://www.igc.apc.org/lpa/program.html and /unions.htm. The AFL–CIO remains attached to the Democratic Party. For Sweeney's approach see Steven Greenhouse, 'Labor Chief Asks Business for a New "Social Compact"', *New York Times*, national edition, 7 December 1995, p. A10. Also, developments can be followed through the journals *Dissent* and *Labor Notes*.

20 'Paises ricos temen que la globalizacion de la economia agrave la desigualdad y pobreza', *La Razón* (Bolivia), 30 June 1996, p. B8. Klaus Schwab and Claude Smadja, 'Davos: mondialization et responsabilité sociale,' *Le Monde*, 17 July 1996, p. 10.

21 On international labour politics and corporate responses from the mid 1960s to the mid 1980s see: Burton Bendiner, *International Labour Affairs: The World Trade Unions and the Multinational Companies* (Clarendon Press, 1987).

22 Since 1949 there have been three global federations. The International Confederation of Free Trade Unions (ICFTU) included social-democratic and trade-unionists, and is the dominant confederation now; the World Federation of Trade Unions (WFTU) included pro-communist and radical unions and is inactive now; and the World Confederation of Labour (WCL), which originally included Christian unions but became non-denominational in 1968. For background see Jean Sagnes, 'Rivalité des organizations syndicales internationales', in Jean Sagnes (ed.), *Histoire du syndicalisme dans le monde: des origines a nos jours*, (Privat, 1994), Ch. 21; Guillaume Devin (ed.), *Syndicalisme: dimensions internationales* (Editions Européennes Erasme, 1990), part 2.

23 Sagnes, *Histoire du syndicalisme dans le monde:*, Parts 1 and 3; Devin, *Syndicalisme:*, Part 5.

24 Lance Compa, ' ... and the twain shall meet? A North–South Controversy over Labour Rights and Standards', *Labor Research Review*, No. 23 (1995), pp. 51–65; Martin Khor, 'WTO: Battle Over Labour Standards', 13 January 1997, at twn[Third World Network]@igc.apc.org/

25 'What is the Social Clause?' at http://www.icftu.org/english/sclause/escdef.html

26 'Los sindicatos recobran su espiritu de lucha', *Presencia* (Bolivia), 23 June 1996, p. 4; Alain Frachon, 'Offensive de la Confédération internationale des syndicats libres contre le "marché mondial"', *Le Monde*, 28 June 1996, p. 2; ICFTU, *Policies Adopted by the 16th World Congress of the ICFTU*, June 25 to 29, 1996, at http://www.icftu.org/

27 Canadian Labour Congress, *Social Dimensions of North American Economic Integration: Impacts on Working People and Emerging Responses*, (Ottawa, 1996), p. 74 and Appendix 3.

28 The ITSs consist of unions in the same broad sectors and are affiliated with the ICFTU. John P. Windmuller, *International Trade Secretariats: The Industrial Trade Union Internationals*, (US Department of Labor, 1995). After the unification of the International Federation of Chemical, Energy and General Workers' Unions (ICEF) and the Miners' International Union (MIF) to create the International Federation of Chemical, Energy, Mine and General Workers' Unions (ICEM) there are currently 14 Secretariats.

29 These were the International Metalworkers' Federation (IMF), the International Union of Food and Allied Workers' Associations (IUF) and the ICEF. The UAW was the union behind the WCCs. For background see Charles Levinson, *Concrete Trade Union Response to the Multinational Company: ICF's [ICEF] Emerging Countervailing Power* (ICF, 1974); H. R. Northrup and R. Rowan, *Multinational Collective Bargaining Attempts: The Record, the Cases and the Prospects*. (Industrial Research Unit, The Wharton School, University of Pennsylvania, 1981).

30 A. Banks, 'Taking on the Global Boss: An Interview with Ron Garver of the IUF [International Union of Food and Allied Workers' Associations]', *Labor Research Review*, No. 21 (1993), pp. 57–69; D. Catherine Sanchez, 'LRR Focus: Solidarity NOT Charity', *Labor Research Review*, No. 23 (1995), pp. 30–33.

31 Larry Cohen, 'Mobilizing Internationally: Global Employee Network Pressures Multinational to Reverse Anti-union Strategy', *Labor Research Review*, No. 21 (1993), pp. 47–55. Background information from Eduardo Diaz of PTTI.

32 ICEM, *Power and Counterpower: The Union Response to Global Capital* (London: Pluto Press 1996). Also, http://www.icem.org/networks/index.html

33 These issues were debated as a result of the Liverpool dockworkers' strike. The dockworkers went on strike in 1995 and utilized the Internet and existing networks of dock-workers to take their struggle international. In the course of their efforts they were at odds both with their own national union and the International Transport Workers' Federation (ITF). The disputes gave rise to an ongoing debate that involves Liverpool dockers, ITF representatives, and international activists over the merits and limitations of the ITSs' and the challenge of labour internationalism. See 'Globalization, Labour Internationalism and the Liverpool Docks Dispute', at http://www. labournet.org.uk/global.html and postings under .../docks/. For background on docker internationalism we are indebted to Peter Waterman's, *From Labor Internationalism to Global Solidarity* (Manuscript, 1997), Ch. 4.

34 We have pointed to the example with ORIT, above. Some additional examples of unions that take a very active interest in international

labour politics are the Congress of South African Trade Unions (COSATU), the Philippine Kilusang Mayo Uno (KMU) and the Danish General Worker's Union. See Waterman, *From Labor Internationalism*, Ch. 5 and http://www.global-labour-summit.sid.dk/

35 Eric Lee, *Internet and the Labor Movement: The New Internationalism* (Pluto Press 1997); Peter Waterman, *International Labor Communication by Computer: The Fifth International?* (Institute of Social Studies Working Papers Series No. 129, July 1992).

36 Examples include the LabourNet at http://www.labournet.org.uk/, the Labornet at http:/www.igc.org/labornet (both components of larger networks) and the SoliNet at http://www.solinet.org/, operated by the Canadian Union of Public Employees.

37 We are very indebted to the thesis of Marsha Niemeijer, *Grassroots Labor Internationalism: The Transnationals Information Exchange* (University of Amsterdam, August 1996). In addition, we have benefited from interviews and material provided to us by Julio Cesar Guerrero (TIE/North America) and by a background interview with Jens Huhn (TIE/Germany).

38 An important influence on the TIE was its contact with Jane Slaughter of *Labor Notes* (Detroit) and her work on lean production. TIE's development, also, owes much to earlier contacts with Brazil's CUT, South Africa's COSATU and activists within the Italian Metalworkers Federation.

39 Even before, however, the European unions had advocated regional industrial relations. See Barbara Barnouin, *The European Labour Movement and European Integration* (Frances Pinter, 1986), Ch. 1. For the role of Jacques Delors's Christian-Socialist union background in encouraging the 'social dialogue' see George Ross, *Jacques Delors and European Integration* (NY: Oxford University Press, 1995), pp. 17–18, 43.

40 European Commission, 'Agreements on Information and Consultation in European Multinationals', *Social Europe*, Supplement no. 5 (1995).

41 'AFL–CIO/ETUC: Closer Cooperation on Setting up European Works Councils in American Multinationals', at http://www.etuc.press/PR0597.htm

42 Jelle Visser and L. Ebbinghaus, 'Making the Most of Diversity? European Integration and Transnational Organization of Labor', in J. Greenwood, J. R. Grote and K. Ronit (eds), *Organized Interests in the European Community*, (Sage Publications, 1992), pp. 206–37. Also Carsten Stroby Jensen, Jorgen Steen Madsen and Jesper Due, 'A Role for a Pan-European Union Movement? Possibilities in European IR-regulation,' *Industrial Relations Journal*, 26, 1 (1995), pp. 4–18.

43 These are the IG Chemie with the British GMB general union. John Hibbs, 'British and German Unions Link', *Daily Telegraph*, 4 March 1997.

44 Patrick Smyth, 'Birth of Euro-demo a Warning to Governments', *Irish Times*, 28 March 1997.

45 For current information see http://www.labournet.org.uk/unemployed/marorg.html

46 Jeremy Brecher and Tim Costello, *Global Village or Global Pillage? Economic Reconstruction from the Bottom Up* (South End Press, 1994); Kim Moody and Mary McGinn, *Unions and Free Trade: Solidarity vs Competition* (*Labor Notes*, 1992). For an analytically informed discussions see

Ralph Armbruster, 'Cross-national Labour Organizing Strategies', *Critical Sociology*, Vol. 21, No. 2 (1995), pp. 75–89 and Thalia Kidder and Mary McGinn, 'In the wake of NAFTA: Transnational Workers Networks', *Social Policy* (Summer 1995), pp. 14–21. For current developments see *Labor Notes*.

47 For a summary of Canadian initiatives and participation see Canadian Labour Congress, *Social Dimensions of North American Integration*, Chs 5 and 6, and its periodical *The Morning NAFTA*.

48 The two cases have met with some success, partly due to the weight that the two unions carry nationally. The STRM is a member of the Congress of Labour, the umbrella organization of all Mexican labour federations and a leader of the *Foro* group of dissident unions and the CWA one of the largest unions in the AFL–CIO. Jon Pattee, 'Sprint and the Shutdown of La Conexion Familiar: A Union-hating Multinational Finds Nowhere to Run', *Labor Research Review*, No. 23 (1995), pp. 13–21. Pamela Prah, 'NAFTA: CWA Drops NAFTA Charge After Mexico Recognizes Workers' Independent Union', *Daily Labor Report*, 17 April 1997.

49 Baldemar Velasquez, 'Don't Waste Time with Politicians – Organize!' *Labor Research Review*, 23 (1995), pp. 45–9; speech to closing session of *Labor Notes* Convention (Detroit, 20 April 1997). FLOC is one of the founding members of the Labour Party.

50 FAT is a federation of unions and community organizations. On UE/FAT collaboration see R. Alexander and P. Gilmore, 'The Emergence of Cross-border Solidarity', *NACLA Report on the Americas*, Vol. 28, No. 1 (1994), pp. 42–8, 51, and Terry Davis, 'Cross-Border Organizing Comes Home: UE&FAT in Mexico and Milwaukee', *Labor Research Review*, No. 23, pp. 23–9. For current information see http://www.igc.apc.org/unitedelect/ Additional information from interview and discussion with Robin Alexander of UE and discussion with Benedicto Martinez and Jorge Robles of FAT.

51 Moody and McGinn, *Unions and Free Trade*, Ch. 8; Dan La Botz and Julio Cesar Guerrero, 'Union Democracy Movement Barred from Ballot at Ford-Mexico plant', *Labor Notes* (October 1996), p. 5. Additional information from presentation by Effren Diaz of the Ford Workers' Democratic Movement, Cuautitlan, at Labor Notes Conference, Detroit, 19 April 1997.

52 For a critical view of the AFL–CIO's foreign policies see Beth Sims, *Workers of the World Undermined: American Labor's Role in US Foreign Policy*, (South End Press, 1992); for recent developments see Frank Borgers, 'The Challenges of Economic Globalization for US Labour', *Critical Sociology*, Vol. 22. No. 2 (1996), pp. 67–88, particularly pp. 78–85.

53 Jeffrey Harrod, *Power, Production, and the Unprotected Worker* (Columbia University Press, 1987). In the USA, where the overall density has fallen, unions in the services and public sectors have grown. Walter Galenson, *The American Labor Movement, 1955–1995* (Westport, Conn.: Greenwood Press, 1996), pp. 3–4.

54 Peter Waterman, 'Social Movement Unionism: A New Model for a New World Order?', *Review*, Vol. 16, No. 3 (1993), pp. 245–78. Jeremy Brecher and Tim Costello, *Global Village or Global Pillage*, Chs 5 and 6, in particular.

55 For stimulating discussions see J. R. Cowie, *The Search for a Transnational Discourse for a North American Economy: A Critical Review of US Labor's Campaign against NAFTA (with Robinson/Cowie debate)*, Latin American Labour Occasional Paper, No. 22, Center for Labour Research and Studies, Florida International University, 1995; Craig S. Benjamin and Terisa E. Turner, 'Counterplanning from the Commons: Labour, Capital and the "New Social Movements"', *LABOUR, Capital and Society*, Vol. 25, No. 2 (1992), pp. 218–48.

11

Globalization and American Common Sense: Struggling to Make Sense of a Post-Hegemonic World

Mark Rupert

Introduction

During the postwar decades, industrial workers in the USA were incorporated into a broad 'middle class', and thereby also brought into an historic bloc which promoted the transnational hegemony of liberal capitalism while seeking to contain the putative menace of expansionist Communism. Now, as capitalism becomes more fully transnational and the Fordist class accommodation is under attack by the state and corporate capital, American industrial workers find themselves largely disempowered and under severe economic pressures. Political ideologies appropriate to an era of Fordist prosperity and Cold War certainties may now begin to appear increasingly anachronistic.

Under these circumstances, 'popular common sense' is being contested in ways which may challenge the hegemony of liberal individualism. In response to the harshness of post-Fordist global capitalism, neo-populist tendencies are arising which frighten some in the power bloc of global capitalism. This neo-populism is not a coherent or clearly defined political ideology, however. It represents a family of related interpretations of the American political tradition, some of which point toward possible worlds in which democratically-oriented progressives might feel at home, and others of which point down the path toward nationalist or racist conflict, and ultimately perhaps fascism. This chapter seeks to sketch out the main currents and tensions flowing within this neo-populism, and to interpret in terms of Gramscian categories the ongoing struggles over the meaning of globalization in 'popular common sense'.[1]

Who's afraid of Pat Buchanan?

The world's most powerful social forces are starting to get worried. Why? Their agenda of global economic openness and integration via the free flow of trade and investment has been progressively realized over half a century. In postwar decades, world trade has grown more rapidly than output, and foreign investment has expanded at least as dramatically.[2] In the early decades of this emerging global order, its architects could justify their project in terms of the manichean categories of Cold War ideology as well as the stories of generalized peace and prosperity associated with the classical liberal tradition. And indeed, American working people (or, at least, a substantial proportion of them) were integrated into a hegemonic global order through access to postwar prosperity and through the stark representations of Cold War politics.[3]

But the Cold War is over and its unambiguous political narrative no longer seems to make sense of the world in ways which are adequate to the realities of life faced by many people in the US and elsewhere. Among those realities has been a major shift in socio-political power at various scales from the local to the global. The 'historic bloc' of social forces and ideologies which formed the core of the US-centred hegemonic world order is being reconstructed.[4] Of particular concern for this paper is the expulsion of US industrial labour from its position as a relatively privileged junior partner in this global power bloc, and the corresponding shift in prevailing interpretations of liberal ideology away from a version which had endorsed more activist and growth-oriented state policies and which legitimized collective bargaining by mass industrial unions. In place of the kinder, gentler liberalism which was hegemonic during the postwar decades – which John Ruggie has famously called 'embedded liberalism' – we now find instead a hard-edged liberalism which strives to focus the violence of market forces directly upon working people through policies which emphasize public fiscal retrenchment, containment of inflation, and 'flexible labour markets' in a context of rigorous global competition. Historical structures which had institutionalized consensual power relations in the nexus between the US and the global political economy now appear less solid and stable, and out of this more visibly fluid environment may emerge new possibilities for re-imagining and reconstructing social relations on a transnational scale.[5]

Mounting evidence of long-term tendencies toward transnational production, corporate 'restructuring,' subcontracting and outsourcing, plant closings and layoffs, concessionary bargaining and union-busting, declining real wages, widening and deepening poverty, intense economic uncertainty, and real fear among average Americans has in recent years been juxtaposed to news of healthy corporate profits and happy days on Wall Street, and breathtaking inequalities of income and wealth unprecedented in postwar experience.[6] The liberal vision of a transnational order institutionalizing the values of freedom and prosperity – most firmly embedded in popular common sense during the postwar decades – may begin to seem bitterly ironic to growing numbers of working people, like a bad joke at their expense.

It is in this context that a new populism is emerging to challenge the formerly hegemonic narratives of liberal peace and prosperity. In the US, among the most visible manifestations of this populist resurgence was the surprisingly strong 1996 presidential campaign of Patrick J. Buchanan. Buchanan stunned the Republican Party with his primary election victories in Louisiana and New Hampshire, and his strong second-place showings in the rust belt states of Michigan and Wisconsin, winning more than 3 million votes overall; but the significance of his campaign cannot be summarized in terms of vote counts. At a time when the historical structures underlying postwar prosperity are visibly degenerating and ideologies of liberal internationalism appear increasingly dubious to average Americans, Buchanan delivered a militant populism to their doorstep along with their morning paper. In his columns and speeches, Buchanan focused attention on the plight of American working people and described NAFTA, GATT and globalization in terms of a narrative of elite betrayal of ordinary people. He depicted the creation of a 'New World Order' in which the profits and power of multinational corporations and giant banks would override the rights and liberties, the way of life and identity of the American 'middle class'. Buchanan's populist agenda centred around an aggressive and unapologetic economic nationalism which harkened back to the ascendant America of the late nineteenth century.[7]

The new populism stoked in the US by Pat Buchanan and company did not go unnoticed by the constellation of capitalists, state managers and intellectuals who have fostered economic globalization as part of a transnational hegemonic project. Even as Buchanan made himself a symbol of popular discontent, a flurry of critical commentaries appeared in the mainstream press bashing his policy proposals as atavistic, crude, isolationist, protectionist, and dangerous. Among these was a warning from James Bacchus, the sole American member of the World Trade Organization appeals panel, who characterized Buchananism as a threat to the system of global liberalization painstakingly constructed through postwar decades: 'It would be economic suicide to throw it all away now'.[8]

Ethan Kapstein, Director of Studies for the Council on Foreign Relations, suggests that the new populism increasingly evident across the OECD countries represents a backlash against the combination of intensified global competitive pressures and a political climate dominated by the interests of investors. The growth-oriented 'embedded liberalism' compromise has been abandoned in favour of anti-inflationary policies which effectively suppresses the real standard of living of working people while maintaining the long-term profitability of investments. Kapstein warns: 'If the post-World War II social contract with workers – of full employment and comprehensive social welfare – is to be broken, political support for the burgeoning global economy could easily collapse.' In the absence of growth-oriented and internationally coordinated measures to ease the plight of those hardest hit by the new global competition – primarily less skilled workers and middle managers – politics in the industrial countries could well take an ugly turn. 'Populists and demagogues of various stripes will find "solutions" to contemporary economic problems in protectionism and xenophobia.' Were that to occur, he suggests, the result would be a loss of the potential aggregate income made available by an extended Smithian division of labour, and the emergence of a zero-sum world in which both peace and prosperity become more difficult to realize.[9]

At the Davos World Economic Forum in 1996, which *The Economist* described as an annual meeting of '2,000 or so top businessmen, politicians and academics' from around the world, the central theme was 'sustaining globalization'. Forum organizers Klaus Schwab and Claude Smadja published an essay in the *International Herald Tribune* suggesting that the process of economic globalization 'has entered a critical phase' in which economic and political relationships, both globally and within countries, are being painfully restructured. Schwab and Smadja acknowledged that these changes are having a devastating impact on large numbers of working people in 'the industrial democracies', with heightened mass insecurity resulting in 'the rise of a new brand of populist politicians'. They feared that in the absence of effective measures to address the social circumstances of working people and the weakened ideological legitimacy of global capitalism, the new populism may continue to gain strength, threaten further progress toward the agenda of globalization, and 'test the social fabric of the democracies in an unprecedented way'. The social forces leading globalization, then, face 'the challenge of demonstrating how the new global capitalism can function to the benefit of the majority and not only for corporate managers and investors'.[10]

In these remarkable statements – by representatives of the constellation of social forces whose hegemony gave birth to long-term processes of globalization – the importance of ideological struggle and the potential threat of populism and nationalism to a sustained liberal hegemony are frankly acknowledged. It is hardly clear however, that this global ruling class is abandoning its consensus on low inflation and fiscal retrenchment, 'flexible labour markets' and free trade, all policies which magnify the impact of market forces on working people. However, expressions of popular disaffection are awakening some among the dominant bloc to the political fragility of globalization and of their continued global social power.

Critical ambiguities of the new populism

We are witnessing the long and painful demise of the Fordist sociopolitical regime through which American industrial workers were incorporated into the hegemonic bloc which constructed the postwar global order. Finding their economic security and their political identity increasingly problematic, the easy certainties of the Cold War no longer providing fixed ideological reference points, American working people are trying to make sense of a rapidly changing world. It is in this context that alternative narratives of globalization increasingly challenge the blandishments of liberal internationalists. Some of these interpretations emphasize the anti-democratic character of transnational capitalism and the need to construct populardemocratic institutions within the world economy.[11] Others view globalization as a process infused with evil intent, the product of un-American treacheries designed to undermine the Constitutional republic and its guarantees of individual rights. These latter interpretations tend to emphasize nationalism as a first line of defence against the insidious forces of globalization.[12] Such alternative visions of globalization are circulating among various segments of the US population, seeking to embed themselves in popular common sense and thus to define the horizons of political action in this period of tension and flux.

This unfolding struggle over the meaning of globalization in popular common sense, with all its tensions and possibilities, is represented in microcosm in the story of Chuck Harder and the United Broadcasting Network (UBN), referred to by the *Wall Street Journal* as 'Populist Inc.'. According to a UBN promotional bulletin, Harder has been a professional broadcaster since the 1960s. As a consumer affairs reporter, he is said to have become disillusioned with 'the "velvet hammer" of corporate media', which dampens anti-corporate messages to avoid offending advertisers. Harder left his mainstream media job in 1987, and invested his life savings to start a radio programme for 'the little guys who had no voice'.[13]

Controversially, in 1989 Harder sold a majority stake in his first venture, the Sun Radio Network, to another network controlled by the Liberty Lobby – a group which calls itself 'populist' but pushes an anti-Semitic agenda of Holocaust denial and tales of global conspiracies by stateless 'international bankers'.[14] After a brief partnership, Harder broke with Liberty Lobby and left Sun to start the People's Radio Network (PRN). Founded in 1991 with 72 stations, PRN grew to around 300 radio stations in all 50 states, as well as 77 TV stations. Writing in April, 1995, journalist Marc Cooper reported:

> More than 40,000 listeners pay a minimum of $15 a year to belong to [Harder's] *For the People* organization. For an extra $19 a year another 30,000 followers subscribe to the biweekly, full color, thirty-two-page *News Reporter* . . . From merchandise sales and memberships, People's Radio Network grossed more than $4 million in 1994.

Broadcast industry surveys showed Harder outperforming such high-profile personalities as Michael Reagan and Oliver North, some ranking him among America's top ten radio talk-show hosts.[15]

Harder's radio show represented itself in the following terms:

> *For the People* seeks to provide a forum for the average citizen to learn about consumer information and the workings of our government. Because the programme is financially supported by listeners rather than advertisers, Harder speaks without fear of corporate censorship or reprisals.

Harder said: 'Our goal is to save the middle class, save the little guy.' Harder and his guests – including such heavy hitters as Ralph Nader and Pat Buchanan – routinely excoriated corporate power and a government which they represented as unresponsive to popular needs and concerns. He and his guests have, on a variety of grounds, been sharply critical of recent trade agreements such as the General Agreement on Tariffs and Trade (GATT) and the North American Free Trade Agreement (NAFTA). During the NAFTA debate, Harder excited the interest of his listeners to such a degree that seven thousand of them bought copies of the full 2,000 page text of the NAFTA agreement which Harder made available at low cost.[16]

In May 1996, Harder's network was purchased by a consortium of investors including the United Automobile Workers (UAW). One of the most historically progressive of American industrial unions, the UAW is investing 'several million' dollars for a share of about 10 per cent in the re-named United Broadcasting Network (UBN) which, according to the *Wall Street Journal*, is 'designed to bring Mr Harder to a wider audience by upgrading technology and buying stations in major markets'. As UAW public relations chief Frank Joyce explained to me, the union views UBN as a broad-based effort to present diverse perspectives on themes important to American working people, especially preserving American jobs. The new network's chairman was economic nationalist Pat Choate, who left UBN temporarily to serve as Ross Perot's presidential running mate. The original team of commentators for UBN included such highly visible opponents of transnational corporate power as Bay Buchanan, sister and political advisor of Pat Buchanan; left-populist Jim Hightower; and, of course, Harder himself.[17]

This was intriguing to me because Harder has been characterized as a promoter of far-right conspiratorial ideologies of globalization. Revisiting Harder's brief association with Liberty Lobby, critics suggested that this might be interpreted as part of a pattern in Harder's activities. They pointed out (correctly) that Harder's radio show *For the People* has offered a receptive atmosphere for far-right organizers and militia activists such as John Trochmann, Linda Thompson, Ken Adams, and Larry Pratt, and even provided a forum for the noxious anti-Semitic conspiratorialist Eustace Mullins. Further, Harder has marketed an array of far-right conspiratorial literature to his listeners (including for a time several of Mullins' books). Critics allege that Harder has told his listeners that the Council on Foreign Relations 'controls the world' and that he routinely promotes the view that America is being led toward incorporation into the New World Order by 'New York power brokers,' 'New York bankers,' 'the global elite', suggesting that Harder speaks to his audience in the lexicon of far-right conspiratorialists.[18]

Harder maintained that he did not promote conspiracy theories or anti-Semitism.[19] And he disavowed any association with far-right armed militias: 'I have never been to a militia meeting.' I have no idea who they are. I have no idea what they do.' He claimed that his radio network presented a forum for a variety of populist voices which 'promote American core values, morality and economic nationalism' – including, for example, *both* Pat Buchanan and Ralph Nader. Critical of politicians from both major parties whom he characterized as 'puppets of the multinational corporations that have brought this country to its knees in the name of profits and globaloney', Harder described himself as 'non-partisan', 'politically neutral': 'I'm on no side. They all despise me. The left-wingers hate me. The right-wingers hate me ... It's very simple. I'm for what's right for the American people.'[20] Harder and his network, it seems to me, represented the tensions and ambiguities of the new populism, a confluence of such currents as the far-right conspiratorial ideologies of the 'Patriot' movement, the economic nationalism associated with Buchanan and Perot, as well as the more progressive and potentially cosmopolitan world-views of Naderites and unionists. It is precisely this sense that the ambiguities and tensions of popular common sense are being played out in the productions of Harder's network that led me to a closer reading of some of those materials.

Reading the new populism: *News Reporter*

Chuck Harder and Richard Osborn[21] of *For the People* made available to me the complete print run of the programme's biweekly tabloid, the *News Reporter*, which was first published in August, 1992. Most of the paper consists of articles and commentary reprinted from Knight-Ridder and other news services, but each edition also contains commentary by Harder, Osborn, and/or others associated with *For the People*. My interpretations here are based primarily upon a perusal of articles authored by Harder between August 1992 and November 1995. I read this material as an embodiment of the tensions and possibilities which have historically resided in the American populist tradition.

According to historian Michael Kazin, the primary characteristic of populist discourse in the American political tradition is its claim to speak for 'the people' – represented as citizen-producers, the social foundation of the American republic – against arrogant and malevolent elites. On this view, populism is 'a language whose speakers conceive of ordinary people as a noble assemblage not bounded narrowly by class, view their elite opponents as self-serving and undemocratic, and seek to mobilize the former against the latter'.[22] Kazin describes successive instantiations of populist language in American political history, speaking on behalf of (often white, male) farmers, craftsmen and small businessmen whose arduous labours are seen to create the material wealth of the republic. The great 'other' of these populist narratives is an aristocratic (and hence implicitly 'un-American') elite, producing nothing and living off the sweat of the average man even as they mocked his manners and mores.

American populist movements have been 'rooted in contradiction', Kazin suggests: 'they championed 'individual enterprise' or equal opportunity in the marketplace but decried the division between haves and have-nots as a perversion of democratic spirit'.[23] Thus they have on the one hand envisioned a small-town mainstreet version of capitalism as their social ideal, while, on the other, they have railed against the undemocratic social power implicit in capitalism's core structure.[24] The former position seems less likely than the latter to serve as a vehicle for the construction of a broad-based social movement encompassing the poor as well as the 'working middle class' and which might aim at the democratization of economic relations. The construction of such a movement, and of cross-border alliances with other people's movements for economic democracy, seems to me a prerequisite for effectively challenging the power of transnational corporate capital. To the extent, then, that the new populism can be reconstructed in such a way that it contributes to this agenda, I would assess its impact as potentially progressive. If, on the other hand, it scapegoats the poor as parasites on the middle class, and takes refuge in an economic nationalism which represents underpaid and underprotected workers in other countries as somehow to blame for deteriorating conditions in America, then the new populism is serving to divide rather than unite the dispossessed and its effect is to enhance still further the power of transnational capital.

In attempting to sort out the various currents of neo-populist ideology running through *For the People*, it seems to me important to ask questions such as the following. Who are 'the people' in whose name claims of injustice are being made, and who are represented as the people's oppressors? Are 'the people' understood in the fashion of a narrowly ethnocentric 'Americanism' – as, for example, the white 'middle class' burdened not only by the exploitation of super-rich bankers but also by an unproductive underclass? Or are 'the people' broadly construed as those whose life chances are constrained by pervasive social inequalities, within the US and transnationally? Is that oppression represented as being rooted in a particular socio-political order, or is it attributed to the intrinsic characteristics of malevolent individuals or groups? What kinds of political strategies seem to flow from these analyses; what kinds of possible worlds do they point toward?

Who are 'the people' addressed by Harder and *For the People*? In a statement of 'editorial and broadcast philosophy', the *News Reporter* put it like this: 'It is our simple belief that all Americans of all colors and creeds must work together to face the problems and rebuild our country and regain our previous standard of living.' Unlike racist elements of the Patriot movement who (more or less explicitly) address 'White Americans', Harder's brand of populist Americanism appears more inclusive.[25] For example, rather than drawing on the familiar racist trope which associates crime and violence with non-whites, Harder suggests a more sociological perspective in which crime is linked with poverty and desperation. Constructing prison cells for non-white citizens thus seems less important than rebuilding the productive base which supports all working Americans. This approach is also reflected in Harder's comments on the roots of the Los Angeles riots: 'Unless all people in the USA have a fair and equal chance at the American Dream, there is no way to avoid more riots of the kind that swept through Los Angeles.' Such language contrasts markedly with Pat Buchanan's view of social unrest in Los Angeles: Buchanan called for military suppression of those he characterized as a lawless 'mob'. Harder's representation suggests instead that issues of social justice uniting middle-class and poor Americans of all races are more fundamental than their differences, thus keeping open the possibility of cross-race solidarity.[26]

Harder's version of 'the people', however, does not seem to be a concept sufficiently elastic to encompass workers in the third world, who are often characterized in the *News Reporter* as 'coolies' and 'peasants', language suggesting that the labours of such unsophisticated peoples could not be worth more than some bare minimum (sub-American) wage. To the extent that American workers are brought into competition with 'coolies' and 'peasants', this seems to imply, their standard of living will inevitably suffer. Accordingly, *For the People* consistently advocates a more militant economic nationalism, urging its audience to 'fix America first' and to 'buy American'. At a minimum, this reinforces feelings of American exceptionalism and does little to encourage cross-border solidarity amongst those dominated by the growing power of multinational corporate capital. In the worst case, it could be interpreted by the racist right as validation of their view of white Americans and Europeans as genetically superior and thus entitled to a higher standard of living than the rest of the world.[27]

Similarly ambiguous are Harder's representations of the causes of popular oppression. While occasionally disavowing conspiratorialism, Harder consistently used language which lends itself quite readily to interpretations grounded in far-right conspiratorial ideology. 'The people' were seen as being oppressed by an elite whose disproportionate power is based in finance, and whose interests diverge from those of 'middle class' Americans. In a sociological sense, of course, this is hardly an outlandish or even implausible claim. Indeed, responding to published critiques which associated him with far-right conspiratorialism, Harder's language took on an analytical tone: 'Wall Street has come to dominate national policy-making in Washington, both through the way we finance our elections and the force of money in the economy. The decision-making, moreover, is highly concentrated. It is not a conspiracy theory ... but a well-documented reality.'[28] Yet, at the same time, Harder repeatedly told of an antidemocratic 'shadow government' in which 'David Rockefeller and his power group' stealthily influence government policy through such organizations as the Trilateral Commission and the Council on Foreign Relations. 'These groups serve as a "Chamber of Commerce" for the ultra-rich industrialists and the world's elite,' wrote Harder. 'Our concern is that the everyday citizen has no voice, input, or real opportunity to balance their doctrines and goals that, historically, become law and official US policy.' According to Harder, American electoral democracy is hollow insofar as 'both parties are controlled and owned by the David Rockefeller crowd – the global greedsters and world industrial overlords who love slave labour and big profits'.[29]

Rhetoric of this latter sort moves away from a more sociological perspective focusing on structured imbalances of social power and moves back toward the scapegoating of nefarious individuals or groups who are held to be ultimately responsible for the deteriorating circumstances faced by ordinary Americans. Thus in another discussion of globalization and deindustrialization, Harder asked: 'Who's doing this? The answer is the global bankers and influence peddlers.' Globalization, and the concomitant deindustrialization of America, was seen as the financial elite's deliberate policy of self-enrichment at the expense of American working people – 'the disposable victims of global corporations chasing larger profits and lower labour costs' by moving factories abroad to take advantage of 'desperate people' in impoverished countries. Free trade agreements (NAFTA and GATT) were depicted as instruments of this elite strategy: 'It's obvious to us that the bankers, who control our USA public policy via their front organizations, have implemented deals like NAFTA.' 'Good jobs in the US are exported to sweatshops where frightened, docile, unarmed peasants do exactly as they are told. This slave-labour force . . . establishes the *base line* for the economic yardstick called "global competitiveness". It is where the US is headed.' Global competitiveness may then be used by corporate employers to batter down the middle-class aspirations of American working people: 'War was silently declared on the "American Dream," as the wealth and lifestyle of the middle-class was drained and turned into profit for a select financial global elite in New York and Tokyo.' In 'corporate America's New World (fascist) Order', Harder warned his readers in language which resonates even more strongly with far-right visions of imminent enslavement, 'People in America could literally be forced to live in poverty at gunpoint in a federal police-state.' Harder cautioned, 'Don't call it a conspiracy because it was just consensus by the elite to do good business.' Yet, there was little analysis of the social conditions under which such practices could be seen as 'good business', or of social reforms which might redefine the conditions of 'good business'. Instead, echoing *The Spotlight* – the hard-core conspiricist tabloid of the anti-Semitic Liberty Lobby – Harder referred to this New World Order as the elite's 'global plantation dream'. In language which would warm the blood of any far-right 'Patriot' or armed militiaman, he condemned globalization boldly and simply as 'TREASON'.[30]

When it was announced in 1996 that German air force pilots would be stationed at Holloman Air Force Base in New Mexico for training, Harder suggested to his radio audience that this could be understood in terms of the New World Order narrative in which

the United Nations subsumes US sovereignty as part of the establishment of an elite-dominated one-world government: Harder
described the basing of foreign forces on US soil as a watershed
event, a cession of US sovereign territory, 'the first part of a global
plan by the United Nations nitwits to control the world'.[31] Harder's
tabloid, the *News Reporter*, devoted a great deal of attention to issues
preoccupying the radical right, such as the FBI killings at Ruby
Ridge, Idaho and the disastrous siege of the Branch Davidian compound outside Waco, Texas. It reprinted articles from the organ of
the conspiricist John Birch Society claiming that the federal government was constructing a 'police state' as part of a 'march toward
global tyranny' and lent its credibility to the suggestion, commonplace in far-right circles, that the Oklahoma City bombing might
have been an American version of Hitler's Reichstag fire.[32] Further,
although Harder's organization stopped selling the most bilious of
the conspiracy literature it had once advertised, as late as August
1996 *For the People* was still marketing texts which promoted an
explicitly conspiratorial vision of globalization.[33]

From formulations like these his audience might readily infer that
the solution to America's problem is to neutralize the perpetrators
who are usurping governmental power in order to subject 'the people'
to an exploitative global government. Resistance to such treason
and tyranny may require an armed and militant citizenry as the
final defence of freedom, as Harder's friendly reception of militia-
related guests seemed to imply.[34] On this view, constructing
broad-based social movements could appear less relevant than building
heavily armed bastions from which to strike against the forces of
globalization and tyranny. Despite Harder's disavowal of violence
and calls for peaceful political resolution of America's problems,
anecdotal evidence suggests that *For the People* contributed to the
environment in which far-right ideology has incubated. For example,
an officer of the Michigan Militia told the *St Louis Post-Dispatch*
that Harder's show 'gives people like me ... a chance to call in and
talk about ... the fear they have of their government ... They are
trying to destroy this country ... some of the people who are in
power ... some of the world bankers ... If they break my constitutional ... rights to come into my house, to take my weapons, yes,
I feel like I have the right to resist.' Harder is cited as an authoritative source of New World Order information on the internet bulletin
boards of the far-right, and their world wide web sites have recom-
mended *For the People* or provided links to the show's home page.[35]

Chuck Harder and the new world order

Whether or not Mr Harder sympathized with the far-right, what is important to me is the fact that his talk-radio networks have served as a vehicle for the contending counter-ideologies of globalization. In this populist stew, the Americanist anti-globalisms of Pat Buchanan, the Patriot/militia movement and Eustace Mullins were juxtaposed with the more cosmopolitan democratic ideology of Ralph Nader and Jim Hightower. In venues such as this, the worldview of neoliberal internationalism – in which states and corporations create the rules for global economic integration – is facing challenges which emphasize different aspects of popular common sense in order to envision alternative possible worlds. Drawing on the democratic strains of popular common sense, what I have called the left-progressive position would construct a world in which the global economy is explicitly politicized, corporate power is confronted by transnational coalitions of popular forces, and a framework of democratically developed standards provides social accountability for global economic actors. The antiglobalist position of the far-right, on the other hand, envisions a world in which Americans are uniquely privileged inheritors of a divinely inspired socio-political order which must at all costs be defended against external intrusions and internal subversion.

The tension between these populist positions could not be contained at UBN, as Harder almost immediately came into conflict with Choate and the network's new management. Choate's UAW-backed team quickly took editorial control of the *News Reporter* from Harder's staff and purged it of its conspiratorial themes while retaining its populist tone and economic nationalist orientation. On the air, they began to undercut some of Harder's message, and encountered dissonance from the more conspiratorially-minded segments of Harder's audience. According to the *Wall Street Journal*, Choate 'spent much of his time on-air dispelling conspiracy theories involving Whitewater, trade officials and Hillary Rodham Clinton that were put forward by the network's callers.' With tensions also building over managerial and money matters, Harder reportedly broke with the Choate team after they 'reprimanded' him for his vociferous anti-Clinton rhetoric. In September 1996 Harder was taken off the air and sent on 'extended vacation'. He then began broadcasting his populist message on a new network of some one hundred stations and hoped to rebuild his audience independent of Choate of UBN.[36]

In ideological contests such as these, the future shape of trans-national political order may be at stake. The emerging historical structure of transnational capitalism may generate the potential for the construction of political identities and projects which transcend state-centric understandings of politics and facilitate transnational movements to contest the global dominance of capital. To the extent that the ambiguities of the new populism are resolved in ways which reconstruct political identities on the basis of economic, cultural, or racial/ethnic nationalism, this potential will be undercut. If, on the other hand, this ambiguous populism can be reconstructed in ways which broaden its core understandings of 'the people' and affirm core values of popular self-determination, it could provide a necessary (but not sufficient) condition for the emergence of transnational social movements oriented toward the democratiza-tion of the world economy.

Notes

1 For Gramsci's reflections on popular 'common sense', see Antonio Gramsci, *Selections from the Prison Notebooks* (International Publishers, 1971), pp. 323–4, 419–25. My own appropriation of this concept is discussed in Mark Rupert, 'Globalization and the Reconstruction of Popular Common Sense in the US,' in S. Gill and J. H. Mittelman (eds), *Innovation and Trans-formation in International Studies* (Cambridge University Press, 1997).
2 Peter Dicken, *Global Shift*, second edition (Guilford Press, 1992), pp. 16–88.
3 Mark Rupert, *Producing Hegemony: The Politics of Mass Production and American Global Power* (Cambridge University Press, 1995).
4 'Historic bloc' is also concept of Gramscian provenance. See *Prison Note-books*, 168, 366, 377. More than a simple coalition of social forces, an historic bloc is rooted in material social relations and unites predomi-nant social forces under the umbrella of a common ideological vision. Formation of an historic bloc is thus a precondition of hegemony.
5 Rupert, *Producing Hegemony*. See also Rupert, '(Re)Politicizing the Global Economy: Liberal Common Sense and Ideological Struggle in the US NAFTA Debate', *Review of International Political Economy*, Vol. 2, No. 4 (1995), pp. 658–92.
6 Lawrence Mishel, Jared Bernstein and John Schmitt, *The State of Work-ing America, 1996–97* (M.E. Sharpe, 1997); Sarah Anderson, John Cavanagh and Jonathan Williams, 'Workers Lose, CEOs Win (II)', (Institute for Policy Studies, 1995); Dean Baker and Lawrence Mishel, 'Profits Up, Wages Down: Worker Losses Yield Big Gains for Business' (Economic Policy Institute, 1995); Edward N. Wolff, *Top Heavy: A Study of the In-creasing Inequality of Wealth in America* (Twentieth Century Fund, 1995); US Census Bureau, 'A Brief Look at Postwar US Income Inequality', *Current Population Reports* (June, 1996); New York Times, *The Downsizing of America* (Times Books, 1996).

7   Patrick Buchanan, 'Where the Real Power Resides', *Washington Times*, 8 February 1995; 'In Their Own Words: Patrick Buchanan', *New York Times*, 8 March 1996; See also the following statements by Patrick Buchanan, obtained from the Buchanan for President web site (http://www.-buchanan.org): 'The Rise of Sovereignty Fears', 1994; 'An American Economy for Americans', 1995; Announcement Speech, Manchester, NH, March 20, 1995. For more on Buchanan's right-populist rhetoric, see Mark Rupert, 'Contesting Hegemony: Americanism and Far-Right Ideologies of Globalization', in Kurt Burch *et al.* (eds), *International Political Economy Yearbook* (Lynne Rienner, 1997).

8   James Bacchus quoted in Jon Nordheimer, 'Buchanan Threatens Longtime Bipartisan Policy, Official Warns', *New York Times*, 25 February 1996. See also Milton Friedman, 'Hong Kong vs. Buchanan', *Wall Street Journal*, 7 March 1996; Robert Hormats, 'The High Price of Economic Isolationism', *Washington Post National Weekly Edition*, 18–24 March 1996.

9   Ethan Kapstein, 'Workers and the World Economy', *Foreign Affairs*, May/June, 1996, pp. 16–17.

10   *The Economist*, 'Off-Piste in Davos', 10 February 1996; Klaus Schwab and Claude Smadja 'Start Taking the Backlash Against Globalization Seriously', *International Herald Tribune*, 1 February 1996.

11   Jon Cavanagh *et al.*, *Trading Freedom: How Free Trade Affects Our Lives, Work and Environment* (Institute for Food and Development Policy, 1992); Ralph Nader *et al.*, *The Case Against Free Trade: GATT, NAFTA, and the Globalization of Corporate Power* (Earth Island Press, 1993); Jeremy Brecher and Tim Costello, *Global Village or Global Pillage: Economic Reconstruction from the Bottom Up* (South End Press, 1994). For more on this line of thinking, see Rupert, '(Re)Politicizing the Global Economy'.

12   Rupert, 'Contesting Hegemony'.

13   Bob Davis, 'Bashing Big Business Becomes a Business for Talk-Show Host', *Wall Street Journal*, 16 May 1996. UBN promotional bulletin retrieved from the world wide web at http://ww2.audionet.com/pub/ubn/harder.htm

14   Chuck Harder, 'Trials and Tribulations at the Telford Hotel: A brief history of *For the People* and the Telford Hotel', *News Reporter*, 21 February 1994; Marc Cooper, 'Cooper Replies [to Mullins and Harder]', *The Nation*, 5 June 1995; Davis, 'Bashing Big Business'. For more on Liberty Lobby and anti-Semitic ideologies of transnational conspiracy, see Rupert, 'Contesting Hegemony'.

15   Marc Cooper, 'The Paranoid Style', *The Nation*, 10 April 1995, 488; Robin DeRosa, 'Tuning In to High-Wattage Talk Show Hosts', *USA Today*, 1 February 1995; Davis, 'Bashing Big Business'.

16   Harder quoted in UBN promotional bulletin, http://ww2.audionet.com/pub/ubn/harder.htm; and Cooper, 'Paranoid Style', 488. On sales of NAFTA texts, see Davis, 'Bashing Big Business'.

17   Davis, 'Bashing Big Business'; telephone interview with Frank Joyce, UAW, 24 May 1996; Sharolyn Rosier, "Workers' voices on the air" *AFL–CIO News*, 7 June 1996; Brooke Gladstone, 'New Radio Network to Offer Full Diet of Populist Fare', National Public Radio, *Morning Edition*, 17 May 1996 (transcript no. 1870–11); Donald Baker, 'Perot Chooses Economist to Fill Reform Party Ticket', *Washington Post*, 10 September 1996.

18 The phrase 'New World Order' carries special significance in far-right ideologies. It is understood to imply a 'one-world government' dominated by super-rich 'international bankers' and their creatures (e.g. the Council on Foreign Relations, Trilateral Commission, United Nations, etc.) who will use their secretive transnational power to escape the political limits of a Constitutional Republic and to exploit the resources and peoples of the world. In this emerging 'global plantation,' the rights and liberties of average Americans, their standard of living and their national identity will all be lost irrevocably. In one of the most directly anti-Semitic versions of this conspiratorial worldview, Eustace Mullins calls for the elimination of those he characterizes as cosmopolitan conspirators biologically predisposed toward social parasitism: Mullins, *The World Order: Our Secret Rulers*, second edition (Ezra Pound Institute of Civilization, 1992), pp. 286–97. For more on the ideology of the New World Order, see Rupert, 'Contesting Hegemony'. For Harder's critics, see Cooper, 'Paranoid Style', and Davis, 'Bashing Big Business'.

19 Arthur Teitelbaum, of the Miami office of the Anti-Defamation League, told the *Wall Street Journal* that his office had not 'seen anything that would cause us to label Chuck Harder as an anti-Semite': quoted in Davis, 'Bashing Big Business'.

20 Chuck Harder, 'Reply', *The Nation*, 5 June 1995; also Harder as quoted in Monica Davey, 'A Big Voice', *St Petersburg Times*, 9 June 1996; Cooper, 'Paranoid Style'; and DeRosa, 'Tuning In'.

21 Osborn is a political commentator and associate of Harder's who has appeared frequently on *For the People* and has edited and written for the *News Reporter*. I would like to acknowledge his willingness to speak to me repeatedly and at length about his worldview and the role of the network, and his assistance in acquiring relevant materials.

22 Michael Kazin, *The Populist Persuasion* (Basic Books, 1995), p. 1.

23 Kazin, *Populist Persuasion*, p. 17.

24 On capitalism's anti-democratic separation of politics from economics, see Paul Thomas, *Alien Politics* (Routledge, 1994); and Ellen Meiksins Wood, *Democracy Against Capitalism* (Cambridge University Press, 1995).

25 For more on white supremicist and anti-Semitic ideologies of globalization, see Rupert, 'Contesting Hegemony'.

26 Harder writing in the *News Reporter*, 10 May 1992; 13 December 1993; 19 October 1992. Compare text of Patrick J. Buchanan's Speech to the Republican National Convention, Dallas, Texas, 1992, reproduced at Buchanan for President web site: http://www.buchanan.org

27 See Rupert, 'Contesting Hegemony'.

28 Harder in *News Reporter*, 8 May 1995; see also Harder, 'Reply'.

29 Harder in *News Reporter*, 11 July 1994; and 31 August 1995.

30 Harder in *News Reporter*, 19 October 1992; 19 July 1995; 13 December 1993; 20 September 1993; 19 June 1995; 8 May 1995; 2 November 1992. See also Scott McLemee, 'Spotlight on the Liberty Lobby', *Covert Action Quarterly* (Fall 1994); and *The Spotlight, Special NAFTA Issue: The Global Plantation* (17 May 1993).

31 Harder quoted in John Mintz, 'Air Force–German Alliance Draws Right-Wing Flak', *Washington Post*, 28 May 1996.

32 *News Reporter*, 24 January, 7 February 1994; and 17 July 1995.

33 In August 1996, I contacted the *For the People* bookstore and was told that Mullins' anti-Semitic tracts were no longer available for purchase, nor were a range of other hardcore conspiracy titles previously advertised through the *News Reporter*. They were, however, selling what might be considered softer conspiracy texts, such as James Perloff, *The Shadows of Power: The Council on Foreign Relations and the American Decline* (Western Islands Publishers, 1988), and James Wardner, *The Planned Destruction of America* (Longwood Communications, 1994).

34 In fairness, however, I must note that when I raised this issue with a representative of *For the People*, Harder responded by directly and explicitly disavowing violence by armed militias while on the air (*For the People* programme tape in my possession).

35 Quoted in William H. Freivogel, 'Talking Tough; On 300 Radio Stations, Chuck Harder's Show Airs Conspiracy Theories', *St Louis Post-Dispatch*, 10 May 1995; see also Peter S. Goodman, 'Mistrustful Share Their Ideas On-Line', *Anchorage Daily News*, 27 April 1995.

36 'No-Talk Radio', *Wall Street Journal*, 6 September 1996; Gail DeGeorge, 'For Pat Choate, Talk Radio Turns to Static', *Business Week*, 4 November 1996; quoted passage from Bob Davis, 'Perot Picks Choate . . .' *Wall Street Journal*, 11 September 1996. Issues of UBN's renamed *National News Reporter* in my possession.

12
Globalization and Emancipation: From Local Empowerment to Global Reform

Jan Nederveen Pieterse

These are dramatic times. We have entered the era of global politics but have grown up in an age of national politics. Globalization generates anxiety because it places people within the reach of forces that are or seem to be outside the range of conventional forms of political control. Along with the sense of powerlessness comes the cognitive and emotional anxiety of conventional frames of reference losing their relevance, without new imaginaries hospitable and welcoming enough being available. Political conventions, analytical frameworks, mental habits and imaginaries are all under pressure.

This reflection seeks to develop two arguments on globalization and politics. The first line of argument is that it is necessary to move from opposition to proposition. Second, the 'new localism' – one of the reactions to and expressions of globalization – can be taken either in an inward-looking or an outward-looking sense; the present argument is for an outward-looking localism, in which local empowerment connects with efforts towards democratization and reform at wider levels of governance. The key argument is that what is needed is to build bridges and strengthen existing bridges between local empowerment and global reform. This reflection discusses combined and uneven globalization, reviews the politics of resistance and civil society networking, looks back at the earlier arena of empire and emancipation, and asks what form emancipations are now taking and could take in the twenty-first century.

Uneven globalization

Globalization refers to a world-wide reach, which may be virtual or actual, but not to an even global spread of gain and loss. Globalization is frequently characterized as 'truncated globalization' concentrated in the triad of Western Europe, North America and Japan. 'Triadization' is another commonly used term. Globalization refers to a new distribution of power, in which it interacts with other trends, of informalization, informatization and flexibilization.

While the development gap between the advanced economies and newly industrialized economies has narrowed, the gap between these and most developing countries is widening. This reflects a partial reversal of an earlier trend of gradual integration of developing countries in the international division of labour. With regard to trade, international capital flows and foreign direct investment, there has been a marked downturn in the participation in the world economy by developing countries since the beginning of the 1980s. Thus, in 1980 the share of world trade of manufactured goods of the 102 poorest countries of the world was 7.9 per cent of world exports and 9 per cent of imports; ten years later these shares fell to 1.4 per cent and 4.9 per cent respectively.[1] Figures for international capital flows and inter-firm cooperation confirm this trend of concentration or reconcentration with the Triad zone. 'In other words, the world economy has been characterized in the last twenty years at least by a gradual *reduction* of the exchanges between the richest and fast-growing countries of North America, Western Europe and Pacific/Asia and the rest of the world – Africa in particular'.[2]

Western societies that have experienced the 'magic of the market place' are referred to as two-thirds societies. We could now speak of a one-third world society considering that the majority of humanity is excluded from life in the global fast lane. The pattern of exclusion, however, no longer runs simply North–South: 'Tiny segments of poor-country populations are integrated into the world economy network, while rich countries are generating their own internal Third Worlds'.[3] The middle class in developing countries participates in the global circuits of advertising, brand name consumerism and high tech services, which, at another end of the circuitry, increasingly exclude the underclass in advanced economies.

The available analytical instruments derive from another world order and seem too blunt to accurately map the new dispensation. For instance, according to Mittelman, 'The foremost contradiction of our time is the conflict between the zones of humanity integrated in the global division of labor and those excluded from it'.[4] This kind of diagnosis lacks precision. 'Contradiction', and the idea of a rank order of contradictions, is familiar neomarxist terminology with reductionist implications (not all forms of exclusion can be meaningfully characterized in terms of contradiction); focusing solely on the international division of labour, while crucial, is likewise reductive; exclusion is not quite accurate, nor does it necessarily translate into 'conflict'. The term exclusion ignores the many ways in which developing countries are *included* in global processes: they are subject to global financial discipline (as in structural adjustment and interest payments, resulting in net capital outflows) and part of global markets (resource flows, distribution networks, diaspora and niche markets), global ecology, international politics, global communications, science and technology, international development cooperation, transnational civil society, international migration, travel, and crime networks. For instance, the public health sector in many African countries is increasingly being internationalized. Thus, it would be more accurate to speak of *asymmetrical inclusion* or hierarchical integration. A classic term for this situation used to be 'combined and uneven development', but now one of the differences is that the units are no longer nations. It is this new pattern of uneven inclusion that generates anxiety and frustration. The disjuncture between global dynamics and existing political infrastructures and intellectual frames generates malaise bordering on Angst and in the process inspires resistance and protest that are seeking effective political forms.

Politics of resistance

Most social science conferences these days address globalization and when it comes to politics 'resistance' is a favourite. A recent conference featured a session on 'People's responses to globalization'. In effect this reduces globalization to corporate globalization and apparently situates people not as participants and agents but as passive bystanders of globalization. What about people as consumers, producers, distributors of transnational commodities and services, as travellers, migrants, participants in transnational communication, international organizations, social movements? If one has first taken people out of globalization, it may be a little difficult and somewhat of a detour to put them back in.

Resistance is not a particularly enabling position, analytically or politically. From resistance there are not many places to go to other than 'anti-globalization'. This points to the option of delinking, the exit option. In some versions of dependency theory, delinking from world capitalism used to be advocated as a radical way out. It may be characterized as the shortest way to Albania.[5] The irony is that delinking as a voluntary exit strategy has now made place for involuntary exclusion. According to one account: 'De-linking is a process through which some countries and regions are gradually losing their connections with the most economically developed and growing countries and regions of the world . . . De-linking concerns almost all countries of Africa, most parts of Latin America and Asia (with the exception of countries from South-East Asia) as well as parts of the former Soviet Union and Eastern Europe.'[6] Thus the very term has changed meaning: from an act of defiance it has become a seal of exclusion. Not that this irony itself is new. The lack of interest of multinational corporations to invest in developing countries was noted already back in the 1960s when it was pointed out that the problem was not merely exploitation by international capital but also *not* being exploited by international capital.

Now what some recommend in relation to globalization is *localism*. This may be where anti-globalization, anti-development, anti-modernity, anti-science, only-small-is-beautiful come together in an 'island' politics – seeking liberated zones 'outside the system', enclaves that provide shelter from the storm, usually in the hope that the system will somehow atrophy or collapse.[7] By implication this is of course the 'crisis of capitalism' thesis revisited, now inspired by ecological dread, apocalyptic risk, and reanimated under the heading of localism or post-development. If the 'gospel of crisis' has paralysed and crippled the left and progressive forces for 150 years (since 1848), why not carry on for another 100 or so?

This is reminiscent of an old choice: drop out or change the system. The step from local struggle to juggernaut reform is not an easy one to take, but globalization presents problems that point beyond the politics of resistance, protest and local struggles to wider horizons. If this premise is accepted it raises questions such as, how can the 'weapons of the weak' become tools of transformation? How can local 'everyday forms of resistance' be integrated in a politics of emancipation? The hiatus that now runs through struggles over resources, niches and futures virtually the world over is the step from resistance to emancipation, from local empowerment to wider engagement. Bridging this gap involves several elements. One is the step from critique to construction. Thus, in post-apartheid South Africa the habitus of activists on the ground had to adjust from struggle to transformation, from opposition to proposition. Another is the step from local to wider horizons. Several such bridges exist or are in construction.

Civil society regionalism

From Africa to the Americas and Asia, local peasant and urban social movements combine in various wider initiatives. Building regional civil society is a theme that runs through many fields of action, often as a stepping stone to wider links. In Pacific Asia it is a matter of combining 'democracy on the spot' with 'transborder participatory democracy'.[8] In Africa democracy often serves as an ideology of domination. 'The only realistic option for reducing corruption, making political systems more responsive, and bettering the lot of the poor', according to Fantu Cheru, 'is to democratize both democracy and capitalism'.[9] Along the way there are several problems: analytical, political, organizational.

A major trend in activist programmes is resistance to arrangements that free trade and capital movement across national borders. Civil society links connect Zapatistas in Chiapas with labour and community activists in the United States and Canada who oppose the free trade regime of NAFTA. In Pacific Asia civil society mobilization focuses on APEC and other market driven hegemonies invading and pervading Asia and the Pacific Basin. With respect to social movements in rural Africa, Cheru notes,

> A comprehensive development alternative cannot go far enough without a basic change in political structures. . . . This implies that the popular sector must have another political agenda over and above its main business of disempowering centralized structures. In other words, it has to come up with a state agenda of its own. . . . Here lies precisely the dilemma of non governmental and people's organizations. By nature their main concern is social politics – in other words, self-governance whose success is measured mainly in terms of the circles or poles of popular power that they create at the base.[10]

For people's organizations and NGOs this leads to problems of their identity getting blurred and confused, to state substitution and parallelism (NGOs/POs setting up bureaucracies and laying claim to territorial jurisdiction) and clientelism. Similar dilemmas arise in parts of Asia and Latin America. It represents as it were the failure of the success of civil society activism. Civil society empowerment comes to a point where either it pursues the path of local autonomy, a path of de facto state substitution, or it accepts being a player in a pluralistic field, side by side with the state and market forces. Cooperation with the state is increasingly accepted in principle; a strong civil society and strong state go together,[11] although in practice it may come at a price of depoliticization. Cooperation with business is often more difficult to conceive and achieve.

When a government lumbers from crisis to crisis, without a policy direction, people shrug their shoulders and call it crisis management. When international NGOs behave in the same way it is regarded as normal. Yet the very growth and scope of civil society networks prompt the question, what lies beyond the politics of resistance? What *forward* programmes inform activist networks? A critique of NICs is a common line of thinking but this is only a critical position. There are more forward propositions but they tend to be of limited scope. Thus, in Africa, elements of an alternative approach include recognizing informal economies, building regional civil society, accommodating peasant resistance to cash crop production, peasant knowledge, facilitating peasant institutional capacity building, and developing a pro-peasant economic policy, including land reform, in the framework of self-reliant development.[12] Forward programmes may take the form of a national alternative development design, as in Walden Bello's programme for equitable and sustainable growth in the Philippines.[13] It may involve attempts to transform corporate driven regionalism into a social and popular regionalism, or the invocation of an alternative principle of organization, such as Muto's 'taking back the economy'[14] through people's accumulation at grassroots level, or Xavier Gorostiaga's 'logic of the majority'.

Are these propositions viable? In scope and comprehensiveness do they add up to an alternative that has the potential to generate a hegemony, 'a shared sense of reality'? A limitation of several programmes is their character of 'third sector' politics, a politics of people, community or civil society. In order to transcend the local struggle and protest mode, however, what would be required is a multi-sector politics, i.e. an outlook and programme broad and attractive enough to accommodate government and business sectors as well. What else would 'democratizing capitalism' be about if not about exploring social market options? In civil society activism, the *social* agenda is usually clear: it concerns questions such as equity, participation, empowerment; the *political* agenda is also clear: it is about democratization, decentralization, de bureaucratization, human rights, citizenship rights, pluralism. What is usually much less clear and less developed is the *economic* agenda. Or, what is on offer under this rubric is the social economy, the cooperative sector, people-to-people trade, fair trade, socially responsible business, eco-business. The problem is that by and large this is a 'Mondragon' type of programme. How many Mondragons are there, what is the scope for the replication of Mondragons, and how real is the Mondragon alternative in the first place? What is missing is an *overall* enabling economic analytic and agenda, rather than an island approach *within* the sphere of economics. Weak links between 'old' (labour) and new social movements (women, identity, community, human rights, ecological movements) are one of the expressions of the relative weakness of economic programmes in civil society activism. The deeper problematic of course is the perplexity of neomarxism upon the collapse of existing socialism. What has been gained, in the meantime, is a cultural turn and epistemological reflexivity; what is missing, in adequate profile, is an alternative political economy.

Often the basis on which social movements mobilize is threat, and hence the project is to erect barricades against inroads into local or national moral economies. In a worst case scenario, it is a matter of uniting the losers in social and economic development, those left with the short end of the stick. Beyond the short term, what would be the outlook for the sustainability and growth of congregations of losers? First, the losers tend to quarrel among themselves indefinitely, preoccupied with conflicts over resource niches and survival politics, and divided along gender, regional, ethnic, religious or ideological lines. Second, they are bound to the winners by multiple strings of clientelism. Third, they are often perceived as irrelevant other than as a minor local nuisance because usually they hardly count in terms of numbers and still less in terms of political proposition, for their concerns tend to be backward and inward looking. If this sounds familiar, it is in many respects a replay of anti-capitalist struggles, but now under vastly different circumstances.

In order to step out of this cul de sac, it would be important to transform loser programmes (defensive, reactive, backward, inward-looking) into winning programmes (forward, proactive, outward-looking). The second step would be to combine – at least in terms of political vision and in organizational terms to the extent that it makes practical political sense – initiatives toward local empowerment and national reform with global reform.

What is missing in this equation so far is a middle ground that intellectually, politically, institutionally bridges the span between local struggles and global reform, between local alternatives and global constraints. Anti-development thinking militantly repudiates the possibility of such a middle ground, and alternative development thinking, while ambivalent on the desirability of such connections, fails to adequately deliver them.[15]

One such middle ground is the human development approach. The importance of human development is that it connects the 'soft' social agenda with 'hard' economic interests. In a brief time span, since 1990 when UNDP published the first Human Development Report, human development has become the major policy orientation and significant intellectual synthesis in development thinking. Unlike alternative development which has found little institutional support except in local niches and among NGOs,[16] human development has found institutional backing in UN and World Bank circles and developing country ministries, to the point of changing the mainstream understanding of development. The human development approach seeks to span the development spectrum from human-scale local development to structural reform.[17] A limitation of human development is that, at its narrowest, it is a human capital strategy of the state supplying the market with packaged human skills. In that human development is in principle concerned with *individual* capacitation its roots are in liberalism and neoclassical economics. The Human Development Index measures individual life expectancy, education and income, aggregated on country basis. Human capital is a vital nexus between equity and growth – a site where social interest and corporate interest meet and can be mediated by government authorities. Education, health and housing policies thus become not merely welfare provisions but supply-side inputs into productivity.

This, however, is not the only place where social and corporate agendas meet. Social capital, in denominations such as institutional densities and civic participatory society, is equally important. This concerns the question of the social and political embeddedness of markets, which is explored in sociology of economics, associative economics and in the extensive literature on local economic development and industrial districts, although it has much wider ramifications, for instance with regard to democracy. Like human capital, social capital can be a meeting place of social and corporate interests, the basis for a social market approach. Further along the road, the human development approach may be opened up and extended in a social framework: not in the sense of social welfare but social development; and not as tidying up after the market but in the substantive sense of rethinking what markets are in the first place.[18]

Empire and emancipation

In order to make explicit what is distinctive about the present arena of globalization and emancipation it may be worth looking back at the past arena of empire and emancipation. Empire (colonialism, imperialism, new imperialism) was fundamentally *political* in that it was driven and orchestrated by states; it was *centred* in that by and large it was directed from the imperial metropoles; and *territorial* in that it was framed by geopolitical and strategic objectives. This is not to say that other elements – economic, cultural, local – did not come in but they generally had to pass through the nodes of state-centred decision making and geopolitical ambition. With regard to the new imperialism of the late-nineteenth century a 'pericentric' theory could make sense because the impetus of empire building was territorial, pre-emptive, competitive. Imperial grandeur, *mission civilisatrice*, prestige and white man's burden, clothed imperial statism in cultural garments.

On the global canvas, the great emancipation movements at the time were those of the working class, women, oppressed minorities, and the colonized peoples. These gave rise to a momentum of democratization, social reform, political revolution and decolonization, which at times resulted in a confluence of anti-capitalist and anti-imperial struggles. Several of these logics continued to be in operation in the bipolar world of the Cold War. Geography mattered in 'spheres of influence', and so did politics and ideology, affecting the way states aligned themselves in relation to the rival hegemonic systems of Washington and Moscow. The confluence of the Vietnam War, the civil rights movement and May 1968 was a conjunction of multiple struggles. There are now attempts to rebuild the anti-capitalist and anti-imperialist coalition, but given fundamentally different circumstances this makes the impression of radical nostalgia politics.

Empire and emancipation have been part of a globalizing momentum and stages in the historical trend of globalization, but there are marked differences between imperialism and globalization. Contemporary globalization – if for now we focus on economic globalization because it is in the forefront of contemporary globalization – is *firm-centred* rather than state-centered, which in effect means it is *decentred*; and *deterritorialized* in that it takes place in virtual space as much as in actual places. The hyperspace of international finance and 24-hour electronic trading, the 'virtual company' as a combine of shifting corporate elements, financial links and supply lines, are cases in point. There are multiple nodes of power to contemporary globalization such as G7, WTO, the Bretton Woods institutions and Washington as superpower headquarters, but all of these are wired in turn to other nodes of power and influence such as the international banking world, major corporations, international institutions, regional bodies as well as transnational civil society organizations.

The general imagery of emancipation has been that of outsiders who want in and the underprivileged who seek transformation. Among the emancipatory movements have been, more or less successively, the bourgeoisie, Catholics, Jews, the working class, women, slaves, minorities, colonized peoples, dependent countries – all have supplied discourses and images of emancipation, discourses of revolution or reform. The overall character of emancipation has not changed; emancipation may be defined as collective actions that seek to level and disperse power and install more inclusive values than the prevailing ones.[19] But the forms and methods of emancipation have largely developed in national political frameworks. Colonized peoples confronted an international opponent, but their typical forms of organization have also been national.

A related question is the relationship between emancipation and regulation. Regulation is a necessary element if we view emancipation not merely as protest but as transformation. According to Boaventura de Sousa Santos, modernity is based on the two pillars of regulation (constituted by the principles of the state, market and community) and emancipation (constituted by the logics of aesthetic–expressive rationality, cognitive–instrumental rationality and moral–practical rationality). In his view, the 'collapse of emancipation into regulation symbolizes the exhaustion of the paradigm of modernity; but at the same time it also signals the emergence of a new paradigm.'[20] This perspective (in an otherwise innovative book) troubles me. It escapes me why emancipation should be grounded in rationality – isn't that just an old Enlightenment habit? More important, as I see it emancipation and regulation have all along been connected, in the sense that successful emancipation struggle translates into forms of institutional regulation that are more socially inclusive than the earlier ones. Thus, yesterday's emancipation struggle if successful yields today's regulation and tomorrow's legislation and institutionalization. This should not be a cause for regret, nor need it occasion a new paradigm, it is rather the general, and on the whole desirable, course of affairs: over time social struggles may or tend to generate more inclusive political arrangements. It is only the very pure who bemoan this as 'the standardization of dissent'.

Recent discussions of emancipation have concentrated on the question of articulation among social movements and concerns: articulation among new social movements, and between old and new social movements, towards a rainbow coalition politics, a politics of difference, an emancipatory pluralism, largely within local or national settings. The problem raised here is a different one. It concerns the articulation of emancipatory movements across different *levels*, across different contexts – local, national, regional, global, North and South. Presently there is a political gap from the local to the global which is only partially being filled by the stretch from local networks to planetary social movements, international NGOs or global civil society. This is not merely an institutional hiatus but as much a programmatic hiatus and a *hiatus of political imagination*. Beyond transforming loser positions into winning programmes (which involves coming to terms with the ideology and psychology of 'winning'), the second general strategy consideration is combining local empowerment and global reform.

Global reform

The question of global reform involves several elements: the need for global reform, the agenda, and the modes of implementation of reform; elements which are only briefly addressed here, by way of evocation rather than discussion.

First, as regards the need for global reform, contemporary

globalization narrows the scope for local and national institutional regulation. The bottom line is that firms who can obtain better terms and opportunities elsewhere can boycott local or national social compromises. Social and ecological dumping indicate the limits to local or national reform. Low bidder localities offering the lowest regulations and the highest return on investment, win out in the global circuit, witness the appeal of minimum-regulation off-shore and cross-border locations. Without foreign investment nations eventually wither for lack of growth, jobs, technology, innovation, financial flows. The familiar outcome is the dynamic of downward convergence, the 'race to the bottom': the generally downward trend of corporate taxes along with the upward trend of government incentives, restrictions on labour rights, social cutbacks, and the failure to set or enforce adequate environmental standards.[21]

The overall trend of growing capital mobility is tempered and modified by the 'new localism', the trend toward relocalization, with firms seeking proximity to markets, high-skilled labour, suppliers, and competitors. This counter-trend of 'flexible specialization', however, tends to be mainly concentrated in industrial districts and technopoles in the Triad zone or in growth sites within NIEs. Relocalization is a winning option that is delimited by the high entry threshold of infrastructure, human and social capital densities; by definition it is available only to few 'top locations' and in the process drains resources away from the others that are left out. Thus it is another island strategy – in this case, a winner strategy – that does not alter overall economic trends.

The need for global reform follows from the transition from national capitalism to global capitalism. In the framework of national capitalism labour and capital could be disciplined and regulated because of the interdependence of capital and state. The national economy setting provided a nexus between enterprise accumulation and national accumulation, reinvestment, human resource development, taxation. Fordism has been one expression of this relationship; Japanese 'corporate paternalism' is another. Regional regulation, as in the case of the European Union, is no safeguard against social dumping, witness the way Britain, which did not sign the EU Social Charter, has been attracting foreign investment.

In global capitalism there is still ample interdependence between capital and state, but now with a view to achieving global competitiveness. With the emergence of globally wired firms the nexus between enterprise accumulation and national accumulation becomes contingent. New wealth is increasingly being generated – for instance in finance and telecommunications – across borders and outside the control of states. In the process the nexus between profits and taxation becomes tenuous, which feeds the fiscal crisis of government authorities, and in turn leads to declining levels of spending on human investment and receding levels of civic trust, which eventually not only erode demand (the Keynesian connection) but also the supply-side of production.

A common historical pattern has been for politics to lag behind innovation, for technological change and enterprise innovation to proceed ahead of social and political regulation. This is not new; what is new is the scale on which this is unfolding, which is global, and the speed of innovation, which is telescoping. National capitalism could evolve social compacts clustered around the national economy; now it is a matter of developing social compacts around the global economy. The only way for localities, nations, regions *not* to be outflanked by the merciless economics of global competitiveness is by changing the rules of the global game itself. Since local, national and regional reform is ultimately checkmated and since what is at issue are processes of a global scope, what is called for is global governance. Increasingly in current realities no authority less than global level authority can issue effective regulation, that is regulation which is not neutralised and outmanoeuvred by corporate exit options. Thus we have effectively entered the epoch of global politics.

Global reform in this context is not viewed as coming *instead* of local, national and regional regulation; rather it plays a dual complementary role. On the one hand, global reform serves as a necessary condition which enables local, national reform, by establishing a global framework for their possible efficacy; and on the other, it is only feasible and conceivable as emerging from and carried by local, national and regional reforms as building blocks toward global reform. In other words, this involves a double movement, from local reform upward and from global reform downward. The idea, at the end of the road, is not a global megastate, but rather a global managed pluralism, in which each level of governance, from the local to the global, plays a contributing part.

It is not that the world economy is presently unregulated. Also casinos have rules. The 1980s wave of national deregulation has installed a global institutional environment of minimal controls. Through the 'Washington consensus', the IMF and World Bank,

WTO, and regional formations such as NAFTA and APEC, the neoliberal regime is gradually being extended. What is at issue is replacing neoliberal regulation with global governance on the basis of a reform programme that reflects broader political and social interests.

Present times are often compared to the nineteenth-century transition of industrialization and laissez-faire capitalism, as a second 'Great Transformation', now on a world scale. Ian Robinson introduces the notion of social democratic globalization. His concern is 'to demonstrate to democratic publics that the neoliberal form of globalization is not natural, inevitable, or desirable. Success in this regard will undercut the hegemony that neoliberal ideas currently enjoy. Putting a simple, yet radical alternative form of globalization on the political agenda weakens the standard argument – "there is no alternative".'[22]

With regard to an agenda of global reform, this may involve, in brief, with respect to the world economy, restrictions on international financial transactions in the form of a Tobin tax to inhibit speculation, and other forms of taxation; it may involve formulating a global development agenda and establishing a world development institution, possibly a combination of international financial and UN institutions; and establishing international labour protection standards and global environmental regulation, possibly as clauses in the WTO. With regard to global politics, a reform agenda may include steps towards global democratization, possibly in the form of regional parliaments, global parties, and reform of the UN.[23]

Thirdly, as regards the possibilities for the implementation of global reform, because of their scope such reforms are often thought of as out of the reach of ordinary politics. This perception may be relativized for instance by considering the precedents of global regulation achieved over the past decades. International law sets human rights standards, regulates the conduct of war, exercises control through the International Court of Justice, and regulates access to resources through instruments such as the Law of the Sea; international treaties and regulatory institutions operate in many fields – the International Energy Agency, the WHO, FAO, ILO, UN agencies, and in international finance the Bank of International Settlements and the IMF. Global reform, against this backdrop, refers to the expansion of a global public sector which de facto exists in a sprawling patchwork of international legislation and institutions, intergovernmental, regional, national and local authorities, international professional and non governmental organizations. The global public sector's multilevel and inter sectoral consultation and cooperation operates ahead of *de jure* regulation in terms of international law and institution building. Such arrangements as exist are referred to under in-between headings such as the 'internationalization of the state' and 'governance without government', which themselves are signposts of our time of transition.

Social (poverty, exclusion) and moral considerations (solidarity, compassion, decency) are weighty but by themselves probably do not provide a broad enough basis and coalition for reform. Indeed the classic retort in the framework of neoclassical economics is that deregulation, liberalization, privatization will generate more jobs and thus, by courtesy of trickle down, benefit the poor eventually. Hence moral considerations tend to fracture along the lines of paradigms and politics. It follows that the major grounds for global reform probably fall under the rubrics of threat and opportunity.

From the point of view of threat, global reform is primarily a matter of global risk management in the global common interest. The risks are thoroughly familiar. The ecological risks are too familiar to rehearse here. Political and security risk arise from instability on account of widening rich–poor gaps in combination with narrowing technology gaps (including military technologies). Civil war, ethnic and religious mobilization, state disintegration, and migration and refugee flows are part of this hazard syndrome. Financial instability due to foreign currency trading and speculation on a volume of traffic that is grotesquely out of proportion to international trade requirements is another growing factor of instability. The neoliberal regime may be in the short-term interest of the larger corporations but involves growing risks arising from market failure. In the advanced economies this takes the form of social polarization due to job loss and jobless growth, and insecurity for small and medium-size business; this may imply a growing mainstream constituency for global reform, at least with a view to containing the competitive threat from low wage economies and the mobility of multinational enterprises. High-growth economies in East and Southeast Asia benefit now but their economies are narrowly based and dependent on outside markets and technology, so that their long-term interest lies in global economic and political stability.

In the past novel forms of regulation have been arrived at prompted by crisis, extreme or manifest risk, or in the aftermath of major upheavals such as war. The dialectics of disaster do not necessarily produce beneficial results. Out of the 1930s Depression came Roosevelt's New Deal and the neo-corporatist settlements of fascism and Nazism. Post-war reconstruction brought the UN system, the Bretton Woods institutions, the Marshall Plan, the framework for decolonization, development decades, and the Cold War. The question is whether current global dynamics and the diverse ways they are perceived are of such a nature that manifest risk generates sufficient pressure and hence convergence of dispersed interests that new settlements are achievable.

A complementary case for global reform is in terms of opportunity. Global reform, in this line of argument, is not merely necessary in order to manage risk but desirable because it serves global common interests, including the interest of firms and high growth economies. Making this case – which lies beyond this discussion – may involve elaborating the arguments of human development and social development on a transnational scale. The structure of rights which corporations require in order to operate globally must be devised such that they include social rights, not merely on the grounds of social justice but also on the grounds of social productivity.

Generally it would be important for NGOs and civil society networks to make global reform proposals part of their agenda, more and more proactively than is presently the case. Presently there is a political hiatus not only from local empowerment to the global level, but also between global reform proposals and local constituencies that are neither informed nor engaged. It is worth noting the rapidity of change of political attitudes even on the intercontinental level. Fifteen years ago the threat of nuclear war dominated the agenda of global concern and now it has virtually vanished. Due to various circumstances coming together it has been possible to find a workable institutional fix. Presently globalization Angst is a growing sentiment. Finding a global institutional fix is thinkable, even though without doubt it will involve long lasting jostling and negotiation among multiple political and social forces of an unprecedented complexity.

Emancipation in the context of globalization in my view means local empowerment and global reform on the basis of inclusive political values and arrangements. What is needed, then, is not merely resistance but transformation, not only local empowerment but global empowerment. The point is not to create new radical

postures but to set forth a global politics of inclusion i
language of the market meets with the aims of human
development. Implementing such an agenda would invo,
cooperation among civil society organizations, includir,   _ur
organizations; and where politically relevant (depending on the
character of local and state government, and the culture of enterprise), developing synergies between civil society, government and
firms. What would be constructive politically is developing multilevel connections from local organizations to international networks
lobbying for and generating global reform.

Notes

1 Petrella, R., 'Globalization and Internationalization: The Dynamics of the Emerging World Order', in R. Boyer and D. Drache (eds), *States against Markets: The Limits of Globalization* (Routledge, 1996), p. 79.
2 *Ibid.*, p. 80.
3 Cox, R. W., 'A Perspective on Globalization', in J. H. Mittelman (ed.), *Globalization: Critical Reflections* (Lynne Rienner, 1996), p. 26.
4 Mittelman, J. H., 'The Dynamics of Globalization', in *Globalization: critical reflections*, p. 18.
5 Nederveen Pieterse, J., 'Delinking or Globalization?', *Economic and Political Weekly*, Vol. 29, No. 5 (1994): 239–42.
6 'Globalization and Internationalization', pp. 78–9.
7 Latouche, S., *In the Wake of the Affluent Society: An Exploration of Post-development* (Zed, 1993).
8 Cheru, F., 'New Social Movements: Democratic Struggles and Human Rights in Africa', in J. H. Mittelman (ed.), *Globalization: Critical Reflections*, p. 155.
9 *Ibid.*, p. 159.
10 *Ibid.*
11 Friedmann, J., *Empowerment: The Politics of Alternative Development* (Blackwell, 1992).
12 Cheru, 'New Social Movements'.
13 Bello, W., 'Equitable and Sustainable Growth in the Philippines in the 1990s', in J. Cavanagh, D. Wysham and M. Arruda (eds), *Beyond Bretton Woods: Alternatives to Global Economic Order* (Pluto, 1994), pp. 16–28.
14 Muto, I., 'For an Alliance of Hope', in J. Brecher, J. Brown Childs and J. Cutler (eds), *Global Visions* (South End Press, 1993), p. 155.
15 Nederveen Pieterse, J., 'My Paradigm or Yours? Alternative Development, Post-development, Reflexive Development', *Development & Change*, Vol. 29, No. 2 (1998): 343–73.
16 Sanyal, B., 'Ideas and Institutions: Why the Alternative Development Paradigm Withered Away', *Regional Development Dialogue*, Vol. 15, No. 1 (1994): 23–35.
17 Haq, M. ul, *Reflections on Human Development* (Oxford University Press, 1995).

18 Nederveen Pieterse, J., 'Growth and Equity Revisited: A Supply-side Approach to Social Development', *European Journal of Development Research*, Vol. 9, No. 1 (1997): 128–49.

19 Nederveen Pieterse, J., 'Emancipations, modern and postmodern', in *Emancipations, Modern and Postmodern* (Sage, 1992), p. 32.

20 Sousa Santos, B. de, *Toward a New Common Sense* (Routledge, 1995), p. 2, ix.

21 Peck, J. and A. Tickell, 'Searching for a New Institutional Fix: the After-Fordist Crisis and the Global–Local Disorder', in A. Amin (ed.), *Post-Fordism* (Blackwell, 1994).

22 Robinson, I., 'Globalization and Democracy', *Dissent* (Summer 1995): 373–80.

23 See Falk, R. A., *On Humane Governance: Towards a New Global Politics* (Polity, 1994); Group of Lisbon, *Limits to Competition* (MIT Press, 1995); Held, D., *Democracy and Global Order* (Polity, 1995); Henderson, H., *Building a Win–Win World* (Berrett-Koehler, 1996).

13

'Corporate Welfare' Campaigns in North America

Kenneth P. Thomas

One important consequence of globalization has been the cumulative shifting of tax burdens from corporations to individuals. While this trend holds for the OECD as a whole, it is especially pronounced within the United States, where the corporate income tax share of total taxes (federal, state, local, and Social Security) fell from 21.51 per cent in 1955 to 7.87 per cent in 1993 (Webb, 1996, p. 8). An equally sharp drop occurred in Canada, with the corporate income tax share falling from 18.5 per cent in 1955 to 6.9 per cent in 1993.[1]

This shift has taken place as a result of competition for investment in the context of increasing capital mobility. This has taken two forms. First, particularly in the 1980s, many governments reduced their rates of corporate income tax to improve their attractiveness to investment in general. Second, governments have resorted more and more frequently to company-specific tax concessions in order to attract individual investments. As these changes have cumulatively reduced the tax burden on firms, governments have had to adjust by increasing taxes on individuals, cutting programmes, running larger budget deficits, or some combination of the three.

In response, a number of citizens' groups in the US and Canada have mounted campaigns to reduce the subsidies and tax concession given to corporations, what many call 'corporate welfare'.[2] This includes national organizations such as Ralph Nader's group Public Citizen as well as numerous local groups throughout the country, often working in conjunction with labour unions. Interestingly, there is also a more conservative strand to this movement (the best example is the libertarian Cato Institute), which criticizes subsidies on economic inefficiency grounds.

This chapter will examine the activities of these organizations, assessing their local successes and failures as well as their prospects to reduce competition for investment and end or reverse the long-run shift in tax burden.

Globalization and competition for investment

While the phenomenon of globalization is often ill-defined, sharing many of the connotations and ambiguities of the term 'interdependence' (Jones, 1995, p. 3), there is no doubt that one of its central economic facets is that of increasing capital mobility. That is, it has become increasingly possible for owners of capital to shift their capital from one location to another, whether that means financial assets or productive investment. In the context of governments' need for investment (Lindblom, 1977; Przeworski and Wallerstein, 1988), increasing capital mobility makes it necessary for states to engage in more intense efforts to compete for investment. The varieties of competition for investment are numerous, including direct grants or firm-specific tax holidays to attract an individual company, more general measures to improve a jurisdiction's 'business climate', such as reduction in tax rates generally, relatively more favourable labor climate (Britain's former opt-out from the Social Chapter of Maastricht; anti-union 'right-to-work' laws in some US states), lower regulatory frameworks, etc. In this chapter, I focus on a subset of these means of attracting investment, those with direct budgetary consequences for governments: grants, tax expenditures,[3] and reductions in corporate income and other business-oriented tax rates. The reason is that their cumulative effect over the last 40 years has been quite dramatic. As governments have competed for investment, they have reduced the relative tax burden borne by corporations (Steinmo, 1993), causing fiscal problems that must be dealt with in one (or a combination) of three ways: increasing the tax burden borne by individuals, worsening their budget balance (in practice, increasing their budget deficit), or cutting government expenditures. The dimensions of the problem can be seen in Table 13.1.

As Table 13.1 shows, the corporate tax share has fallen within US states,[4] within the US as a whole, within the G-5, and in Canada. As Webb shows, the overall G-5 decline is not due simply to the US fall, but there have been declines in the UK, France, Germany (Japan saw a rise from 1955 to 1960, stability until 1990, then a

Table 13.1 Corporate tax share of total government revenues

	1948	1955	1975	1991	1993
US states	8.6%			6.6%	
Total US		21.51%	10.79%		7.87%
G-5 mean		13.11%	9.55%		7.41%
Canada		18.5%	13.6%		6.9%

Sources: For US states, Howard, 1994; total US and G-5 mean, Webb, 'Taxing Transnational Capital'; Canada, personal communication from Michael Webb, 30 May 1996.

fall back to 1955 levels in 1993), as well as in the smaller OECD members (Webb, 1996, p. 8).

The dramatic shift in tax burden away from corporations in the US has helped fuel the perception that individuals are highly taxed, as illustrated by the 'Tax Revolt' beginning with California's Proposition 13 (reducing property taxes) in 1978. In fact, the US tax burden as a proportion of GDP is virtually the lowest among all industrialized countries (Steinmo, 1993, p. 40). Yet the perception does illustrate well the dilemma countries face as their competition for investment reduces the corporate tax burden: increase the individual burden, run greater deficits, or reduce services.

Popular response

A wide variety of organizations in the US and Canada are involved in efforts to reduce the subsidies and tax expenditures given to corporations. This section will demonstrate the numerous activities taking place organizing around these issues.

These efforts can be categorized in two ways. First, are the organizations national, local, or a combination of the two? Second, what is the motivation behind the group's efforts?

National US organizations active in the corporate welfare movement include Essential Information (organized by Ralph Nader), the Cato Institute (a libertarian think-tank), Friends of the Earth, and the American Federation of State, County and Municipal Employees (AFSCME). The first two focus more on research and education, while Friends of the Earth and AFSCME have been more active in lobbying efforts and are more connected to local organizations. The Association of Community Organizations for Reform Now (ACORN) is a national organization with local chapters in most parts of the country, while the Grassroots Policy Project is a research and education group with close contacts with a number of local groups. Examples of local groupings include the Louisiana Coalition for Tax Justice, Minnesota Alliance for Progressive Action, and the Southwest Organizing Project (based in New Mexico).

In Canada, the New Democrats have highlighted corporate welfare since their 1972 electoral campaign, and the Canadian Federation of Students has also drawn the connection between cutbacks and corporate tax expenditures. In recent years, the Canadian Taxpayers' Federation (CTF) has moved to the forefront of this issue, providing a government waste-efficiency critique of subsidies and generating substantial publicity over Department of Industry programmes. At the provincial level, organizations like the Ontario Federation of Labor and the Ontario Coalition for Social Justice have addressed the problem, along with provincial New Democratic Party (NDP) governments.

The question of motivation revolves around the implicit criticism of subsidies animating each group's activities. Broadly speaking, there are three possible reasons for objecting to subsidies. First is an efficiency argument, which suggests that subsidies should be eliminated because they are inefficient. Location subsidies, in this view, are simply a disguised barrier to free capital movements. This efficiency critique has motivated the efforts of the European Commission to control state aid with the EU (Commission of the European Communities, 1991). In the US context, it is also behind the participation of the Cato Institute and some of the member organizations of the Friends of the Earth's' 'Green Scissors' coalition, such as the Concord Coalition and Citizens for Common $ense. Second is an environmental argument, which criticizes only those subsidies that encourage environmentally harmful practices, such as subsidized electricity rates by the Bonneville Power Administration (encouraging overuse of energy and harming salmon runs) and subsidies to the nuclear power industry. This is behind the involvement of the environmental groups taking part in the Green Scissors campaign.[5] Finally, there is the equity argument implicit in this chapter. On this view, mobile firms use their bargaining power to extract concessions from jurisdictions, whereas in the past they made investments without expecting or receiving financial inducements. The aggregate effect of this pattern of bargaining over location is to shift income from labor to capital, making the distribution of income within countries less equal (Robinson, 1993, pp. 34–5). This is exacerbated by the cumulative shift in the tax burden onto lower income groups and budget pressure to reduce spending for social programs. This motivates many of the citizen's groups as well as union participants.[6] Interestingly, this contrasts sharply with the experience of the European Union, where the vast majority of subsidy or state aid control is motivated by efficiency considerations, and the Left is critical of EU state aid policies.[7] The main reasons for this difference, I believe, are the larger state-owned sector in most EU countries, and the greater use in some European states of subsidies as a tool of economic intervention.[8] Much state aid goes to public-sector firms, and cuts, such as those enforced especially during the tenure of Competition Commissioner Leon Brittan, meant the loss of thousands of jobs. This has muted criticism of state aid on equity grounds, even though, as the Commission pointed out in its *First Survey on State Aid*, the amount of money given to EU firms in state aid exceeded the amount collected in corporate income tax (Commission of the European Communities, 1989, p. 3).

National efforts in the US

Friends of the Earth (FoE) sponsors the 'Green Scissors' campaign, targeting subsidies to polluting activities. According to Gawain Kripke, Green Scissors is made up of several dozen environmental organizations as well as several 'taxpayer' or 'free market'-oriented groups, such as the Concord Coalition and Taxpayers for Common $ense.[9]

Despite the broad base, three organizations make up the 'core' of the campaign: Friends of the Earth, US Public Interest Research Group (US PIRG), and Taxpayers for Common $ense. The latter replaced the National Taxpayers Union (NTU), which withdrew under pressure from Republican Party leaders. Long-time NTU staffer Jill Lancelot then teamed up with FoE's Ralph De Gennaro to form TC$. US PIRG provides the grassroots backbone through its affiliates on college campuses throughout the country. Friends of the Earth itself has 30,000 members nationally, in addition to 54 affiliates in other countries.[10]

According to Cuff, Lancelot pioneered the coalescing of conservative and environmental groups when she was with NTU in the early 1980s. The first big effort between FoE and NTU resulted in the 1993 publication of 'The Green Solution to Red Ink', which changed its name to Green Scissors in 1995.

Kripke sees the campaign as a way 'to build bipartisanship on environmental issues', giving Friends of the Earth 'a bridge to work with the Republican leadership' of Congress. This has been possible, he says, because 'targeted items are mainly pork barrel and [narrow] corporate interest'. In the last few years, the Coalition has claimed success in eliminating some $24 billion in spending and subsidies, including the TPX fusion reactor and Advanced Neutron Source project, both of which created substantial waste disposal problems. Their sixth report, *Green Scissors '99*, identifies 72 programmes, with a heavy focus on energy, water, agriculture and highway programs (Friends of the Earth, 1999).

Another national example of politics making strange bedfellows is the joint campaign of the Cato Institute (libertarian), Progressive Policy Institute (part of the centrist Democratic Leadership Council, once chaired by then-Governor Bill Clinton) and Ralph Nader's Essential Information (Left, by US standards). In June of 1995, the three groups released a 'Dirty Dozen' of corporate subsidies which they unanimously agreed should be ended. According to Janice Shields, 'The list included eliminating maritime operating subsidies, OPIC [Overseas Private Investment Corporation] loans and insurance, the MPP [Market Promotion Program of the Department of Agriculture], the Export Enhancement Program, subsidies for military exports, and more' (Shields, 1996, p. 5). The five-year savings of the Dirty Dozen were projected to be $16 billion.

The three organizations also provide separate analyses that give much higher estimates of the total of corporate welfare. Essential Information suggests that the total of federal subsidies alone in fiscal 1995 was more than $167 billion (Shields, 1996, p. 1), by far the highest of the estimates. Cato's estimate is considerably lower than Essential Information's: $87.3 billion in fiscal 1995 (Moore and Stansel, 1996, p. 13). The Progressive Policy Institute had the smallest estimate of the three, $53 billion annually (Shapiro, 1995, pp. 17–24). These figures run from 0.64 per cent of 1995 GDP for the PPI estimate to 2.30 per cent of GDP for the Essential Information estimate. By comparison, in the European Union, total 'state aid' (which includes direct subsidies, tax expenditures, soft loans, etc.) in 1992–4 was only 1.7 per cent of the GDP of the then-twelve Member States.[11]

Not only do their estimates differ, but as Shields (1996, pp. 6–7) points out:

> While conservatives and progressives agree on the need to cut corporate welfare, old differences re-emerge when the groups are

faced with the question of the freed funds. The Competitive Enterprise Institute, for example, would use budgetary savings to reduce the deficit. Essential Information would ensure that needy people have access to safe shelter, nutritional food, affordable health care and quality education.

Cato, by contrast, would eliminate tax expenditures in return for lower overall tax rates, with an overall result of revenue neutrality or a tax cut (Moore and Stansel, 1996, p. 8).

Another national organization, Citizens for Tax Justice (CTJ), provides an estimate of business and investment tax expenditures given to corporation of $69.2 billion in fiscal 1996. Two things are especially noteworthy about CTJ: its focus on tax expenditures only (as opposed to grants, below cost services such as mining land, etc.) and its very explicit emphasis on distributional issues. Its 1996 study, *The Hidden Entitlements*, documents the extent to which upper-income taxpayers receive the vast majority of benefits from both corporate and personal tax expenditures. A number of CTJ studies in the early 1980s highlighted the massive increase in corporate tax expenditures as a result of the so-called 'Reagan Revolution', and helped to lay the groundwork for the 1986 Tax Reform Act, which sharply decreased corporate tax expenditures from 201 per cent of corporate income taxes in 1986 (versus 72 per cent in 1980) to only 41 per cent in 1996 (Citizens for Tax Justice, 1996, p. 6).

Canadian efforts

In Canada, the New Democratic Party ran has long focused on tax fairness, in fact running its 1972 campaign on the theme of corporate welfare. Its efforts have primarily focused on the tax system and its entrenched inequities, as opposed to direct subsidies. This has also been true of the work of the labour movement and social organizations on corporate welfare. Since most tax subsidies occur at the federal rather than provincial level, this has meant that more efforts have been devoted to campaigning against corporate welfare federally as opposed to provincially.[12]

The Canadian Taxpayers' Association made waves with an exhaustive critique of Department of Industry subsidy programmes in April 1998. Of C $11 billion in funds. The CTF documented that five companies received about one-fifth, and that C $2.1 billion, in the form of repayable contributions was unlikely to be repaid even by very profitable corporations (Leblanc, 1998). CTF was also involved with the drafting of the Alberta Financial Assistance Limitation Statutes Amendment Act in 1996.[13]

Sub-federal corporate welfare in the US

Data for state-level subsidies to business is fragmentary, while information on business support by local governments (most commonly in the form of property tax or rates exemptions) is virtually non-existent. Nothing comparable to the European Union's *Surveys* of state aid exists. Moreover, since most corporate welfare at the state and local level comes in the form of tax expenditures rather than through grants or other on-budget items, general budgets are of little help. Only tax expenditure budgets can provide useful information, and in very few states are they sufficiently developed to give an indication of states' support for enterprises. According to an analysis of tax expenditure budgets for 11 states, corporate income tax breaks amounted to $6.3 billion in 1992, while in addition New York state both before and after 1992 gave approximately $1 billion annually in such tax expenditures (Lynch, 1996, p. 3). One could easily imagine the total for all 50 states exceeding $15 billion annually. Moreover, Iris Lav of the Center on Budget and Policy Priorities suggests that local tax expenditures are as high as state tax expenditures. This is due to the near-universal use of property tax (rates) abatements by local governments.[14] If she is correct, then, it would imply at least $30 billion annually given in location incentives by sub-national governments in the US. The next section examines several examples of efforts to combat state and local level subsidies.

Local struggles

The Louisiana Coalition for Tax Justice (LCTJ) was founded in May 1990, and has over 20 member organizations, including four local LCTJ chapters, seven unions, and a number of tenant, community and environmental organizations. According to Dan Mills, the group's efforts have focused on the very substantial property tax exemptions given to companies located in the state.[15] From January 1991 to June 1995, the state Department of Economic Development signed 2,613 10-year Industrial Property Tax Exemption Program (IPTEP) contracts exempting $1.5 billion in local property taxes, receiving job creation commitments for 16,921 jobs, or $89,855 per job (LCTJ, 1995, pp. 19–22). LCTJ points out that because of these large reductions (the top ten IPTEP recipients had far more tax forgiven than they actually paid), Louisiana parishes (the equivalent of counties) had to rely on regressive sales taxes for funding. Moreover, the IPTEP law does not give parishes any say in the exemption decisions which decide their fiscal fate, instead vesting it in the appointed State Board of Commerce and Industry. Finally, LCTJ criticizes the programme because the subsidies go to heavily polluting industries such as chemicals, petroleum and paper. 'In all, Louisiana's chemical plants, after releasing 430 million pounds of toxins in 1993, have had $311 million exempted since 1994, and have created 762 jobs. Three of these plants are counted among the worst four polluters in the nation' (LCTJ, 1995, pp. 19–22). Moreover, Louisiana has the highest level of toxic emissions per manufacturing job in the nation (Guarisco, 1996).

While proponents of the tax breaks contend they help attract investment, Mills says LCTJ research shows that 96 per cent of the contracts go to companies already located within the state. The group's lobbying efforts have focused on the state legislature. Their biggest success came in 1990, when the legislature approved a bill reducing the property tax exemptions to a percentage of what companies had previously been due, based on an 'environmental scorecard.' Firms with a perfect 100 per cent score thus received their full tax exemption, while polluting firms saw their tax breaks reduced. However, when Governor Buddy Roemer was replaced by Edwin Edwards, the latter was receptive to the repeal of the environmental scorecard. Despite this defeat, LCTJ has remained active, successfully lobbying for a disclosure bill requiring firms receiving property tax exemption to list complaints brought by the Occupational Health and Safety Administration and the Environmental Protection Agency, as well as showing what the companies paid in taxes and what they had exempted.

In Minnesota, the Minnesota Alliance for Progressive Action (MAPA) has focused on the wages paid by firms receiving tax exemptions. The group successfully lobbied for a law requiring any company receiving $25,000 or more in tax exemptions to set and meet job and wage goals within two years or be liable to repay the subsidies.[16] This law was strengthened in 1999 (MAPA, 1999).

Wages have figured prominently in other local campaigns on subsidies. For example, when the Walt Disney Company proposed building a theme park in the state of Virginia, not only was it opposed by conservationists and by Civil War historians who feared the Disnification of American history, a number of other opponents scored the proposed $163 million investment incentive package offered to the company, allegedly to create 2,700 full-time jobs. During the course of public debate on the issue, it developed that 73 per cent of the jobs 'would have been part-time and seasonal' (LeRoy, 1994). As a result, the firm would have been rewarded for creating thousands of poverty-level jobs whose employees needed further subsidies from the government, including 'Medicaid, unemployment compensation, food stamps and earned income tax credits'. Only the project's defeat prevented this drain on the state and federal budgets.

Wages have also been an important focus of campaigns by the Association of Community Organizations for Reform Now (ACORN), a national alliance of low- and moderate-income citizens' action groups. It has been one of the participants in the Minnesota campaigns mentioned above, as well as the organizer of efforts in St Louis, Chicago, New York and Boston. In Chicago, the group has introduced an ordinance in the City Council that would require city contractors and all firms receiving tax abatements (with some exceptions for small business) to pay $7.65 per hour to their workers.[17] In St. Louis, the group was behind the 1987 passage of a 'First Source' law requiring tax abatement recipients to hire city residents in return for the financial assistance they receive. A renewed 'living wage' campaign began in the autumn of 1999. In New York, ACORN negotiated directly with a major recipient of city subsidies (Viacom) for a training and job programme.[18]

Conclusion

The foregoing histories are only the tip of the iceberg, but they nonetheless give a taste of the wide variety of organizing taking place around the issue of corporate welfare in the US and Canada. As the discussion makes clear, the corporate welfare campaign in the United States is by no means a unified movement reacting to the excesses of globalization. In particular, at the national level, there is substantial participation by conservative and even libertarian organizations whose overall economic agenda is supportive of globalization. These groups attack corporate welfare on the basis of its alleged economic inefficiency, or on the more general supposed inefficiency of government. Nevertheless, both at the national and grassroots levels, there is widespread recognition that government fiscal crisis derives in large part not from excessive spending but from the ability of corporate actors to reduce their tax burden while increasing the subsidies they receive from government. Many, such as the Minnesota Alliance for Progressive Action, recognize the superiority of federal efforts to reduce competition for investment.

In Canada an issue that was once a preserve of the Left has now taken on the same multi-critique pattern seeen in the United States. So far, there has been no cooperation on corporate welfare across the ideological divide, but it would not be surprising if this occurs in the future.

The campaigns against corporate welfare represent a response to the effects of rising capital mobility, even if the causal chain is not apparent to all the participants. Since competition for investment has allowed corporations to reduce their tax burden, it has meant higher burdens on individuals, higher budget deficits, and cutbacks of government services. The losers from this process are responding to one of the main symptoms, even if they do not all agree on the cause. And there are clear signs that their efforts are not futile. As the 1986 tax reform in the United States shows, corporate welfare does not always increase. The victories claimed by such local organizations as MAPA and ACORN also provide examples of successful resistance to corporate welfare and to its use as an organizing tool. It may be the case, then, despite Cerny's pessimistic claim that 'Polanyi's "Great Transformation" is over' (1994, p. 339), that society is yet trying to protect itself from the ravages of the market.

Notes

1 Personal communication from Michael Webb, 30 May 1996.
2 Other groups use different names, because this term might imply that welfare given to individuals is a bad thing. Due to its widespread use, however, I will keep the term, without quotation marks, in this chapter.
3 Note, however, that tax expenditures are often treated as 'off-budget', particularly in the United States. This chapter follows the practice of the European Union and Organization for Economic Cooperation and Development, which acknowledges the real budgetary impact of tax expenditures.
4 Note also that Richard McKenzie and Dwight Lee have shown that tax rates are lower at the state level than at the federal level precisely due to capital mobility. See McKenzie and Lee (1991).
5 Telephone interview, Gawain Kripke, Friends of the Earth, 21 May 1996.

6 AFSCME is an especially good example of this; see their publication, Howard, *A Corporate Welfare Reform Agenda*.

7 See, for example the divide between Liberals and Socialists on state aid in the European Parliament reported in 'MEPs Split Over State Aid and Liberalization', *Reuter European Community Report*, 14 February 1996, BC Cycle.

8 I want to thank Barbara Jenkins for this latter point.

9 Telephone interview, 21 May 1996. In the US context, 'taxpayer' and 'free market' groups essentially favour balanced budgets and oppose government spending. Their political discourse tends toward the 'efficiency' critique of subsidies, as noted previously.

10 Personal interview with Courtney Cuff, Friends of the Earth, 7 June 1996.

11 Commission of the European Communities (1997), p. 35, Table 15. Note that these figures are far from comparable. On the one hand, the US figures do not include sub-federal amounts, while the EU data do. On the other hand, the US numbers may fall relative to the EU statistics because: (1) Accelerated tax depreciation, included in many of the US estimates, is considered a 'general measure' in the EU and therefore not counted (but probably is less than 0.1 per cent of EU GDP); (2) Shields includes over $59 billion in non-taxed pollution as a subsidy, which again is not counted in EU statistics; and (3) the EU figures have some missing data for national aid to agriculture (i.e., exclusive of the Common Agricultural Policy), which may increase the EU figure by about 0.1 per cent of GDP. My own best estimate of total federal, state and local support to business is $112.5 billion (1.55 per cent of GDP), including accelerated depreciation, or $80.3 billion (1.11 per cent of GDP) without it, lower than the EU average, but within the range within which EU member states fall. See Thomas (forthcoming).

12 Telephone interview, Jim Turk, Canadian Union of Public Employees, 5 September 1996. On the provincial level, the Rae NDP government in Ontario introduced a corporate minimum tax. Telephone interview, Judy Randell, Canada's New Democrats, 11 September 1996.

13 Telephone interview, Walter Robinson, CTF Federal Director, 23 July 1999.

14 Personal interview, Iris Lav, Center on Budget and Policy Priorities, 7 June 1996.

15 Telephone interview, 20 May 1996.

16 Interestingly, though it is common practice in Europe to include such 'clawback' clauses in investment subsidy agreements, as of May 1995 only nine US states and four cities had adopted such practices. See Leroy (1995).

17 Telephone interview, Jen Kern, ACORN, 28 May 1996.

18 Telephone interview, Jen Kern, ACORN, 28 May 1996.

References

Cerny, Philip G. (1994), 'The Dynamics of Financial Globalization: Technology, Market Structure, and Policy Response', *Policy Sciences*, Vol. 27.

Citizens for Tax Justice (1996), *The Hidden Entitlements* (Washington: author).

Commission of the European Communities (1989), *First Survey on State Aid* (Brussels-Luxembourg: author).

Commission of the European Communities (1991), 'Fair Competition in the Internal Market: Community State Aid Policy,' *European Economy* no. 48 (September).

Commission of the European Communities (1997), *Fifth Survey on State Aid* (Brussels-Luxembourg: author).

Friends of the Earth (1999), *Green Scissors '99*, electronic version, http://www.foe.org/eco/scissors 99

Guarisco, Tom (1996), 'Louisiana Lures Jobs with Tax Breaks', *Sunday Advocate* (Baton Rouge, Louisiana), 24 March 1996, p. J1.

Howard, Marcia (1994), *A Corporate Welfare Reform Agenda* (American Federation of State County and Municipal Employees Public Policy Department).

Jones, R. J. Barry (1995), *Globalisation and Interdependence in the International Political Economy: Rhetoric and Reality* (Pinter).

Leblanc, Damel (1998) 'Aerospace Industry Supports R&D Loans' *Ottawa Citizen*, 17 April.

LeRoy, Greg (1994), 'State Subsidies for Real Jobs', *St Louis Post-Dispatch*, 2 December 1994, p. 15D.

LeRoy, Greg (1995), 'No More Candy Store: States Move to End Corporate Welfare', *Dollars and Sense*, May/June 1995.

Charles Lindblom (1977), *Politics and Markets* (Basic Books).

LCTJ (Louisiana Coalition for Tax Justice) (1995), 'IPTEP: Industry's Pet that's Eroding Parishes', *Louisiana Parish Government*, September 1995.

Lynch, Robert G. (1996), *Do State & Local Tax Incentives Work?* (Economic Policy Institute).

McKenzie, Richard and Lee, Dwight (1991), *Quicksilver Capital* (Free Press).

'MEPs Split Over State Aid and Liberalization', Reuters European Community Report, 14 February 1996, BC Cycle.

MAPA (1999) 'Legislature Reins in Corporate Welfare', *MAPA Bulletin*, 18 May 1999.

Moore, Stephen and Stansel, Dean (1996), *Ending Corporate Welfare As We Know It*, electronic edition, http://www.cato.org/main/pa225.html

Ontario Coalition for Social Justice and Ontario Federation of Labour (1996), *Unfair Shares: Corporations and Taxation in Canada* (Toronto: author).

Przeworski, Adam and Wallerstein, Michael (1988), 'Structural Dependence of the State on Capital', *American Political Science Review*, Vol. 82 (March).

Robinson, Ian (1993), *North American Trade As If Democracy Mattered* (Canadian Centre for Policy Alternatives).

Shapiro, Robert (1995), *Cut-and-Invest: A Budget Strategy for the New Economy* (Progressive Policy Institute).

Shields, Janice (1996), 'Ending (Corporate) Welfare As We Know It,' electronic version, http://www.emf.net/~cr/govreform/corpwelf-012596.

Steinmo, Sven (1993), *Taxation and Democracy* (Yale University Press).

Thomas, Kenneth P. (forthcoming), *Competing for Capital: European and North American Responses* (Georgetown University Press).

Webb, Michael (1996), 'Taxing Transnational Capital: Transfer Prices in US Policy and the OECD,' paper presented to the Workshop on Capital Mobility, Princeton University, Princeton, NJ, March 1996.

14
Neoliberal Globalization, Social Welfare and Trade Unions in Southeast Asia

Johannes Dragsbaek Schmidt

Southeast Asia's political elite has deliberately encouraged economic growth by emphasizing international competition through a calculated export-led strategy and avoidance of social welfare programmes. The strategy is essentially based on an anti-entitlement attitude which has laid the groundwork for a stable societal order based on pragmatic political ideology and a specific set of social values. Policy-making in this regard has promoted a political culture which claims that public welfare reduces productivity. Despite decades of high economic growth rates, little emphasis has been devoted to education and health. Social welfare expenditures are primarily located in the private domain and concentrated on public employees. The explicit purpose of this course is to avoid wage increases and in general neutralize labour and oppositional policy groupings. This particular strategy has been implemented either through co-opting, repressing or linking economic growth and increases in employment opportunities with control by the government. Nevertheless, these societies experience pressures from the workforce on the state to adopt and implement social security related legislation and policies.

Globalization and social welfare

In the past two decades the high growth rates of the NICs (South Korea, Singapore and Taiwan) and the would-be NICs (Thailand, Malaysia, Indonesia and to some extent the Philippines) have been cited as successful examples of development with a small state sector, minimal public expenditure, light regulation and low taxation.

220

Accordingly, the market mechanism is claimed to allocate wealth which automatically 'trickles-down' and thereby minimizes social inequalities. The objective of this liberal position is to rationalize the competition between different national economies in order to offer transnational capital the best conditions possible. Since investment in manufactured production and services increasingly favours those countries with low wages, minimal social security, health, safety and environmental costs, global competition increasingly becomes a zero-sum social game.

The societal arrangements which have been reached in both East and West are related to the constraints and possibilities which the world market imposes. Hence the above propositions about social welfare make the question of how states and policy-makers have controlled the nature and impact of globalization an important one. It is essentially a matter of how individual capitalist states adapt and respond to the neoliberal policies of keeping wages below productivity growth and downsizing domestic costs which have led to an unstable vicious circle of 'competitive austerity': 'Each country reduces domestic demand and adopts an export-oriented strategy of dumping its surplus production, for which there are fewer consumers in its national economy given the decrease in workers' living standards and productivity gains all going to the capitalists, in the world market. This has created a global demand crisis and the growth of surplus capacity across the business cycle.'[1] Furthermore, the convergence between low welfare expenditures and export orientation has become part and parcel of the tendency to position national economies in the international system.

Social policies are the outcome of contemporary struggles between classes and the state. They are essentially a national political issue but an issue which is being undermined by the logic of the hegemony and discourse of the 'Washington Consensus' on globalization and neoliberalism.

Contemporary development of social welfare policies

Throughout most Southeast Asian countries the primary social welfare roles were historically assumed by the family, and sometimes by the local community. It might thus be argued that to a large extent, economic growth substituted for social welfare during most of the post-war period.

Until the formation of an industrial working class and urbanization, pressures for social protection on governments were limited. Thus policy-makers have been able to interpret the past in order to justify their lack of enthusiasm for the Western-type welfare state. In conventional thinking in Southeast Asia, whatever the social benefits, these were regarded as an act of political philanthropy to somewhat undeserving populations. Witness the view expressed in 1983 by the Prime Minister of Thailand: 'culturally the Thai behaviour and way of life are inactive ... Lack of ambition is the big enemy of the Thai way of life ... The democratic government must take some action by the establishment of the Department of Public Welfare as the tool for action.'[2] This paternalistic attitude has meant that the prevailing welfare ideology of Thai policy-makers is more inclined to charity than services. In Singapore, 'the influence of the Poor Law Tradition, particularly the idea that the public money should not be "wasted" on the "undeserving" and the belief in the thesis of the perverse effect are strong in Singapore's public assistance programmes. Not only are these schemes limited in scope but they are also very strictly administered.'[3]

These common features of Southeast Asia show that traditional social values emphasize the duty of the family to support their members in need of help. Ideologies of meritocracy have meant that those who fail in society have little to fall back on and are seen to be responsible for their own failures. Stigmatization of the underprivileged is common throughout the region, which is clearly seen in the views taken by political elites who characterize the poor as 'lazy'.[4] Hence the dominant discourse of policy elites is that financing social security should primarily be based on individual and family responsibility.

Nevertheless, there exists a large gap between constitutional statements concerning the obligations of the state to provide social welfare and the reality of entitlement. For example, the Filipino 1973 Constitution proclaims the people's right to social services. The Declaration of Principles and State Policies commands that the state shall establish, maintain and ensure adequate social services to guarantee the people a decent standard of living.[5] The system consists of a mandatory basic universal coverage, supplemented by occupational pension plans. Obviously, the Philippines, with its high foreign debt, has never been able to implement these policies. Southeast Asia introduced legislated social security programmes, as early as the mid-1950s, covering the following: old age, survivors and invalidity; and except for Malaysia, sickness, maternity and medical care; while programmes covering work injury were inaugurated as early as in the 1920s, 1930s, and late 1950s. However, the small coverage is by and large employment-based and not universal.

In the beginning of the 1980s, Thailand spent less than 0.5 per cent of the total budget on social benefits.[6] 'Official social security schemes (covered by the Social Security Act) are available only to formal sector workers in the civil service and those working in enterprises employing ten workers and more. Those working in the informal sector do not receive protection under the labour law, nor are they covered by social security provisions.'[7] 'Thailand does have problems of social exclusion due to uneven development and unfair institutional arrangements, such as inadequate provision of basic social goods . . .'[8] In contrast, Singapore, which is classified as a high-income society, spends only 2.15 per cent of total expenditure or 0.49 per cent of GDP in 1989 on social security and welfare.[9] In Indonesia, the percentage of the labour force covered by social security was 4–5 per cent in 1985, and confined to civil servants, the armed forces, and industrial workers and their dependants.[10] In Malaysia public expenditures on social security as a percentage of total government expenditure rose in the period from 1980 to 1993 by 1.84 per cent, and as a percentage of GDP by only 0.32 per cent. The figures in the same period for the Philippines were 0.67 and 0.39 per cent, respectively; Singapore 2.58 and 0.39 per cent; and finally Thailand 1.27 and 0.08 per cent (figures for Indonesia n.a.). Health, education and housing saw only very marginal increases both in terms of percentages of total government expenditure and GDP. The exception is Thailand where public expenditures on health, covering the same period as above, rose from 4.09 to 8.15 per cent and 0.78 to 1.10 per cent, respectively. In Singapore, the government's share in total health expenditure declined from 40.1 per cent in 1970 to 27.4 per cent in 1989.[11]

The status of social welfare in the 1990s

In general, the status of welfare in Southeast Asia is not entirely different from the Japanese, South Korean and Taiwanese cases where, 'welfare policy has been dominated by economic rather than social considerations supported by some underlying ideas of anti-welfarism and, especially, by resistance to the provision of government-guaranteed social welfare. The ruling elites have generally only accepted the institutional concept of social welfare when confronting political crisis; when this is overcome they return to the "residual concept of social welfare" (Park 1990) by drawing on "Confucian" cultural ideologies.'[12] This explains how social welfare became subordinated to the state's economic priorities and how the state managed to manipulate national support for its growth strategy and deflect public pressure for social welfare development. It has done so by effective use of the education system, by control of the media and through the political exclusion of labour and peasant organizations. There is no doubt that Southeast Asian policymakers in their 'Look East' policy also are very aware of Japanese and NIC historical experience in social welfare, because of the vital emphasis laid on control of agenda setting for the public debate.

This is evident in Malaysia, where the relatively higher provisions of social welfare are related to ethnic antagonism which has shaped the role of the state, economic policies, and in particular the union movement where the level of Bumiputra (ethnic Malay) participation now accounts for more than half. In the name of Malay favouritism, the New Economic Policy implemented a series of programmes intended to extend social welfare, from small scale-housing materials grants and land development schemes to subsidizing Bumiputra business and education. But in the beginning of the period, poverty eradication swallowed the largest amount of expenditures, with some success.[13]

The Philippines has one of the oldest social security systems with the widest coverage and range of products.[14] The social security programmes are of the defined benefit type, based on pay and contributory service, but they are not being implemented, because the Philippines has been under IMF and World Bank surveillance which has meant major public programmes have seen cuts.

The question of financing social security systems is of major importance to provide an understanding of public attitudes towards welfare policies. In the Philippines a serious erosion of social conditions occurred during the past three decades. Corruption, and lack of finances and state capacity to implement existing schemes were serious. In Indonesia, multilateral aid conditionalities forced the government to repay its debt in the amount of up to 50 per cent of total government expenditures. Thus, two of the most important welfare institutions received declining funding. Sjahrir asked, 'Is it fair for Indonesia, a "good boy" in World Bank/IMF terms, to receive a foreign aid cut?'[15] Throughout 25 years of development, only around 25 per cent of the Indonesian workforce has come under the protection of the Labor Law, while two-thirds of the economically active population struggles between unemployment and underemployment.[16]

In Indonesia there are separate social security schemes of a corporatist kind for civil servants, military personnel, and private sector workers covering endowment insurance, pension and health care.[17] In general, civil servants and military personnel, which make up slightly more than half of those covered, enjoy a much higher level of benefits than those in the private sector and state enterprises. Indonesia's reliance on foreign capital, along with the relatively small proportion of the workforce employed in the formal sector, will limit social security coverage and benefits in the foreseeable future.

The social security systems in Malaysia and Singapore are of the mandatory defined-contribution type, supplemented by other minor programmes. This is also known as the national provident fund method which requires contributions by employer as well as from employees with both record-keeping and investment functions undertaken centrally by the government statutory board. The policy-making framework for this kind of social security system 'requires a paternalistic government which is able to isolate economic decision-making from interest-group politics.'[18]

In Malaysia, out of several complementary social security schemes and institutions, it is the EPF-scheme based on individual provision which is the most important. In 1991, 45 per cent of the labour force was contributing to the EPF. Singaporeans' contribution of 40 per cent of gross wages and salaries to the CPF is the highest in the world.[19] These schemes do cover a considerable part of the population, but are insufficient and create a highly segmented class structure and social polarization between those inside and those outside the provident Fund system. Furthermore, the CPF scheme does not cover foreign workers who constitute about 20 per cent of the labour force.[20]

High saving rates may be connected with the lack of state provision of welfare, especially in old age. The special connection between savings and welfare and the conscious rejection of state involvement in Southeast Asia is mirrored in the fact that, 'Singapore's high savings rate can be largely explained by public policies rather than by any other factors.'[21] This explanation is also plausible in the case of Malaysia, contra the much celebrated myth about Southeast Asian households' high savings, which in fact have relied on policies and not on cultural characteristics.

The nexus of labour response and state regulation

During the 1960s and 1970s Left-wing forces in Southeast Asia mobilized labour in rural and urban areas against dictatorship and the intrusion of domestic and foreign capitalism. The socialist project was either crushed by US interference or failed simply as a consequense of the conflict between the Vietnamese and Chinese versions of socialism. Even if the situation in the Philippines is treated as more similar to the Latin American model of strong interference in economic policy-making from landed aristocrats (a feudal landowning class) and the business sector, the general pattern in the region has been one of dominance by the technocracy and high degree of dependency on external forces. The crushing of organized labour and the Left laid the ground for the Export Oriented Industrialization (EOI).

The implementation of EOI in Southeast Asia has differed from the Korean and Taiwanese experience. In the Thai case, 'the external factors for policy reform were the inflow of international capital and the relocation of light industries into the country. The internal factors were pressure from the local business sector, liberal technocrats and foreign advisors advocating a more liberal development strategy.'[22] Labour discipline and industrial peace is always a prerequisite for EOI development based on cheap labour. Disciplined labour, since the mid-1970s, resulted from political exclusion of labour which was guaranteed by the indirect intervention of the state. First, the state created a legal framework for industrial relations which encouraged weak and fragmented unionism. Another form of indirect control of labour is the establishment of institutional conditions for wage negotiation in the labour market. Wage bargaining in Thailand and Singapore have been governed through the minimum wage policy implemented under the supervision of the tripartite National Wage Committee.

In Malaysia there is no generally applicable minimum wage. However, workers in individual industries can seek the protection of a minimum wage and by 1991 less than 2 per cent of workers had done so. In Thailand and Indonesia minimum wages are relatively small proportions of average wages, and have shown no upward trend in real terms, and have lacked serious implementation.[23]

In Thailand and the Philippines, the stress on EOI led to a policy of wage restraint and attempts to promote institutional frameworks which could limit conflicts in industrial relations.[24] In these two countries, there have been periods of repression and periods of freer organization of labour, but the development strategy has largely been built around the 'political exclusion' of labour. The same type of labour market regulation has had the effect that trade unionism in the region has been severely weak or co-opted by the state. This has been the case in Malaysia and Singapore; whereas Indonesia, Thailand and the Philippines have been characterized by more inclusionary and repressive policy regimes.

Nevertheless, the general policy pattern of labour market regulation has been tight and repressive, and perhaps with the exception of Malaysia, trade union organization has been extremely difficult or under state guidance. In some countries like Thailand and Indonesia the fight for labour welfare, that is, improvement in pay and working conditions, is a dangerous and sometimes deadly affair. For instance, killings of labour activists in Indonesia were the result of attempts to organize labour in East Java and Medan.[25]

In Thailand, labour cutbacks in the textile industries, associated with the development of new managerial styles, resulted in strikes and protests by workers. According to a former director-general of the Labour Department, 'there is now an awakening among low level workers about their rights and privileges under the law... There is a rise in expectations. Chandravithun states that "only an estimated 30 per cent of companies paid the minimum wage of Baht 125 a day... In the textile industry workers on average were paid only Baht 4,000 a month for a 60-hour week, often in poor working conditions."'[26]

In Malaysia, the debate concerning existing limitations on labour union activity, particularly in the sensitive electronic components industries, erupts whenever the GSP privileges between the US and Malaysia are reviewed. From 1988, the American AFL–CIO has petitioned Washington to withdraw its GSP privilege pointing to the 120,000 Malaysian electronics workers who are being denied the right to organize into a nation-wide union. Dissident union leaders also place pressure on the government by taking the issue of government control over unions to international forums. The MTUC has several times tried to persuade the government to ratify ILO convention 87 on freedom of association, but without result. The Mahathir leadership has maintained strict containment of union activity, particularly since low-cost labour is considered to be the country's chief asset in attracting foreign investment. In Free Trade Zones, labour unions are prohibited and payment in the electronics industry is roughly one-third to one-quarter of similar wage levels in Singapore. According to Rajasekaran, executive director of the Metal Industries Employees Union, 'many companies are prepared to pay higher wages but the government asks them to keep them down.'[27] The result is a balkanization of unions in Malaysia and numerous small fragmented unions. The general problem of membership levels has stimulated larger unions to use incentives of small welfare schemes to members including services such as as retirement, sickness, death, and educational benefits.[28]

However, due to international pressure and the democratic opening, times are also changing in Southeast Asia. An embryonic demise of the legitimacy of state-sponsored and employer-dominated labour unions and the reemergence of independent, representative organizations are growing in militancy.[29] This is also the result of international organizations lobbying Western countries to impose trade sanctions in retaliation for the general disbanding of unions and ban on strikes. There is no doubt that labour welfare campaigns and common strategies aimed at the establishment of social security systems and other solidarity measures are increasing all over the region.[30]

Organized labour was an important force for achieving political change in the Philippines with the election of Aquino in 1986. Since that period, however, the class coalition that has consolidated state control has not included labour organizations, nor have they been directed at a fundamental change in socio-economic structures. As a result, real incomes in the country continue to be below the poverty line and the harassment and dismissal of union officials and violations of labour standards continue to be the main courses of industrial dispute.[31]

In Indonesia, independent unionism continued to grow despite the militarization of labour relations. Conservative estimates of the official government statistics reveal that strikes increased from 19 in 1989 to 310 for the first six months of 1994, often involving large-scale factories of between 2,000 and 12,000 workers. The increasing influence of big business led to growing concern about uneven development and economic inequality. This is further exacerbated by the expansion of rentier capitalism, which is not labour-intensive. It should be noted that these developments have taken place in an economy which must accommodate newcomers to the workforce at an annual rate of 2 million workers, where only a limited number of jobs are available.[32]

In Thailand, 'where unions have been able to preserve previously won gains and security through resistance to privatization, out-sourcing, flexibilization, and so forth, they evoke continued coercive state controls. Thus, for example, Thai labour repression has been sustained in the state enterprises sector, where unions effectively blocked privatization efforts and provided national leadership in labour's successful struggle to force the passage of expanded social security legislation in 1990.'[33] In Malaysia, the strong MTUC, with a membership of 500,000, has recently evoked moves aimed at trans-forming the federation into a representative and active organization. There have been strikes in the past few years that would have been previously unthinkable.

Labour regulation in the region takes on different forms. In In-donesia, it took the form of direct military intervention. In Thailand fewer than 5 per cent of industrial workers are in unions, although the public sector is better organized. In Malaysia, labour market relations are mediated through bureaucratic unionism similar to Japanese-style enterprise unionism, combined with harsh internal security laws that have been used to incarcerate labour activists. In the Philippines weak enterprise unionism is combined with state-sponsored violence against alternatives in the form of vigilante action. Despite the differing forms, they all reveal a high degree of coer-cive state intervention against the interests of labour.[34]

The aim of labour legislation has essentially been to attract foreign capital and to encourage EOI. In the case of TNCs, one study found that, since 1985, a significant number of Japanese firms have sought to undermine union organization with a range of tactics; these include sacking union leaders, forming pro-company second unions, employing temporary workers to break strikes, and match-ing union wage demands with their own 'counter demands' for worse conditions. While Japanese TNCs may preach co-operative industrial relations, the study notes that, 'in Thailand [they] do not practice what they are required [to] by the traditions in their own country.'[35]

TNCs tend to be less sensitive to social concerns as well as politi-cal pressures of national and regional authorities.[36] Thus, TNC workers in the region are much more exploited and inhibited from partici-pating in labour union activities. They are effectively prevented from having autonomous workers' organizations defending their standards of living through collective action and are almost wholly depen-dent upon the goodwill of management. Recent data show that the state intervened directly in slightly over one-half (51.9 per cent) of labour actions between 1968 and 1983. Workers experienced firings in 49.0 per cent of the events; detentions in 12.2 per cent; injuries in 8.2 per cent; and coerced terminations in 32.7 per cent. At least one form of repression occurred in two-thirds (67.3 per cent) of the cases.[37]

The suppression of ASEAN trade unions for the purpose of EOI has caused the erosion of real wages. The industrial working class is small and with a restrained political potential and mobilization. It has been easy for the state and policy elites to establish domination over the labour movements. During the colonial era in Malaya, the British fostered the formation of the MTUC as an alternative to the Communist unions. The MTUC today continues to be a moderate organization, hemmed in by many restrictive laws. In Indonesia a government-sponsored labour federation replaced independent unionism, which collapsed with the crushing of the Communist Party in 1965. Unions in Thailand have traditionally been small and fragmented, and occasionally under the influence of factions in the military and the government. Only in the Philippines does the leftist labour movement represent some sort of challenge to the government, but it is still not a potent force.[38]

The lack of bargaining power of the working class is also accentuated by uenemployment and the widespread underemployment in Thailand, Indonesia and the Philippines. Considering the sectoral distribution of production structures and labour force it is significant that none of the countries have experienced a substantial shift to agro-industrialism. The proportion of the work force in manufacturing and construction is only 13 per cent in Indonesia and the Philippines, 15 per cent in Thailand and 14.5 per cent in Malaysia. Omitting Malaysia, the share of the labour force in agriculture is more than half, revealing a low level of employment transition and mobility.

Another issue of importance has been foreign investors' interest in an environment of low production costs, including labour! What is interesting is the strategies and policies of TNCs and the push and pull factors behind social welfare.[39] What is argued here is that there is a convergence between the official views of the Southeast Asian elite and international corporate interests to support free trade and suppress labour costs in a unregulated environment.

Globalization of financial and capital markets is a matter of profits versus taxes and involves a punishment (for instance by increasing the risk premium and therefore borrowing costs) of those countries that deviate from conservative policy-making. Fiscal concerns are of utmost importance because social welfare expenditures have to be paid for through an increased tax burden, which would involve other standards with regard to ideology and political culture, and a radically new policy priority of the emerging NICs.

Two-tier non-welfare corporatism or militant labour welfare

It is possible to discern two scenarios. One scenario is related to a possible replication of the two-tier non-welfare corporatist approach in Japan. The second scenario is related to the increasing militancy of labour, which is a response to the growing unevenness and unequal distribution of wealth. 'Asian values', as they have been presented by the old developmental and paternalist guard, might soon be changing.

Southeast Asia might enter a period of corporatism 'without labour', which denotes a highly policy co-ordinated system but with a relatively small organized workforce belonging to company unions whose national federations are weak and politically marginalized. At the micro level this implies a system of private welfare corporations consisting of an array of workforce training facilities as well as assurances of employment security, reinforced with an array of corporate social welfare services. Private welfare corporatism is presented as a way of showing labour's interests and achieving consensus. Thus Japan is a two-tier system combining statist 'Corporatism without labour' with enterprise 'Welfare Corporatism'. This two-tier approach also exists elsewhere in East Asia, notably in Singapore, Taiwan and South Korea.[40] However, this model might also be called 'employer paternalism', indicating a particular mode of government (indirect control/support) which paradoxically can be seen as an outcome of the official belief in laissez faire. In Malaysia the percentage of in-house unions was 54.5 per cent in 1988. With government support, this type of unionization will probably increase significantly in the near future, implicating some success in emulating their Northeastern counterparts.[41]

The capacity for nation-wide social pacts is closely connected to future potential political instability in the region, such as labour unrest, foreign domination of national corporate sectors, and unequal economic development exacerbated by competition for capital investment and markets in similar products. The middle class has high expectations, particularly related to the infrastructure of cities, and is pressuring governments and the private sector to place higher priority on urban environmental improvement.[42]

Some political leaders such as Mahathir and Lee Kuan Yew paradoxically see their countries' economic future in terms of an educated workforce. 'This obviously implies growing commitments to education, health, and social services,'[43] and might well undermine the current non-welfare regime. What seems even more irreversible is an 'attitudinal shift from the dynastic to the life-cycle view of income and consumption under which accumulated savings are more likely to be spent than bequeathed.'[44]

This is a critical point, because it shows the paradox of embryonic welfare state construction in Southeast Asia. It is globally unique and represents a hybrid of existing welfare state characteristics with a content close to the ideal neoliberal model. It emphasizes familialism and an aversion to public social services. Another concern is with the possible negative impact on savings. The Asian tigers' economic miracle was premised on high saving rates rather than Keynesianism: Families save for lack of adequate social security coverage. 'A genuine welfare state, it is feared, will undermine this incentive.'[45] This view is well reflected in Karto's remarks about the priorities of the Malaysian policy elite: 'What contributions social security can make to economic development has become the priority rather than the social protection.'[46]

Although policy elites claim that social structures remain intact, they still try to reinforce a distinctive Asian culture. The situation in Singapore shows that so far the state has been able to maintain the primacy of societal or group interests over those of the individual, but affluence and widespread Western-based education and economic and social ties are likely to increase the tension between the two.[47]

Furthermore, the extended family is on the decline. What is at stake is the collapse of the traditional social support networks. The situation of social security in Indonesia 'will depend essentially on the economic development of the country until employment in the formal sector can be expanded considerably – and the organizational prerequisites for comprehensive social security thereby fulfilled – traditional forms of insurance will continue to predominate.'[48] However, even in Indonesia 'villages become urbanized, access to land denied, and workers are losing the informal social security net that had supported them in times of need. The other safety device, namely the high labour absorption capacity of the informal sector that had earlier supported industrial workers and their families is now also endangered.'[49]

The explosions of labour protest in Indonesia in the 1990s can be interpreted as a revolt against the idea that labour, rather than investors or management, should pay the cost of corporate globalization. 'The doctrine that prevails in international business today is that maximizing return on capital has priority over any other management responsibility. This priority, like the notion that increased industrial productivity and competitiveness must be exacted primarily from the labour force, is the result of arbitrary decisions.'[50]

Workers are demanding basic rights and reforms. In Indonesia, 'early stages of a shift in consciousness from passivity and resigned acceptance to a growing class consciousness ... expressed in an upsurge of collective strike action that will threaten Indonesia's image as a foreign investment haven.'[51] was observable from the early 1990s onwards. Indeed a militant form of independent unionism continued to grow despite the militarization of labour relations by the state.[52] Such trends played a key role in the revolution that eventually overthrew the Suharto dictatorship.

In Thailand, there is increasing evidense that because of the very low state schemes for improving the income and welfare of employee, workers initially concentrated on demands for wage increases. But this pattern has been changing. This is clear from the fact that 'major issues of labour disputes from 1987 to 1989 concerned welfare (33 per cent) wages (20 per cent) conditions of employment (18 per cent) and other issues (29 per cent).'[53] In the 1980s, the renewed pressure through public demonstrations and campaigns from the Labour Congress and Trade Union Congress resulted in the promulgation of the Social Security Act of 1990.[54] The first phase was implemented in 1992 and covers health insurance, maternity benefit, disability benefit and death benefit. The scheme is financed by employers, employees and the government, each paying 1.5 per cent of wages as contributions, but there is serious debate about the second phase.[55]

The impact of globalization and neoliberalism in Thailand has recently demanded privatization of the energy sector, but unions are fiercely trying to halt privatization. Thamyudh Suthivicha, president of the State Enterprises Employee Association, delivered an ultimatum to the government: 'Drop EGAT's privatization ... or the union will more than double the number of protesters on Bangkok's streets from the present 20,000 – mostly members of the Assembly of the Poor.'[56] The privatization programme called for laying off nearly half of EGAT's 33,900 workers.

The tactics used by the Indonesian and Thai governments and employers remain current in other Southeast Asian countries, but the new response on the part of labour against co-optation and repression are duplicated throughout the region. In the Philippines, the militant KMU has been able to win several battles against TNCs and thereby improve working conditions.[57] Furthermore, the KMU and other trade unions are involved in organizing a popular front working for the improvement of social standards in the country.

Corporate anti-union efforts in Malaysia are multi-faceted, and 'there have been strikes that would have been previously unthinkable.'[58] According to Jomo, 'labour's interests may be served by extending social security beyond the existing provisions for occupational disease and employment injury to cover unemployment benefits, sickness, maternity benefits, family allowances, invalidity pensions, old age pensions and survivors' pensions... However, the effective advocacy and advancement of labour's interests requires an institutionalized framework reflecting a social contract between capital and labour, which does not appear anywhere on Malaysia's political horizon for the time being.'[59] Nevertheless, the Malaysian trade union movement seems to be the most docile and weak in Southeast Asia.

The rise in public protest is tied to the stages of globalization. What is rising in Southeast Asia is a double-movement against downsizing in state expenditures on public benefits and wage constraints. It is essentially the opposite of Philippine leader Fidel Ramos' message to industrialists: 'I don't want to hear talk of wages and productivity gains going hand in hand. What makes sense is that wage costs must be kept in check. Grasp this point well for it is the price of your survival and the means for enhancing our international competitive capabilities.'[60] Flexibility is the buzzword meaning dismantling of the welfare state, even the sort of hybrid welfare state in Southeast Asia, but this issue is being contested from below by demands for democratization and social reforms.

Southeast Asia between neoliberalism and the quest for welfare

The hitherto distinctive 'Asian values' as the place of hierarchy and social conservatism, which originally encouraged discipline, now seem to stifle innovation and new ideas. Social harmony is waning and leisure is no longer managed by paternalist social relations. Will the younger urban generation accept the privatized systems of welfare in Singapore and Malaysia?[61] In the former, workers are compelled to contribute a substantial amount of their earnings to the CPF scheme which exists in a vacuum of a proper system of social security benefits and subsidized health. This is further exacerbated by a severe demographic problem consisting of massive migration into urban industrial centres, a process which undermines traditional forms of social protection. In Southeast Asia, this poses a dilemma between hypothetical welfare construction and corporate plans, and the traditional stress on familialism with its care obligations.

The approach of non-welfare by the elites is only possible to implement if an autocratic political system is in place to restrict the rights of individuals, to ban labour rights and to enforce controls of the media. The real achievement of such a system is not social security but social control.[62]

The debate about social and cultural values can be used for various political purposes. Singapore's philosophy regarding social security discourages any kind of system akin to the European model. To its leaders, it is important that Singaporeans do not lean on social security, be spoiled and become 'soft'.[63] Singapore is probably the first high-income country in the world which attempts to provide social security while rejecting the main foundations of the welfare state. This is done through a system of individual provisions, rejection of social insurance, and an extremely limited public assistance system based on the Poor Law tradition.[64]

The problem of social welfare in Southeast Asia has closely followed the neoliberal ideology of globalization which is essentially a matter of identifying needs, solving problems and creating opportunities at the individual level. The causes behind the needs for support are believed to rest overwhelmingly in individuals and subcultural defects and dispositions. Responsibility is deflected from states and national economic, administrative and legal organizations to individuals and groups. Little or no attention is paid to the interacting consequences of economic and social change for families, employment, taxation, housing, social security and public services. Laissez-faire individualism and the legitimation of discrimination are in fact the intellectual sources of this tradition.

This particular version of social welfare is in practice closely based on welfare theories about social philanthropy. It is difficult to discern any specific 'Asian value' in this context, except for the fact that it rests on a particular ideology which is used as a repressive tool to discipline labour's demands for social security and demands which could humanize and socialize work, living conditions and economic relations.

With the advent of the East Asia crisis following the devaluation of the Thai baht in July 1997, it is necessary to conclude by discussing the reasons for the crisis, its impact on social welfare, and its potential impact on resistance to neoliberal globalization. As to the first point, four basic problems can be identified as key factors causing the Asian financial crisis:

1 global overproduction and the fact that all the economies prefer EOI;
2 forced deregulation of financial and monetary controls in East Asia, encouraged by the IMF and the World Bank, in collaboration with international productive and financial capital;
3 the revaluation of the Yen and the devaluation of the Chinese Yuan, which caused tremendous competitive pressure on the EOI economies of Southeast Asia in particular; and
4 the growing influence and pressure of national business sectors on policy-makers to liberalize the economies, resulting in over borrowing by the private sector. In short, the problem may be termed 'market failures'.

To the second problem, the double pressure from the World Bank and other Western dominated organizations, and by domestic labour, on national policy elites to increase public entitlements and social welfare increased as the crisis deepened. Thirdly, the so-called financial crisis is actually more what Peter Drucker has termed a 'social crisis'. There is no doubt it is also a crisis of 'neoliberal globalization'. The re-invention of nationalist economies, protectionism, and control of foreign capital may strengthen the popular forces and the anti-Americanism throughout the region. Resistance against neoliberal globalization and foreign control over the local economies may once again become much stronger (in a Polanyian double movement); thus strengthening local democratic control over economic development.

Notes

1 Gregory Albo, 'Competitive Austerity' and the Impasse of Capitalist Employment Policy', in Ralph Miliband and Leo Panitch (eds), *Between Globalism and Nationalism, Socialist Register 1994* (Merlin Press, 1994), p. 147.
2 Yupa Wongchai, 'Thailand', in John Dixon and Hyung Shik Kim (eds), *Social Welfare in Asia* (Croom Helm, 1985), p. 357 and p. 363.
3 Mukul G. Asher, *Social Security in Malaysia and Singapore: Practices, Issues and Reform Directions* (Institute of Strategic and International Studies (ISIS Malaysia), 1994), p. 56.
4 Yupa Wongchai, *op. cit.*, p. 378.
5 Evelina A. Pangalangan, 'Philippines', in Dixon and Kim, *op. cit.*, pp. 247.
6 Yupa Wongchai, *op. cit.*, pp. 363.
7 Pasuk Pongpaichit, Sungsidh Piriyarangsan and Nualnoi Treevat, 'Patterns and Processes of Social Exclusion in Thailand', in Gerry Rodgers, Charles Gore, José B. Figueiredo, *Social Exclusion: Rhetoric, Reality, Responses* (ILO, 1995), p. 151.
8 *Ibid.*, p. 159.
9 Asher, *Social Security in Malaysia and Singapore*, p. 33.
10 Amira Tyabji, 'Social Security in the Asian-Pacific Region', *Asian-Pacific Economic Literature*, Vol. 7, No. 1, p. 62 (1993).
11 Asher, *Social Security in Malaysia and Singapore*, p. 63.
12 Roger Goodman and Ito Peng, 'The East Asian Welfare States: Peripatetic Learning, Adaptive Change, and Nation-Building', in Gøsta Esping-Andersen, (ed.), *Welfare States in Transition: National Adaptions in Global Economics* (UNRISD and Sage, 1996), p. 198. The reference is Byung Hyun Park, 'The development of social welfare institutions in East Asia: case studies of Japan, Korea, and the People's Republic of China 1945–89', Ph.D. thesis, School of Social Work, University of Pennsylvania, 1990 (quoted in Goodman and Peng, p. 223).
13 Donald K. Crone, 'States, Social Elites, and Social Welfare in Southeast Asia', *World Development*, Vol. 21, No. 1 (1993), p. 62.
14 Mukul G. Asher, 'Financing Old Age in Southeast Asia: An overview', *Southeast Asian Affairs 1996* (Singapore: ISEAS, 1996), pp. 80–3.
15 Sjahrir, 'Challenging "Business as Usual", in Jan-Paul Dirkse, Frans Husken and Mario Rutten (eds), *Development and Social Welfare. Indonesia's Experiences Under the New Order* (KITLV, 1993), p. 40.
16 Wardah Hafidz, 'Poverties Beyond Economics', in Jan-Paul Dirkse *et al.*, *op. cit.*, p. 220.
17 Asher, 'Financing old Age', pp. 74–6.
18 Asher *Social Security in Malaysia and Singapore*, pp. 5–7, and pp. 15, 21, 45, 54 and 74.
19 Tyabji, *op. cit.*, p. 56.
20 Asher, 'Financing Old Age', pp. 79 and 89.
21 *Ibid.*, p. 88.
22 Sungsidh Piriyarangsan and Kanchada Poonpanick, 'Labour institutions in an export-oriented country. A case study of Thailand', in Gerry Rodgers (ed.), *Workers, Institutions and Economic Growth in Asia* (ILO, 1994), pp. 249–50.

23 Azizur Rahman Khan, 'Structural Adjustment, Labour Market, and Employment', *Asian Development Review*, Vol. 13, No. 2, p. 88.

24 Frederic C. Deyo, *Beneath the Miracle: Labor Subordination in the New Asian Industrialism* (University of California Press, 1989).

25 *Economist*, 9 July 1994, p. 60.

26 Cited in Jacques Bierling, 'The "Developing Powers": Thailand, Malaysia, the Philippines and Indonesia', *Current Sociology*, Vol. 43, No. 1 (1995), p. 104.

27 *Ibid.*, p. 104.

28 Ponniah Arudsothy and Craig R. Littler, 'State Regulation and Union Fragmentation in Malaysia', in Stephen Frenkel (ed.), *Organized Labor in the Asia-Pacific Region. A Comparative Study of Trade Unionism in Nine Countries* (ILR Press, 1993), p. 126.

29 See Rob Lambert and Donella Caspersz, 'International Labour Standards: Challenging Globalization Ideology?' *The Pacific Review*, Vol. 8, No. 4 (1995), pp. 572, 580 and 583.

30 Andrew Brown and Stephen Frenkel, 'Union Unevenness and Insecurity in Thailand', in Frenkel (ed.), *op. cit.*, pp. 82–106.

31 Bierling, *op. cit.*, pp. 104–5. See also Barry Gills *et al.*, *Low Intensity Democracy: Political Power in the New World Order* (Pluto Press, 1993), who argue that democratic change has not been oriented to genuine reform in the socio-economic structure.

32 Jan-Paul Dirkse, Frans Husken and Mario Rutten, 'Poverty in Indonesia: Policy and Research', in Dirkse *et. al.*, *op. cit.*, p. 8.

33 See Frederic C. Deyo, 'Capital, Labor, and State in Thai Industrial Restructuring: The Impact of Global Economic Transformations', in David A. Smith and Jozsef Borocz (eds), *A New World Order? Global Transformations in the Late Twentieth Century* (Greenwood Press, 1995), p. 141.

34 Rob Lambert, *Authoritarian State Unionism in New Order Indonesia*, Working Paper no. 25 (October) (Murdoch University: Asia Research Centre 1993), p. 34, fn 9.

35 Hugh Williamson, 'Japanese Enterprise Unions in Transnational Companies: Prospects for International Co-operation', *Capital & Class*, No. 45 (Autumn, 1991); and Somsak Kosaisuk, *Labour Against Dictatorship*, Friedrich Ebert Stiftung Labour Museum Project (Bangkok: Arom Pongsangan Foundation, 1990).

36 The classic example being Nike, the American sports shoe supplier which uses about 40 factories; 20 have closed in the past five years (1992) or so and another 35 have opened. *Far Eastern Economic Review*, 5 November 1993. The basic reason why Nike has made substantial investment in Indonesia is because of the extremely repressive Labour regime. For details, see William Seaman, 'The Current Crisis in Indonesia. Interview with Benedict Anderson', ZMagazine December 1996.

37 Note that 12 countries are included in the sample. David Kowalewski, 'Asian State Repression and Strikes Against Transnational', in George A. Lopez and Michael Stoll (eds), *Dependence, Development and State Repression, Contributions in Political Science*, No. 209 (New York: Greenwood Press, 1989), pp. 73.

38 Harold Crouch and James W. Morley, 'The Dynamics of Political Change',

in James W. Morley (ed.), *Driven by Growth: Political Change in the Asia-Pacific Region* (New York: M. E. Sharpe, 1993), p. 285.

39 Johannes Dragsbaek Schmidt, 'The Challenge from Southeast Asia. Social Forces between Equity and Growth', in Chris Dixon and David Drakakis-Smith (eds), *Uneven Development in Southeast Asia*, (Avebury: 1997).

40 Sanford M. Jacoby, 'Social Dimensions of Global Economic Integration', in Jacoby (ed.), *The Workers of Nations: Industrial Relations in a Global Economy* (Oxford University Press, 1995), p. 21.

41 See the details in Ponniah Arudsothy and Craig R. Littler, 'State Regulation and Union Fragmentation in Malaysia', in Frenkel (ed.), *op. cit.*, pp. 128–30.

42 Douglass Webster, 'The Urban Environment in Southeast Asia: Challenges and Opportunities', *Southeast Asian Affairs 1995* (ISEAS, 1995), p. 89.

43 Esping-Andersen, 'After the Golden Age? Welfare State Dilemmas in a Global Economy', in Esping-Andersen (ed.), *op. cit.*, pp. 9 and 10.

44 Mukul G. Asher, 'Social Security Systems a Regional Challenge', *Bangkok Post*, 18 May 1995, p. 16.

45 Esping-Andersen, 'After the Golden Age?' p. 24.

46 D. Karto, 'Social Security in Malaysia', *ASEAN Economic Bulletin*, Vol. 3, No. 1 (1985), quoted in Amina Tyabji, *op. cit.*, p. 63.

47 Asher, *Social Security in Malaysia and Singapore*, p. 34.

48 M. Queisser, 'Social Security Systems in South-East Asia', *International Social Security Review*, Vol. 44, No. 1–2 (1991). Quoted from Amina Tyabji, *op. cit.*, p. 63.

49 Hans-Dieter Evers, 'The Growth of an Industrial Labour Force and the Decline of Poverty in Indonesia', *Southeast Asian Affairs* (ISEAS, 1995), p. 169.

50 William Pfaff, 'Why should workers bear the brunt of globalization pain?' *International Herald Tribune*, 13 January 1997.

51 Rob Lambert, *Authoritarian State Unionism in New Order Indonesia*, Working Paper No. 25 (Murdoch University: Asia Research Centre, October 1993), p. 33.

52 Lambert, *ibid.*

53 Sunsidh Piriyarangsan and Kanchada Poonpanich, *op. cit.*, p. 241.

54 Andrew Brown and Stephen Frenkel, in Frenkel (ed.), *op. cit.*, p. 104.

55 Mukul G. Asher, 'Social Security Systems a Regional Challenge', *Bangkok Post*, 18 May 1995, p. 16.

56 Vissuta Pothong, 'Union Uses Shock Tactics to Halt Thai Power Selloff', *Asia Times*, 18 March 1997.

57 'Recolonizing Southeast Asia', *Multinational Monitor*, November 1993.

58 Lambert and Caspesz, *op. cit.*, n. 29 p. 579.

59 K. S. Jomo, 'Capital, the State and Labour in Malaysia', in Juliet Schor and Jong-Il You, *Capital, the State and Labour: A Global Perspective* (Edward Elgar & UNU/WIDER, 1995), p. 236.

60 Quoted from Frederic Clairmont, 'The G-7 and the Spectre of Job Destruction', *Third World Resurgence*, No. 44 (1994), p. 22.

61 Mukul G. Asher, *Social Adequacy and Equity of the Social Security Arrangements in Singapore* (Times Academic Press, 1991), p. 1.

62   See also Johannes Dragsbaek Schmidt *et al.*, *Social Change in Southeast Asia* (Longman, 1997).

63   Quoted in Tyabji, *op. cit.* n. 10, p. 66.

64   See Mukul G. Asher, 'Financing Old Age in Singapore: Are There Lessons for the Welfare States?, Paper prepared for the Third International Research Seminar on Issues in Social Security, 11–14 May 1996, Sigtuna, Sweden, pp. 4–5.

15
Globalization, Islam and Resistance

Mustapha Kamal Pasha

The ascendancy of hyperliberalism on a world scale with emphases on post-Fordist strategies of flexible accumulation, the retrenchment of the state in the social economy, and the marginalization of large populations in the global political economy, gives the present phase of capitalism a distinct flavour as the apotheosis of a unified materialist order. Imbued with mysterious and unbounded powers, homogenizing in scope and content, and with scant respect for cultural difference, this order, understood as 'globalization', takes on the appearance of inevitability. Though challenges to its singular compulsion and logic assume diverse forms, they are received either as a rejection of modernity,[1] that is, particularistic responses to a universal civilization with its centre in the West, or reversionary exercises of a dying order.[2] Globalization represents the high drama of world politics; opposition to globalization recedes into the background. Focusing on the Islamic cultural areas, this chapter proposes an alternative to hyperliberal notions of globalization and offers new understandings of resistance to economic globalization.

Assuming a basic cleavage between a global market project and a politics that is encoded in a religious idiom, one is likely to reproduce the universal–particular dualism which renders resistance merely as a mirror of localism.[3] This dualism has been an integral part of thinking about economic, social, political, and cultural differences between rich and poor countries, the industrialized powers in the North and peripheral areas in the South.[4]

Rather, if economic globalization is approached as a specific, uneven, incomplete, and contradictory phenomenon, the re-articulation of Islam acquires a more open-ended character, one with competing tendencies.[5] This alternative vantage-point avoids the propensity

to reify globalization, recognizing instead the practical consciousness of agents and their ability to constitute meaning in diverse
ways.[6] Despite the apparent inevitability of globalization, then, social
processes can be seen as contested terrains. Similarly, the unidirec-
tional thrust of economic globalization can be questioned.

Globalization and resistance

Global hyperliberalists equate *culture with consumption*. Advancing
a particular notion of individual, society, and community, they
acknowledge the presence of some common innate propensity in
humans to seek fulfillment via consumption of commodities. The
social order envisaged to realize this human capacity rests on the
dominance of exchange as *the* organizing principle of social life.
On this view, community and social cohesion are incidental products of atomistic self-seeking actors. Fulfilling the Smithian propensity
to truck, barter and exchange, human beings construct a high social
order, free of natural constraints or anarchy. Though circumscribed
by space and time, hyperliberals present their model as a universal
blueprint for international society. Denying its own historicity,
proponents of hyperliberalism do not see its claims arising within
a certain phase in the development of *a disembedded economy on a
world scale*. Nor is the idea of a disembedded economy seen in the
wider *political* context within which it has emerged.[7] More immediately, the post-socialist world order poses no ideological competition,
nor is it able to mount an effective challenge to economic
globalization. Without the discursive parsimony of the Cold War,
resistance to hyperliberalism appears in a patently *cultural* form,
pushing out of focus alternative issues of marginality, poverty, inequality, and exploitation. Instead, social injustice and its political
expressions in the Muslim World become recognizable only as *religious* protest or *cultural* resistance. The necessary, though complex
nexus between social dislocation under globalizing conditions, and
Islam is subordinated to a link between modernity and tradition.

Contra the hyperliberal view, the idea of globalization captures
an intricate phenomenon, a set of discontinuities inscribed on our
social existence. A radical departure from established modalities of
organizing economic and political life, globalization underscores the
reconstitution of polity, economy, and identity: i.e. the re-articulation of political space in favour of the translocal over the local;
the rise of a 'borderless economy'; and the permeation of unstable

identities.[8] To the point, it congeals a fruition of technological and economic development linked to historical patterns of capitalist exchange, production, and consumption. With the compression of time and space, old patterns have dissipated, yielding new challenges.[9]

In this expanded idea of globalization lies the recognition that social processes are porous, interlinked across 'national' space. 'Globalization' denotes the growing subordination of national, domestic, or local elements in the social process to transnational forces via the internationalization of finance, production, and the state.[10] In the final analysis, the processes are ultimately *social*; the global order is not 'some immense communicational and computer network'.[11]

Islam and 'resistance'

Global neoliberalism increasingly takes on the appearance of cultural homogenization, sustaining the fiction that allows Islamic politics *in its entirety* to appear as merely a *cultural* 'reaction' to globalization. With neither an internal centre nor agency, the re-articulation of Islam in the quotidian practices of Muslims across geographic frontiers, spanning varied local contexts, becomes subsumed under the common rubric of resistance to globalization. Ironically, by making the epithet of resistance fit every conceivable political and social practice in the Muslim World, the neoliberal view of globalization, gives actual resistance quixotic properties. Even critiques of globalization that stress the impact of flexible accumulation on human relations on a world-scale end up denying the *internality* of social processes in the Muslim world. In celebrating opposition to homogenization, resistance itself is *homogenized*. An indiscriminate mixing of diverse social movements, actors, attitudes, passions, and interests in the Muslim World produces the misguided effect of shifting focus away from contradictory social impulses in favour of elements that privilege religious affinities. Reducing politics to economic globalization, in turn, empties out the cultural content and its *particularized* expression in diverse local contexts.

Islam and globalization

Islamic social movements are both a moment *of*, and a reaction *to*, neoliberal globalization. In either case, they are only an aspect of globalization. At base, these movements embody multilayered historical forces and currents; the sources and modalities of Islamic resistance to globalization are themselves diverse and complex. Invariably, they are conditioned by local circumstance, the form neoliberalism has embraced, and the relative strengths and weaknesses of social forces combating the materialist order. Thus, the character of Islamic politics offers a heterodox picture: Algeria, Iran, Turkey, or Pakistan, for instance, have demonstrably distinctive patterns.[12] The conflict between Algeria's secular nationalists and the Islamic Salvation Front (FIS) may be interpreted as the culmination of a virtual cultural partition of the country, traceable to French colonialism and its uneven effects on Algerian society. The case of Iran on the other hand, is inexplicable without recognition and comprehension of notions of authority and legitimacy drawn from Shi'a Islamic constructions of political order, and the experience of the Shah's failed revolution from above. Turkey's political and cultural ambivalence is linked to Ottoman distemper as to the form modern or secular nationalism has taken. The sectarian character of Pakistan's numerically small, yet forceful, Islamic movement may represent local anxieties and political inheritance, rather than global concerns.[13]

Recognizing the 'horizontal' and 'vertical' aspects of Islam,[14] we need to recognize that the Muslim world is a complex of *living* societies. While there may be a broad agreement on the status of God's centrality in the Muslim worldview and the corresponding, subordinate role of human beings (the vertical dimension), there is tremendous variation within the world of Islam in the nature of social institutions and practice. The historically received awareness of a spatial (or horizontal) separation between the Islamic and the non-Islamic cultural areas, is also complemented *internally* by differences in wealth, power, and economic capacity. Islam, itself, is seen 'as a system of ideal social behavior and as a path toward experiential knowledge of God'.[15] Belief in a revealed scripture and vision of an ideal Muslim society produces complex permutations: the Islam of the *'ulama* and the Islam of the *sufis*, for instance, is quite different.[16]

Yet, there are common signs of a basic rupture in the social lifeworld of Muslim countries. Ever since the decline of the Ottoman, Safavid, and Mughal empires and the consolidation of European power, Muslim states and society have been in the process of reconstitution. Crucial to this process was the inauguration of a cultural chasm *within* Muslim society over the nature of the ideal political community, legitimacy, and identity. Throughout the seventeenth and eighteenth centuries, Muslim society witnessed reformist, revivalist or 'scripturalist' movements.[17] In part responses to endogenous problems, but largely an expression of a quest to establish new identities under conditions of foreign rule and subordination, these movements instituted a growing cultural divide. In vast regions of the Muslim lands, these movements became the basis of anti-colonial resistance, either in an India or an Indonesia, under the leadership of religious and spiritual authorities.[18] A similar pattern was detectable in Central Asia and North Africa, where *sufi* movements waged struggles against Russian, Chinese, or West European expansion.

Key to an awareness of Islamic resurgence is the historical appreciation of the European colonial impact, especially in its role in eroding the traditional self-image of Muslims themselves, notably in the area of cultural self-sufficiency.[19] In this vein, the current phase of resurgence can be viewed as the articulation of hidden or suppressed sensibilities in Muslim collective consciousness, but more accurately as a continuation of an unsuccessful process of decolonization. By projecting resurgence of a revolt against the West, a new 'national consciousness' can be created.[20]

The roots of the re-articulation of Islam under globalizing conditions are, therefore, quite extensive and deep. But there is a marked difference in the character of 'political' Islam in the twilight of the twentieth century. Islamic movements are not simply a response to Western conquest and control, but a movement against western-centred globalization, promoted by fractions *within* Muslim society, and a movement *for* realizing an alternative to secular-nationalism. To the extent that alternatives for building a (religious) community, society, and state do not emerge in a pure form, themselves shaped by the experience of subordination, they carry all the antinomies of a derivative discourse of modernity.[21] With neoliberal globalization, the contradictions of Muslim society, which appear as cultural polarization, have acquired a new form.

Time–space compression reinforces the image of Islamic resurgence as a transnational volcano, ready to *simultaneously* erupt in different locales. To attempt to homogenize this phenomenon is to privilege the putative goals of its passionate adherents or its opponents rather than to acknowledge the silences that undergird its narrative. It is in the recognition of its own problems that Islamic resurgence under globalizing conditions is lent a true distinction. Economic dislocation, re-articulations of space and time, and dispersion of collective and personal identities are producing a heightened awareness of marginality in the midst of affluence; a condition now facing a 'universal culture of consumption and communication.'[22] By rejecting the notion that social change necessitates secularization, one can encounter different forms of negotiations *in*, and not simply *with*, the modern world.

In short, the key to linking globalizing tendencies to 'resistance' in the Muslim world is a delineation of those material and symbolic intrusions that are affecting the *local* character, composition, and content of Islamic resurgence. Implicit in this thinking is an acknowledgement of the historical basis of Islamic movements, and their relative autonomy from homogenizing global currents. There is also the recognition of an analytical separation between local and *globalizing* processes, a separation ostensibly blurred by globalization. Resistance straddles the two, interlinked, worlds.

In breaking up communities built around principles of redistribution or reciprocity, global capitalism is no doubt an equal opportunity offender. Yet, there are multiple vectors of instituting the market and numerous patterns of defiance. Hence the need for recognizing the *differentiated* character of Islamic resurgence and the alleged forms of resistance to globalization. There is considerable temptation to lump heterodox phenomena under the heading 'Islamic fundamentalism', to bracket disparate forms of 'Islamic' consciousness as 'resistance to globalization', or to see Islam as 'an irrational and backward form of human consciousness'.[23]

Generally, resistance to globalization has arisen in civil society. Seen as a 'moral defence' against alien values, Islam offers to its adherents the resources of an 'endogenous ideology with redeeming powers', but in the context of the failures of secular-nationalism, a site to conduct a 'war of position' in order to capture and reconstitute the state.[24] Paradoxically, the major thrust of globalization also lies in civil society. Taking civil society as an arena for realizing its promise and peril, neoliberal globalists undernourish the state. In this regard, civil society ends up playing a contradictory role: i.e. as the site of deepening globalizing tendencies and resistance to globalization. The Islamic movements embody the twin character of being both a moment of and resistance to globalization. The burden of welfare retrenchment and marginalization has fallen on those social sectors least capable of negotiating globalization. With major demographic shifts, migration flows, and the growth in the population of college-educated students, often without jobs, the scale of the problem is only getting larger. Growing inequities are undermining efforts to provide adequate schooling, and the character of education imbibes the neglect it has generally received in the Muslim world, except in Turkey and parts of Islamic South-east Asia. Without the development of educational infrastructures, knowledge production has increasingly assumed 'lumpen' forms of schooling, with obvious effects. Social and scientific truths are often sacrificed in favor of dogmatism.

For the sake of simplification, two sets of processes can be identified here: first, the insertion of an 'Islamic' texture into the social fabric of everyday life and the growth in religious centers, notably mosques, and pietist associations.[25] Broadly viewed, this is the *zone of piety*. The basic thrust of Islamization here is a 'war of position' that takes cultural institutions as the bridgehead to the transformation of society and state.[26] This 'civil' arena of Islamic politics offers a counter-discourse to the failed policies of secular nationalists, but it also underscores the withdrawal of the state from responsibility for welfare in the context of globalization. The role of the Muslim Brotherhood across the Middle East, for example, fits the characterization of Islamicists in this sphere.

The social world of the cities is invariably complex, indeterminate, and paradoxical. At one level, the ambivalence towards secular modernity, clearly more pronounced in the urban areas, may confirm the tensions inherent in an ongoing sexual (or gender) revolution in the world of Islam.[27] Removed from established patterns of rural life, the vast majority of Muslim youth who now inhabit the congested cities, confront unexpected sexual encounters with the opposite sex. Both men and women now face the pressures to reconcile employment with social conservatism. From urban living to employment to mobility, the new social universe transmits multiplicities of sexual messages. Globalization has only accentuated communication. In this context, Islam serves as a coherent internal center to filter out disturbing external tensions. The sexual revolution in the Islamic cultural areas is implicated in the zone of piety. By promising to transform society, that is, *Islamizing* it, an ideal city can be built. Vital to this promise is the notion of building a *'dar ul Islam'* (realm of Islam); the intrusion of 'impure' elements, mainly from the West, carried by secular nationalists, are recognized as ingredients of *'dar ul harb'* (realm of war).

Second, by contrast, the Muslim world is also the home of 'wars of manoeuvre' designed to strike an un-Islamic state and society directly, as in the case of the Iranian Revolution, and the recent Islamic movements in Algeria, the Sudan, and Afghanistan. Weakened by internal contradictions and with a weak political base, state structures in several Muslim states have become a target of assault from politically better organized social forces *outside* the state. This is mostly the case in the countries with more authoritarian rule. Facing threat of extinction, state managers here often rely on external support, notably from Western powers, to prop up their faltering regimes. Gravitation towards the West, usually in the name of secular and liberal alternatives, widens the gap between the westernizing elites and the rest of (Islamic) society.

Differences between the two strategies are not absolute. It would be a mistake to essentialize the difference between Islamic movements that are seeking to overturn the status quo in society and those that want to capture political power. These movements are united by context, history, and memory. At the same time, the sources and compulsions of Islamic re-assertion are heterodox: the pattern shows considerable variation and diversity, since the social forces in local contexts originate from very different sets of historical conditions. From the near-success of the Islamic Salvation Front (FIS) in Algeria in capturing power, after an electoral victory in December 1991, to the growing assertion of religion in Central Asia, and South-east Asia,[28] contemporary Islamic movements want to reconstitute both state and society. During the colonial period, the privileged and under-privileged parts of society pursued two radically opposed rhythms. The same appears to be the case in the Muslim world. However, with globalization, the character of polarization is now of a *hybrid* variety.

The terms of Islamic discourse reveal a creative tension between sensibilities that draw from the pre-colonial society and those that have arisen primarily as a response to external intrusion.[29] A wide discursive space of disparate voices has long existed in the Muslim World. Sometimes united by appeals to Islamic iconography, but often divided by local conditions and interests, Islamicists (those who pursue the project of Islamizing polity, economy, or society) demonstrate an ambivalence towards modernity. For some, modern society is inherently godless, unjust and authoritarian, an embodiment of *jahiliya* (period of ignorance, or pre-Islamic times).[30] The central point is to understand how Muslims themselves envision their role, recover their culture, and constitute community.

The contradictory nature of Islamic social movements is vividly captured in the Islamicist stance toward the technical-instrumental and cultural aspects of modernity, enthusiastically accommodating the former, but rejecting wholesale the latter. European hegemony is clearly implicated in Muslim modernism. Notions of the modern state, state–society relations, and social transformation are products of an interface between Islam and the West. A curious instance of this interface lies in the composition of contemporary Islamic movements. For the most part, the mainstay of Islamicist youth groups are not students in the humanities and the arts, but those who have an interest in computers, technical knowledge, physics, and above all, engineering. The willingness of youth in several Muslim countries to pursue higher education in technical subjects without displaying an outward sign of accepting secular modes of life congeals the contradictory aspects of modernity in the Muslim world.

However, to align reform simply with westernizing elements is to caricature the attempts by Muslim intellectuals, including Sayyid Ahmad Khan, (1817–98); Jamal al-din-al-Afghani (1839–97), Muhammad Abduh (1849–1905) and the contemporary Islamic movements to blend modernist and reformist tendencies. There are autonomous wellsprings of Islamic discourse and established mores of formal and informal knowledge and practice. Responses to globalization arise within the parameters of Muslim culture and civilization, but in an environment that has *always* been changing.

Historically, the Western impact produced two interlocking rhythms of change in the Muslim World, each tied to a different temporal vision. There appears to be a collusion between two temporal visions, a vision that draws from the past, and a vision that denies the past. The Western impact pushed Muslim society towards an externally-driven modernization project under secular-nationalists. Alternatively, many Muslims were drawn towards building society mainly in line with 'its own internal movement, and partly in reaction to forces coming from outside'.[31] Neither tendency has been autonomous, i.e. from mutual influence. Between these modular forms lies an army of voices that gives the spatial world of Islam a quintessentially heterodox character. The inclination for *Islah* (reform) versus *taqlid* (imitation) operates within the same cultural milieu.[32]

Against the backdrop of orientalist constructions of the Muslim world, on the one hand,[33] and the totalizing rhetoric of economic globalization, on the other, the re-articulation of Islam in the political and personal spheres of social life appears basically anti-modernist.

Challenging the linear prognosis of historical evolution, with secularization as a crucial plank of societal development, Islamic assertiveness
offers a competing image of change. A less parochial periodization
of time would reject linearity and allow a different perspective. The
origins of an *Islamic* politics predates both European and Western
hegemony. The religious component of anti-colonial struggles is
only a part of the story. In the face of European colonialism, and
under conditions of western-centered globalization, the context of
politics has experienced perceptible changes.[34] Even those who have
considered themselves insulated from *western-centred* modernity have
had to face social conditions deeply touched by external impact.
For a very long time, the seeds of transformation have been conditioned by political and cultural contact.

The failure of secular-nationalism

With the failure of secular-nationalism in much of the Third World,
including Muslim countries, new centers of cultural assertion have
arisen. The imposition of neoliberal policies gives these centers both
a *raison d'être* and appeal. Given the transformation of both economy
and state under conditions of neoliberal globalization, social forces
in the periphery must organize or perish. Originally designed to
provide self-help, the new Islamic movements have become the
sources of resistance and alternatives to materialism. Hence, the
traditional domain for social welfare of the state is now occupied
by private Muslim schools, clinics, even garbage collection. Self-
help centres for women provide important social services. What
usually passes as the delegitimation of the state is more precisely
state retrenchment. Islam is not simply a set of religious rituals,
but the social cement that binds communities that are being abandoned by the neoliberal state. Seeking support in the private sector,
Muslim associations service the religious and social needs of an
economically disenfranchised population. Hence, they have become
the mainstay of providing public services, setting up institutions
that cater to the needs of large sectors of the bottom half of society.

Appealing, to those with neither power nor privilege, Islamic resistance is primarily a cry of the disinherited.[35] Ostensibly tackling
questions of core values in building a social order,[36] Islamicists are
drawn from the peripheral sectors of Muslim societies, the shanty
towns in burgeoning metropolis or universities, with growing armies
of the reserve army of the unemployed *lumpen*-intellectuals. The

connection between the assertiveness of Islam and marginalization is not casual: it is in the marginal sectors of Muslim society that religious awareness 'and desire to bring Islam back to the center of Muslim thought and practice' are more pronounced.[37] Social rigidities, widespread corruption, and political distemper may be important correlates, yet they always appear as cultural forms of resistance to globalization. *Islamic resurgence is not about religion per se.*[38] Ultimately, the assertiveness of Islamic identities is an expression of marginality itself; the re-articulation of Islam is both an expression of marginality and a cry against it. Without addressing the social context of the resurgence, one is likely to dismiss it as a lingering presence of a traditional society.

The rise of Muslim communities of self-help in many parts of the Islamic cultural areas, however, is also tied to the growing petit bourgeois artisans, merchants and students, and sections of the middle class, not only the dispossessed. The rise of new social groups, linked to the oil economies, especially migrant workers, as in Pakistan, who have re-entered society as a non-proletarian element, gives globalization its palpable rendition.[39] The global division of labour, a key element of globalization, may be responsible for engendering new social forces and disrupting old social hierarchies.[40]

Conclusion

Drawing its vitality from a wide spectrum of memory, resistance to neoliberal globalization is congealed in Islamicization movements that take the failure of the post-colonial state, but especially its incapacity to manage peripheral economies and preserve the life-lines of Islamic culture, as their starting-point. Islamic resurgence appears to have replaced the previously dominant ideologies of secular nationalisms and Marxism.[41] Many Islamicists propose alternative forms of social engineering drawn from modernist assumptions of societal development and political power. While these views are often glossed over in covering Islam in the West, they guide policy and ideology.[42] The terms of discourse and modes applied by Islamicists are quite distinct from the ones used by westernizing elites. But underpinning the Islamicist discourse is not only popular memory, with an autonomy of the sources of consciousness rooted in Islam, but also modernism.

An analysis of contemporary Islamic movements defies the hyper-liberal promise of a world unified by markets, telecommunications, or consumer culture. Although, there are several homogenizing forces at work, the *social* context of change and transformation necessitates recognition of both the diversity of forms of life and the irreducible capacity of human beings to resist unilinear pathways towards the future. The re-articulation of Islam under globalizing conditions underscores the point that it is human beings that make their own history.[43]

Notes

1   John O. Voll, 'The Mistaken Identification of "The West" and "Modernity"', *American Journal of Islamic Social Sciences*, Vol. 13, Spring (1996), pp. 1–12.

2   Bassam Tibi, *Islam and Cultural Accommodation of Social Change*, translated by Clare Krojzl (Westview Press, 1990), especially pp. 119–34.

3   The sources of this dualism have a long genealogy. As Asad notes: 'The European Enlightenment constitutes the historical site from which Westerners typically approach non-Western traditions. That approach has tended to evaluate and measure traditions according to their distance from Enlightenment and liberal models.' Talal Asad, *Genealogies of Religion: Discipline and Reasons of Power in Christianity and Islam* (Johns Hopkins University Press, 1993), p. 200.

4   Huntington's foreboding thesis on the coming conflict between West and the Muslim World, for instance, is only the latest version of inherent conflicts between a 'rational–modern' civilization and civilizations based on 'traditional' world-views about how to organize the social world. Samuel P. Huntington, 'The Clash of Civilizations?' *Foreign Affairs*, Vol. 72, No. 3 (1993), pp. 22–49.

5   Mustapha K. Pasha and Ahmed I. Samatar, 'The Resurgence of Islam', in James H. Mittelman (ed.), *Globalization: Critical Reflections* (Lynne Rienner, 1996), pp. 187–201.

6   Anthony Giddens, *The Constitution of Society: Outline of the Theory of Structuration* (University of California Press, 1984), p. xxiii.

7   Karl Polanyi, *The Great Transformation* (Beacon Press, 1944).

8   For a discussion of globalization themes, see the contributions in Mittelman (ed.), *Globalization, op. cit.*

9   David Harvey, *The Condition of Postmodernity: An Enquiry into the Origins of Cultural Change* (Blackwell, 1989).

10 Robert W. Cox, *Production, Power, and World Order: Social Forces in the Making of History* (Columbia University Press, 1987).

11 Frederic Jameson, 'Postmodernism, or the Cultural Logic of Late Capitalism.' *New Left Review*, 146 (1984), p. 79.

12 Esposito classifies Muslim attitudes toward change under four groupings: secularists, conservative, neo-traditionalist, and Islamic reformist. See John L. Esposito (ed.), *Voices of Resurgent Islam* (Oxford University Press, 1994). Also see, his *The Islamic Threat: Myth or Reality* (Oxford University Press, 1993). For a useful survey of the literature of resurgence, see Yvonne Haddad, *The Contemporary Islamic Revival: A Critical Survey and Bibliography* (Greenwood Press, 1991).

13 Ira M. Lapidus, *A History of Islamic Societies* (Cambridge University Press, 1990).

14 Robert W. Cox, 'Towards a Post-Hegemonic Conceptualization of World Order: Reflections on the Relevancy of Ibn Khaldun', in James N. Rosenau and Ernst-Otto Czempiel (ed.), *Governance without Government: Order and Change in World Politics* (Cambridge University Press, 1992), pp. 132–59.

15 Albert Hourani, 'How Should We Write the History of the Middle East', *International Journal of Middle East Studies*, Vol. 23, No. 2 (1991), p. 130.

16 According to Shahrani, 'a substantial part of the corpus of the high tradition of Islamic knowledge has been mediated by the social production and reproduction of vernacular popular Islamic texts, and thereby made available to the masses of non-literate Muslims.' M. Nazif Shahrani, 'Local Knowledge of Islam and Social Discourse in Afghanistan and Turkistan in the Modern Period', in Robert L. Canfield (ed.), *Turko-Persia in Historical Perspective* (Cambridge University Press, 1991), p. 177. For a background on 'official' and 'unofficial' Islam, see Ernest Gellner, *Muslim Society* (Cambridge University Press, 1981).

17 Ira M. Lapidus, *Contemporary Islamic Movements in Historical Perspective* (University of California Press, 1983).

18 *Ibid.*

19 William M. Watt, *Islamic Fundamentalism and Modernity* (Routledge, 1988), especially the Introduction.

20 Nikki R. Keddi, 'Islamic Revival as Third Worldism', in Jean-Pierre Digard (ed.), *Le Cuisinier et Le Philosophe: Hommage à Maxime Rodinson* (G. P. Maisonneuve et Larose, Paris), pp. 275–7.

21 Partha Chatterjee, *Nationalist Thought and the Colonial World: A Derivative Discourse* (University of Minnesota Press, 1986).

22 Olivier Roy, *The Failure of Political Islam*, trans. Carol Volk (Harvard University Press, 1994), p. 202.

23 Lapidus, *Contemporary Islamic Movement*, *op. cit.*, p. 2.

24 Antonio Gramsci, *Selections from the Prison Notebooks*, ed. Quintin Hoare and Geoffrey Nowell Smith (International Publishers, 1971).

25 Giles Kepel, *The Revenge of God: The Resurgence of Islam, Christianity and Judaism in the Modern World*, trans. Alan Braley (Polity Press, 1995), p. 13.

26 Gramsci, *Selections from the Prison Notebooks op. cit.*

27 Nazih N. Ayubi, 'Rethinking the Public/Private Dichotomy: Radical Islamism and Civil Society in the Middle East', *Contention*, Vol. 4, No. 3 (1995): 79–105.

28 Ali Rahnema (ed.), *Pioneers of Islamic Revival* (Zed Books, 1994), pp. 1–10.

29 As Lapidus points out: 'The legacy of Mediterranean, European, and Middle Eastern confrontation has for Europeans and Americans largely been smoothed over by the large century of European domination and by forgetfulness of history, but it is very much alive in the lately colonized Middle Eastern and Muslim world.' Lapidus, *Contemporary Islamic Movements op. cit.*, p. 3.

30 Kepel, *The Revenge of God, op. cit.*

31 Hourani, 'How Should We Write the History of the Middle East?' *op. cit.*, p. 129.

32 John Voll, 'The Nature of Islamic Revival', in James P. Piscatori (ed.),

Islam in a World of Nation-States (Cambridge University Press, 1986), pp. 24–39.

33 Edward Said, *Orientalism* (Vintage, 1978). Also see Norman Daniel, *Islam and the West: The Making of an Image* (Edinburgh University Press, 1958).

34 Extrapolating Voll, one can argue that under conditions of globalization, 'there is a major reduction in the possibility of maintaining separate and "pure" cultural repertoires as a basis of traditions of discourse or separate discourse-based world systems . . . there is emerging new, broadly cosmopolitan cumulative cultural repertoire.' Voll, 'Mistaken Identification', *op. cit.*, p. 9.

35 Rehnema (ed.), *Pioneers of Islamic Revival, op. cit.*

36 Kepel, *The Revenge of God, op. cit.*

37 Ameer Ali, 'Religiocultural Identity and Socioeconomic Development in the Muslim World', *American Journal of Islamic Social Sciences*, Vol. 12, No. 3 (1995), p. 331.

38 Peter Beyer, *Religion and Globalization* (Sage Publications, 1994), especially Introduction. Also see, Samir Amin, 'Culture and Ideology in the Contemporary Arab World', *Rethinking Marxism*, Vol. 6, No. 3 (1993), pp. 9–27.

39 Jonathan Addleton, *Undermining the Centre: The Gulf Migration and Pakistan* (Oxford University Press, 1992).

40 Mittelman (ed.), *Globalization, op. cit.*, pp. 1–19.

41 Sami Zubaida, 'Is there a Muslim Society? Ernest Gellner's Sociology of Islam', *Economy and Society*, Vol. 4, No. 24 (1995), pp. 151–88.

42 The tendency to represent the Muslim World as a repository of violence overrides analysis of the ideological moorings of Islamicists.

43 Karl Marx, *The Eighteenth Brumaire of Louis Bonaparte* (International Publishers, 1957; originally published 1852).

16
Mexico, Neoliberal Restructuring and the EZLN: A Neo-Gramscian Analysis[1]

Adam David Morton

'. . . the capacity of some social movements to speak to the poverty of the contemporary political imagination . . . gives them significance beyond their immediate demands, achievements and even failures.'[2]

'To the politilogue, the EZLN is located much closer to Antonio Gramsci than Karl Marx.'[3]

Introduction

This chapter develops a *critical* analysis of mutually reinforcing connections between social forces in Mexico and the global political economy. The term *critical* refers to the enquiry of how norms, institutions, or practices emerge and what forces may be changing or transforming a certain operational framework.[4] Using (neo)Gramscian tenets in relation to the Institutional Revolutionary Party (PRI) in Mexico, I attempt to explain how internal socio-political coherence in Mexico is mutually reinforced by external linkages.[5] The initial issue to address is the claim that the (neo)Gramscian approach to IPE has not seriously considered questions of political strategy in the world economy.[6] The (neo)Gramscian approach can be criticized for leaving a 'host of questions' concerning resistance to global forces to 'future research'[7] and failure to analyse concrete alternatives to neoliberalism within the current historical conjuncture.[8] Craig Murphy recognizes the 'lack of efficiency' of solutions posed by intellectuals of the *critical* tradition to North–South conflicts.[9] As André Drainville has noted, what is needed is 'more active sorties against transnational neo-liberalism, and the analysis of the concepts of control must beget original concepts of resistance.'[10]

The chapter is structured in four stages. The first section offers a summary of (neo)Gramscian tenets. It will be argued that hegemony, involving the co-optive mechanism of *trasformismo*, emerges from the mutually reinforcing global and local structures of social forces. As Barry Gills has argued the entire global social formation is probably better characterized as a set of 'inter-linking hegemonies',[11] in this case between the linkages of international institutional organization and the state/society complex of the PRI, though the mutually reinforcing aspects of hegemony are never monolithic or complete.[12] Therefore, the second section attempts to answer the question: Does the expansion of a *reformismo* (reform-centred) agenda in Mexico, coalescing around the EZLN, exhibit the potential to overcome the mechanisms of *trasformismo* articulated by the PRI and mutually reinforcing global social forces?

The second section is sub-divided to address what Robert Cox has called the 'developmental potential within the particular.'[13] In seeking out the *reformismo* possibilities of the EZLN, the antecedents of the Zapatista organization will be drawn on as well as contemporary factors that have influenced the uprising and its subsequent impact. As the EZLN represents a break with the guerrilla movements of the past, its manifestations of 'post modern resistance' will be examined. The third section argues that the formation of a 'supra-intersubjectivity' across the region will be a *sine qua non* for the consolidation of a successful *counter* hegemony. The fourth section identifies areas for future research.

A conceptual framework

The primary task of this section is to explicate the central tenets of (neo)Gramscian theory in relation to the PRI in Mexico, attempting to explain how internal coherence in Mexico is mutually reinforced by external linkages of institutional organization. The fundamental proposition here is that the internal hegemonic order in Mexico, involving the political structures of the PRI, is linked to a transnational hegemony which can be explained from a (neo)Gramscian perspective. Two key questions are addressed:

1 How might (neo)Gramscian theory explain the changes underway in Mexican society?;

2 Does such consensus derive from a real convergence of core–periphery interests or from a hegemony of core international institutions and ideas?[14]

A focus is maintained on the notions of hegemony, *trasformismo*, historical bloc, passive revolution, and the strategies of 'war of movement' and 'war of position' related to the struggle of *counter* hegemony. An understanding of these concepts has been developed from classical Gramscian writings from the *Prison Notebooks*[15] and a plethora of (neo)Gramscian writings. Despite the difficulty of methodologically 'using' Gramsci,[16] the aim is to take up the call to develop Gramscian analysis by drawing on the, 'incipient changes in the global political economy.'[17] By balancing calls for contextual considerations alongside understanding general historical experiences and conditions we may thus be able to discern the 'contemporary resonance of Gramsci'.[18]

The concept of hegemony has been central to the adjustment of classical Gramscian tenets to the conditions of recent historical circumstances. Gramsci proposed that the spheres of the state and civil society were integrally linked, so that the formal institutions of state power (government, political parties, military) could exercise and channel indirect domination through the informal organizations of civil society (church, media, education).[19] Hence, Gramsci's view of an extended state: the creeping intrusiveness of the state into realms of civil society. Through analysing the relations between the state and civil society Gramsci thus articulated the forms and functions of the concept of hegemony. However, rather than restricting hegemony to brute material force as a form of domination the concept was widened to refer to cultural and moral factors of influence. Thus hegemony was argued to involve domination and intellectual and moral direction, coercion and consent, across the fused spheres of the state and civil society.

Hegemony is more than simple dominance: 'Hegemony is a form in which dominance is obscured by achieving an appearance of acquiescence . . . as if it were the natural order of things.'[20] Hegemony involves a combination of coercion *and* consent expressed through the institutions of the global political economy. Consequently, the state may be seen as a conduit for internationalizing forces, such as particular models of economic development and world trade, which are subsequently supported by institutions of the global political economy. The latter may involve a 'machinery of surveillance' involving organizations such as the Group of Seven (G-7), the

International Monetary Fund (IMF), the World Bank, the Bank for International Settlements (BIS) or it may include trade arrangements that 'lock in' economic agreements, such as the North American Free Trade Agreement (NAFTA).[21] These instruments engender 'policy harmonization' through the process of ideological osmosis that develops an interpenetrating of national and international policy-making processes.[22] It is thus possible to conceptualize the spread of ideas, institutions, and material capabilities across the global political economy as a form of hegemony between states and other global social forces. Hegemony is at once more than the state due to the transnational structure of influence and less than the state due to the existence of possible *counter* hegemonic forces.[23] Hegemony must therefore never be seen as monolithic, one-dimensional, or complete, but rather as transitory, as oppositions can always develop from the contradictions arising from the process of social change.[24]

The process of *trasformismo*, or co-option, is also essential to the exercise of hegemony. The term was used by Gramsci to refer to the convergence of alternative programmes until there ceased to be any substantive difference between them.[25] Similarly, Cox defines the process as, 'a strategy of assimilating and domesticating potentially dangerous ideas by adjusting them to the policies of the dominant coalition.'[26] Ideas that potentially threaten the hegemonic doctrine may be co-opted to make them consistent with the hegemonic project. Therefore the consensual form of hegemony is an indispensable element in the process of *trasformismo* which equally reinforces the importance of an appearance of acquiescence when there is actually a veil of control. The relationship between coercive/consensual control and the mechanisms of assimilation and co-option are summarized so that, 'Hegemony is like a pillow: it absorbs blows and sooner or later the would-be assailant will find it comfortable to rest upon.'[27] This point can now be linked to the further elucidation of (neo)Gramscian tenets to explain how neoliberal economic ideas have engaged in a struggle *vis-à-vis* embedded mercantilist perspectives across Latin America,[28] that is particularly represented by the agenda of social transformation in the state/society complex of Mexico.

Mark Rupert notes that Gramsci developed the notion of historical bloc to refer to an ensemble of social relations that encompasses political, cultural and economic aspects to form not just a simple alliance of classes but a particular constellation of social forces that is capable of articulating a world view.[29] This in turn would be grounded in historically specific socio-political conditions and production relations, lending substance and ideological coherence to such social power.[30] Craig Murphy has extended this notion to present a globalist perspective of hegemony on 'North–South' relations, but the approach is equally relevant to the narrower consideration of US–Mexico (or Latin America) relations. Consequently, an historical bloc represents a regime of accumulation and a mode of regulation within which a certain industrial and developmental paradigm is circumscribed.[31] In this case the perspective is that of neoliberalism which is portrayed as a Gramscian overarching structure or historical bloc. The post-1945 (*pax Americana*) era has witnessed the rise of a regime of accumulation cemented by an international historical bloc centred in the United States whilst the present historical juncture exhibits vestiges of this bloc as well as mutations of this structure of accumulation. Consequently,

> The concept of 'historical bloc' with its axiom that the regional asymmetry of power within a society, and the involvement of this society in the world economy, constitute one and the same reality, allows one to think simultaneously of the international, national and local dimensions of the development of the . . . State.[32]

It is the contention here that throughout the Americas, and particularly with respect to US–Mexico relations, there has been a steady introduction of neoliberal market economics that can be linked to the above notions of ideological hegemony within a North American/globalist historical bloc.

During the administration of Carlos Salinas de Gortari in Mexico (1988–94) the economic goals of reducing inflation via wage and price controls, privatization of state enterprises, and trade liberalization, can be presented within the above framework of hegemony, *trasformismo*, and historical bloc. For instance, the prescriptions of neoliberalism have been strongly backed by an intellectual–financial complex employing discourse structuring terminology.[33] The World Bank is recognized as the lead agency in articulating a certain conception of development and thus a particular development agenda. Also, since the 1982 debt crisis, the parallel leverage of the International Monetary Fund (IMF) in Mexico has been staggering. These institutions, along with prestigious academic establishments, stand as 'regulated colleges of learning' in which what counts is not what people think but what they are taught to think.[34]

Further elaboration of the development of such a consensus can be made in relation to the post-1987 implementation of the Pacto de Solidaridad Economíca (PSE: Pact for Economic Solidarity) in Mexico. Despite the existence of so-called heterodox measures within the policy, such as wage and price controls aimed at halting inflationary pressures, the mutually reinforcing internal and external aspects of institutional organization did influence the initial formation of the PSE.[35] Common perspectives on the importance of fiscal discipline and market-oriented reforms between officials of shared social backgrounds, attending elite schools and possessing advanced degrees in economics from US graduate programmes, were crucial to the forging of such priorities.[36] The PSE initiated the emergence of a new financial élite centred around brokerage houses with a subsequent dependence upon holders of internationally mobile assets.[37] In this sense the PSE can be highlighted as one of the recent factors of the length and depth of PRI hegemony in Mexico. The political structures of the PRI have been extremely pervasive and the ruling party has ensured political stability through a network of corporatist institutions since the 1920s.[38] The tenure of the PRI bears out the point that hegemony, in the contemporary and historical context of Mexico, develops by securing the appearance of acquiescence.

Such changes also exemplify Gramsci's concept of passive revolution. Due to tumultuous economic restructuring, changes are being introduced in Mexico, and across Latin America, without mass participation. Yet the impetus for such change may be seen to arise not out of 'vast local economic development' but as a 'reflection of international developments which transmit their ideological currents to the periphery.'[39] In Mexico, the interior conservative dynamics of the PRI can be linked to the exterior dynamics of hegemony exercised within the international political economy so that revolutionary changes within the social formation in Mexico are occurring but without an *actual* revolution.[40] This is the contemporary essence of Gramsci's concept of passive revolution, the dialectic of 'revolution/restoration' or 'revolution without a revolution'[41] and may just as adequately be described as a 'silent revolution'[42] that is affecting Mexico and much of Latin America.

However, as outlined earlier, hegemony is never complete. Thus, we need to consider the role of the Ejército Zapatista de Liberacíon Nacional (EZLN) uprising in the southern Mexican state of Chiapas since 1 January 1994. This rebellion was a direct challenge to the above strategy of accumulation and *salinismo*, the economic model implemented by President Salinas, as a political discourse. The date of the rebellion was deliberately arranged to coincide with Mexico's entry into effect of NAFTA.[43] Crucially, the EZLN represent a break with guerrilla movements of the past in many ways. The movement is distinct from the *foquista*-insurrection (*foco*) strategy of a small band of rebels launching a sporadic conflict of revolutionary warfare. Instead, the rebellion is a plan for a guerra *prolongada* involving the Indian population and a front in the international community.[44] As Neil Harvey notes, the EZLN represents a Gramscian war of position aimed at shifting the balance of forces in favour of popular and democratic movements, to penetrate and subvert the mechanisms of hegemonic diffusion on the cultural front within civil society, rather than a Peruvian *Sendero Luminoso* 'war of movement' attempt to destroy the state.[45] As a result of such challenges to the hegemony of the PRI and the international configuration of power, the EZLN may well be regarded as a *counter* hegemonic force.

A *counter* hegemony, in the 'strict' Gramscian sense,[46] must represent and attempt to create a new conception of the world at the ethico-political level whilst also transcending common economic-corporate interests. In short, it has to develop the organizational capacity to establish a rival historical bloc to the prevailing hegemony by sustaining a long war of position. According to Cox, a coherent conjunction of rival ideas/institutions/material capabilities may assert a *counter* hegemonic project through the world order, different forms of state, or contending social forces.[47] Consequently, as a radical social force, the EZLN may represent imminent tendencies in the present order which might facilitate progressive change. Yet a counter hegemony may also simply entail tackling prevailing norms and rules without actually supplanting the old hegemony to construct a new hegemony.[48] Consequently, the EZLN may also be counter hegemonic in a 'loose' sense whilst still possessing the potential to supplant the old hegemony of the PRI.

The Ejército Zapatista de Liberacíon Nacional (EZLN)

Antecedents, autochthonous roots, influencing factors and political impact

The armed uprising on 1 January 1994 by a small band of rebels assaulting and capturing four cities in the Los Altos region of Chiapas (San Cristóbal de las Casas, Las Margaritas, Altamirano, and Ocosingo) should not be seen as a spontaneous, externally implanted, offensive. Instead a conjunction of events impacted on the rebellion that involved: a deep struggle between the interests of estate owners and ranchers and the interests of *campesino* (peasant) and Indian communities over the control of land; an acute social crisis involving extreme poverty for the majority of the local population; and a climate of violence and discrimination.[49] In its present form, the social base of the EZLN, made up principally of Indians from the Lacandón forest and central highlands of Chiapas,[50] mobilized latent unrest against the above events. Yet there were precursors to the EZLN that deserve discussion.

Luis Hernández Navarro cites three main currents of *campesino* organization throughout the 1970s that can be considered as the antecedents of the EZLN.[51] Firstly, the Unión de Uniones Ejidales y Grupos Campesinos Solidarios de Chiapas (UdU: Union of Ejido Unions and Peasant Organizations) emerged in the areas of the Lacandón forest, the Northern Zone and the Sierra Madre, becoming the largest independent *campesino* organization in Chiapas struggling for appropriation of the production process whilst avoiding direct confrontation. Secondly, the Central Independiente de Obreros Agrícolas y Campesinos (CIOAC: Independent Confederation of Agricultural Workers and Peasants), active in the Simojovel, Huituipan and El Bosque municipalities, aimed to mobilize labourers on coffee and cattle ranches in line with the old Partido Comunista Mexicano (PCM: Mexican Communist Party) and the Partido Socialista Unificado de México (PSUM: Unified Socialist Party of Mexico). Thirdly, the demands of communal landholders in Venustiano Carranza were incorporated within the Organización Campesina Emiliano Zapata (OCEZ: Emiliano Zapata Peasant Organization), who struggled for land and against repression by engaging in direct confrontation with the state. From the above three groups, by the late 1980s, the Alianza Campesina Independiente Emiliano Zapata (ACIEZ: Emiliano Zapata Independent Peasant Alliance) was formed in the Selva and Altos regions, later emerging in Altamariano, Ocosingo, San Cristóbal, Sabanilla, and Salto de Agua.[52] Crucially, by 1992, ACIEZ gained support from ethnic communities, including for example Tzotziles, Tzeltales, Choles, Tojolabales, Mames and Zoques, had altered its name by adding the 'Nacional' (National) component and eventually went underground to begin training for the armed rebellion to later emerge as the EZLN.[53]

The autochthonous roots of identity formation and organization were pivotal within this process of mobilization in Chiapas. The rebels themselves have called for *revindicación étnica*: the reclaiming of rights and autonomy based on the equation of shared poverty with indigenous identity from the colonial period to the present.[54] Furthermore, such mobilization has also mixed with the popular Church which has been another factor of local activism. This mix, as Neil Harvey has noted, has involved Catholic priests building support for more autonomous forms of representation beyond the corporatist links of the PRI, with the largest base of support for the EZLN coming from communities indigenous to the Selva region.[55] In this context, the longstanding role of Bishop Samuel Ruiz García has been crucial,[56] and the indigenous adoption of Maoist ideas has been linked to him.[57] These various antecedents of the EZLN eventually fulminated following the revision of agrarian land reform under Article 27 of the 1917 Constitution, announced in November 1991 and passed into law, almost by personal fiat, in February 1992.

The reform of Article 27 must be seen as a paramount factor inducing the protest of the EZLN movement. Previously, Article 27 had enshrined the central gains of the Zapatistas in the 1910–19 Mexican Revolution, ensuring the collective status of *ejidos* and *comunidades agrarias* lands.[58] However, the previous status of the *ejido* system as a 'political sacred cow'[59] became transformed by a radical overhaul of the agricultural sector that involved the privatization of state-owned enterprises (SOEs) and the gradual elimination of agricultural price supports and import subsidies. Unsurprisingly, the adoption of these policies by the Salinas administration was linked to World Bank conditions involving the disbursement of new structural adjustment loans.[60] According to Harvey, there have been four particular modifications of Article 27: *ejido* and *comunidades agraria* lands can now be legally sold, bought, rented, or used as collateral for loans; private companies can purchase lands; new associations between capitalist developers and *ejidatarios* are allowed; and provisions that existed for *campesinos* to petition for land redistribution have been deleted thus giving primacy to the security of private property.[61] As a result, one can view the resistance of the EZLN as a societal response to changes in production relations, as represented by both commercial assaults on indigenous forms of economic organization and assaults on indigenous modes of governance by the PRI.[62] Resulting protests over these measures led to the coercive repression of *campesino* organizations, notably in Chiapas the UdU, CIOAC and OCEZ groups, which again influenced the form and content of the subsequent EZLN reply demanding work, land, housing, food, health, education, independence, freedom, democracy, justice, and peace. After the initial military phase of the rebellion, which was concluded by the Zapatistas in early January 1994, the political phase followed encompassing methods of symbolic warfare.[63] Throughout 1995, PRI vacillations have involved an army crackdown, human rights abuses and arrests followed by an amnesty law, the Congress approval of the Law for Dialogue, Conciliation and Peace with Dignity in Chiapas, and peace negotiations. Notably, a National Mediation Commission (CONAI), an eight-person body created and chaired by Bishop Samuel Ruiz, was set up during this period whilst peace negotiations continued. Although military events have subsided,[64] the political impact of the uprising has had diverse implications.

The immediate political impact of the Chiapas rebellion was felt by the political institutions in Mexico with the Secretary of the Interior, Patrocinio González, removed from office – replaced by Jorge Carpizo MacGregor – and the Cabinet reshuffled in favour of moderates over hard liners.[65] Notably the Governor of Chiapas, Elmar Setzer, resigned as early as 19 January 1994. In the longer term, the uprising initiated debate on national political/electoral reform.[66] As one study argues,

> The demands of peasant groups were taken up by a broad spectrum of local, regional, professional, and nongovernmental organizations, all pressuring the government to open the political system to more just and democratic elections, decision-making processes and politics.[67]

Furthermore, the *consulta*, a nationwide consultation, was precipitated by the EZLN, challenging the government's policy of *concertación* or consensus building.[68] This generation of a wider, more organic support base, allows the further possibility for more autonomous political organizations to emerge, organized around new interests and principles.[69] However, the quintessential challenges to concertación must be the Convención Nacional Democrática (CND: National Democratic Convention), held by the EZLN from 6–9 August 1994 in San Cristóbal and Aguascalientes, and the Intercontinental Gathering for Humanity and Against Neoliberalism, the Intergalactic, again organized by the EZLN, over late July/early August 1996 in Chiapas. The former *coyuntura*, or coming together,[70] involved more than 5,000 delegates, and importantly 600 press representatives, aimed at articulating changes within the national political process and a new vision of federalism based on a multinational state with territorial autonomy for indigenous peoples as part of a Mexican nation.[71] The latter aimed to generate trans-boundary left-wing sympathies during a conference involving somewhere between 2,000–7,000 participants from 48 countries. These unique features of the EZLN will now be discussed to discern the potential for *counter* hegemony as well as questioning whether other facets of the organization substantiate the reading of the EZLN as a *critical* social movement with elements of post modern resistance.

Manifestations of post-modern resistance: a *counter* hegemony?

There is a danger of romanticizing the Zapatistas. As Robert Cox has said, one should avoid the disposition to regard such movements as *ipso facto* benign or progressive.[72] Yet, many features of the EZLN movement break with guerrilla organizations of the past. The Zapatistas do not represent a *foquista (foco)* strategy of insurrection aimed at seizing absolute control of the state. Instead the rebellion is an attempt to move beyond the politics of modernity with the objective not to take state power in the name of revolution, along traditional Leninist lines, but to activate a mass movement throughout the civil society of Mexico.[73] In Gramscian terms the EZLN can be seen to be initiating a broad-based political dialogue, even articulating a national-popular movement, thus giving political drive to the community as a whole.[74] A grand strategy is not advocated but instead an inclusionary arena: any proposals are simply recognized as one possibility among many alternatives.[75] There is no attempt to construct a formal and rigid model but merely ecologically sound alternative development paths.[76]

This open-ended emphasis is also evident in the organizational structure of the EZLN. There is an attempt to eschew centralized leadership tendencies with strategic decisions decided at the community level through the Clandestine Revolutionary Indigenous Committee (CCRI). According to Harry Cleaver this framework of collective and democratic decision-making has been developed out of local traditions.[77] Similarly, Roger Burbach perceives the EZLN governing structure to be fluid, consultative and based on a policy of rotating members.[78] Also, from the Zapatista Army of National Liberation (EZLN) heralds the Zapatista Front of National Liberation

(FZLN), an organization directly targeting civil society, which provides an example of how a concrete expression of resistance can continually propel itself into new and innovative forms by articulating a war of position.[79] Even the representative of the overall EZLN movement is deliberately humbled by the title sub-Commandante Marcos.

It is also widely acknowledged that the EZLN is sensitive to gender autonomy within the diverse Indian cultures of Chiapas.[80] Women have played a role as EZLN members in negotiations with the Mexican government as well as participating in the armed struggle with as much as 30 per cent of the combatants believed to be women.[81] Alongside the initial EZLN revolutionary declaration on 1 January 1994 – the 'Declaration from the Lacandón Jungle' – there was also the 'Women's Revolutionary Law' with many of the issues underlying this policy adopted across Mexico in grassroots coalitions. In addition to the organization of the National Democratic Convention (CND), there was a Chiapas Women's Convention formed in July 1994.[82] Therefore, an appreciation of the gender dimension of the EZLN is paramount to understanding the wider struggles of those at the bottom of the Mexican social pyramid.[83] Finally, a further feature of the EZLN has been the use of the media and technology to establish a global forum in which to communicate their messages. This has been hailed as the 'electronic fabric of struggle'.[84] Consequently, the emphasis on the politics of inclusion, the egalitarian organizational structure, the gender dimension and the use of global telecommunications has led to the EZLN collapsing space and time via local–global linkages within their struggle. Simultaneously, the past, present and future have been connected through instrumental invocations of 'tradition', everyday mobilizations against repression, and aspirations for alternatives. These features have led James Rochlin to state:

> Overall, the emergence of a diversity of groups with an assortment of political agendas parallels a central argument of *some veins of postmodern conceptual approaches* – one that emphasizes the increasing significance of the 'many voices' that are speaking more loudly.[85]

It must be clear that the term 'post modern' is specifically understood here as a rejection of 'modernity' as well as relating to the restructuring of a normative commitment. This position accords with the similar argument developed by Nick Rengger and Mark Hoffman.[86] Therefore, as a series of commentators have argued, in the broadest sense of the term, post modern social forces may be perceived to be reaching beyond traditional left analysis whilst still developing a normative commitment.[87] In this sense, Roger Burbach strongly upholds the post modern interpretation due to a reaction against the modernization project in Chiapas and the attempt to build new, equitable societies in which indigenous cultures are central rather than peripheral.[88] Similarly, June Nash[89] regards the Zapatistas as the first post modern movement in the 'Third World' with Harry Cleaver,[90] James Rochlin,[91] and Ana Carrigan[92] sharing this inter-pretation. In contrast Daniel Nugent severely criticizes the approach 'northern intellectuals' have taken to label the EZLN as post mod-ern, arguing that the Zapatistas of the EZLN are no more post modern than their predecessors of the 1910–19 Mexican Revolution.[93] Nugent overlooks the way the EZLN have articulated symbolic guerrilla warfare, often with only wooden guns, whilst occupying international media space, and thus the way the Zapatistas have proceeded locally, regionally and internationally through a diversity of forms. Con-sequently the *form* the EZLN struggle has taken may be understood as post modern although the *content* may not have been designed with this explicit aim. In short, because the rebels represent a poli-tics of difference, they defy grand-theorized strategies of revolutionary thought, and they have developed innovative resistance, they *may* be regarded as post modern.

This reading of the Zapatistas may be linked to the understand-ing of *critical* social movements, expressing elements of post-modern resistance, developed separately by R. B. J. Walker[94] and Jim George.[95] Although neither author refers to the particularities of the Chiapas case, it is held that there are common concerns between their dis-cussions of social movements and the manner in which the EZLN have been presented within this argument. The term *critical*, as defined earlier, involves self-consciousness about how prevailing practices emerge and what forces may change or transform such practices. According to Walker, a *critical* social movement is able to look be-yond the immediacy of the struggle, to understand the wider connections and possibilities between local and global structures, and thus discover new spaces in which to act and to even recon-struct social processes.[96] Crucially, in relation to this interpretation, *critical* social movements express scepticism about the possibility and desirability of taking over the state as the primary objective of political activity[97] and instead embark on consciousness-raising as a form of emancipatory politics to overcome the 'politics of closure.'[98] Similarly, Jim George argues that the non-traditional agenda of such movements involves newly formulated developmental, ecological, gender, and cultural themes as well as new levels of democratic decision-making and participation processes.[99] Despite the generalities of this literature it is held that there is a link between the particular way Walker and George perceive *critical* social movements and the *critical* approach that has pervaded this argument. Therefore, one may even perceive the EZLN as a *critical* social movement that links the 'common thematic concerns' of those interested in restructuring the project of 'modernity' with a post-modern reading of world politics.[100] As a result, the EZLN may well represent the emerging politics of *critical* social movements combining elements of post-modern resistance as

> It is *post*modern in the sense that while it is always directly (and sometimes violently) engaged with modernity, it seeks to go beyond the repressive closed aspects of modernist global existence.[101]

Finally, in accord with Jim George, it is hoped that the struggles of *critical* social movements, and notably the EZLN, will engender a reflective attitude toward the questioning of routines and apathy within oneself so that the former may energize 'the creativity and critical capacities of people learning about their world in their own ways and through their own struggles.'[102] To continue George's argument,[103] such critical social movements, along with critical social theorists, may become engaged in re-conceptualizing and re-articulating emancipatory concepts and practices. This could involve constructing a true *counter* hegemony by expanding the *reformismo* (reform-centred) agenda, by at first overcoming the mechanisms of *trasformismo* articulated by the PRI in Mexico and then overturning the mutually reinforcing aspects of institutional organization at the level of global social forces.

Supra-intersubjectivity

To prevent such a nascent *counter* hegemony from ossifying, opportunities need to be created to develop what Robert Cox has distinguished as the mutual recognition of supra-intersubjectivity.[104] This involves providing a bridge between distinct and separate subjectivities of different coexisting civilizations without necessarily reconciling differences in goals.[105] As Robert Cox asks:

> Is it possible to evolve out of the different realms of intersubjectivity expressive of different coexisting traditions of civilization a supra-intersubjectivity that would consolidate norms consistent with all traditions of civilization without any one tradition being superimposed on others?[106]

At a simple level this involves creating ethics of mutual understanding, as exhibited by the development of a global moral community following the favourable attention the EZLN rebellion gained from the world's press. June Nash argues that this may even set the standard for a more egalitarian redistribution of profits from production as well as financial speculation.[107] At a more complex level, it involves moving from 'attitudinal' (nationalist) convergences in Latin America/Mexico to 'longitudinal' convergences.[108] This entails a search by the Latin American left for convergences with diverse interlocutors in the US, concerning the development of trans-boundary organization, on a co-operative North–South axis rather than a divisive nationalist axis.[109] Contrary to Timothy Wickham-Crowley, this is not seen as 'totally illusory',[110] due to the international network of grassroots groups that coalesced around the NAFTA debate that, although initially unsuccessful, may mobilize around the EZLN–Chiapas situation. The result could well be a 'multiplicity of rhizomatically linked autonomous groups' connecting struggles throughout the Americas, that Harry Cleaver has emphasized[111] and Harry Browne[112] has elaborated upon.

To summarize the argument, then, previous sections have analysed the Ejército Zapatista de Liberacíon Nacional (EZLN) by considering the antecedents, the autochthonous roots, the influencing factors and the political impact of the movement. It is held that the potential for *counter* hegemony does exist within the possibly post modern resistance of the *critical* social movement of the EZLN. Such a statement has been based on the reading of the Zapatistas as an organization that is capable of sustaining a Gramscian war of position and building an alternative polity and thus a new historical bloc. This possible new form of state is even beginning to draw sufficient international support to protect its national base, as exhibited by the recent Intercontinental Gathering for Humanity and Against Neo-liberalism (July/August 1996). This is essential if the *counter* hegemony is going to assert itself through the wider world structure and generate a wider supra-intersubjectivity.

However, one must avoid triumphalism in the analysis of the potential of such a *counter* hegemony. Just as it is possible to change power relations and overturn irreducible realities,[113] it is equally conceivable that social movements may ossify, or in the extreme, be crushed. Thus, whilst the optimism for *counter* hegemony is inexhaustible, the limits may well be on sustaining such concrete possibilities. Yet, even if the existing practices of *counter* hegemony falter it is held that the EZLN will have significance beyond immediate circumstances that may lead to the reassertion of similar tactics elsewhere in the international political economy. This point is substantiated by Jorge Castañeda when noting the striking ability of the national-populist sector across Latin America to resurrect itself despite the consequences of immediate conjunctural events.[114] Similarly, the cyclical process of ideas and ideological currents may be emphasized to the extent that, 'The apparent exhaustion of Marxism among the popular social movements and political parties across Latin America during the early 1990s may signal an eventual resurgence of Marxist thinking adapted to new and changing conditions.'[115] In addition, the EZLN needs to be aware of the 'classic contradiction' of the Latin American left when, on those moments of success, assimilation occurs along with the consequent association with the status quo and its unpopularity.[116] This particular contradiction may affect the EZLN if it considers becoming a political party. As a result of these processes one may heed the proviso, made in a different context but equally relevant to this case, that the fluidity of events, 'may require us to postpone our judgement or to qualify it in the light of things that have not yet happened.'[117]

Conclusion

'Theory follows reality. It also precedes and shapes reality.'[118]

'. . . we must recognize that theory, as it develops out of practice and develops into practice, plays its own transforming role in the process.'[119]

As a critique of disciplinary orthodoxy, it is hoped that this chapter has implicitly highlighted the precepts Craig N. Murphy emphasizes as necessary in the recasting of International Political Economy (IPE). These are: the allowance for greater connection to subjects; the engagement of the perspectives of the disadvantaged; and the avoidance of closure.[120] A central part of opening up such debate has been the adoption of a *critical* perspective that rejects the orthodox imposition of Manichean oppositions to analysis. Such an orthodoxy, supporting fact/value, subject/object distinctions, is seen as too simplistic and should therefore be avoided. In contrast, the need to eschew such orthodoxy has hopefully been highlighted by implicitly emphasizing a dialectical understanding of fact and theory, politics and economics, state and society, or even hegemony and *counter* hegemony. Within each couplet one is dialectically implicated in the nature of the other. With a strong Gramscian tone it was argued that the Mexican social structure is experiencing a re-composition of state–business–labour relations linked to a hegemonic core of international institutions and ideas rather than a real convergence of interests. As a consequence, linkages were traced between the internal coherence of the Institutional Revolutionary Party (PRI) in Mexico and mutually reinforcing international institutional aspects of persuasion and collaboration. The 'lock-in' guarantee, or 'new constitutionalism', of the North American Free Trade Agreement (NAFTA) is particularly apposite as an example of such ideological osmosis.[121] Overall, particular tenets of (neo)Gramscian theory, such as hegemony, *trasformismo*, historic bloc, and passive revolution, are especially useful in explaining the changes underway in Mexican society.

As a result of these changes, in the global political economy in general and Mexico in particular, it is now widely recognized that a new Polanyian double movement is occurring.[122] This involves the thrust of the self-regulating neoliberal market and the corollary of counter movements reasserting self-preservation in an attempt to curb the disintegrating and alienating consequences of such economic forces. In Mexico, the first movement in itself contains a further dual pincer movement based on the technocratization of government agencies and the modernization of corporate organizations. The second movement has involved the expansion of a *reformismo* (reform-centred) agenda exhibiting the potential to overcome the mechanisms of *transformismo* articulated by the PRI and mutually reinforcing social forces. EZLN, a *critical* social movement with some possibly post modern manifestations, has the potential to sustain a prolonged Gramscian war of position against the PRI and *ipso facto* the very neo-liberal paradigm that sustains it. The EZLN may even engender a successful *counter* hegemony. To propel future debate on the possibility of radical reform and progressive social change the EZLN could be considered, along with other transnational movements, in relation to the process of 'transformative multilateralism'. This involves the articulation of non-state forces in the activity of international organization and hence maximum emancipatory participation by popular movements within the current juncture of global restructuring.[123] The task for future research is to conceptualize this response further by discerning the links between changes in the production process, including the ascendancy of financial interests, and the changes in the structure of the state/society complex in Mexico and the wider world order which sustains it. This area would need to draw on the changes between the global structure of social forces and local configurations of social forces following the 1994–5 devaluation/*tesobonos* crisis and the subsequent US–Mexico Framework Agreement.[124]

It will also be necessary to question the potential for *counter* hegemonic consolidation. A central question in such an endeavour, to adapt Cox's analysis, could be: *Have the EZLN acquired the degree of self-consciousness, organizational capacity and ideological maturity to become the basis of a counter hegemony that can be consolidated concurrently across several countries?*[125] Further research would also need to address the crucial issue of abstracting Gramscian tenets from a particular time and place to a different context and culture.[126] Recent work that questions the validity of some of the (neo)Gramscian claims,[127] could propel debate and discussion.

Finally, whilst there currently seems to be a case for much concern and pessimism in relation to global economic restructuring, there need not be limits to the possible optimism arising from the concrete responses of local social forces to politico-economic interests articulated at the level of the global social formation. EZLN *does* speak to our own world and thus rather than silencing such voices we should begin to listen and learn from the political perspicacity of this local response to global processes. It is from such responses and within oneself that a truly transformative agenda can be conveyed.

Notes

1   The research on which this chapter is based has been funded by the Economic and Social Research Council (ESRC). It forms part of the author's doctoral thesis 'Social Forces in the Making of Mexico: Hegemony and Neoliberalism in the International Political Economy'.

Acknowledgements and gratitude are extended to the following who have all read drafts of the paper: Andreas Bieler, Steve Hobden, Roger Tooze,' and Pinar Bilgin. The biggest debt is owed to just one individual: Julie Dawn Brookes.

2   R. B. J. Walker, 'Social Movements/World Politics', *Millennium: Journal of International Studies*, Vol. 23, No. 3 (1994), p. 679.

3   John Ross, *Rebellion from the Roots: Indian Uprising in Chiapas* (Common Courage Press, 1995a), p. 292.

4   Robert W. Cox, 'Editor's Introduction', in Yoshikazu Sakamoto (ed.), *Global Transformation. Challenges to the State System* (United Nations University Press, 1994a). Also see Robert W. Cox, 'Social Forces, States, and World Orders: Beyond International Relations Theory', *Millennium: Journal of International Studies*, Vol. 10, No. 2 (1981), pp. 126–55.

5   Robert R. Kaufman, Carlos Bazdresch and Blanca Heredia, 'Mexico: Radical Reform in a Dominant Party System', in Stephen Haggard and Steven B. Webb (eds), *Voting for Reform. Democracy, Political Liberalization and Economic Adjustment* (University Press 1994), p. 397.

6   André Drainville, 'International Political Economy in the Age of Open Marxism', *Review of International Political Economy*, Vol. 1, No. 1 (Spring 1994), p. 105.

7   William I. Robinson, *Promoting Polyarchy: Globalization, US Intervention and Hegemony* (Cambridge University Press, 1996), p. 382.

8   *Ibid.*, pp. 382–3. See also William I. Robinson, 'A Case Study of Globalization Processes in the Third World: A Transnational Agenda in Nicaragua', *Global Society: Journal of Interdisciplinary International Relations*, Vol. 11, No. 1 (1997), pp. 61–91.

9   Craig N. Murphy, *International Organization and Industrial Change: Global Governance since 1850* (Polity Press, 1994), p. 273.

10   André Drainville (1994), p. 125.

11   Barry Gills, 'The Hegemonic Transition in East Asia: a Historical Perspective', in Stephen Gill (ed.), *Gramsci, Historical Materialism and International Relations* (Cambridge University Press, 1993), p. 190.

12   *Ibid.*, p. 210.

13   Robert W. Cox with Timothy J. Sinclair, *Approaches to World Order* (Cambridge University Press, 1996), p. 53.

14   Kelly Lee, 'A Neo-Gramscian Approach to International Organization: An Expanded Analysis of Current Reforms to UN Development Agencies', in John Macmillan and Andrew Linklater (eds) *Boundaries in Question: New Directions in International Relations* (Pinter, 1995), p. 157.

15   See Quintin Hoare and Geoffrey Nowell Smith (eds), *Antonio Gramsci: Selections from the Prison Notebooks* (Lawrence & Wishart, 1971).

16   It has been claimed that the *Selections from the Prison Notebooks* volume is a 'corrupt' text. See the interview with Edward Saïd, 'Orientalism and After', in Peter Osbourne (ed.), *A Critical Sense: Interviews with Intellectuals* (London: Routledge, 1996); Perry Anderson, 'The Antinomies of Antonio Gramsci', *New Left Review*, No. 100 (November 1976–January 1977), pp. 5–78. For a revised version of the *Prison Notebooks* see the first two volumes of a proposed six–seven volume series by Joseph A. Buttigieg, *Gramsci's Prison Notebooks* (Columbia University Press).

17 Roger Tooze, 'Understanding the Global Political Economy: Applying Gramsci', *Millennium: Journal of International Studies*, Vol. 19, No. 2, (1990), pp. 278–9.
18 Joseph Femia, *Gramsci's Political Thought* (Clarendon Press, 1981), p. 19.
19 Hoare and Smith (eds) (1971), pp. 206–76.
20 Robert W. Cox, 'THE FORUM: Approaches from a Historical Materialist Tradition', *Mershon International Studies Review*, Vol. 38, Supplement 2 (1994b), p. 366.
21 This broad grouping has been generically termed the 'G7 nexus', see Stephen Gill, 'Theorising the Interregnum: The Double Movement and Global Politics in the 1990s', in Björn Hettne (ed.), *International Political Economy Understanding Global Disorder* (Zed Books, 1995), p. 86.
22 Robert W. Cox, *Production, Power and World Order: Social Forces in the Making of History* (Columbia University Press, 1987), pp. 253–8.
23 Cox with Sinclair (1996), pp. 106–7.
24 Cox (1994b).
25 Hoare and Smith (1971), p. 58, n8.
26 Cox with Sinclair (1996), p. 130.
27 *Ibid.*, p. 139.
28 Gills (1993), p. 35.
29 Mark Rupert, 'Alienation, Capitalism, and the Inter-State System: Towards A Marxian/Gramscian Critique', in Gill (1993), p. 81.
30 *Ibid.*
31 Craig N. Murphy, 'Freezing the North–South Bloc(k) After the East–West Thaw', in Paul R. Viotti and Mark V. Kauppi, *International Relations Theory: Realism, Pluralism, Globalism* (Macmillan, 1993, 2nd edition), p. 518.
32 Jean François Bayart, *The State in Africa. The Politics of the Belly* (Longman, 1993), p. 193.
33 Joel S. Samoff, 'The Intellectual/Financial Complex of Foreign Aid', *Review of African Political Economy*, No. 53, (1992), pp. 60–87.
34 This phrase was coined by Edward Saïd, *Orientalism* (Penguin Books, 1977), p. 197.
35 Kaufman *et. al.* (1994), p. 396.
36 *Ibid.*, pp. 397–8.
37 Mónica Serrano, 'The Legacy of Gradual Change: Rules and Institutions Under Salinas', in Mónica Serrano and Victor Bulmer-Thomas (eds), *Rebuilding the State: Mexico After Salinas* (Institute of Latin American Studies, 1996), p. 15.
38 In 1929 the National Revolutionary Party (PNR) was founded and was renamed the Party of the Mexican Revolution (PRM) in 1938, becoming the Institutional Revolutionary Party (PRI) in 1946 after the pivotal presidency of Lázaro Cárdenas (1934–40). The network of corporatist institutions has principally involved *the labour sector* – the Confederación de Trabajadores Mexicanos (CTM: Confederation of Mexican Workers); *the peasants* – the Confederación Nacional Campesina (CNC: National Peasant Confederation), and the *heterogeneous popular sector* – formerly the Confederación Nacional de Organizaciones Populares (CNOP:

National Confederation of Popular Organizations), renamed since 1993 to become the Federación Nacional de Organizaciones y Cuidadanos (FNOC: National Federation of Organizations and Citizens). See Nikki Craske, *Corporatism Revisited: Salinas and the Reform of the Popular Sector* (London: Institute of Latin American Studies, Research Paper No. 37, 1994).

39 Hoare and Smith (eds) (1971), p. 116.
40 See Adam David Morton, 'Social Forces and Politico-Economic Interests: A Neo-Gramscian Analysis of Mexico in the International System', *Research Institute for European Studies, Occasional Paper* No. 7 (July 1997).
41 Hoare and Smith (eds) (1971), pp. 105–20. The already established dominant groups maintain their power, so that 'Everything changes so that everything stays the same'. See: Bayart (1993), p. 119.
42 Duncan Green, *Silent Revolution: The Rise of Free Market Economics in Latin America* (Latin America Bureau, 1995).
43 Neil Harvey, 'Rebellion in Chiapas: Rural Reforms and Popular Struggles', *Third World Quarterly*, Vol. 16, No. 1 (1995), p. 62.
44 Jorge G. Castañeda, *Utopia Unarmed: The Latin American Left After the Cold War* (Vintage Books, 1994), p. 93, n7.
45 Neil Harvey (1995), p. 39
46 Hoare and Smith (eds) (1971), pp. 180–5.
47 Cox (1981).
48 Gregg J. Legare, 'Neorealism or Hegemony? The Seven Sisters' Energy Regime', in Claire Turenne Sjolander and Wayne S. Cox (ed.), *Beyond Positivism: Critical Reflections on International Relations* (Lynne Rienner, 1994), p. 103, n12.
49 Luis Hernández Navarro, 'The Chiapas Uprising', in Neil Harvey *et al.*, *Rebellion in Chiapas: Rural Reforms, Campesino Radicalism, and the Limits to Salinismo* (University of California, Centre for US–Mexican Studies, 1994), pp. 58–9.
50 Neil Harvey, 'Rural Reforms and the Zapatista Rebellion: Chiapas 1988–95', in Gerardo Otero (ed.), *Neo-liberalism Revisited: Economic Restructuring and Mexico's Political Future* (Lynne Rienner, 1996), p. 210.
51 Luis Hernández Navarro (1994), p. 53.
52 *Ibid.*, p. 62.
53 *Ibid.*
54 June Nash, 'The Reassertion of Indigenous Identity: Mayan Responses to State Intervention in Chiapas', *Latin American Research Review*, Vol. 30, No. 3 (1995), p. 10.
55 Neil Harvey (1995), p. 57.
56 Samuel Ruiz has been the Diocese of San Cristóbal as well as a human rights campaigner. During the 1970s he sponsored an Indian Congress, the 'Fray Bartolomé de las Casas Congress of Indigenous Peoples', 12–15 October 1974, that brought together 1,000 communities, representing 400,000 people. There was a liberation theology emphasis, with a network of disciples – 'catequistas' – moving amongst communities to precipitate empowerment. See: Roger Burbach, 'For a Zapatista Style Postmodernist Perspective', *Monthly Review* (March 1996),

p. 119; and Ross (1995a), p. 220. Similarly, the consciousness-raising effort carried out by priests and lay workers in the region of Chiapas, not unlike the influence of *comunidades eclesiales de base* (Christian Base Communities) across Latin America, as well as the organizational work undertaken by agrarian semi-Maoist activists from the north of the region has been emphasized by Jorge G. Castañeda, *The Mexican Shock: Its Meaning for the US* (New Press, 1995), p. 41. Whilst Samuel Ruiz is not regarded as having orchestrated the EZLN movement, his actions over a period of thirty years constitute the consolidation of a social power bloc that has been solidified subsequently by the Zapatistas. See: Bishop Samuel Ruiz, 'Lessons of the Zapatista Uprising', Pastoral Letter, 23 February 1994 (Catholic Institute of International Relations).

57 See: Dan La Botz, *Democracy in Mexico: Peasant Rebellion and Political Reform* (South End Press, 1995), p. 34.

58 *Ejido* lands are those the state has redistributed through the break-up of private holdings whilst *comunidades agraria* lands are those historically held by indigenous communities. Both types became protected *de jure* from the onslaught of extensive capitalist land development, yet the *de facto* situation increasingly involved this.

59 Merilee S. Grindle, 'Reforming Land Tenure in Mexico: Peasants, the Market, and the State', in Riordan Roett (ed.), *The Challenge to Institutional Reform in Mexico* (Lynne Rienner, 1995), p. 47.

60 Neil Harvey (1996), p. 193.

61 *Ibid.*, pp. 94–5.

62 Randall Germain, personal correspondence, 17 January 1997.

63 Stephen J. Wagner and Donald E. Schultz, 'Civil-Military Relations in Mexico: The Zapatista Revolt and Its Implications', *Journal of InterAmerican Studies and World Affairs*, Vol. 37, No. 2 (Summer 1995), p. 15.

64 Reports suggested continuous army manoeuvres with increasing military patrols and aircraft flights and increasing violence outside the guerrilla zone. See: 'Zapatistas Muster International Left', *Guardian*, 7 July 1996.

65 Luis Hernández Navarro (1994), p. 59.

66 After more than nineteen months of negotiations it seemed that a consensus on electoral reform had been reached between government and officially recognized political parties. This involved controls on electoral campaign spending, the removal of government from involvement in Mexico's electoral tribunal, the introduction of proportional representation in elections to the senate, and direct elections for governor of Mexico City. The negotiations did not include the EZLN and are not irreversible. For reports on the electoral agreement see: 'Zapatistas Muster International Left', *Guardian*, 7 July 1996 and 'Now for Action', *The Economist*, 10 August 1996, p. 46.

67 Grindle (1995), p. 52.

68 Catholic Institute of International Relations, *Mexico: Free Market Failure* (CIIR, 1996).

69 Grindle (1995), pp. 52–3.

70 John Ross, 'The EZLN, A History: Miracles, *Coyunturas*, Communiqués',

in *Shadows of Tender Fury* (The Letters and Communiqués of subCommandante Marcos and the Zapatista Army of National Liberation), (Monthly Review Press, 1995b).

71 Nash (1995), pp. 32–3.
72 Robert W. Cox, 'An Alternative Approach to Multilateralism for the Twentieth-first Century', *Global Governance: A Review of Multilateralism and International Organization*, Vol. 3, (1997), p. 107. A less sanguine assessment of the EZLN is made by Carlos M. Vilas, 'Are There Left Alternatives? A Discussion from Latin America', in Leo Panitch (ed.), *The Socialist Register: Are There Alternatives?* (Merlin Press, 1996).
73 Roger Burbach, 'Roots of the Postmodern Rebellion in Chiapas', *New Left Review*, No. 205 (May/June 1994), p. 113.
74 Harry Cleaver, 'Introduction', in *Zapatistas, Documents of the New Mexican Revolution* (Autonomedia, 1994), p. 19.
75 *Ibid.*
76 For a wider analysis of 'indigenous ecology' in Mexico, see: David V. Carruthers, 'Indigenous Ecology and the Politics of Linkage in Mexican Social Movements', *Third World Quarterly*, Vol. 17, No. 5 (1996), pp. 1007–28. Also, for analysis of the fundamental connections between the people of Chiapas, the EZLN social movement, and the centrality of land issues see: George Collier, *BASTA! Land and the Zapatista Rebellion in Chiapas* (Food First, 1994); and Tom Barry, *Zapata's Revenge: Free Trade and the Farm Crisis* (South End Press, 1995).
77 Harry Cleaver (1994).
78 Burbach (1994), p. 114.
79 The 'silhouette' of the FZLN emerged after the Fourth Declaration of the Lacandón Jungle, declared 1 January 1996. See the EZLN home page http://www.ezln.org, and http://www.peak.org/~joshua/fzln/4th-decl
80 Cleaver (1994), p. 19.
81 June Nash and Christine Kovic, 'The Reconstitution of Hegemony: The Free Trade Act and the Transformation of Rural Mexico', in James H. Mittelman (ed.), *Globalization: Critical Reflections* (Lynne Rienner, 1996), pp. 182–3.
82 Lynn Stephen, 'Democracy for Whom? Women's Grassroots Political Activism in the 1990s, Mexico City and Chiapas', in Otero (1996), pp. 174–80.
83 Cynthia Enloe, 'Margins, Silences and Bottom Rings: How to Overcome the Underestimation of Power in the Study of International Relations', in Steve Smith, Ken Booth and Marysia Zalewski (eds), *International Theory: Positivism and Beyond* (Cambridge University Press, 1996).
84 Harry Cleaver, 'The Zapatistas and the Electronic Fabric of Struggle', in John Holloway (ed.), *The Chiapas Uprising and the Future of Revolution in the Twenty-first Century* (Pluto Press, 1997). Also see http://www.eco.utexas.edu:80/Homepages/Faculty/Cleaver/zaps.html#*
85 James Rochlin, 'Redefining Mexican 'National Security' during an Era of Post-Sovereignty', *Alternatives*, Vol. 20, (1995), p. 387 [emphasis added].
86 Nick Rengger and Mark Hoffman, 'Modernity, Postmodernism and International Relations', in Joe Doherty, Elspeth Graham and Mo Malek (eds), *Postmodernism and the Social Sciences* (Macmillan, 1992).

87 Roger Burbach, Orlando Núñez and Boris Kagarlitsky, *Globalization and Its Discontents: The Rise of Postmodern Socialisms* (Pluto Press, 1997). For an alternative view of the potential of such postmodern social forces see: Richard Gott, 'No Future for Rebels Trapped in Past', *Guardian*, 21 December 1996.

88 Burbach (1994, 1996).

89 Nash (1995), p. 36.

90 Cleaver (1994).

91 Rochlin (1995).

92 Ana Carrigan, 'The First Post-Modern Revolution', *Fletcher Forum*, Vol. 19, Part 1, (1995), pp. 71–98.

93 Daniel Nugent, 'Northern Intellectuals and the EZLN', *Monthly Review* (July–August 1995), pp. 124–37.

94 R. B. J. Walker, *One World, Many Worlds: Struggles for a Just World Peace* (Lynne Rienner, 1988).

95 Jim George, *Discourses of Global Politics: A Critical (Re)Introduction to International Relations* (Lynne Rienner, 1994).

96 R. B. J. Walker (1988), Chap. 4.

97 *Ibid.*, p. 83.

98 *Ibid.*, p. 79.

99 Jim George (1994), p. 213.

100 See Richard Devetak, 'The Project of Modernity and International Relations Theory', *Millennium: Journal of International Studies*, Vol. 24, No. 1 (1995), pp. 27–51 and Rengger and Hoffman (1992).

101 George (1994), p. 214.

102 *Ibid.*, p. 213.

103 *Ibid.*, p. 214.

104 Cox with Sinclair (1996), p. 152.

105 *Ibid.*, p. 168.

106 Robert W. Cox, 'Civilizations in World Political Economy', *New Political Economy*, Vol. 1, No. 2 (1996), p. 147. Also see Robert W. Cox, 'Civilizations: Encounters and Transformations', *Studies in Political Economy*, Vol. 47 (1995), pp. 7–31.

107 Nash (1995), p. 35.

108 Castañeda (1994), Ch. 10.

109 *Ibid.*, p. 311.

110 Timothy Wickham-Crowley, 'An Epitaph for Latin American Revolutionaries' (feature review of Jorge G. Castañeda, *Utopia Unarmed: The Latin American Left After the Cold War*), *Third World Quarterly*, Vol. 15, No. 3 (September 1994), pp. 530–1.

111 Cleaver (1994), p. 21.

112 Harry Browne, *For Richer, For Poorer: Shaping US–Mexican Integration* (Inter-Hemispheric Resource Centre, 1994), Ch. 3.

113 George (1994), p. 215.

114 Castaneda (1994), p. 49.

115 Ronald H. Chilcote, 'Left Political Ideology and Practice', in Barry Carr and Steve Ellner (eds), *The Latin American Left: From the Fall of Allende to Perestroika* (Latin America Bureau, 1993), p. 184.

116 Castañeda (1994), p. 118. In Mexico this contradiction has been

exemplified by the intractable difficulties the Partido de la Revolucíon Democrática (PRD: Party of the Democratic Revolution) has experienced since becoming a political party (under the leadership of Cuauhtémoc Cárdenas) after existing as a broad front of organizations prior to the 1988 presidential elections. As stated by one commentator, in a classic Gramscian *sotto voce*: 'The PRD does not seem to have been able to make the jump from being a conjunctural coalition of anti-PRI forces to creating an organically new political force.' See Barry Carr, 'Mexico: The Perils of Unity and the Challenge of Modernisation', in Carr and Ellner (1993), p. 92.

117 E. H. Carr, *What is History?* (Penguin, 1990 edition), p. 129.
118 Cox with Sinclair (1996), p. 145.
119 E. H. Carr, *The Twenty Years Crisis* (Papermac, 1995 edition), p. 14.
120 Craig N. Murphy, 'Seeing Women, Recognizing Gender, Recasting International Relations', *International Organization*, Vol. 50, No. 3 (1996), p. 526. Also see Craig N. Murphy and Roger Tooze (eds), *The New International Political Economy* (Lynne Rienner, 1991).
121 Stephen Gill, 'Globalization, Market Civilization, and Disciplinary Neoliberalism', *Millennium: Journal of International Studies*, Vol. 24, No. 3 (1995), pp. 399–423.
122 Karl Polanyi, *The Great Transformation: The Political and Economic Origins of Our Time* (Beacon, 1957).
123 James H. Mittelman, 'Rethinking the International Division of Labour in the Context of Globalization', *Third World Quarterly*, Vol. 16, No. 2 (1995), pp. 282–3. One may even argue that the EZLN epitomize some of the issues recently raised as crucial to the project of transformative multilateralism, see Cox (1997), pp. 113–14.
124 Central questions in any such project could ask: How were the sociopolitical relations in Mexico – central to PRI hegemony – themselves constructed? What were the historical qualities of the Mexican state/society complex which fostered the local configurations of neoliberalism?
125 Cox (1987), p. 390.
126 As a methodological cue to this point one could argue that a certain historicist approach, associated with Coxian historicism, as well as the approach of others such as Joseph Femia, could provide insight into how these issues may be addressed.
127 Michael Kenny and Randall Germain, 'Gramsci and IR Theory: A Critical Engagement', paper presented to the annual conference of the International Studies Association, Toronto, Canada, 18–22 March 1997.

17
Globalization and Local Resistance: The Case of Shell versus the Ogoni

Cyril I. Obi

Introduction

The extractive and polluting activities of Shell, the Anglo-Dutch global oil giant which produces slightly over half of Nigeria's oil, has spawned alienation, protests and resistance across the local host communities of the oil-rich Niger delta region in the past two decades. These took a turn for the worse from the mid-1980s in the wake of a deepening economic crisis, the throes of structural adjustment and a political transition. The Movement for the Survival of Ogoni People (MOSOP) was driven by the quest for self-determination; their aim was to force Shell and the Nigerian state to accept their right to control their own land, and the proceeds therefrom.

To stem the further 'production of environmental degradation' and the expropriation of the oil-rich Ogoni ecology, MOSOP waged a popular-based campaign against Shell and the state in Nigeria, locally and globally. The Nigerian state remains a significant factor in the local–global nexus. Entirely dependent on externally re-alized oil rents for its reproduction, this state is an expression of a fragile yet strong power bloc seeking to impose its hegemony and legitimacy on the Nigerian 'nation', while guaranteeing the local conditions for unimpeded global accumulation in Nigeria. The case of the Ogoni reflects how the balance of social forces influences outcomes locally. The environment becomes a contested terrain reflecting social and political relations of power over production, distribution and access.

The dialectics of globalization and local resistance

The politics of local resistance is a collective action directed at blocking further alienation, expropriation and environmental degradation. It represents a mass project of restitution and self-determination. To grasp the dialectics of globalization and local resistance in the context of the Ogoni struggle, we should situate our analysis in the structure of the on-going project of globalization. This avoids the limitations of state-centric approaches and the tendency for mainstream international relations theory to inadequately address the politics of global environmental change (Williams, 1996: 42). In considering the global logic of capital and its connections with environmental degradation and local resistance, attention will be paid to the 'national' context of the struggle, the social and political forces locked in the conflict, and their position in the global accumulation of capital at the local level.

Globalization, Shell and local resistance

Shell's interaction with the Ogoni environment is at the root of the conflict. The Ogoni – the indigenous landowners – have been increasingly alienated from the products of their land. Shell has polluted the ecosystem and damaged the livelihood of the local Ogoni peasantry without paying sufficient heed to initially peaceful demands for restitution.

To get at the root of Ogoni resistance, one needs to 'focus on the underlying structural conditions that give rise to expropriation and environmental degradation at the local level (Woodhouse 1992), and its connection with global accumulation. Conceptually, one cannot separate the environmental crisis in Ogoni land from the process of globalization. What then is Shell's role in the process of globalization?

A lot has been written about the immense power, political clout, wealth and global spread of the seven leading oil multinationals (Sampson, 1973). What is important is the strategic link between the oil giants and the energy needs of the industrial powers, particularly the G-7 countries. Oil is strategic as the most viable source of energy for transforming nature into commodities, which are exchanged to realize surplus. Thus, control of oil is directly linked to the reproduction and expansion of capital on a global scale.

Shell[1] is located in 'a global structure of material accumulation which simultaneously concentrates wealth and energy both in certain locales and at certain social levels of extracting and dispossessing from other locales and social levels' (Saurin, 1996: 87). In the Ogoni context, Shell need not 'attend to either (local) labour needs or local ecological propriety'. As Saurin argues (*ibid.*: 88):

> the destruction of Ogoni lands in Southern Nigeria by oil companies including allegedly Royal Dutch Shell satisfies the covetous and distanced shareholders who derive huge financial benefit from these lands and people. At the same time, the Ogoni pay the permanent costs of ecological degradation and repression, whilst relinquishing their control over what happens to their land, to the oil, or the product of their labour.

As observed by MOSOP, Ogoni indigenous people were not employed by Shell, their locality lacks basic infrastructure, and pollution has destroyed the local economy: farming, fishing, hunting and petty trading. What was at stake was the very existence of the Ogoni – the right to be. It is this struggle for achieving control of the land, and re-imposing environmentally sustainable local economic practices, that pitched the Ogoni against the further penetration of global capital.

Shell versus the Ogoni: from the local to the global

Having been marked out and given to Shell since 1938 (Soremekun and Obi, 1993a) Ogoni land was integrated into 'globalized capitalist relations' (Giddens, 1990: 18). The specificities of the Ogoni struggle for self-determination have been variously treated. Apart from the writings, interviews and speeches of its prominent spokesperson and leader of MOSOP, the late Ken Saro-Wiwa,[2] other writers have treated it in terms of a struggle against 'internal colonization' (Naanen, 1995), ethnic minority elite agitation (Osaghae, 1995) or the unresolved minority nationality question in Nigeria's federalism (Ngemutu-Roberts, 1994). Welch presents the Ogoni struggle within the context of the risks involved in the quest for social justice and self-determination in sub-Saharan Africa (Welch, 1995). A common thread linking these works is the broadly state-centric descriptive approach, which pays inadequate attention to the critical nexus between local resistance and the contradictions arising from the global social relations of production. Steeped in positivist social science, this approach glosses over the economic and political impact of Shell's interventionism on the Ogoni ecosystem, while treating the social forces in conflict as undifferentiated ethnic 'wholes' without considering the differences in their location on the 'basis of the power relations between dominant classes among interacting ethnic groups' (Syahuka-Muhindo, 1995). The vital trans- and inter-class coalitions which cut across ethnic and national lines, and the ways these reflect the balance of social forces and power are therefore lost. The important question is not the identification of the ethnic appearance of 'minority group resistance', but how the transnational class coalition subverts the ranks of the social and political forces which resist global accumulation in their locality.

This approach enables us to transcend analysis which queries the Ogoni struggle on the grounds that they were not the only marginalized ethnic minority group in Nigeria, or others that catalogue how the 'majority ethnic groups'[3] controlled the oil wealth to the exclusion of the Ogoni. The transnational class, made up of factions of the dominant class at the global, national and local levels, benefits from the expropriation and degradation of the oil-rich Ogoni ecology. It is also necessary to examine the role of the state, and its structural inability to resist globalization.

Shell and the state in Nigeria: the unequal partnership

The state in Nigeria is the product of colonialism. Its early form was clearly interventionist, directed at the forceful integration of Nigeria into the global capitalist system: as a source of supply for cheap raw materials, and a ready market for finished products from the global centres of industrial capital. The task of integration and the process of defining the territoriality of the colonial state involved the process of forcefully bringing together people of diverse nationalities and pre-capitalist modes of production (Soremekun and Obi, 1993b, 1995). The centralized nature of colonial patrimonialism gave factions of certain numerically superior ethnic groups a head start in the sharing of spoils within the colonial state. This in turn gave them effective control over cash-crop based accumulation and a role in exercising power at the regional level (Obi, 1995). The consequence of this was that the dominant factions found in ethnicity a ready tool for access to resources and power. In the equation of colonial patrimonialism, the ethnic minorities often lost out. Their response was one of using ethnicity to push for self-determination – usually expressed in the form of demands for exclusive space, or state creation, which would give them room to exercise autonomy over resources, and protection from having resources taken away by factions from the majority ethnic groups.

As far back as 1889, 1907 and 1914, the colonial state had legislated the monopoly of oil concessions in Nigeria to 'British or British-allied capital' (Lolomari, 1976: 14; Soremekun and Obi, 1993a: 8). Under the 1914 law, Shell in 1938 (and later Shell-BP) was granted an oil exploration licence covering the entire mainland of Nigeria, an area of 367,000 square miles (Shatzl, 1968: 24–6). Shell's monopoly was exercised without local participation. Shell exercised this monopoly over Nigeria's oil until 1959 – one year prior to independence in 1960 – when it reduced its acreage to 16,000 square miles. Between 1938 and 1956, when it first struck oil in commercial quantity at Oloibiri, and the commencement of oil exports in 1958, Shell was able to establish control over the most promising oil acreage and reserves, and concretized its head start over the other oil majors.[4] The wider implications of Shell's advantaged position, and the global control of Nigeria's oil *vis-à-vis* the role of the state, did not become obvious until the collapse of the cash crop economic base in the mid-1960s.

Thus, from the 1970s onwards, oil became the fiscal basis of the Nigerian state, accounting for over 80 per cent of national revenue and 95 per cent of foreign exchange earnings (Soremekun and Obi, 1993b: 209). Due to the social relations spawned by global oil, Nigerians were excluded from production, while the local dominant class factions engaged in a zero-sum contest for niches in the distribution of oil surplus, mediated by the state's formal authority over the collection (and allocation) of oil rents.[5]

It is important to note the shift by the state from non-participation to participation in the oil industry. This cemented the ties between national and global capital. From being content to be a mere collector of taxes or rents, starting with the 1959 Petroleum Profits tax, the state began to acquire participation rights in the operating companies mining oil in Nigeria. This also provided a cloak of legitimacy, via economic nationalism, for the state, and increased its access to oil rents.

The 1969 Decree No. 51, which abrogated the 1914 Petroleum Act, theoretically transferred the control of oil from the oil giants operating in Nigeria to the state. It also vested all oil revenues –

on-shore and off-shore – in the state. The state also took up equity interest in the joint ventures it had with the oil companies. The state took up equity in Shell–NNPC joint ventures to the tune of 60 per cent then 80 per cent (with the nationalization of BP assets in Nigeria in 1979). By the late 1990s it was about 55 per cent to the Nigerian National Petroleum Company (NNPC), 10 per cent to Elf and 5 per cent to Agip, while Shell owned 30 per cent equity participation. Shell remains Nigeria's largest operator and the state's interest in oil surplus is mostly represented in its joint venture with Shell and its critical role in Nigeria's Liquefied Natural Gas Project. Thus, the state and Shell have a common stake in the creation of oil surplus, and global oil-based accumulation (Shell, 1993). In the mid 1990s, Shell derived 14 per cent of all its oil from Nigeria (Greenpeace, 1995), while the oil-dependent state of Nigeria relied on Shell to produce 51 per cent of 'its' oil.

Due to the dependence of the Nigerian state on oil surplus it is integrated into the global relations of production which expropriates the oil resources of its own territory and people. Its role of mediation reflects the divisions within the ranks of the domestic ruling class and the balance of forces in society. Indeed, the ruling coalition has remained riven by 'regional political and ruling structures that have overlapped with historical patterns of economic and educational opportunity to create distinct regional fractions of the bourgeoisie that are hegemonic in their respective sectors' (Lubeck and Watts, 1994: 210). It is this ruling coalition and its global partners who have 'privatized' the state. At the local level, the oil minorities faction have found themselves playing a marginal role, often co-opted by the dominant groups but left out of the 'commanding heights' of the power bloc. Therefore, control over oil, being the key to Nigeria's participation in global accumulation, is a contested terrain by all social groups, while the state, as the sum total of relations arising from the global character of oil production, is a site of constant struggles for access to power and accumulation. The state's existence and that of the ruling coalition depends on the global oil giants which produce the oil, particularly Shell.

Apart from its role in defining the parameters of Nigeria's oil for the global market, Shell's status as a power house of global capital renders the state in Nigeria a weak partner. Providing a picture of Shell's might, Miller (1995: 35) notes that:

> Shell Oil's 1990 gross national income was more than the com-
> bined GNPs of Tanzania, Ethiopia, Nepal, Bangladesh, Zaire,
> Uganda, Nigeria, Kenya and Pakistan – countries that represent
> almost one-tenth of the world's population.

Shell runs fully integrated oil operations in over one hundred
countries and has substantial interests in gas, chemicals, mining
and real estate (Obi, 1997). Its joint venture partner (and competitor),
the NNPC, is no match for Shell.

Thus, Shell's position in Nigeria's political economy and its role
as the cutting edge of the global control of Nigeria's oil, offers its
'unequal' partner – the state – little autonomy *vis-à-vis* the imperatives
of globalization. Thus the state in Nigeria defends its partner from
contending social and political forces, repressing local opposition
to Shell. By reinforcing its control over the political, the state protects
global accumulation and the interests of the transnational class,
while still projecting itself as the protector of the national interest
in order to retain its legitimacy. The objective role of the state and
the interests of the ruling coalition perceive the Ogoni resistance
as subversion, an act obstructive of the expansion of global oil capital
in a period of crisis.

The Ogoni versus global oil

The Ogoni struggle against Shell goes back to 1958. It had its background in the forceful integration of Ogoni into the global oil
economy. As oil capital penetrated deeper into the Ogoni ecosystem,
it spawned relations of production which alienated the landowners
and producers from the products of their land, while degrading
the environment and destroying the basis of livelihood in the agro-
based peasant economy. This led to the clash between Shell and
the Ogoni people.

Several developments acted as catalysts in the escalation of this
clash of opposing forces: the Nigerian civil war, the impact of
structural adjustment on social and power relations, and changes
in global politics in the post-cold war era.

The Nigerian civil war led to some shifts in the balance of social
and political forces in Nigeria. At the onset of the war, the four
regions were split into twelve states,[6] satisfying to some extent the
age-old quest of ethnic minorities for self-determination. With respect to the ethnic minorities of the Niger delta, they soon found

out that what they gained within the twelve state–federal structure was lost in terms of non-access to oil revenue. What this implied politically was that the regionally defined factions of the dominant class, particularly those which had defeated Biafran claims to the oil fields of the Niger delta, were now in control of the distribution of oil-rents, while the oil minorities faction found itself marginalized.

A new struggle was defined within the dominant class, in which oil minorities factions were variously either co-opted or sacrificed. In the struggle between the dominant class and the oil minorities faction, the latter mobilized popular forces against the former on the grounds of the solidarity of the oppressed, the quest for justice and self-determination, and the need to resist further marginalization.

The response of the oil minorities faction immediately after the war was largely one of disappointment that its tactical support for the federalist dominant class did not translate into compensation in the form of access to oil surplus. Rather, it led to the blockage of access (Saro-Wiwa, 1984, 1995). The oil minorities factions were basically united by the quest for more access to oil surplus, increased autonomy and power at the local level, and restitution for ecological damage by oil companies. Internal debate between those who believed in limited protest, and full co-optation into the hegemonic agenda of the transnational class, and an opposing faction which believed in confronting the transnational coalition with evidence of its atrocities and using popular power to wrest restitution, increased autonomy and power at the local level.

Ogoni resistance can also be linked to the high concentration of global capital in its region. As Claude Welch (1995: 636) puts it:

> the Ogoni live atop some of the richest real estate in Africa yet few Ogoni benefit from jobs, developments or amenities in the oil industry. Instead, they suffer serious environmental degradation that has polluted streams and fresh water sources, poisoned land through spills and blowouts, and created an atmosphere fouled by decades of flaring natural gas.

Within an area of 404 square miles, Ogoni is host to six oil fields with numerous pipes crossing overland, connecting various oil installations, two refineries, a huge fertilizer plant, petrochemical plants and an ocean port (Naanen, 1995). Ogoni represents the paradox of capitalist accumulation – as the poorest and yet most industrialized enclave in Nigeria (Naanen, 1995). At the heart of this contradiction lies the roots of the Ogoni revolution. It pitched the global against the local; accumulation against resistance. The immersion of Nigeria in economic crisis, and its socially harsh programme of economic adjustment in the midst of a political transition, sharpened these contradictions, leading to open confrontation between the opposing forces.

The politics of adjustment in Nigeria has received academic attention (Olukoshi, 1993). Its immediate impact was the deepening of the social and economic crisis. This took place within a political context marked by authoritarianism and the shrinking of political space to exclude all those opposed to the military wing of the power bloc (*ibid.*). Thus, the initially peaceful protests of the social movements of the Niger delta assumed more frequency as the harsh effects of adjustment sank deeper. The situation was worsened by the deregulation of the oil industry, which underscored the desperation of the state to get more oil rents to service its huge external debt (Obi, 1994).

For global oil, it was an equally desperate period with the competing oil giants keen to build up their reserves and expand the process of capital accumulation. The deregulation of the oil industry in Nigeria gave the oil companies better leverage to expand investments. The consequence of the foregoing was the deepening of contradictions between the transnational coalition and the people of the Niger delta. It was the balance of power between the feuding oil minorities' factions *vis-à-vis* the transnational coalition and the coercive apparatus of the state that eventually defined the outcome of the struggle.

Under structural adjustment, the state reinforced its political functions, and remained central to the process of oil-based accumulation. The radicalization of the Ogoni struggle which had become evident in the demands listed in the 1990 Ogoni Bill of Rights, gave notice to the state that the struggle was directed against oil-based accumulation – the very basis of state power, dominant class hegemony, Shell and Nigeria's place in the global capitalist system:

> Justifying Ogoni resistance, Ken Saro-Wiwa stressed its moral advantage ... Over the past thirty years, Ogoni has given Nigeria an estimated US thirty billion dollars and received NOTHING in return, except a blighted countryside, an atmosphere full of carbon dioxide, carbon monoxide and hydrocarbons, a land in which

wildlife is unknown, a land of polluted streams and creeks, of rivers without fish, a land which was in every sense of the term an ecological disaster (Saro-Wiwa, 1995: 74).

The formation of the Movement for the Survival of Ogoni People (MOSOP) in 1991, under the leadership of a broad coalition of the Ogoni faction of the Oil Minorities took the struggle to a higher level. It was in the thick of this struggle that the cracks within the Ogoni widened, and the radical and more militant faction of MOSOP assumed ascendancy to the desperation of the more conservative elements and their transnational allies. The basic issues on which the MOSOP-led resistance against Shell and the state were based included the following: the need for social justice for minorities, equity in power sharing in Nigeria, compensation for environmental devastation and the restoration of the environment, payment of economic rents to oil-producing areas, human dignity and self-actualization (Saro-Wiwa, 1994: 17). There is no doubt that these considerations ran against the logic of the expansion of global capital and domestic accumulation in Nigeria. By 1993, MOSOP decided to apply more pressure. According to Saro-Wiwa, MOSOP had the moral advantage and 'time and world opinion was on the side of the Ogoni struggle'.

From 1991 onwards, MOSOP internationalized its struggle, taking its case to Amnesty International, Greenpeace and the Geneva-based organization – the Unrepresented Nations and Peoples Organization (UNPO), the London Rainforest Action Group and eventually, the United Nations (Saro-Wiwa, 1995; Greenpeace, 1994, 1995; Rowell, 1994). It waged its campaign through lecture tours, newspaper articles, and documentary films showing the atrocities being committed against the Ogoni by Shell and the state in Nigeria. This way the dimensions of the ecological disaster and denial of rights which the Ogoni suffered from Shell and the state was used in shocking the global community into putting pressures on the 'unequal partnership' to respect the rights of the Ogoni to self-determination.

The Ogoni strategy of internationalizing its struggle was partly based on its reading of certain developments at the global level: 'the end of the cold war, increasing attention being paid to the global environment, and the insistence of the European Community that minority rights be respected in the USSR successor states and in Yugoslavia' (Saro-Wiwa, 1992: 7). By 1993, MOSOP had been transformed by the dialectics of the struggle into a popular social movement. The conservative leadership was pushed aside by the more militant cadres in the National Youth Council for the Survival of Ogoni People (NYCOP) and the Federation of Ogoni Women's Associations (FOWA). NYCOP and FOWA were able to mobilize the Ogoni masses under the leadership of MOSOP. As tensions rose, they became more militant. The final split in MOSOP took place when the conservative faction lost a crucial vote to prevent the Ogoni from boycotting the 12 June 1993 presidential elections. The radicals, who had demonstrated their strength earlier in the year when they successfully organized a huge peaceful rally marking Ogoni day, purged the leadership of MOSOP of the conservatives, and voted Ken Saro-Wiwa as the leader. Under his leadership, the radicalization of the social movement grew very fast and before long the people had been able to block access to oil wells in Ogoni, forcing Shell to stop operations and costing the Shell–state partnership an estimated daily loss of N9.9 million from May 1993 (Izeze, 1994: 1). Equally significant was that some oil communities, following the MOSOP example, drew up Charters of Demands and raised pressure on Shell and the state (Obi, 1995). The developments of 1993 and 1994 clearly convinced the transnational alliance that the danger they faced was the possible subversion of oil-based accumulation in Nigeria. To the domestic dominant class, the revolutionary activities of MOSOP were a direct threat to its hegemony, as well as the legitimacy of the oil minorities faction aligned to the dominant class.

Neither Shell nor the state acceded to the demands of MOSOP. Shell's strategy was to deny responsibility, insisting that MOSOP was making unreasonable demands, sabotaging oil installations and exaggerating the extent of ecological damage in Ogoni (Shell, 1994, 1995; Achebe, 1996). The state on its part viewed MOSOP activities as subversion and economic sabotage.

Consequently, the struggle became militarized with the state mobilizing armed troops to force through the continued global project of controlling the Ogoni environment. These troops occupied Ogoni villages and unleashed a reign of terror against suspected MOSOP cadres and the peasantry who sympathized with the MOSOP cause. Entire villages were sacked, people lost their lives, and many took to hiding in the bush. Nothing was spared in crushing the MOSOP revolution. At the same time, the conflict between the radicals and the conservatives raged within the Ogoni elite. The local conservatives, backed by global and state forces, became the target of MOSOP militant cadres, and were increasingly despised by the social and political forces ranged against the transnational coalition. It was during one such incident that four leading members of the Ogoni political class suspected of being 'counter revolutionaries' were murdered by a mob in Ogoni land. The state moved in, and in November 1995, nine leaders of MOSOP, including Ken Saro-Wiwa were hanged on the orders of a tribunal, after being convicted on counts of inciting a mob to murder the four Ogoni chiefs.

After the conviction and hangings the Ogoni struggle went into retreat locally, while the international campaign was sustained by Ogoni activists in exile (Owens Wiwa, 1996). The international campaign sought to mobilize support for the imposition of sanctions on Nigeria, and 'calling Shell to order' (Ake, 1996), and the release of MOSOP activists (Sakaar, 1996).

Outcomes and lessons

It is difficult to predict the eventual outcome of local resistance of the Ogoni against Shell and the state. However, at the conjuncture of the aftermath of Ken Saro Wiwa's execution, it spelt tragedy for local resistance. Nevertheless, the domestic ruling coalition suffered from internal contradictions and a crisis of governance. Tensions ran high just below the surface. Violent unrest burst out into the open again in the Niger delta in the autumn of 1998, revealing the continued possibility of the rise of local resistance. The recent return to democracy in Nigeria may offer possibilities for dialogue not possible previously.

The primary lesson of the reversal of the Ogoni revolution is the danger in underestimating the capacity of global capital and the local state to defend oil-based accumulation in Nigeria. The Ogoni resistance failed partly because it took place ahead of its time, and partly because MOSOP did not work hard enough to build solid tactics and local or regional alliances. Indeed the revolution hardly spread beyond Ogoni land. Without strong linkages to neighboring oil communities or movements outside the Niger delta, it was easy for the state to isolate the Ogoni locally and stifle their protest.

Equally important is the overestimation of the pressure that the global civil society could bring to bear on Shell and the state in Nigeria, not knowing the extent to which organizations such as Amnesty, Greenpeace and UNPO could go in actually stopping the ecological devastation of Ogoni, and the limitations they faced if they attempted to block Shell and the vital interests of the G-7 countries.

It is not clear if MOSOP had an advanced ideological clarity about the ramifications of its struggle. A lot rested on the moral advantage and the justness of its cause. Anger, bitterness and personality differences played a major role in sowing discord in the ranks of Ogoni leadership. The infiltration of the movement by 'counter revolutionary forces' of the transnational coalition paved the way for its subversion from within.

The remnants of MOSOP's cadres in Ogoni continue to carry on the struggle. The lesson of the Ogoni tragedy for other social movements seeking to make a revolution at the dawn of the twenty-first century is that the task is much more difficult, and requires rigorous preparation based on the correct reading of the balance of social and political forces and their position in the globalized empire of capital.

Notes

1 Shell Petroleum Development Company (Nigeria) Limited is a local subsidiary of Shell International Petroleum Company.

2 Ken Saro-Wiwa and eight of his MOSOP colleagues were hanged in a Port Harcourt Prison on 10 November 1995.

3 The three dominant ethnic groups in Nigeria are the Hausa-Fulani, Ibo and the Yoruba.

4 The oil companies included Mobil, Gulf (now Chevron), Agip, Safrap (now Elf), Tenneco and Amoseas (Texaco/Chevron).

5 Formal state control was enshrined in Decree 51 of November 1969 which vested in the state entire ownership and control of oil. While Decree 38 of 1971 extended the limits of Nigeria's territorial waters, and gave the Commissioner of Mines and Power (later Petroleum Resources) the power to grant oil exploration, oil mining and oil production licences.

6 From the initial number of twelve states, the number has now risen to thirty-six.

References

Achebe, Emeka (1996), 'Shell and the Truth', *The Guardian*, 25 January.

Ake, Claude (1996), 'Shelling Nigeria Ablaze', *Tell*, Vol. 129 (January).

Giddens, A. (1990), *The Consequences of Modernity* (Cambridge University Press).

Greenpeace (1994, 1995), *Shell (Nigeria) Campaign*.

Izeze, Ifeanyi (1994) 'Nigeria Loses N2.732 billion to Ogoni Crisis', *Daily Sunray*, 3 February.

Lolomari, Odoliyi (1976), 'The Evolution of Nigeria's Oil Policy', in *Edited Proceedings of the 1976 Annual Conference of the Nigerian Economic Society* (Nigerian Economic Society).

Lubeck, Paul and Watts, Michael (1994), 'An Alliance of Oil and Maize': The Response of Indigenous and State Capital to Structural Adjustment in Nigeria', in Bruce Berman and Colin Leys (eds), *African Capitalists in African Development* (Lynne Rienner).

Miller, Marian (1995), *The Third World in Global Environmental Politics* (Lynne Rienner).

Naanen, Ben (1995), 'Oil-producing Minorities and the Restructuring of Nigerian Federalism: The Case of the Ogoni People', *Journal of Commonwealth and Comparative Studies*, Vol. 32, No.1.

Ngemutu-Roberts, F. O. (1994), 'Federalism, Minorities and Political Contestation in Nigeria: From Henry Willink to the MOSOP Phenomenon' Paper presented to the 20th Nigeria Political Science Association Conference, Ile-Ife, 28 February to 2 March.

Obi, Cyril (1994), *Structural Adjustment, Oil and Popular Struggles: The Deepening Crisis of State Legitimacy and Governance in Nigeria.* Research Report submitted to CODESRIA, Dakar.

Obi, Cyril (1995), 'Oil Minority Rights versus the Nigerian State: Environmental Conflict, Its Implications and Transcendence'. Paper presented to CODESRIA's 8th General Assembly and Conference, Dakar, 26 June to 2 July.

Obi, Cyril (1997), *Oil, Environmental Conflict and National Security in Nigeria: Ramifications of the Ecology-Security Nexus for Sub-Regional Peace* (ACDIS Occasional Paper).

Obi, Cyril and Soremekun, Kayode (1995), 'Oil and the Nigerian State: An Overview', in Kayode Soremekun (ed.) *Perspectives on the Nigeria Oil Industry* (Amkra).

Olukoshi, Adebayo (ed.) (1993), *The Politics of Structural Adjustment in Nigeria* (James Currey).

Osaghae, Eghosa (1995), 'The Ogoni Uprising: Oil Politics, Minority Agitation and the Future of the Nigerian State', *Africa Affairs*, Vol. 94, No. 376.

Rowell, A. (1994), *Shell-Shocked: The Environmental and Social Costs of Living with Shell in Nigeria* (Greenpeace).

Sakaar, Dornu (1996), '19 More Ogoni's for the Justice Auta Special Military Tribunal'. MOSOP Crisis Management Committee Press Release.

Sampson, Anthony (1973), *The Seven Sisters: The Great Oil Companies and the World They Shaped* (Viking Press).

Saro-Wiwa, Ken (1984), *On a Darkling Plain* (Saros).

Saro-Wiwa, Ken (1992), *Genocide in Nigeria: The Ogoni Tragedy* (Saros).

Saro-Wiwa, Ken (1994), 'Oil and the Basic Issues at Stake', *Guardian*, 1 April.

Saro-Wiwa, Ken (1995), *A Month and a Day: A Detention Diary* (Penguin).

Saurin, Julian (1996), 'International Relations, Social Ecology and the Globalization of Environmental Change', in John Vogler and Mark F. Imber (eds) *The Environment and International Relations* (Routledge).

Shatzl, Ludwig (1968), *Petroleum in Nigeria* (Oxford University Press).

Shell Petroleum Development Corporation (1993), *Nigeria and Shell: Partners in Progress* (Shell).

Shell International Petroleum Corporation (1994), 'Shell Briefing Note' (Press Release).

Shell International Petroleum Corporation (1995), 'Clear Thinking in Troubled Times' (Press Release).

Soremekun, Kayode and Obi, Cyril (1993a), 'The Changing Pattern of Private Foreign Investments in the Nigerian Oil Industry', *Africa Development*, Vol. 18, No. 3.

Soremekun, Kayode and Obi, Cyril (1993b), 'Oil and the National Question', in *Edited Proceedings of the Nigeria Economic Society 1993 Annual Conference* (Nigerian Economic Society).

Syahuka-Muhindo, A. (1995), 'The Rwenzururu Movement and the Democratic Struggle', in Mahmood Mamdani and Ernest Wamba-dia-Wamba (eds), *African Studies in Social Movements and Democracy* (CODESRIA).

Welch, Claude (1995), 'The Ogoni and Self-determination: Increasing Violence in Nigeria', *Journal of Modern African Studies*, Vol. 33, No. 4.

Williams, Marc (1996), 'International Political Economy and Global Environmental Change', in John Vogler and Mark Imber (eds) *The Environment and International Relations* (Routledge).

Wiwa, Owens (1996), 'The Agony of the Ogoni', *Africa Notes* (March).

Woodhouse, P. (1992), 'Environmental Degradation and Sustainability', in T. Allen and A. Thomas (eds), *Poverty and Development in the 1990s* (Oxford University Press).

18

Structural Adjustment and the Response of Civil Society in Bangladesh and Zimbabwe: A Comparative Analysis

Sandra J. MacLean, Fahimul Quadir and Timothy M. Shaw

Introduction

Structural adjustment policies (SAPs) are now a commonplace, even ubiquitous, manifestation of the established dominance of neo-liberalism in an era of intensified globalization of economies, institutions and social relations. Both SAPs and globalization have led to myriad forms of popular resistance which have begun to inform a set of 'second wave' analyses of civil societies. Academic fascination with 'new' social movements and non-governmental organizations (NGOs) has intensified since the 1980s because organized responses and resistance have proliferated as the shocks attendant on one- and a-half decades of initially economic and now political reform conditionalities have become ever more apparent.[1]

Introduced at the outset of the Third World debt crisis as conditionalities for loans by the International Monetary Fund (IMF) and the World Bank to severely indebted countries, SAPs are designed to restore macroeconomic balances in economies. According to the international financial institutions (IFIs), such imbalances are the results of inappropriate policy choices by national governments. By contrast, critics of SAPs argue that the sources of the problem exist in broader international and/or global political economy contexts. Regardless of causality, because of the severity of the debt crisis and the lack of alternative sources of capital, many Third World countries have become heavily reliant on the IFIs either to supply loans directly or to provide a 'stamp of approval' that other external lenders can accept as assurance that their investments will be protected. In either case, regimes are obliged to agree to bring their economies in line with open market practices. Although each country is treated as a separate economic unit, there is a set formula of structural adjustment measures that includes devaluation, deregulation, desubsidization and privatization.

Critics of SAPs observe that there is a fairly consistent list of problems which ensue from their implementation. These include disinvestment, deindustrialization, decreased employment, and increased social problems and inequities. Indeed, after a decade and a half of their existence, a well-established literature on the subject indicates that it is at least debatable whether SAPs, even if followed to the letter, could simultaneously promote sustainable economic growth in all the countries where the programmes are now in place: i.e. a fallacy of composition may be in operation. Equally unlikely is that it is *politically possible* to implement SAPs; that is, the 'good governance' conditionalities imposed secondarily by the IFIs are not necessarily or obviously compatible with the economic ones which were initially implemented. Moreover, many observers question whether SAPs are *morally justifiable*, given that they are imposed by industrial countries (as the dominant member-states of the IFIs) on poor countries and because they cause severe social distress, especially for the poorest and most vulnerable members of society.

There is a common assumption that in agreeing to implement SAPs, Third World governments at best acquiesce to the IFIs' demands and, more usually, resist – either openly or passively by failing to comply. Second, in debating the effects of SAPs on civil societies, it is often implied that the latter are homogenous entities and that the various groups which comprise are similarly affected. However, some government officials may be ideologically predisposed to favour orthodox economic prescriptions and/or may benefit personally or politically from their implementation. Also, groups in civil society may be favourably affected by SAPs while others are disadvantaged. To some extent, who loses and who benefits from structural adjustment varies from country to country depending upon the specific histories of state–societal relations and (political) cultures, and the dialectics of the latter's interaction with regional, international and global actors and forces. Nevertheless, in most countries the number of those who are disadvantaged by structural adjustment appears to be growing, as is the opposition to these economic policies and the governments that impose them.

This Chapter examines forms of resistance by social movements/ groups to the articulation and implementation of SAPs in two Third World political economies. The comparative analysis reveals sophistication in such reactions over time, characterized by both opposition and coping; i.e. elements in civil society have both resisted and also provided services to compensate for reduced state roles and expenditures. Such bifurcation may have moderated their opposition, while it also informed their alternative provision of basic needs. New regimes in both Bangladesh and Zimbabwe introduced statist policies soon after achieving formal independence. Nevertheless, the pressure of globalization and the hegemony of neoliberalism could not be denied for long. The social dynamics of advocates and detractors of SAPs have varied in the two cases; in part in reflection of their distinctive political economies/cultures/histories. Comparative analysis across continents reveals interesting similarities as well as contrasts in SAP sequences and responses. As we suggest in the conclusion, comparative insights into 'globalization and resistance' constitute a promising field for both analysis and praxis as we anticipate the new millennium. Such dialectics will surely characterize the next decade and century given patterns of exponential incorporation and differentiation.[2]

The case of Bangladesh

Moving towards the market

Bangladesh's journey to a 'free market' began long before the issue of structural economic reforms had been presented as a panacea for all the economic and financial problems of the developing world. Given the apparent failure of a socialist model to meet the enormous challenge of poverty reduction and rapid economic growth, General Ziaur Rahman's (1975–81) military regime embarked upon market-oriented reforms as early as in the mid-1970s. In December 1975, the regime introduced an economic reform programme through the announcement of the Revised Investment Policy (RIP). Based on an export-led economic growth strategy, the policy aimed at reducing levels of budget deficit and inflation, increasing domestic savings and promoting long-term growth. More specifically, it emphasized the need for transferring state-owned enterprises (SOEs) to the private sector and encouraged private entrepreneurs to invest in all but eight strategically important sectors. The policy opened up new opportunities for foreign investors and facilitated the formation of the country's first Export Processing Zone (EPZ) in the port-city Chittagong.[3]

Zia's liberalization programme also attempted to improve the macroeconomic framework in order to ensure both competitiveness and higher economic growth. Complying with the conditionalities laid down in the International Monetary Fund (IMF)/World Bank sponsored adjustment and/or Extended Fund Facility (EEF) programmes, the military regime undertook measures for controlling of budget deficit, reforming the public sector, reducing subsidies on such items as food, fertilizer and petroleum and liberalizing the trade regime. Besides, the government made attempts to develop a competitive exchange rate policy primarily through the devaluation of the taka – the unit of currency. Also, it took a variety of additional measures, namely reforming the tax system, lowering inflation, and increasing exports to improve the country's foreign exchange reserves.[4]

However, it was not until the assumption of power by General Hussain M. Ershad's (1982–90) military regime in March 1982 that the country witnessed the adoption of a radical path to the market. Soon after the seizure of power, unlike Zia's hesitant strategy, Ershad initiated a more defined and aggressive approach to liberalization. His reform programmes, for instance, aimed at accelerating the process of privatization, improving the policy framework to institutionalize the role of the private sector in development and to strengthen the on-going processes of adjustment and stabilization. In particular, his liberalization measures further limited the role of the public sector and focused on the urgent need to ensure macro-economic stability of the country.

In order to liberalize the financial sector, Ershad's military regime undertook quite a few important measures during the 1980s. It decided, for instance, to allow private commercial banks to operate in the country and transferred the ownership of two nationalized banks, namely Uttara Bank and Pubali Bank in 1984. As well, it deregulated the interest rates by permitting banks to determine deposit and lending rates within the limits set by the Central Bank. Moreover, it adopted a policy of ensuring greater autonomy of financial institutions, making them able to develop more appropriate lending mechanisms.[5] The government's reforms also included the liberalization of trade in Bangladesh. The policy focused on phasing out the quantitative restrictions, reducing the number of tariff rates, eliminating protection-related non-tariff barriers, streamlining import procedures and simplifying custom clearance of imported goods.[6]

Contrary to what both of the military regimes had expected, however, the country's hope to meet its myriad developmental challenges through market-oriented reforms has been frustrated by disappointing economic outcomes of the liberalization programme. Throughout the 1980s, for instance, the economy grew at an estimated 4 per cent annually, much lower than the 7–8 per cent required for alleviating poverty. Rehman Sobhan, a well-known economist of South Asia, essentially blamed donor sponsored SAPs for the failure of the economy to grow at a faster rate. He examined both the pre-adjustment and post-adjustment performance of the economy and suggested that the country did much better during the pre-adjustment period. According to him, real GDP grew at an average 5.7 per cent annually between 1972 and 1981, while the growth rate remained below 4 per cent in the 1982–90 period.[7]

No wonder that such a slow GDP growth has had serious implications for human development in general, and poverty alleviation in particular. Indeed, most studies suggest that both rural and urban poverty increased during the early years of structural adjustment. Using the daily calorie intake method, most estimates show that almost half of the population, about 47.5 per cent, has remained trapped below the poverty line in 1995–6.[8] The situation is much worse when the Capability Poverty Measure (CPM) is used to determine the nature of poverty. According to the *Human Development Report 1996*, the CPM value for Bangladesh is 76.9 – one of the highest in the world.[9]

What is even more important to mention is the growing inequality between the rich and the poor in both urban and rural areas. The Gini coefficient rose from 0.372 in 1985 to 0.430 in 1995 – a clear indication that inequality is on the rise. Similarly, the number of landless people significantly increased over the last two decades. The rate of the landless in Bangladesh rose from 34 per cent in 1972 to 68.8 per cent in 1996.[10] Part of the reason for growing inequality is that, as most studies suggest, adjustment programmes have consistently benefited a small group of mainly financial and economic elites of the country.

Problems of democratic consolidation in the era of structural adjustment

The dominant orthodox perspective on the relationship between democracy and the market suggests that market-oriented reforms and democratization are mutually reinforcing. While authors are divided as to whether economic liberalization contributes to democratization or vice versa, many argue that economic reforms lead to the creation of a favourable environment for both political liberalization and democratic consolidation. Bangladesh's experience, however, disproves such a thesis. The recent breakdown of democracy in the country suggests that while market-oriented reforms enabled the nation to make a transition to formal, multiparty democracy, contradictions generated by economic liberalization undoubtedly impeded the process of institutionalizing a sustainable democracy.

On the one hand, contrary to what is claimed by many established liberal authors, market-oriented reforms virtually became the primary source of generating popular discontent in the country. Continued cuts in social services, privatization of SOEs, trade and monetary liberalization and removal of hitherto existing subsidies from basic consumer goods, such as fertilizer, petroleum and electricity, strengthened resistance to economic reforms, enabling civil society organizations to play a crucial role in the country's struggle for democracy. Rejecting General Ershad's market-oriented reforms, a variety of civil society groups, such as student associations, trade unions, professional and cultural organizations, women's groups and peasants associations, continued to shape and reshape Bangladesh's movement for democracy throughout the 1980s. They sincerely hoped that a democratic transition would enable them to construct a political environment in which they could make politicians more responsive to their socio-economic demands. Thus, long before mainstream political parties managed to establish political platforms, civil society groups got united and launched a series of programmes to oust the military regime from power, which eventually led to the collapse of General Ershad's military regime.

To the surprise of many, within a year and half of the transition to democracy, Bangladesh began to witness the erosion of a socio-political consensus achieved through a decade-long struggle for democracy. Renewed conflicts between the ruling Bangladesh Nationalist Party (BNP) and mainstream opposition – composed of the AL, General Ershad's Jatiya Party (JP) and the Islamists Jammat-i-Islami – shattered the hope of democratic consolidation. Claiming that the BNP regime would manipulate the polling to increase its chances of re-election, the opposition demanded a constitutional amendment that would allow a neutral caretaker government (NCG) to conduct the next parliamentary elections scheduled to be held in early 1996. They also charged Mrs Zia's regime with corruption, demanding the dissolution of the parliament and early elections. However, the BNP regime rejected these charges and maintained that the election would be fair.[11] The politics of distrust approached a precarious stage in February 1994 when the opposition began a boycott of parliament, alleging that Mrs Zia's BNP rigged a by-election and would do anything to stay in power. With the failure of several negotiation attempts to resolve the political impasse, 147 opposition MPs resigned en masse from the JS on 28 December 1994, plunging the country into a crisis.

However, it was not until the involvement of civil society associations in the anti-BNP agitation that the political stand-off entered an extremely dangerous phase. Utterly frustrated with the economic policy of the BNP regime, civil society groups decided to lend their unequivocal support to the opposition movement. Part of their frustration resulted from the fact that, contrary to what civil society groups had expected, the BNP regime made no attempt to abandon or even slow down the pace of market-oriented economic reforms. After coming into power, Prime Minister Khaleda Zia's democratically elected regime adopted an even faster approach to economic liberalization. Although her reforms registered some success in improving the economy's fiscal health, it clearly failed to accelerate GDP growth, improve the poverty situation and generate employment.[12] With great disappointment, ordinary citizens experienced a deteriorating standard of living on the one hand, and a widening gap between the rich and the poor on the other.

Thus, civil society groups did not wait long before they lent their support to the opposition's movement to unseat the BNP regime. Together with civil society, mainstream opposition organized a 'resistant movement' that ultimately created the 'most terrifying episode' in the entire political history of post-liberation Bangladesh. The country virtually witnessed what is often called a 'statelessness syndrome', where politics was clearly overtaken by violence. Luckily, Bangladesh narrowly escaped a total breakdown, when the BNP regime finally agreed to step down on 30 March 1996.

Popular movements for democratic development

Somewhat ironically, the contradictions generated by market-oriented reforms have led people to search for alternatives, giving the emergence of the NGO sector, which is playing a crucial role in creating a momentum for democratic development in Bangladesh. Indeed, the emergence of NGOs as key development actors has been reflected in their phenomenal growth over the past few years. 'There are probably more NGOs in Bangladesh', according to Lewis, 'than in any other country of the same size in the world.'[13] Available statistical information suggests that the number of NGOs registered under the Voluntary Social Welfare Agencies (Registration and Control) Ordinance vary between 13,000 and 19,000. Of the total, it is estimated that about 1000 NGOs are mainly engaged in implementing foreign donor-supported development projects. Financial support for their projects from official external donors increased from US$ 158 millions in the 1990–1 fiscal year to US$ 441 million in 1994–5, coming to account for about 20 per cent of the nation's public investment programmes.[14]

Emphasizing the need for enhancing the self-management capabilities of the poor, developmental NGOs, namely the Grameen Bank (GB), Bangladesh Rural Advancement Committee (BRAC), Proshika Manobik Unnayan Kendra (Proshika), Nijera Kari and Gonoshasthaya Kendra (GK) and UBINIG (Policy Research for Development Alternative) have begun to focus on such issues as empowerment, participation and the creation of alternative organizational structures for vulnerable groups. The GB, for instance, has effectively developed and implemented the concept of 'credit without collateral'. Rejecting the conventional banking assumption that the poor are not 'bankable' social groups, the GB provides credit and necessary organizational assistance to rural people who have no access to formal lending agencies. Through its 1056 branches, it has extended credit activities to 35,726 villages over the last few years. More important perhaps is the fact that its programmes have created rare opportunities for women to get involved in a variety of income-generating activities, thus challenging the traditional childbearing role of women in rural Bangladesh. By one estimate, some 93 per cent of its loans went to women that enabled them to obtain relatively secure livelihoods. Empirical studies suggest that participation in GB's projects have given women the 'power' to take action against different forms of malpractice, such as wife abuse, dowry and male-originated divorce.[15]

Likewise, BRAC has succeeded in mobilising hundreds of thousands of marginalized rural women, men and children. Focusing exclusively on the landless poor in rural areas, BRAC initiates programmes to organize them into co-operative groups. In addition to supporting income-generating enterprises, BRAC also provides training to raise the awareness of disempowered groups. It renders legal-service to enable the rural poor to act as 'para-legal counsellors in such matters as land conflicts and registration, civil rights and unfair practices'.[16] Similarly, GK initiates a variety of programmes to empower the growing pool of marginalized people – particularly rural poor women. It gives functional education and practical training to rural women and supports activities for income generation, thus enabling women to break out of stereotyped female occupations. Likewise, Proshika, another large development NGO in Bangladesh, is engaged in helping the poor to broaden their participation in development programmes.

In brief, development NGOs are seemingly working together for constructing a broader framework for democratic development in Bangladesh in the twenty-first century. They are making efforts to ensure that the poor can advance their interests without solely relying upon either the state or the market.

The Zimbabwean case

From liberation to liberalization

Like Bangladesh, Zimbabwe 'moved toward the market' by implementing a structural adjustment programme. Also, as in the Bangladeshi case, Zimbabwe's new direction was not only a concession to global pressure but also was reflective of changing preferences and political considerations of the governing elite. Finally, Zimbabwe, like Bangladesh, is experiencing symptoms of the worldwide democratizing wave in struggles by civil society for greater control over political and social decisions that are dialectically related, if not directly in response to, structural adjustment.

Zimbabwe was established in 1980, following the end of a protracted war of independence from Britain. On winning the national elections which were held that year, the Zimbabwe African National Union (ZANU–PF) formed the Government of National Unity. The new regime was faced with daunting problems, the most intractable being the social disparities which resulted from the colonial juxtaposition of class and race: a dominant class of white-settler owners of production and a subordinate class of black workers and marginalized poor. ZANU–PF had campaigned on promises to reduce the extreme inequalities that were a legacy of the racist policies of the preceding Rhodesian government, but redistribution depended upon the generation of high economic growth levels. Therefore, the government asserted in its first economic doctrine, Growth with Equity: An Economic Policy Statement (1981), that it would strongly support the (re)vitalization of the productive sector while also meeting the basic needs of the poor.

Early into its mandate, the government signalled that it was genuinely committed to the policy of redistribution by significantly increasing its spending on social services.[17] However, its promotion of socialist developmentalism was impeded because 'it had no fundamental control over the productive forces in the country (and) had to rely on the investment decisions of private capital to ensure adequate economic growth'.[18] Therefore, the government began to buy out or acquire shares in a variety of enterprises and to introduce various measures of price control, actions justified as necessary to implement the promised reforms. Yet, despite increased state intervention in the economy, the party's professed Marxist-Leninist sympathies, and Prime Minister Mugabe's declared intention to create a one-party state, socialism was never firmly consolidated in Zimbabwe. Instead, the state-capitalism that developed did not differ essentially in form from the previous colonial system in which the Rhodesian state had served as a buffer, protecting white elites and workers from political and economic competition from the black masses and the small vulnerable economy from external shocks and pressures.[19]

Economic protectionism persisted in post-independence Zimbabwe and the ZANU–PF government undertook to reconsolidate a state corporatism which balanced tight control by the regime with continuing advantages to labour and business.[20] However, while the white agrarian and entrepreneurial bourgeoisie retained their privileged economic position and power in this system, they lost direct political control to a black state-based bourgeoisie. Although this new ruling elite was careful to accommodate white business leaders, it was also sensitive, initially at least, to the needs of the subordinate classes of black peasants and workers who had fought beside the new rulers in the liberation struggle and had provided ZANU–PF with its electoral victory.[21]

Maintaining a corporatist system in Zimbabwe's racially-divided society depended upon preserving a delicate economic equilibrium of growth with equity. Initially, in 1980–1, the hope that this precarious balance might be preserved was fuelled by an economic boom which helped to finance the substantial increase in expenditures on social services. However, such prosperity was short-lived and for the remainder of the 1980s, the annual growth rate hovered around 3 per cent, net investment levels were low (3.6 per cent average), gross fixed capital formation declined, and the budget deficit increased (due to the costs of emergency drought relief as well as expenditures on social services). Yet, at the same time,

> Zimbabwe diversified exports in the direction of manufactures, repaid its debts without resort to rescheduling, expanded education and health services, created food security sufficient to enable it to ride out the devastating drought of 1987 without imports – and all this in face of a daunting battery of constraints, including destabilization, rigged export markets, donor hostility and four drought years.[22]

On balance, given the constraints that Zimbabwe faced, and compared with the experiences of many other countries at the time, Zimbabwe's economic record for the 1980s might be described as modestly successful. Therefore, when the Economic Structural Adjustment Programme (ESAP) was implemented in 1990, considerable debate ensued on the logic of and motivation for the decision to change direction.[23]

The political economy of structural adjustment

Although few developing countries have evaded the global trend away from state capitalisms and socialisms and towards a market-oriented transnational capitalism, and although the 'home-grown' ESAP bears the hallmarks of the IMF adjustment formula, some scholars believe that Zimbabwe was not 'pushed' but rather that it 'jumped' into adjustment, and that the 'ideological shift and change of development strategy' was due largely to the growing 'embourgeoisement' of the state-based elite.[24] The increasing Africanization of the Zimbabwean bourgeoisie provided the ruling class with both an incentive and a justification for a market-first strategy. Indigenization of the economy has been one of the cornerstones of the government's development policy both as a concession to anti-colonialism and as a mechanism to establish a more racially-equitable economic balance. By pointing to an increasing number of successful black Zimbabwean entrepreneurs, the government could claim some success for its indigenization policy while arguing that the latter thrives on a market-friendly environment. With several of its leading members now heavily involved in the economy (through both legitimate and corrupt practices),[25] the government has been struggling to maintain a state-corporatist structure despite the state-reducing rigours of adjustment. To do this, it has delayed such measures as privatization of parastatals while putting most of the burden of reform on ordinary citizens. It has been an onerous burden. Real wages have declined, unemployment has increased and the cost of living has escalated throughout the 1990s. Also, reduced government spending on health and education during this period has led to a serious deterioration of social conditions.[26] In the late 1990s, with a soaring inflation rate, rapid decline in the value of the Zimbabwean dollar, and dramatic increases in prices of necessity items including fuel, the economic situation has reached crisis proportions.

Clearly, to date, the government's and the IMF's projections for economic progress under ESAP have not been realized and long-term prognoses appear to be increasingly ominous. Some ESAP supporters have placed the blame for the intensifying problems on the government's unwillingness to adhere strictly to the adjustment programme. However, many ordinary Zimbabweans feel that ESAP itself is responsible for their deteriorating living standards.[27] Also, in recent years, as evidence of bureaucratic corruption has continued to surface, popular opposition to the government as well as to ESAP has grown. Not only has the level of violent anti-government protest recently escalated, but there is evidence that numerous groups in civil society are now seeking in non-violent ways to locate, advance and/or take advantage of openings of political space in which to press for both immediate regime-change and sustainable democratic consolidation.

Responses by civil society

Democratizing pressure has emerged in several sectors of civil society in the 1990s although it has not been particularly well coordinated. There has been an increase in labour agitation and strike action opposing ESAP as well as growing student resentment of and protest against the government's authoritarianism.[28] As well, efforts by these traditional social movements are reinforced by pressures for democratic reform from church groups, the media and both established and new members of a rapidly growing NGO community. Indeed, following a tradition of NGO cooperation with or, in some instances, cooptation by the government, vibrant pockets of anti-government and -SAP resistance now exist within these organizations.[29] Various civil and human rights organizations, in particular, are persistent in bringing rights abuses to public attention, in pointing out constitutional inadequacies, and in providing various fora for educating the public on legal, constitutional and human rights issues.

Such organizations often disseminate information through the publication of their own newsletters or pamphlets or through collaboration with sympathetic newspapers or journals from among a burgeoning and sharply critical oppositional press. Moreover, they are linked with various grassroots church groups and welfare organizations, often by electronic communications systems and/or through their membership in the national umbrella organization – NANGO (National Association of Non-Governmental Organizations) – or in regional organizations such as MWENGO (Mwelekeo wa NGO). Finally, there is considerable support for local, national and regional initiatives through an extensive network of organizations of an emerging transnational civil society as most indigenous NGOs and much of the oppositional press and communications system are funded or otherwise abetted or encouraged by inter-/trans-national NGOs. The variety and growing inter-connectedness of these various organizations, together with what Sylvester has described as fugitive forms (meaning largely informal, diffuse or covert) of resistance to authoritarianism,[30] offer considerable promise for deepening and extending democracy in Zimbabwe.

Although civil society's resistance to the government has clearly strengthened throughout the 1990s, it did not result in ZANU–PF's defeat in the last national election held in 1995. Nevertheless, although the party captured 76 per cent of the votes cast, cracks in the regime's authority were becoming evident. A boycott of the election by nearly one-half (43 per cent) of registered voters suggested a form of protest against ZANU–PF and especially against the latter's use and misuse of constitutional provisions and/or intimidation tactics to weaken its opponents and prevent the establishment of a reasonable alternative.[31] Moreover, even if the increasing antipathy to the regime was obscured to some extent by ZANU–PF's clear victory at the polls, the rejection of several incumbent government members in the primaries before the election indicated that opposition was mounting by 1995. Since then, the discontent has become much more overt. Protests opposing the economic policy and demonstrations against government corruption have increased and the level of violence associated with these events has intensified.[32] Furthermore, recent defections from ZANU–PF of some high-profile members indicate a growing rift within the party ranks (likely to intensify with the impending process of choosing a successor to 75-year-old President Mugabe).[33] Thus threatened from within as well as from without, and forced to capitulate to the IMF's insistent demands for further privatization, the government will have considerable difficulty in maintaining the corporatist arrangements it has nurtured since independence, whether economic growth occurs or not. While the inevitable erosion of these relations may open more space for democratization, pressures for reform increase as economic growth continues to elude Zimbabwe. With a soaring unemployment rate (up to 50 per cent in some sectors by some reports)[34] and a 30 per cent increase in prices since a currency devaluation in November 1997, popular opposition to structural adjustment and to the government continues to grow and fewer resources or incentives are available to sustain a state corporatism. Morgan Tsvangirai, a labour leader who has been identified as a likely leader if the present regime is defeated, claims that 'the time is ripe for change. Things are falling apart because the government has lost the capacity to manage the economy'.[35]

Yet, the demise of the present regime does not necessarily mean that a sustainable democracy will be immediately consolidated. As Macumbe points out, civil society in Zimbabwe, as in most of Africa, is 'fairly weak and beset with constraints of a financial, organizational, operational and even environmental nature'.[36] If the surge of popular opposition against the present regime is to lead to democratic transition and consolidation, it must be carefully nurtured. Although in the past decade many academics have been enthusiastic in describing or predicting the development of vibrant civil societies in Africa, several hurdles must be overcome before civic activism is transformed into the construction of a democratic system of governance. Pressures of globalization and neoliberalism may have unleashed anti-governmental forces in Zimbabwe, but it is not yet certain that the civil society is intrinsically democratic, nor that sufficient amounts and appropriate types of external support will be forthcoming to support a transition to a sustainable democracy.

Conclusions

As indicated at the beginning of this chapter, we encouraged comparative analysis of the incidences and impacts of globalization and resistance. Such comparative insights should inform related fields of study, from comparative politics/development to international relations/organizations, now including the extremes of anarchy and the 'peace-building nexus' – i.e. collapsed or failed states – and of (already and near-) Newly Industrializing Countries and authoritarian regimes. Our two cases of diminished yet continuing middle powers are perhaps typical of a set of 'Third World' Less but not Least Developed Countries. These national regimes and civil societies reveal some degree of persistence in their institutional and ideological characters, including vigorous debates about SAPs. These informed a range of on-going discourses about globalization/adjustments and civil societies/NGOs which now constitute the core of contemporary comparative politics/development.

Among the comparative insights which emerged from the above case studies are:

1 the place of internal as well as external advocates of structural adjustments, who to be sure are connected in a 'transnational' alliance to advance globalization/integration given the apparent logic of market forces;

2 the new space for and level of resistance from both direct opposition and indirect provision of basic needs whether formal political contestation is particularly democratic or not;

3 the diversities of civil societies and strategies both within and between our two cases and the emergence of social/religious fundamentalisms in response to persistent market fundamentalism;

4 the importance of periodization of adjustment policies and popular responses, which change over time, particularly with the end of the Cold War and the proliferation of political as well economic conditionalities;

5 the relevance of both regional and global contexts; i.e. transnational relations of both incumbent regimes and dominant classes as well as civil societies and NGOs; and

6 the profound longer-term effects of such state downsizing and

policy reforms on state–economy/society relations over time in the balance of power and division of labour between state and civil societies/national economies; i.e. Asian and African states at the end of the twentieth-century are quite transformed by contrasts to their post-colonial inheritance.

Notes

1　See, for example, M. B. Brown, *Africa's Choices: Thirty Years of the World Bank* (Penguin, 1995); J. Clapp, *Adjustment and Agriculture in Africa: Farmers, the State and the World Bank in Guinea* (Macmillan, 1997); N. Heyser *et al.* (eds), *Government–NGO Relations in Asia* (Macmillan, 1995); L. Macdonald, *Supporting Civil Society* (Macmillan, 1997); P. Nelson, *The World Bank and NGOs: The Limits of Apolitical Development* (Macmillan, 1996): and T. Skålnes, *The Politics of Economic Reform in Zimbabwe* (Macmillan, 1996).

2　UNDP, *Human Development Report 1996* (Oxford University Press, 1996) and UNRISD, *States of Disarray* (UNRISD, 1995).

3　Ministry of Finance, *Bangladesh Economic Survey: 1975–76* (Ministry of Finance, Government of Bangladesh, 1976), pp. vii–viii, 228–9.

4　M. Rahman, *Structural Adjustment, Employment and Workers: Public Policy Issues and Choices for Bangladesh* (University Press, 1994), pp. 13–14.

5　A. Hossain and S. Rashid, 'Financial Sector Reform', in M. G. Kibria (ed.), *The Bangladesh Economy in Transition* (University Press, 1997), pp. 224–31.

6　M. Alam, *Trade and Financial Liberalization in Bangladesh* (Desh Prakashan, 1995), pp. 20–25.

7　R. Sobhan, 'Structural Maladjustment: Bangladesh's experience with market reforms', *Economic and Political Weekly*, 8 May 1993, p. 931.

8　See Bangladesh Bureau of Statistics, *Summary Report of the Household Expenditure Survey 1995–96* (Bangladesh Bureau of Statistics, 1997).

9　UNDP, *Human Development Report 1996* (Oxford University Press, 1997), p. 112.

10　UNB, 'Rate of Landless on the Rise', *Daily Star*, 19 August 1996, pp. 1 and 12.

11　S. Kamaluddin, 'Politics of Distrust: Opposition Agitates for Polls on Its Own Terms', *Far Eastern Economic Review*, Vol. 156, No. 1 (1993), p. 24.

12　Centre for Policy Dialogue, *Experiences with Economic Reform: A Review of Bangladesh's Development 1995* (University Press, 1995), pp. 24–8.

13　D. J. Lewis, 'Overview', in J. Farrington and D. J. Lewis (eds), *Non-Governmental Organizations and the States in Asia: Rethinking Roles in Sustainable Agricultural Development* (Routledge, 1993), p. 50.

14　Government of Bangladesh, *Flow of Foreign Grant through NGO Affairs Bureau* (Prime Minister's Office, June 1996).

15　A. N. Mizan, *In Quest of Empowerment: The Grameen Bank Impact on Women's Power and Status* (University Press, 1994), p. 152.

16　P. Ekins, *A New World Order: Grassroots Movements for Social Change* (Routledge, 1992), pp. 116–17.

17 Government expenditures on health increased by 33 per cent in real dollars in 1980/81 and 20 per cent in 81/82 and on education by 60 per cent in 1980/81 and then 5 per cent per year until 1990/91. From 1980 to 1990 infant mortality dropped from 88/1000 in 1980 to 61/1000, under age five mortality decreased from 104/100 to 87/1000, and maternal mortalities fell at similar rates. In education, enrolment increased from 1.2 million in 1980 to 2.1 million ten years later. See Government of Zimbabwe/UNICEF, *Programme of Cooperation 1995–2000* (Harare, October 1993).

18 B. Raftopoulos, Beyond the House of Hunger: Democratic Struggle in Zimbabwe', *Review of African Political Economy*, No. 54 (1992), p. 64.

19 J. Herbst, *State and Politics in Zimbabwe* (University of California Press, 1990), p. 18.

20 T. M. Shaw, 'Beyond Neo-Colonialism: Varieties of Corporatism in Africa', *Journal of Modern African Studies*, Vol. 20 (1982), pp. 239–61.

21 H. Dashwood, 'The Relevance of Class to the Evolution of Zimbabwe's Development Strategy, 1980–1991', *Journal of Southern African Studies*, Vol. 22, No. 1 (1996), pp. 27–48.

22 C. Stoneman, 'The World Bank: Some Lessons for South Africa', *Review of African Political Economy*, No. 58 (1993), p. 94.

23 B. MacGarry, *Growth? Without equity?* Silveira House Social Series, No. 4 (Mambo Press, 1993); J. Makumbe, 'What Alternatives to ESAP?' *Social Change and Development*, No. 36 (December, 1994), pp. 11–12; W. Naude, 'Macro-economic Change in Zimbabwe: Implications for South Africa', *Africa Insight*, Vol. 26, No. 1 (1996), pp. 57–64.

24 L. Cliffe, 'Were They Pushed or Did They Jump? Zimbabwe and the World Bank', *Southern African Report* (March, 1991), pp. 25–8; H. Dashwood, 'The Relevance of Class'.

25 J. Makumbe, 'Bureaucratic Corruption in Zimbabwe: Causes and Magnitude of the Problem', *Africa Development*, Vol. 19, No. 3 (1994), pp. 45–60; A. Meldrum, 'The Land Scandal', *Africa Report* (Jan–Feb, 1995), pp. 28–31.

26 M. Chiszo, *Government Spending on Social Services and the Impact of Structural Adjustment in Zimbabwe* (1993); M. Chiszo and L. Munro, *A Review of Policy Dimensions of Adjustment in Zimbabwe 1990–9* (UNICEF, 1994); B. MacGarry, 'Double Damage: Rural People and Economic Structural Adjustment in a Time of Drought', Silveira House Social Series, No. 7 (1994); UNICEF, *Children and Women in Zimbabwe: A Situation Analysis Update 1994* (UNICEF, 1994).

27 A. Meldrum, 'Economic Jitters', *African Business* (November, 1995), reprinted in *Zimbabwe Press Mirror*, Vol. 24, No. 23 (11 November 1995), p. 3.

28 The University of Zimbabwe was closed in June, 1998 because of student unrest and did not reopen until early in 1999.

29 The 1995 Welfare Organizations Amendment Bill which allows the government to limit and scrutinize NGOs' activities, both indicates and reinforces the growing state-NGO rift.

30 C. Sylvester, 'Whither Opposition in Zimbabwe?' *Journal of Modern African Studies*, Vol. 33, No. 3 (1995), pp. 403–23.

31 M. Sithole and J. Macumbe, 'Elections in Zimbabwe: the ZANU (PF)

Hegemony and its Incipient Decline', *African Journal of Political Science*, Vol. 2, No. 1 (1997), pp. 122–39.

32   The political unpopularity as well as the financial costs of the government's recent deployment of troops to support Laurent Kabila's threatened regime in the Republic of the Congo has aroused strenuous popular opposition. Considerable antipathy was created as well by the government's handling of allegations involving the Zimbabwe National Liberation War Veterans Association's apparent misuse of the War Victims' Compensation Fund. With such political resistance combining with hostility towards economic policies, the intensity of opposition continues to rise and in early November of this year, riot-squad troops were used to contain destructive and violent protests set-off by fuel price hikes.

33   See, for example, Sithole and Macumbe, 'Elections in Zimbabwe', pp. 134–7.

34   *Ibid.*

35   *Ibid.*

36   J. Makumbe, 'Is There Civil Society in Africa?' *International Affairs*, Vol. 74, No. 2 (April 1998), p. 318.

Index